INTEREST
GROUP
POLITICS
in the Southern States

INTEREST GROUP POLITICS

in the Southern States

Edited by
Ronald J. Hrebenar
and
Clive S. Thomas

1992

The University of Alabama Press
Tuscaloosa and London

Library of Congress Cataloging-in-Publication Data

Interest group politics in the southern states / edited by Ronald J.
Hrebenar and Clive S. Thomas.
      p.   cm.
    Includes bibliographical references (p.   ) and index.
    ISBN 0-8173-0568-8 (alk. paper)
    1. Pressure groups—Southern States. 2. Southern States—Politics
and government—1951–   I. Hrebenar, Ronald J., 1945–   .
II. Thomas, Clive S.
JK1118.I567   1992   91-40803
322.4'3'0975—dc20   CIP

British Library Cataloging-in-Publication Data available

This book is dedicated to
Harmon Zeigler,
a southerner and a pioneer in the study of state
interest groups

CONTENTS

PREFACE

In 1949, in his preface to *Southern Politics in State and Nation*, V. O. Key, Jr., expressed surprise that despite a vast literature on the South there was no comprehensive treatment of its politics. Radical changes in southern life and politics, as well as Key's pioneering efforts, have spurred publication of several comprehensive studies over the ensuing forty years. There have also been a plethora of articles, book chapters, and monographs that have analyzed various aspects of southern politics from a comparative perspective. In terms of sheer volume, when all this is added to the writing on individual southern states, the scholarly literature on southern politics far outstrips that of any other region of the United States. Yet this body of literature includes no study, comprehensive or otherwise, of the role of interest groups in southern politics.

We believe that such a study is important for two reasons. First, because parties have been traditionally weak, leadership unstable, factionalism rife, and southern political systems often in a state of flux, the enduring nature of various entrenched interest groups has often provided political stability by filling several political voids. That is, because of the weakness and fragmentation of southern political institutions, interest groups have often performed political functions that in many other states were the province of parties, leaders, and public officials. These functions included recruiting candidates, financing campaigns, and determining and implementing public policies. Second, as a result of interest groups' stabilizing and quasi-political institutional role, plus the nature of state constitutions that made them easy to amend, interest groups have exerted enormous influence on the public policy-making process of all southern states. In fact, in most cases they have been the dominant political forces. Together, these two factors meant that in most southern states interest groups were more important to the functioning of the political and governmental system and more powerful than in all but a few other states in the nation.

This is not to say that the literature on southern politics ignores interest groups and their importance. It would be well-nigh impossible to do that. There are many treatments of group systems in the literature on individual states, and to varying degrees groups are treated in comparative studies of aspects of southern politics as well as in the more comprehensive books on the politics of the South. Yet in virtually all these studies interest groups are treated only incidentally. Patterns of factionalism within the Democratic party, the rise of the Republicans, increased political participation by blacks, the effects of economic growth and changing demographics, and the South's role in national politics tend, not without good reason, to be the dominant themes and foci of treatments of southern politics.

By focusing on interest groups, we provide a different perspective on the politics of the South and its individual states, although augmenting the general understanding of southern politics was not our major purpose when we first considered a book on interest groups in the South. This book was conceived as the third in a series of four books on interest groups in all fifty states, each focusing on a region of the country. The first covered the thirteen western states; the second, the Midwest; this one, the South; and the fourth, the northeastern states. A fifth volume will compare all fifty states. Seventy-eight political scientists were involved in the research, which took over five years to complete and has resulted in the most extensive treatment of interest groups in the states yet produced. As with the other three regional books, this one on the South grew out of a sense of frustration. We, and several colleagues throughout the country who teach and research in the area of interest groups, were particularly concerned about the dearth of material, and especially hard data, on groups at the state level.

In planning this fifty-state study we identified five primary objectives. One major objective was to provide the first overall analysis of interest groups in states where there was no existing research on the subject. About twenty states fell into this category. Second, we wanted to provide an update on group activity in states where there was some previous work. Together, these first two purposes would provide an up-to-date data base for the comparative analysis of state interest groups to an extent that had never before been possible—our third major objective. Our fourth was to be able to assess our findings against previous research on state groups by scholars such as Harmon Zeigler, Sarah McCally Morehouse, Wayne Francis, and Belle Zeller. From such an assessment we could suggest modifications to existing theories and develop some new theories and propositions of our own.

As interest groups are so central a part of all political and governmental systems, we realized that, if our methodology and analysis were rigorous enough, our study would also throw light on state and regional politics in general. This was our fifth objective. As our research progressed we found that studying interest groups provided a perspective on the politics of southern states and of the region that had not been previously explored or, at least, expressly treated. Nevertheless, this remains a book on state interest groups that focuses on the South, and not a treatment of southern politics that focuses on interest groups. First and foremost we are interest group specialists and, despite immersing ourselves in the relevant literature for the past four years, we do not claim to be experts on southern politics. We leave to such experts the task of discovering the deeper implications of our study for understanding politics in the region.

In the first chapter we use a conceptual framework combined with a historical methodology to set the scene for understanding the place of interest groups in southern state politics. We bring the story of the development of southern interest groups up to the early 1970s and explain our methodology. The twelve state chapters—covering the eleven states of the old Confederacy plus Kentucky—are organized into two sections, the Peripheral South and the Deep South. With the addition of Kentucky to the Peripheral South, this is the division used by Earl and Merle Black in their 1987 groundbreaking work, *Politics and Society in the South*. To provide some background for understanding the specifics of interest group activity in each state, we begin each chapter with a brief, pertinent overview of the state and its politics. In the concluding chapter we bring the story of southern interest groups up to the present day, using the conceptual framework set out in Chapter 1 and drawing on the information in the state chapters to provide a comparative analysis of the current role, operating techniques, and power of southern state interest groups. We also compare recent developments in southern interest group politics with those in other regions.

To steal a line from countless prefaces, this book could not have been written without the help of many people and organizations. Many there are, but in this case, they are not too numerous to mention. At the top of the list are our eighteen contributing authors. In particular we appreciate their willingness to bear the cost of their own research, and to stick with us when things were not working out quite the way we had planned. The work of the fifty-eight contributors to our project from the other three regions made possible the comparisons with the rest of the country that we make in this book. Earl Black, Robert P. Steed, and Charles G. Bell read the manuscript and made several useful suggestions. We benefited greatly from their efforts. We thank Malcolm MacDonald, director of the University of Alabama Press, for his support and enthusiasm for our project. Our editors, Pamela Ferdinand, Ellen Stein, and their colleagues were of immense help. Sue Ogden and Debbie Frye helped type the manuscript and aided us in mastering the intricacies of computer software. The University of Utah and the University of Alaska Southeast provided us with some basic resources—not least of which was regular employment. And finally, our families were very understanding. Most importantly, they sensed those times, those countless hours, when we just had to be left alone to think, research, and write.

A few comments about how we shared the work in putting together this book: at times each of us felt that he was doing the bulk of the work. The truth of the matter is, however, that in the final tally we each did 51 percent. That is not to say that we shared equally in each of the myriad tasks involved in producing an edited book; like all good partnerships, ours is based on the fact that we complement each other. But how successful our partnership has been in this instance is a question that we will leave for others to judge.

Ronald J. Hrebenar
Salt Lake City, Utah

Clive S. Thomas
Juneau, Alaska

INTEREST
GROUP
POLITICS
in the Southern States

1

UNDERSTANDING INTEREST GROUP ACTIVITY IN SOUTHERN STATE POLITICS

Clive S. Thomas

For much of this century, down to the 1960s, Texas politics was dominated by four powerful interests—oil, chemicals, railroads, and the Texas Manufacturers Association. The wheeler-dealer lobbyists who represented these Big Four interests used their tremendous influence to achieve purposes far beyond their clients' narrow policy goals. "They advocated the establishment's number one priority—a good business climate, which in those days meant weak unions, low taxes and minimum regulation."[1] In other words, more than any other forces or facets of Texas life, the Big Four interests could largely determine what state government did or, more importantly, what it did not do.

Such a situation, with interest groups exerting a stranglehold on state politics, was common in many states during this period. But, largely because of the special circumstances of southern political life, interest groups played a crucial and in most cases a dominant role in all southern states with the possible exception of Virginia, although even in Virginia they were extremely influential. And the power of southern interest groups lives on today. In fact, in some respects their political significance is greater than ever. Interest groups have been such an important and dominant feature of southern politics for so long that studying their development and contemporary activities provides perspective both comprehensive and unique on past and present southern political life.

No life-style—particularly no political life-style—of any region of the United States has been the subject of more negative stereotypes than that of the American South. The South has been seen as racist and staunchly white supremacist; as backward, rural, poverty-stricken, and economically stagnant; as rife with demagogs and corrupt politicians; and as politically elitist and conservative to the extreme. Yet, and perhaps mainly because of these long-standing stereotypes, in the last thirty years the South has been the subject of a largely positive press. This is because the region has gone through some major, if often painful, changes that have brought its social, economic, and political system more in line with the rest of the nation.

Change—often fundamental change—has affected almost every aspect of southern life and culture. As one commentator put it, "the South has changed so much in the past decade or two that change itself has become Dixie's most identifiable characteristic."[2] Volumes of writing, both popular and academic, have documented, traced, analyzed, and speculated about these changes. As integral and resilient features of southern life, interest groups have been both affected by this change and instrumental in helping bring it about.

Two words closely associated with change are *transition* and *growth*. Change inevitably produces a transition, whether to a less or more favorable state of affairs. By the standards of democratic theory, recent changes in interest group activity in the South have set in motion a largely positive transition. In Texas, for example, several groups not previously represented have entered the political fray in Austin, which in turn has challenged the power of the Big Four. Change does not necessarily produce growth; it might produce decline or contraction. In the recent history of southern interest group politics, however, change has very much been linked with growth. Once again, Texas is fairly typical. Here there has not only been a growth in the number of groups in Austin, but also in the strata of the population represented by interest groups, as well as a growth in the professionalism of lobbyists and group leaders. Explaining exactly what the nature of this change, transition, and growth has been in recent developments in southern interest group politics is our primary objective in this book.

To achieve this we combine an in-depth analysis of individual states with comparative analysis of the region as a whole. This involves four distinct but interrelated lines of inquiry. First, we provide an overview of the types of groups operating in each state and the tactics they are now using to achieve their goals. For several states this constitutes the first comprehensive treatment of interest groups past or present. Second, we assess changes in interest group politics in the South as a whole, especially in the role that groups play in the public policy-making process. Third, we place the South in context by comparing its past and present trends with those in other regions. Finally, by combining the findings from these three lines of inquiry we hope to enhance general theories of interest group activity in the states.

Most importantly, this first chapter sets out an analytical framework for understanding the changes, transition, and growth in southern interest group politics. We will review the existing state of knowledge on southern groups; briefly trace the development of groups in the South up until the 1970s, and the factors that have affected change; explain some key definitions and our methodology; and identify some recent changes in other regions as a means of assessing the developments identified by the authors of chapters on the individual states. However, neither in this chapter nor in this book do we claim to provide more than a cursory treatment of southern politics. We simply highlight those topics and themes that are essential for an understanding of southern interest group politics.

The South Defined

The South has long been considered one of the most distinctive of American regions, encompassing the eleven states of the Old Confederacy. This was the definition used by V. O. Key, Jr., in his 1949 classic, *Southern Politics in State and Nation*,[3] and most subsequent academic treatments of southern politics have followed suit.[4] There are, indeed, good arguments based on cultural, social, economic, and political factors for defining the South in this way. A case can be made, however, that recent changes have weakened the cohesiveness of this regional definition. Southern Florida, northern

Virginia, and west Texas can justifiably be no longer considered as part of the South, if they ever were. On the other hand, parts of Maryland and West Virginia, the southern parts of Missouri, Indiana, and Illinois, eastern Oklahoma and most of Kentucky could easily be considered southern.

Furthermore, even within the traditional eleven-state region some distinct subregional patterns have long been identified, as well as intrastate regionalism. Distinctions have been made, for example, between the Upper South—North Carolina, Virginia, Tennessee—and the Deep South—Arkansas (sometimes considered an Upper South state), Louisiana, Mississippi, Alabama, Georgia, South Carolina, and Florida. Exactly which category Texas fits, if either, has never been clear. Another, and more analytically sound, division is between the Deep South and the Peripheral South: Five states (South Carolina, Georgia, Alabama, Mississippi, and Louisiana) are classed in the first, and the remaining six in the latter category.[5] As to intrastate divisions, within several southern states the division between the lowlands and the uplands dates back to colonial or territorial days.

Consequently, while the South is less amorphous a region than the West or the Midwest, scholars disagree over its extent. Faced with these problems, we settled on a definition of the South that includes the eleven states of the Old Confederacy plus Kentucky. Listed alphabetically these are:

Alabama	Kentucky	South Carolina
Arkansas	Louisiana	Tennessee
Florida	Mississippi	Texas
Georgia	North Carolina	Virginia

Our rationale for embracing these twelve within our definition is based on a combination of their distinctiveness and convenience of analysis. As most of the existing comparative data on southern politics use Key's definition, it was most logical to include these states for comparisons with our data. Kentucky was added because it is predominantly more southern than midwestern or northeastern in terms of its social, economic, and political variables. Maryland, West Virginia, Oklahoma, Indiana, and Missouri were excluded because they are not predominantly southern in these respects. In organizing the sequence of discussing these twelve states, we took the division of Peripheral and Deep South as being the one that best represents recent political developments in the region. However, as we will see throughout this book, the distinction between southern states in regards to their contemporary interest group systems is much less clear than in other areas of southern politics.

Southern Interest Groups: Research and Definitions

Despite the extensive literature on southern politics, very little material exists on southern interest groups. For very good reason, research on southern politics has followed the mold cast by Key over forty years ago. The bulk of research has focused on patterns of factionalism within the Democratic party, the rise of the Republicans, increased political participation by blacks, the effects of economic growth and changing demographics, and the South's role in national politics. Yet the South is not alone in its dearth of research on state interest groups; the bulk of research on interest groups in the United States has focused on group activity at the national level.

As to southern interest group politics specifically, until now no comprehensive comparative analysis has been produced. Seven types of studies have, however, treated—or more often touched on—some aspects of interest group activity in the South. First, at the most general level and written for a popular readership, there are books that have dealt with southern politics, and to some extent southern interest groups, as part of a general treatment of the life of the states. These include John Gunther's *Inside USA* and the series of books on the regions of the country by Neal R. Peirce.[6] Despite their shortcomings, in the absence of comprehensive and comparative academic information scholars have often turned to these books to piece together an understanding of southern interest groups. In fact, Sarah McCally Morehouse used Peirce's books to put together the first list of the most effective groups in the fifty states.[7]

The second category of literature on southern interest groups comprises academic works, books treating the government and politics of individual southern states, and books that include southern states as examples or case studies. While at some time all twelve states are written of in some text, the treatment of interest groups varies widely. Some researchers devote a separate chapter to interest groups, others do not.[8] These authors also display a wide variety of approaches, from the purely anecdotal to the highly conceptual and quantitative. They also vary in scope and depth of treatment. Most such studies are now outdated. And while many chapters in books that include southern states as examples or case studies are well written, length limitations preclude their authors' paying more than cursory attention to interest groups.[9]

Third, beginning with Key, scholars have to some extent treated interest groups in general texts on southern politics. Yet, as we mentioned above, these treatments have usually been only incidental. No book, for example, has analyzed the role that groups have played over the years in southern states' political systems.

Fourth, in more recent years books have been published on specific aspects of southern politics, whose authors have focused on or included treatments of particular interest groups in the South. Most notable is the series of books edited by Robert P. Steed, Tod A. Baker, and Laurence W. Moreland.[10]

A fifth category includes a small body of literature that focuses on public policy in which researchers have taken a case-study approach to investigating the impact of individual groups. For example, several years ago Harmon Zeigler studied the impact of the Florida Milk Commission (which was controlled by the dairy interests) on milk prices in that state. More recently Joseph Stewart and James Sheffield studied the use of the courts by black interest groups in Mississippi.[11]

In a sixth category of literature scholars have taken what might be termed a microapproach to the study of group theory, looking at either some specific aspect of the internal organization and operation of groups or at how they affect some specific part of the political process, such as the legislature. Sometimes these researchers have been concerned solely with specific states—for example, an early 1980s study of Arkansas lobbyists by Charles Dunn and Donald Whistler.[12] Most often, however, those using this approach have taken one or more southern states as part of a larger study. Zeigler and Michael Baer, for example, used North Carolina as one of the four states in their study of lobbying in state legislatures; and Charles Bell, Keith Hamm, and Charles Wiggins used Texas in their recent three-state study of group impact on certain areas of public policy.[13]

These six categories are a useful starting point in a study of southern interest groups, particularly group activity in individual states, and we will make numerous references to them throughout this book. Yet, because of their great variation in methodology and scope and depth of analysis, they are of very limited value for purposes of comparative analysis (and often for individual state studies). There is, however, a seventh category of literature, comparative in focus and including the southern states as part of nationwide studies of state interest group activity. Authors within this category have taken what we might term a macroapproach, attempting to understand interest groups in the context of the individual state and particularly in relation to that state's political and governmental systems. The most notable work here has been conducted by Belle Zeller, Harmon Zeigler, and Hendrik van Dalen, and by Sarah McCally Morehouse.[14]

In none of these studies, however, have scholars conducted systematic research on all the southern states. Their attempts at comprehensive analysis of both the South and other regions are based upon original data from only a few states and draw on other information (such as that referred to above) that varies in its methodology from the impressionistic to the highly quantitative, a divergence that is not ideal for comparative analysis. The theories and propositions developed from these studies were thus arrived at by extrapolation, or by reliance on secondary sources, and sometimes, in the absence of data, through speculation. Yet these comments should not be interpreted as understating the significant contribution of these studies. Each was a major source for evaluating interest groups at the subnational level—including the South—at a time when little other data existed. Zeller was the first to categorize states into strong, moderate, or weak interest group systems. Zeigler, and Zeigler and van Dalen, developed several theories and propositions about how a state's economic, social, and political system influences the composition, operation, and power of the state's interest group system. Most notably they developed a four-category classification of group power within strong interest group states; and advanced knowledge on the relationship between party strength and group power. More recently Morehouse built on this work. In particular, she expanded on the relationship of parties and groups, and refined the threefold classification system (strong, moderate, or weak) of interest group power vis-à-vis a state's political system. And, as mentioned above, she developed the first listing of the most "significant" groups in all fifty states. All this has acted as a benchmark for scholars conducting subsequent research. It certainly provided our study with an important point of departure.

One of the problems that reduces the usefulness of existing studies of southern interest groups for purposes of comparative analysis, be this within a state over time or between states past or present, is the variation in definition of key terms. Five of the most important of these terms are *interest group, interest, lobby, lobbyist,* and *group power.* It is not surprising that scholars have used various definitions of these terms, whether explicitly or not, as disputes over their meaning have plagued the academic study of interest groups for years. Therefore, for the purposes of methodological and analytical consistency we developed definitions of these terms for use by our contributors in all fifty states. Here we will define the first four, leaving group power for later in this chapter when we explain our methodology in more detail.

The terms *interest group, interest,* and *lobby* are used here to denote three levels of political group classification that are useful for analyzing interest group activity. At the most specific level is the interest group itself. Just a cursory reading of the literature reveals that over the years researchers have used a variety of operational definitions of this term. Most commonly they have used the legal or regulatory definition, making their focus of study those groups required to register under federal and state laws, and excluding those not required to do so. In certain limited cases such a definition may be adequate; but for most research on state interest groups and particularly that with a comparative focus or component, it has some serious shortcomings.

The major problem with this legal or regulatory definition is that the fifty states vary considerably in what groups and organizations they require to register as lobbying entities. Some states, such as

Oregon, have relatively broad rules requiring even state agencies to register. Others, such as Georgia, have very narrow regulations.[15] Common sense would lead us to surmise, and research on Georgia demonstrates, that most of the types of groups that appear on Oregon's registration lists but are not required to register in Georgia are, in fact, also very active in Georgia's public policy-making process. Ignoring these unregistered, or "hidden," groups and lobbies, and especially state governmental agencies, provides a very distorted understanding of the role and impact of interest groups in Georgia's public policy-making process. For these reasons, using group registration lists as the sole basis for comparative state interest group research is largely unsatisfactory. This is particularly true in the South where lobby registration laws tend, like Georgia's, to be narrow and laxly enforced.

In an attempt to overcome these problems and embrace these unregistered lobbying forces, we defined an interest group in our fifty-state study as *any association of individuals or organizations, whether formally organized or not, that attempts to influence public policy.* The Alabama League of Municipalities is an example of a specific interest group, as is the Tennessee Farm Bureau. This is a variation of David Truman's definition, probably the most widely used definition of interest group. However, our definition is shorter and more concrete; embraces, by implication, the various concepts that Truman included; and at the same time eliminates some of the shortcomings of his definition.[16] Obviously, as do all definitions of interest group, ours has its problems. It is very broad and, as some of the contributors to our Hrebenar-Thomas study discovered, creates some problems in securing data. However, the research results from this project demonstrate that this definition produces a view of interest group activity in the states, including many aspects previously unnoticed or only superficially treated, that is much more comprehensive and balanced than that of many previous studies. This has proved to be especially the case with the South.

In contrast to an interest group, lobby has a much broader connotation. In our study we use it as a collective term, defined as *two or more individuals, groups, or organizations concerned with the same general area of public policy, but that may or may not be in agreement on specific issues.* One example will suffice. The local government lobby in most states, including the South, is composed of state municipal leagues or associations of cities and counties (e.g., the Alabama League of Municipalities); public employee groups such as county and city workers (clerks, police, firemen, and teachers); associations of elected officials such as mayors, judges, and school board members; state agencies concerned with local government; and individual towns, cities, and districts that use or hire their own lobbyists. All of these have a general interest in promoting legislation and funding to enhance the quality of local government. However, on specific issues members of this lobby may be on opposite sides. For instance, individual cities and districts often find themselves in conflict with their state municipal league or other associations to which they belong over such issues as changing local governmental powers, taxation policy, and particularly the allocation of funds for capital projects.

The term *interest* has a broader connotation than interest group but is more specific than a lobby. We can refer again to local government groups as an example. Individual cities and towns such as Louisville, Kentucky, and Miami, Florida, often lobby directly and thus can be considered as specific interest groups. These, as we noted above, are also members of the local government lobby in their state. But they can also be considered as part of the interest category of cities and towns or local governmental jurisdictions. This might embrace several specific groups such as state municipal leagues and associations of counties. Exactly where an interest ends and a lobby begins is not always clear. But it is often a useful distinction to make, for two reasons. Public officials often refer to similar types of interest groups that often act in concert as an interest; and the term provides a useful means for categorizing similar types of groups for purposes relating to such activities as analyses of the types of groups operating in state capitals, group tactics, and group power.

Finally, we define a lobbyist as *a person designated by an interest group to represent it to government for the purpose of influencing public policy in that group's favor.* From our definition of interest group we know that the interest represented by the lobbyist need not necessarily be a formal organization such as the Tennessee Farm

Bureau or the Virginia Bankers Association. It includes informal and ad hoc groups such as a group of union members disaffected from their leaders or an informal association of businesspeople. Or it could be an individual representing himself or herself or pursuing some heartfelt cause. Neither do we confine the term *lobbyist* to those representing groups required to register under state law, for the reasons we mentioned earlier.[17]

It is important to understand, however, that to lump all lobbyists together as lobbyists clouds an understanding of their role and of various aspects of interest group activity, just as an understanding of the organization and operation of the legal profession would be clouded by referring to all its members as attorneys. Lobbyists, like attorneys, musicians, baseball players, and teachers, can be divided into various categories or types. There are five major categories of lobbyists:

- Contract lobbyists: those hired on contract for a fee specifically to lobby; they may represent more than one client
- In-house lobbyists: employees of an organization, association, or business who as all or part of their job act as lobbyists; these represent only one client—their employer
- Government lobbyists, or legislative liaisons: employees of state, local, and federal agencies who as part or all of their job represent their agency to the legislative and executive branches of state government; these also represent only one interest
- Citizen or volunteer lobbyists: persons who, usually on an ad hoc and unpaid basis, represent citizens' and community organizations or informal groups; they rarely represent more than one interest at a time
- Private individual, "hobbyist," or self-styled lobbyists: those acting on their own behalf; since the only "organization" they "officially" represent is themselves, they are for all practical purposes their own "interest group."

While these five categories of lobbyists have the identical goal of influencing public policy, their background and experience, the resources they have behind them, and the organizations they represent mean that they are perceived differently by those they seek to influence, and thus they have to gear their methods of operation accordingly.

A Framework for Understanding
Interest Group Activity in the States

As a basis on which to build an understanding of interest group activity in the states, including the southern states, it is useful to consider the basic factors that influence that activity—that is to say, what determines the types of groups that are active; the methods they use in pursuing their goals; and the role that groups play within state political systems and, in particular, the power that they exert within those systems. Existing research in this area is rather sketchy. Scholars agree, however, that the answers to these basic questions about group activity lie in a complex set of economic, social, cultural, legal, political, governmental, and even geographical variables; and that these will vary in their combinations from state to state, giving each state a unique interest group system. Nevertheless, we can identify eight specific sets of factors that appear to be of particular importance in all states. These we develop into a conceptual framework set out in Table 1.1.

This conceptual framework for understanding the environmental influences on group activity in the states is a synthesis of previous research and of findings from our Hrebenar-Thomas study. While all eight factors and their various elements are not new, what is original is the way that many of these elements have been used here, and the integration of the factors into a single conceptual framework. These eight factors and their components are very much interrelated in that they influence each other. A change in one may reflect or lead to a change in one or more of the other factors. Any change at all is likely to affect the nature of group activity, and major changes will have a significant impact on the interest group and lobbying scene in a particular state or the states as a whole.

With this information about the use of terms and the conceptual framework in mind, we can now begin our exploration of interest groups in the southern states.

Table 1.1 Eight Major Factors Influencing the Makeup, Operating Techniques, and Impact on Public Policy of Interest Group Systems in the States

Factor 1. State Policy Domain

Components
- Constitutional/legal authority
- Policy areas actually pursued and those not exercised
- Reduction in budgets and policies exercised
- Policy priorities

Explanation

The policy domain of a state, as defined in its constitutional/legal authority, constitutes the areas over which it can formally exercise policy decisions. This will determine which interests will attempt to affect state policy. As policy authority expands, it will increase the number and types of groups lobbying.

The types of groups that are active will be partially a consequence of the policy areas actually pursued. The existence of other types of groups will be the result of efforts to get state government to pursue policies that it has chosen not to exercise. Although this category of reformist-type groups will be much smaller than the first, interests not adversely affected by state policies pursued or not pursued will either not be organized or will lie politically inactive. Reductions in budgets and policy areas pursued will likely not reduce lobbying activity but actually increase it, as groups fight more intensely to protect their interests. The policy priorities of a state government at any time will tend to increase the importance to public officials of the groups affecting those policies, thus enhancing their access and influence.

Factor 2. Intergovernmental Spending and Policy-Making Authority

Components
- Federal/state/local policy and spending authority
- Changes in federal/state/local policy and spending authority
- Centralization/decentralization of state/local policy and spending authority

Explanation

Factor 2 refers to the policies exercised and the amount of money spent by state governments, versus policies and spending by federal and local governments. The extent and intensity of lobbying at these three levels of government will be determined by the intergovernmental distribution of spending and decision-making authority. Changes in these responsibilities between levels of government will tend to affect the types of groups that lobby federal, state, and local governments, and the intensity of their lobbying efforts.

The greater the federal devolution of policy and funding responsibilities, the greater the centralization vis-à-vis local governments of policy-making in the state capital, and the higher the percentage of state versus local spending on individual programs and services, the more intense will be lobbying in the state capital. This increased group activity in the states may well have the effect of making both individual interest groups and group systems more significant and powerful in state politics, counteracting such factors as increased socioeconomic diversity and increased governmental professionalism, which might otherwise reduce the political impact of groups.

Factor 3.   Political Attitudes

Components   • Political culture
                 • Conservative/liberal ideology

Explanation

Political culture is a shared set of knowledge, attitudes, and symbols that helps to define the procedures and goals of politics.[a] Conservative/liberal ideology denotes specific attitudes to the role of government. Political attitudes influence the types and extent of policies performed; the level of integration/fragmentation and professionalization of the policy-making process; what are and are not acceptable lobbying techniques; and the comprehensiveness and stringency of enforcement of public-disclosure laws, including lobby laws.

In states where a moralistic political culture and liberal attitudes are prevalent, individual interest groups tend to have less freedom of action; the overall impact of the group system on state politics also tends to be less; and more stringent public-disclosure laws usually exist. Conversely, in states with a predominantly traditionalistic political culture and conservative orientation, the opposite situation tends to be the case in these three respects. States with varying combinations of political culture and ideology fall somewhere in between.

Factor 4.   Level of Integration/Fragmentation of the Policy Process

Components   • Strength/weakness of political parties
                 • Power of the governor
                 • Number of directly elected cabinet members
                 • Number and authority of independent boards and commissions
                 • Extent and use of methods of direct democracy initiative, referendum, and recall

Explanation

The level of integration/fragmentation of the policy process is the extent to which the policy-making process is centralized or dispersed within a state. This will have an impact on patterns of group access and influence. Generally, the more integrated the system the fewer the options available to groups. Conversely, the more fragmented the system the larger the number of access points and available methods of influence.

The policy system is likely to be more integrated when political parties are stronger, the formal and political power of the governor greater, and the number of directly elected cabinet members fewer; when independent boards and commissions are fewer and have less authority, and when methods of direct democracy are more limited in extent and less frequently used. The greater is the reverse situation with these five components, the more fragmented the policy process. The influence of both individual interests and the group system as a whole tends to be greater when the policy process is more fragmented, and vice versa.

Factor 5.   Level of Professionalization of State Government

Components   • State legislators
                • Legislative support services
                • The bureaucracy, including the governor's staff

Explanation

The extent to which legislators are full-time, receive adequate compensation, and have adequate support services such as office space, staff, research services, and interim funding and support influences the level of professionalism. So does the extent of merit as opposed to political appointees in the bureaucracy, and its level of training and support services. Professionalization makes more-varied sources of information available to policymakers. It also creates a higher demand for information by policymakers and an increased demand for technical information from groups and lobbyists. Also, the higher the level of professionalization the more likely is the state to pursue liberal policies, and vice versa.

It was previously believed that an increase in independent sources of information would undermine group power by reducing groups' role as purveyors of information. This does not appear to be the case. In fact, groups may have increased their role and influence in this regard as the demand for information outstrips policymakers' ability to absorb it. Increased professionalism of policymakers does appear to increase the level of professionalization of the interest group system and especially of lobbyists, and to increase the amount of lobbying of the administration and the use of the courts to achieve group goals. More-professionalized states tend to encourage the development of more social-issue groups as a result of more-liberal policies. The result is a more pluralistic and varied group life. This is in contrast to less-professionalized and more-conservative state governments.

Factor 6.   Level of Socioeconomic Development

Components   • Social development
                • Economic development

Explanation

Social development is defined as an increase in urbanization, middle-class residents, and the number of professionals in the population. Economic development is defined as an increase in nonagricultural employment and in the industrial and service sectors, and a decrease in disparities in income distribution and wealth. The consequence of economic development is increased economic diversity; social development increases the number of people joining groups because urban dwellers and the middle and upper classes are more likely to join groups than rural residents and the working class.

Greater social and economic development will tend to produce a more diverse and competitive group system; a decline in the dominance of individual groups (but not necessarily a decline in the overall impact of groups, which may actually increase because of other factors); the development of new and more sophisticated techniques of lobbying such as an increase in professionalism of lobbyists, a growth in contract lobbyists, an increase in the number of lawyers acting as lobbyists, the emergence of multiclient and multiservice lobbying firms, and the development of sophisticated public relations techniques and systems of contacting members.

Factor 7. Extensiveness and Enforcement of Public Disclosure Laws

Components
- Lobby laws
- Campaign-finance laws
- Regulation of political action committees (PACs)
- Conflict-of-interest provisions

Explanation

Lobby laws provide for the registration of lobbyists and their employers/clients and in most states for the reporting of expenditures. Campaign finance laws require the reporting of campaign contributions over a specified amount. Most states have separate laws regulating PACs and PAC contributions. Conflict-of-interest provisions disclose the financial connections between public officials, especially elected officials, and interest groups, in an attempt to lessen corrupt practices. Public-disclosure laws work to provide public visibility, primarily through the press, of the activities of interest groups and their connections with public officials.

Disclosure appears to have little effect on reducing the overall power of the group system. In fact, restricting campaign contributions may actually lead to the proliferation of interest group PACs, which tends to increase the power of both individual groups and the group system as a whole. However, these laws do appear to change group tactics, and in some cases affect the power of certain specific groups and lobbyists. Increased public visibility has tended to make many old-style lobbying practices less acceptable to politicians.

Factor 8. Level of Campaign Costs and Sources of Support

Components
- Level of campaign costs
- Level of aid and funds going to the candidate directly from political parties and party PACs
- Level of aid and funds from interest groups, including their PACs, going directly to candidates

Explanation

By campaign costs and sources of support, we mean the amount of money and other aid needed to get elected and where resources, particularly money, come from. An increase in campaign costs and aid needed to get elected puts increased pressure on candidates to raise funds and secure campaign workers. The more funds and aid coming from their party, the more control the party will have over them once elected. The more support coming directly to candidates from groups and their PACs, the more candidates are beholden to them.

The rapidly increasing cost of campaigning has been met primarily by interest group PACs, not by parties. This has helped contribute to the decline of parties and reduced their effectiveness as coordinating influences on policy-making. As professionalism increases among politicians, especially legislators, they tend to become more dependent on contributions from groups' PACs. Thus, through their use of PACs, interest groups may come to exert increasing influence in states with more professionalized political systems. The increasing role of groups' PACs appears to have more than compensated for other developments that might otherwise have worked to reduce both the power of certain individual groups and group systems as a whole.

---

[a] See Hyde and Alsfeld, "Role Orientations of Lobbyists in a State Setting," 10.

Sources: The Hrebenar-Thomas study; and Mark S. Hyde and Richard W. Alsfeld, "Role Orientations of Lobbyists in a State Setting: A Comparative Analysis," paper delivered at the Annual Meeting of the American Political Science Association, New Orleans, 1985; Wayne L. Francis, *Legislative Issues in the Fifty States: A Comparative Analysis* (Chicago: Rand McNally, 1967); Sarah McCally Morehouse, *State Politics, Parties and Policy* (New York: Holt, Rinehart and Winston, 1981); John C. Wahlke, et al., *The Legislative System* (New York: John Wiley, 1962); L. Harmon Zeigler, "Interest Groups in the States," in *Politics in the American States: A Comparative Analysis,* ed. Virginia Gray, Herbert Jacob, and Kenneth N. Vines, 4th ed. (Boston: Little, Brown, 1983); Harmon Zeigler and Hendrik van Dalen, "Interest Groups in State Politics," in *Politics in the American States: A Comparative Analysis,* ed. Herbert Jacob and Kenneth N. Vines, 3d ed. (Boston: Little, Brown, 1976); and Harmon Zeigler and Michael Baer, *Lobbying: Interaction and Influence in American State Legislatures* (Belmont, Calif.: Wadsworth, 1969).

Old-Style Southern Politics, the Interest Group System, and Transformation in Southern Life

The stereotypes about the South that have become indelibly printed on the American mind mask the fact that the region and its politics have always exhibited considerable diversity. In his *Origins of the New South*, C. Vann Woodward demonstrated that complexity, not similarity, was the hallmark of the region in the post–Civil War period.[18] And historians, sociologists, and political scientists alike have shown that throughout the so-called era of the Solid South the region was no monolith, politically or otherwise.[19] There were, for example, periodic challenges to the power of the ruling elite from populist forces of the up-country areas. The diversities and complexities within the South continue today and are perhaps greater than ever, as we will show. Nevertheless, we can identify certain themes that were common to southern political life for three-quarters of a century, down to the 1960s.

What set the South apart from the rest of the nation during this period can be traced to its historical experience and certain socioeconomic factors. Of major significance was the Civil War and Reconstruction, the region's racial composition, the populist revolt of the 1890s, the region's overwhelming economic dependence on agriculture, its prolonged status as a predominantly rural society, and its poverty. Together these factors produced a unique political system with a distinctive approach to political participation and to the provision of public services.[20]

The central influence on southern politics during this period was race: "In its grand outline the politics of the South revolves around the politics of the Negro."[21] This led to a political system in which everything was subordinated to keeping "the Negro" politically impotent. The scheme was masterminded by the well-to-do whites of the Black Belt counties in the rural South. With the help of businessmen from the larger towns of the region, this rural, small-town elite of lawyers, doctors, planters, and businessmen was able to dominate southern state politics and national politics for over half a century.

The major means of control was to disenfranchise the Negro, and along with him most poor whites, whose populist leanings were always a concern to the rural elite. The poll tax, literacy tests, and various other means were used to achieve this disenfranchisement. The power of the rural elite, or "courthouse rings" as they were often termed, was also buttressed by extremely malapportioned legislatures that were weighted heavily in favor of rural interests. All this occurred in an environment of one-partyism; the Democratic party reigned supreme—at least in name. In actual fact party was irrelevant to politics, which was a series of shifting alliances focused around personalities, an issueless politics dominated by a tradition-alistic political culture that endeavored to maintain a McKinley-like laissez-faire philosophy of government. The extensive problem of poverty was ignored for fear that trying to address it might upset the delicate balance consisting of control by the rural elite and the sub-ordination of the Negro.

The interest group system that this political situation produced was one of a very narrow range of interests in terms both of the types of interests represented and of those that wielded power. This be-comes easier to understand when we consider the factors, set out in Table 1.1, that influence interest group activity in the states. In this period all southern state economies were almost entirely dependent on agriculture; industry was sparse. So, agricultural groups, espe-cially planters and other large landowners, were very prominent. Also, because of the power of the small-town elites, county court-houses and local governments in general wielded some considerable influence. Churches, especially the Baptist church, also possessed political influence. In states where there was a major industry, such as sewing-machine manufacturing in Arkansas, textiles in South Carolina, and steel in Alabama, industrial groups were an important interest. But in most southern states large, or even medium-sized, industry was not a significant political interest.

At least in terms of its narrow range of interests the South was not unique; its situation was similar to that in most other states during the period. Down to the 1960s the development of the interest group system in the South (and in the rest of the nation) followed a pattern. The railroads were an important force in all southern states by the 1880s. Beginning around the turn of the century, agricultural groups such as state farm bureaus, and stockmen's and commodity associa-tions began to develop a political voice in southern state capitals. From the late 1930s on these were joined by local government groups, labor unions, and educational interests, especially school-teachers. Together, these five interests—business, agriculture, labor, local government, and education—formed the major interests oper-ating in state capitals in the South, and in the states in general, in the early 1960s.

One long-lasting aspect of the state lobbying scene that these loose environmental constraints produced both in the South and elsewhere was that most famous, or perhaps notorious, of stereotypical lobbyists: the wheeler-dealer. His style is easier to recognize than to define, but in general it refers to a powerful lobbyist who operates aggressively and flamboyantly and is willing to use a variety of methods, some of which may be legally and morally suspect, to achieve his goals. As with many other aspects of the pre-1960s lobbying community, it is impossible to determine how widespread the wheeler-dealer was in the states. The nature of politics at the time, resulting in part from the lack of public disclosure and professionalism, leads to the conclusion, however, that this was a prominent lobbying style in all the states and particularly in the South.

Like most major changes in southern history, the major thrust that was to change the life-style of the South, and thus its politics, came from outside. The changes began in the 1940s and 1950s but did not manifest themselves to any large degree until the 1960s. Of the numerous changes that took place, the most publicized were those stemming from the movement for racial equality spearheaded by Martin Luther King and eventually involving the federal government through the Civil Rights Act of 1964 and the Voting Rights Act of 1965. But there were other changes. Six are of particular importance for our task in this book: (1) increased political participation by blacks and lower-income whites; (2) the rise of the Republican party and the emergence, in most states, of two-party competition; (3) extensive reapportionment of state legislatures; (4) increased economic diversity and the decreasing importance of agriculture; (5) increasing urbanization accompanied by a growing middle class; and (6) increased demand for state and local governmental services and a consequent expansion in the role of these governments. If we refer back to our conceptual framework we will see that all of these had some impact on group activity in the South. Exactly what this impact was forms a major theme in our discussions of the individual states. But first we need to explain the methodology that we used in our investigation of southern interest groups.

Methodology

The ideal approach to a project of this type would be to use an identical research methodology, including identical survey instruments, in each of the southern states (and indeed in each of the fifty states in our overall project). Practical reality, however, does not permit such absolute methodological consistency on such a scale without extensive resources being devoted to it. In fact, we know of no study in the area of state and local government of such a magnitude as ours that has come even close to achieving absolute methodological consistency for all fifty states.

Several factors precluded the imposition of an identical methodology in our fifty-state interest group study. First, in some states literature on interest groups already existed, while in others—the majority—our contributors had to start from scratch. Second, because the registration and reporting requirements vary so much between states, some information—for example, on lobbyists' fees or the percentage of campaign funds contributed by political action committees (PACs)—is just not available. Third, to attempt to impose an identical and restrictive methodology would prevent individual contributors from identifying certain unique and perhaps crucial aspects of their state's interest group system that would be valuable both for an understanding of that system and for comparative purposes.

Even if an identical methodology could be imposed, we strongly believe that a purely quantitative approach would be inadequate. This is because political scientists have not yet reached the stage of being able to understand the role, influence, and impact of interest groups by simply quantifying their activities (unlike other areas of political science, such as voting behavior or the assessment of mass political attitudes). A purely quantitative approach would fail to convey the highly personalized and dynamic nature of several key aspects of interest group activity. One of the most important of these is the interaction between lobbyists and group leaders on the one hand and policymakers, both elected and appointed, on the other. Much of the dynamics of this relationship, and especially what ultimately determines influence, requires a qualitative as opposed to a quantitative methodology. A purely quantitative approach has similar shortcomings when it comes to assessing the various aspects of group power.

This is not to say that a quantitative approach has only a minor role to play in the study of interest groups. On the contrary, we believe that it has a major place. But in some areas it needs to be combined with a qualitative approach, "soaking and poking" as Richard Fenno would say—interviews, observation, and simply hanging around with lobbyists, group leaders, legislators, bureaucrats, and the like. Accordingly, we encouraged our contributors to use qualitative methods in conjunction with quantitative research and to place both within a conceptual framework.

Given these practical problems and the inadequacy of both a uniform set of research tools and the use of a purely quantitative approach, we devised a methodology that would maximize two elements. First, we sought to obtain as much quantitative and usable qualitative data as possible to maximize our ability to make comparisons between states. Second, we wanted to give each contributor the leeway to identify the unique aspects and the nuances of interest group activity in order to convey the essential nature or flavor of that activity in his or her state. To achieve this we developed a set of guidelines that required each contributor to use a methodology incorporating common elements such as the development of group activity over the last twenty years, the types of groups operating today, the tactics that groups use to achieve their goals, and a consideration of the makeup of the lobbying community, among others. Another of the common elements of our methodology, as noted earlier, was the use of a common definition of interest group, interest, lobby, lobbyist, and group power. We have already explained the first four of these terms. It remains, then, to explain our approach to group power.

The concept of interest group power can denote two separate though interrelated notions. It may refer to the ability of an individual group, coalition, or lobby to achieve its policy goals. Alternatively, it may be used to refer to the strength of interest groups as a whole within a state's political and governmental system; or the strength of groups relative to other organizations or institutions, particularly political parties. First, we explain our definition and method of assessment of individual group and lobby power.

Anyone even slightly acquainted with interest group theory will know that group power is a problematic concept. The problems, however, relate much less to the question of definition than they do to the method of assessment. There are so many variables affecting both long- and short-term group power that it is difficult to develop a methodology to assess and predict it in more than a general way. Three methods have been used for assessing individual group power: (1) the use of purely objective or empirical criteria; (2) the perceptual method, relying on the perception of politicians, bureaucrats, and political observers; and (3) a combination of these two approaches. Our approach was this last course. We used the perceptual method but attempted to inject a high degree of objectivity and consistency into the research by using quantitative techniques to analyze the responses. Our definition of individual group power, which also incorporates our method of assessment, is that *the power of any particular interest group or lobby is its ability to achieve its goals as it defines them,* and as perceived by the various people directly involved in and observant of the public policy–making process (e.g., present and former legislators, aides, bureaucrats, other lobbyists, and journalists).

While we have no illusions as to the definitive nature of either our methodology or our results, our findings do provide the first comprehensive assessment, based on a consistent research method in all fifty states, of the most effective interest groups and lobbies in each state of the Union.[22]

Group power as a whole within a state's political system is even more problematic. In fact, this is probably the most difficult aspect of interest group activity to assess, primarily because there are so many variables to consider, many of which have not yet been identified, let alone defined. Consequently, assessments of overall group power are crude at best. Many scholars, however, have taken a valiant stab at the question. We mentioned earlier that Zeller, Zeigler and van Dalen, and Morehouse developed a classification of states into strong, moderate, or weak in the overall impact of their interest group system. One of the key factors here is the inverse relationship between party strength and group strength. But this is a relationship that does not always stand up to investigation.

Faced with these problems involving overall group power, we decided to specify no definition or methodology at all. There was a very good reason for this. With nearly eighty researchers involved in our fifty-state study, eighteen of whom were investigating southern states, we saw an opportunity to set some of the most knowledgeable minds to work on the problem. As a starting point we asked them to consider existing methods and the findings on overall group impact. They were to critique these and offer alternative methodologies and assessments. This is probably the largest number of people who have ever focused on this problem at any one time (the individual state chapters and Chapter 14 explain some of the results of this process). Because no previous investigation included all fifty states (or even the twelve southern states), this study enabled us to add considerably to our knowledge of interest groups in state politics. Perhaps of equal importance is the ability to verify or suggest modifications in those general theories and propositions based on extrapolation from information on a handful of states. And we gained also the ability to compare the South's interest group system with those of other regions.

Southern Interest Group Politics in Relation to Other Regions

As our central theme is change, transition, and growth in southern interest group politics, it is useful as a basis for comparison to identify the major changes and trends that are occurring in the other three regions—the Midwest, the West, and the Northeast. Then, as the analysis of the individual states is explored, the changes and trends in the South can be assessed against the other regions. This will provide yet another dimension for understanding southern interest groups.

In other writings we have gone into considerable detail on these changes and trends.[23] For our present purposes, however, we need only list their essence. Ten such changes and trends appear to be of major importance in the other regions.

1. The number of groups active in state capitals has substantially increased.

2. Simultaneously, the diversity or types of groups that attempt to affect public policy in the states has expanded.

3. Most notable in the broadening of interests is the rise of public-service unions (especially teachers' and public employees' associations), state and local governmental agencies as lobbying forces, and public-interest and citizens' groups.

4. The first three developments have led to an increased intensity of lobbying—more groups and a wider variety of groups are spending more time and money on lobbying than ever before in the history of state government.

5. Interest group tactics are becoming much more sophisticated. They now include public relations campaigns, networking (using a member-contact system), and grass-roots lobbying, as well as coalition building, newsletters, and more-active participation in campaigns.

6. There has been a phenomenal rise in the use of PACs by certain groups as a means of channeling money to favored candidates. Business, labor, and professional groups account for the bulk of PACs and their contributions.

7. There have been some notable changes in the background and style of contract lobbyists. The wheeler-dealer is being replaced by the technical expert. And more and more contract lobbying is being taken over by multiservice lobbying firms, law firms, and public relations companies.

8. Public monitoring of interest group activity has increased through the passage and strengthening of lobby laws, as well as campaign-finance and conflict-of-interest regulations.

9. There have been some major shifts in interest group power in the states, both of individual groups and of groups as a whole. Business is having to share power with an increasing diversity of groups; and group influence as a whole appears to have benefited from, among other factors, the decline of political parties.

10. Overall, and partly because of this decline in parties, the role of interest groups within state political systems has expanded. In particular, they have become more important as vehicles of political participation.

One way of describing these changes is to say that interest group activity in the thirty-eight state capitals outside the South is becoming much more professionalized and more and more like the interest group system operating in Washington, D.C.

We have set the scene for understanding southern interest group politics in three contexts: in individual states; in the region as a whole; and in the context of the fifty states. Our eight-factor conceptual framework, a review of major recent changes in southern society and politics, and the identification of the ten most significant changes in interest group activity in other regions are our major means for understanding group activity in these three contexts. Our central theme in this analysis is to examine the extent of change, growth, and transition in southern interest group politics. Besides this, bearing in mind three other, related questions will help to place the chapters on the states in perspective. Simply stated, these three questions are:

1. Over the years the South's politics may have been quite different from that in the rest of the states, but was its interest group system notably different as a result?
2. Have there been and are there still some common elements in southern interest group politics?
3. How different (if at all) are southern interest group politics today from those of other states and regions?

PART I

THE PERIPHERAL SOUTH

2

KENTUCKY

ADAPTING TO THE INDEPENDENT LEGISLATURE

Malcolm E. Jewell and Penny M. Miller

Kentucky, more than most states, is often described in terms of stereotypes—the Bluegrass State, famous for bourbon, fast horses, burley tobacco, and coal mining. Not surprisingly, these are among the interests taken as important in previous accounts of Kentucky politics and interest groups.[1] In the late nineteenth and early twentieth centuries the Louisville and Nashville Railroad appeared to be the strongest single interest in the state. During the first quarter of this century politics was dominated by a Bipartisan Combine, an alliance of political leaders with Kentucky's major racetrack, liquor, and coal-mining interests. During the New Deal period labor unions, particularly the United Mine Workers in the coalfields, challenged these dominant business interests and were prominently involved in several statewide races.[2] But Kentucky, like most southern states, is becoming more diverse and outgrowing the stereotypes of the past, as evidenced by a wider range of interests and a much larger number of interest groups represented in Frankfort in recent years.

Kentucky, like Tennessee, is divided into regions. Eastern Kentucky is mountainous, a part of Appalachia and a center of coal mining. Central Kentucky is the Bluegrass region, with the metropolitan center of Lexington surrounded by rolling hills and horse farms. Lexington, Louisville, and the suburbs of Cincinnati, Ohio, are the major metropolitan areas. As one moves farther west (except for several cities along the Ohio River), the state becomes rural, more southern in its culture, and more Democratic in its politics; the Bible Belt influence also strengthens. Regionalism produces both diversity and, sometimes, disunity in state politics.

Kentucky has a remarkably high level of ethnic homogeneity and considerably fewer blacks (7%) than any other southern state. Consequently racial conflicts have played a very small role in Kentucky politics. The influence of black interest groups on public policy has been relatively small and seems not to have been affected much by trends in other southern states toward greater black political power.

There is usually a moderate, nonideological tone to politics in Kentucky. Most governors have been Democrats, the most recent Republican serving from 1967 to 1971. Consequently the Democratic primary is usually decisive for state offices. The Democrats have continued to hold comfortable majorities in both houses of the legislature, averaging an approximate three-to-one margin. In recent years the Republican party has had serious difficulty recruiting competitive candidates for major statewide office despite the fact that the party usually polls at least 40 percent of the vote in statewide races. One base of Republican voting support are suburban parts of metropolitan counties; a second are the mountains of southeast Kentucky. In contrast to other southern states, in Kentucky there has been a remarkable stability in the pattern of party identification in the last decade or so, with the Democrats holding an approximate two-to-one lead.[3]

Kentucky is changing in a number of ways that affect the influence of interest groups in the state. Despite a back-to-the-country movement in the 1970s, there has been a gradual shift of population to metropolitan areas. While coal production doubled between 1960 and 1980, the number of persons employed in coal mines has declined, and in recent years coal income has slumped. The major industrial center of Louisville has lost some of its employment in heavy industry, such as automobile and appliance manufacturing, while Lexington and surrounding communities have continued to grow—most notably with the recent acquisition of the Toyota plant in Scott County, just outside of Lexington.

In recent years there has been one particularly important change in Kentucky politics that has had major implications for interest groups: a shift in the balance of power between the governor and the legislature. For many years the governor played a dominant role in the legislative process. The General Assembly was handicapped by the constitutional limitation on its sessions: sixty days every two years. There was high turnover of membership and limited staff resources. The governor dominated the budgetary process, and the legislature was accustomed to approving the budget rapidly and without change. Each new governor became accustomed to selecting the legislative leaders (the House speaker, Senate president pro tem, Democratic floor leaders, and committee chairs), a practice that gave him great leverage in guiding his program through the General Assembly while blocking bills that he opposed.

The change in gubernatorial-legislative relations has come slowly, however. Since 1968 the legislature has gradually developed a strong interim committee system, enabling it to study issues and draft bills between regular sessions, and enabling members of the joint Appropriations and Revenue committees to study budgetary questions in considerable detail. The legislature has begun to review the executive budget more carefully, sometimes making significant changes in it, and has also established several interim committees dealing with oversight of the executive. Meanwhile, as the General Assembly has become more active and powerful, the rate of turnover, specifically voluntary retirement, of members has dropped sharply. As the legislature has assumed a larger role, it has attracted more members who have a long-term interest in a political career.

Changes have also occurred as a result of the action, or inaction, of recent governors. Gov. John Y. Brown, elected in 1979, chose not to influence the selection of legislative leaders. His successor, Martha Layne Collins, made no effort to reassert such authority. Neither Brown nor Collins maintained the kind of day-to-day contact with legislators practiced by some of their predecessors, nor did they try to influence the outcome of more than a small proportion of bills, concentrating their efforts on their budgets and tax measures. Wallace Wilkinson, elected in 1987, was more aggressive but not more skilful in his legislative leadership. It remains to be seen how much success a stronger, defter governor might have in reasserting influence over legislative decision making.

The implications of these changes for interest groups are far-reaching. In the past, lobbyists devoted much of their time to trying to persuade the administration to support or oppose bills. This meant contacting the governor if possible, as well as his aides and the heads of agencies. Only if the governor were unwilling to take a stand, or asked for help in getting a bill passed, was it necessary to devote time and effort to legislative lobbying.

Legislative reform has also led to changes in the tactics of legislative lobbying. Over the last twenty years there has been a steady increase in the frequency and length of committee hearings, making it possible and necessary for all groups to present testimony at such hearings. The growth of legislative independence and power has made the lobbyist's job more complicated. More decision makers must be contacted over a longer period of time. These changes have also made the decision-making process more open, enabling a wider variety of groups to participate. These changes in the legislative system, together with the growing complexity and variety of issues considered by the legislature, have contributed to the growing numbers of interest groups represented by lobbyists in Frankfort.

Regulation and Types of Interest Groups

Kentucky's statutes regulating lobbying date back to 1916, and there have been no major revisions since then—a reflection of the state's conservative, traditionalistic political culture.[4] According to the Lobbying Act of 1916 (Kentucky Revised Statutes [KRS] 6.250), "lobbyist means any person employed as legislative agent or legislative counsel to promote, oppose or act with reference to any legislation which affects or may affect private pecuniary interests as distinct from those of the whole people." Therefore, certain individuals are exempted from the act, including elected or appointed officials acting in an official capacity, private individuals who lobby about issues without pecuniary interests, and individuals who lobby for issues affecting the "public as a whole." KRS 6.280 to 6.290 require that all lobbyists file with the attorney general; unlike some other states, Kentucky imposes no registration fee. KRS 6.300 specifies that each lobbyist must file with the attorney general, within thirty days after the close of the session, a statement of expenses incurred in promoting or opposing legislation. KRS 6.310 prohibits lobbyists' going on the floor of either house while in session, except at the invitation of that house. KRS 6.320 prohibits any form of corrupt lobbying (e.g., by coercion, intimidation, or bribery).

According to the attorney general, in 1974 there were 215 registered lobbyists in Kentucky; by 1990 the number had almost tripled, to 603.[5] Concomitant with this increase in the number of lobbyists, interest groups have proliferated, increasing from 162 to 383 and representing a wide variety of issues. Since there have been no legislative changes in Kentucky's lobby law that would account for these increases, the dramatic growth in registered lobbyists and interest groups can be traced to the increased level of competition required by a shrinking base of governmental revenue resources. Each piece of the budgetary pie becomes harder to acquire or to preserve.

A list of groups employing registered lobbyists is one indicator of the scope of interest group activity in Kentucky. In Table 2.1 the number of groups represented by lobbyists for each of sixteen categories of groups for the 1974 and 1990 legislative sessions is shown. Our focus is on the increase in the number of interest groups represented, rather than the number of lobbyists representing each type of interest group, because in Kentucky some interest groups employ many part-time lobbyists, whereas others employ one or two full-time agents. Moreover, some contract lobbyists represent more than one special interest. Therefore, the number of lobbyists employed by particular types of interests would not be an accurate accounting of the power and political clout of those groups.

As depicted in Table 2.1, many types of interest groups have grown substantially in number during this fifteen-year period in which a more independent legislative body has emerged. There are many noteworthy trends. The growth has been much less of public-interest groups than it has been of specific economic interests. An abundance of trade associations, national corporations, specific individual companies, and other groups have engaged lobbyists to pursue specialized goals of business. In their drive to turn economic clout into political power, these diverse business groups have enlisted the time and skills of professional lobbyists and forged relationships with prominent law firms and banking institutions. Medical/health groups and hospital associations have significantly

Table 2.1 Interest Group Involvement in the Kentucky Legislature, 1974 and 1990

Interest Groups Categories	Number of Organizations Represented		
	1974 only	1974 and 1990	1990 only
Education			
Adult groups (KEA)	4	5	6
Student organizations	3	—	—
Labor	7	7	15
Government			
Cities and counties	1	1	7
Local officials	1	2	13
Professionals (nonhealth)	2	2	7
Health			
Medical facilities	—	1	19
Professionals (e.g., AMA)	7	7	24
Insurance	3	4	16
Real estate	3	3	4
Banking and finance	19	6	19
Businesses			
Broad purpose (e.g., Chamber of Commerce)	1	5	4
Single industries (e.g., Kentucky Restaurants Assn.)	8	9	21
Individual companies	6	—	62
National corporations	2	3	12
Horse industry	1	—	7
Transportation	3	2	7
Utilities	1	6	13
Energy (coal, oil, etc.)	4	6	26
Special issues	8	2	13
Nonprofit organizations	5	—	8
Agriculture	—	2	7
Total	89	73	310

grown in number and political power; health professionals (e.g., doctors, dentists, nurses, optometrists, chiropractors) all compete in the legislature for scarce health-care funds from government. Labor groups have increased in number by more than 100 percent; labor's strength has been enhanced by its convergence of interest and activity with educational, public employees', farm, and minority groups. Substantial legislative presence has also been achieved by groups representing various facets of the horse industry (e.g., horse racing, breeding), by energy-related interests (e.g., coal, oil), and by utilities. Insurance interests and special-issue groups have also demonstrated considerable growth.

The most important interest groups in Frankfort that are not registered are the various agencies of state government. The Departments of Commerce, Human Resources, Education, and Natural Resources are among the most active in lobbying the legislature. These agencies are influential in part because of their ability to mobilize skilfully their constituencies and client groups. Moreover, the agencies are respected because they provide legislators with detailed information and expert judgment on legislation. The University of Kentucky, University of Louisville, and six regional universities are also powerful, partially because of their ability to mobilize faculty and alumni. Legislators are likely to be particularly responsive to concerns of universities in their area, their alma mater, or both. Local governments and organizations of local officials (such as sheriffs and county clerks) often have considerable influence over the narrow issues of particular concern to them (although lobbyists for some of these groups are often registered).

Overall there has emerged a growing pluralism of special interests. That growth shows no signs of abating; nor should a different pattern be expected. A slow growth of tax receipts, along with new demands on government, can be anticipated. Old turfs will require more-active protection, and new interests will appear at the General Assembly's door.

Categories of Lobbyists and Their Spending Patterns

Frankfort's lobbying community consists of four categories of lobbyists: in-house; contract; government; and citizen lobbyists. The largest category of registered lobbyists are in-house company or association lobbyists—persons who are employed by or are members of a company or organization, who engage in lobbying as part—often a major part—of their duties. This broad category of lobbyist represents three basic types of institutions: business firms or individual companies (e.g., First Security National Bank and Baker Petroleum); voluntary associations (e.g., Kentucky Education Association [KEA], Kentucky Farm Bureau, and the Kentucky Coal Association); and organizations of local governments or public officials (e.g., Kentucky Municipal League and the District Judges Association of Kentucky).

A few organizations such as KEA are large enough so that on their payroll are one or two persons who spend a great deal of time lobbying and specialize in legislative matters, year in and year out. But for many other companies and associations this work is done by various individuals (e.g., the company president, in-house lawyers, or public relations experts), and their lobbying efforts—primarily during the legislative session—represent only a small proportion of their overall designated activities. In the last few legislative sessions there has been a significant growth in the number of individual companies that have registered in-house lobbyists; these businesses want a voice in policy-making that affects their specific interests.

A second category, contract lobbyists, consists of individuals who are hired by a client on a contractual basis specifically to lobby. Of the 603 lobbyists registered with the attorney general in April 1990, seventeen contract lobbyists each represented five or more clients.

Those in the third category, government lobbyists, are not officially lobbyists; state and local governmental entities are represented in the legislative arena by either the state department or city/county executive leaders, or by designated specialized legislative liaisons. Much of the formal testimony and informal, "hard-hitting" lobbying is probably carried out by the powerful, politically experienced agency or local governmental leaders—the official spokespersons. Although most state employees are not allowed to lobby in their official capacities, the governor's office and the various departments, commissions, and other agencies usually employ at least one person each as a legislative liaison. Legislative liaisons engage in many types of activities: They monitor bills affecting their agencies;

testify as specialists in legislative hearings; represent their agency to the legislature and often to the governor's office; and prepare technical information requested by legislative and executive bodies.

The larger Kentucky local governments utilize the lobbying skills not only of their politically savvy executive leaders, but also of specially trained legislative liaisons. For example, Lexington designated Jane Vimont its first legislative liaison in August 1986; she had been serving as research director of Lexington's Urban County Council for five years. "The need for her position became evident during the 1986 General Assembly, when Mayor Scotty Baesler sent her to Frankfort to stay abreast of the more than 1,000 bills that directly affected Lexington."[6]

Another category of lobbyists, citizen lobbyists, generally represent both registered and unregistered groups that include nonprofit, social-service, public-interest, and special-interest groups—such as the state chapters of the National Organization of Women (NOW), the League of Women Voters, and other women's groups; community and neighborhood associations; the state Parent-Teacher Association; the state chapter of the American Association of Retired Persons (AARP); Kentucky War on Drugs, Mothers Against Drunk Driving (MADD), and other alcoholism- and drug-prevention groups; Grandparents Visitation Rights and Grandparents' and Grandchildren's Rights groups; groups for gifted and handicapped children and for day care; and sports groups such as the League of Kentucky Sportsmen. These groups, which have experienced significant growth in numbers, are largely staffed and run by unpaid volunteers, and they form the core of Kentucky's citizens' lobby. In 1990 the AARP was represented by seventeen unpaid senior Kentuckians.

Kentucky lobbyists flocked to Frankfort in greater numbers for the 1990 General Assembly and spent more than ever before. The 603 registered lobbyists, representing 383 organizations, spent $4,163,757; four years earlier 440 lobbyists spent $3,083,325, setting what was then the record. In 1986 and 1990, although most of the money was spent on salaries, hotel rooms, and transportation, lobbyists also claimed as expenses such items as chili dinners, flowers, and candy. The largest single amount in the 1986 reports to the attorney general's office was $82,500, which Buddy Adams of Bowling Green listed as salary and expenses in representing Traffic Safety

Now, a Detroit, Michigan, organization supported by the automobile industry that backed an unsuccessful bill to make using seat belts mandatory. Adams is a former state representative and former secretary of the state Human Resources Cabinet who operates a governmental affairs and public relations firm. He reported a total of $176,430 in compensation and expenses in representing eight companies and trade associations. According to Ron Adams, the president of People's Finance and Investment Company, "it's expensive to stay away from home." The bulk of his expenses were for hotel rooms and meals.[7] The largest single amount in the 1990 reports was $129,987, which W. Dixon Jones of Louisville listed as salary and expenses in representing Management Registry, a Kentucky health-care company.

In 1986 Blue Cross and Blue Shield of Kentucky had seven registered lobbyists who received a total of $104,375 for salaries and expenses, the largest amount being paid to Louisville attorney D. Paul Alagia, Jr. Blue Cross's legislative goals included passage of a bill to allow it to operate as a mutual insurance company and defeat of a sweeping health-care bill that would have required Blue Cross to cover some Medicaid patients as part of its contract for state employees' health insurance. Both of these goals were achieved.

In 1990 Humana had five registered lobbyists who received a total of $118,503 for salaries and expenses. Also appearing on behalf of the hospital conglomerate were its chair and president. Humana's primary legislative goal was an exemption from state regulation of hospital expansions. After much divisive debating, Humana got what it wanted.

At the other end of the scale in 1990, eighty-seven of the 603 registered lobbyists reported spending nothing. In Table 2.2 spending during the 1986 and 1990 sessions and interims is set out by twenty-one categories of special interests.

Interest Groups' Role in Elections

Interest groups may participate electorally in several ways. The most obvious, and most easily measured, is through PACs. Of major importance here is the level of PAC contributions in Democratic

Table 2.2 Spending by Lobbyists, 1986 and 1990 Sessions of the General Assembly

Category	Spending Level (in Dollars)	
	1986	1990
Business and industry	420,485	724,192
Health and medical	356,032	720,955
Insurance	256,253	317,284
Transportation	228,087	136,343
Utilities	204,180	258,319
Oil, gas, steel	193,787	359,693
Banking, finance, collectors	188,926	231,325
Public officials, government	173,595	191,104
Education	155,980	56,150
Contractors, homebuilders, real estate	143,515	132,963
Labor	139,441	142,020
Equine racing	136,310	135,414
Miscellaneous	130,833	105,021
Agriculture	123,925	197,878
Coal	95,646	223,948
Law	63,826	49,331
Liquor, temperance	36,479	63,440
Media communications	15,444	99,985
Retirement	15,406	5,788
Senior citizens	4,324	6,415
Women's issues	853	6,188

Source: Figures for 1986 are from the Louisville *Courier-Journal,* August 12, 1986, sec. B, 1, 4. Those for 1990 are from reports filed in the state attorney general's office.

primaries and in general election campaigns for governor and for the legislature. (Kentucky does not have the initiative or referendum, except for voting on constitutional amendments. In such votes interest groups usually do not play a large role.)

Since the 1968 election the Kentucky Registry of Election Finance has served as a repository of campaign reports for all state and local offices. Contributions of more than $100 from individuals and groups must be recorded by campaign treasurers and submitted to the registry. Before 1968 there were unrealistic limits on contributions and haphazard, minimal reporting, and thus there was a dearth of comprehensive and accurate campaign-finance data. Starting in mid-July 1986, the maximum contribution an individual could make to a candidate in one state or local election was raised from $3,000 to $4,000. The 1988 General Assembly put a cap on PAC contributions: PACs were limited to giving $4,000 per candidate; contributions to PACs to $2,000 per individual.

In Tables 2.3 and 2.4 we see, by type of interest group, how much the PACs spent in the gubernatorial and legislative races. Seventeen interests were identified, and money given by PACs within each was aggregated. Most of the categories in the tables are self-explanatory; the special-issues category includes groups supporting such issues as right to life and gun regulation. Although these categories do not include all potentially significant groups, they were chosen because of their recognized political and economic power in Kentucky, the frequency and total sums of their giving, and—in most cases—their unity on issues affecting them.

Overall, there has been a substantial increase in PAC contributions in both statewide and legislative races. In Kentucky, as in many other states, there has emerged in the last ten years a plethora of PACs representing numerous occupational groups and special issues.

Gubernatorial Elections

In Table 2.3 we can see that in 1983 (as in 1979) only two organized interests—labor and education—made major contributions through PACs to the gubernatorial races. These interests have a tradition of organized campaign efforts in Kentucky Democratic primaries and general elections. Most of the other organized interests made very little use of PACs for these races. In 1987, however, several other types of PACs made substantial contributions to gubernatorial races—notably professional groups and several business groups, particularly banking and finance, and insurance.

Table 2.3 Contributions to Gubernatorial Candidates in Primary and General Elections, by Categories of Interest Groups (in Dollars)

	1983			1987		
	Primary	General Election		Primary	General Election	
	Democratic	Democratic	Republican	Democratic	Democratic	Republican
Education	70,864	2,250	1,190	53,000	—	35,000
Labor	221,366	78,360	1,621	78,000	44,000	—
Public employees	6,000	350	—	6,500	5,000	—
Professionals	7,000	12,700	6,000	90,000	8,000	—
Health and medical	500	1,750	—	13,000	19,000	1,000
Insurance	—	1,000	500	25,500	32,000	1,500
Real estate	5,200	7,000	—	13,000	2,000	—
Construction	1,000	1,000	4,000	12,000	21,000	—
Banking and finance	6,900	21,000	10,500	131,050	13,500	2,500
Business and industry	17,775	16,390	4,100	19,000	41,700	—
Horse industry	1,000	3,000	—	16,300	5,000	—
Transportation	7,500	500	—	16,750	10,000	—
Utilities	1,400	—	—	9,500	7,500	—
Oil and gas	3,000	—	500	16,000	6,000	—
Coal	1,000	500	—	1,000	—	—
Liquor	4,000	2,000	2,000	6,500	—	—
Special issues	3,200	—	—	2,300	—	—
Total group contributions	357,705	147,800	29,96-	509,400	216,700	40,000
Total receipts	4,408,910	1,770,551	1,221,617	12,324,038	2,610,075	255,788
Percentage of receipts from groups	8.1	8.4	2.5	4.1	8.2	15.6

Compiled from records at the Kentucky Registry of Election Finance.

Table 2.4 Contributions to Legislative Candidates in Primary and General Elections, by Major Categories of Interest Groups (in Dollars)

| | House | | | | Senate | | | |
| | Primary | | General | | Primary | | General | |
	1981	1984	1981	1984	1981	1983	1981	1983
Education	32,156	34,730	16,400	73,107	28,368	31,320	14,350	17,657
Labor	18,000	36,287	14,025	33,917	1,600	9,234	2,000	16,915
Public employees	375	905	150	1,200	—	—	—	1,000
Professionals	900	200	5,450	2,750	—	3,650	1,050	1,750
Health and medical	26,650	23,950	25,470	38,550	31,000	31,150	10,950	26,576
Insurance	1,400	750	1,550	3,075	—	1,400	1,000	200
Real estate	11,700	4,200	13,900	18,600	5,500	10,000	6,500	4,000
Construction	1,700	7,750	3,600	4,100	250	250	1,050	3,200
Banking and finance	15,720	23,455	18,400	23,670	14,700	20,250	9,520	4,350
Business and industry	14,650	14,400	23,598	14,800	10,800	8,150	12,750	5,650
Horse industry	25,800	17,500	17,000	29,700	6,100	12,500	4,950	12,600
Transport	1,850	2,500	1,325	5,150	1,400	2,800	650	—
Utilities	1,080	1,450	550	9,500	2,900	5,850	1,950	3,600
Oil and gas	900	800	600	200	400	700	—	—
Coal	—	4,700	—	2,150	3,200	3,200	3,500	1,000
Liquor	875	—	200	150	1,000	1,600	200	1,450
Special issues	1,400	800	1,900	6,350	2,100	—	1,800	6,750
Total group contributions	155,156	174,378	144,118	266,969	109,318	142,054	72,220	106,704
Total contributions	674,351	944,670	431,967	749,037	434,719	613,287	193,391	255,782
Percentage from groups	23.0	17.5	33.4	35.6	25.1	23.2	37.3	41.7

Compiled from records at the Kentucky Registry of Election Finance.

In 1983 only about 8.2 percent of all funds raised by Democrats in the primary and general elections came from PACs. In 1987 the absolute amount of PAC contributions to Democratic primary candidates rose, but the percentage coming from PACs fell to only 4.1 percent. The reason was that the candidates, particularly Wilkinson, raised unprecedented amounts from individual contributors. In the general election the proportion of Republican funding from PACs rose to 15.6 percent, simply because educational PACs favored the Republican candidate, while individual contributions to his campaign were minimal.

For those interest groups making relatively small contributions to candidates, the contributions by individuals have often dwarfed those made by PACs. Because campaign-finance reports list the occupations of contributors, it is possible to calculate individual contributions of specific occupational groups. In the 1983 Democratic gubernatorial primary, for example, coal operators contributed $111,803; farmers, $63,540; insurance agents, $42,421; and bankers, $39,490—in each case a much larger figure than was contributed by the corresponding PACs. In the 1983 general election campaign, individuals in the construction business gave $162,000; coal operators, $87,000; and bankers, $73,000, most of it going to Democrats.[8] It appears that many persons in these fields were more concerned with benefits their own business might gain from an administration than with broader state policies.

Legislative Races

The cost of legislative campaigns for all the House seats and half the Senate seats doubled between 1979 and 1983/84, from $1.327 million to $2.613 million. During the same period the proportion of these costs contributed by PACs increased from 15 to 26.4 percent, growing from almost $200,000 to nearly $700,000. The rapid increase in the rate of PAC contributions to legislative campaigns reflects the growing power of the legislature vis-à-vis the governor, a trend that a number of interest groups have clearly recognized.

Overall, as depicted in Table 2.4, the leading PAC contributors to House and Senate electoral campaigns have been education, health and medical, labor, the horse industry, banking and finance, business and industry, and real estate interests. The educational lobby, through its statewide and county PACs, has been in the forefront for targeting funds to legislative candidates. Because of growing conflicts within the health industry, and particularly the increased competition for shrinking governmental funds, health and medical PACs have dramatically increased their funding to Senate and House legislative leaders, members of key committees, and other incumbents who are friends of the health profession. Labor has also substantially increased its funding of legislative races, with most of its funds going to Democratic candidates.

How can we assess the impact of PACs on public policy-making? PACs' campaign contributions might affect public policy-making in two ways: influencing the outcome of elections and thus affecting future policy-making; or influencing the outcome of policy-making by causing elected officials to be more responsive to them. As noted above, in the very costly gubernatorial races direct PAC contributions were small; therefore, we might conclude that these contributions were not large enough to do either of these things—to influence the outcome of elections or to give them greater access to the elected governors. In contrast, as state legislative races are getting more expensive, PAC moneys are becoming a much larger proportion of total campaign receipts, and certainly a much larger proportion of total receipts than in the gubernatorial races. As significant contributors to legislative races, PACs can affect policy-making either by helping candidate X beat candidate Y, or by making candidate X more responsive to their special interests in the policy-making arena.

Interest Group Strategies in the Legislature

As the General Assembly's independent influence has grown, interest groups have found it necessary to adapt new strategies to accomplish their objectives. It is no longer sufficient to enlist the support of the governor and the pertinent executive agencies in order to get legislation passed or defeated. A greater variety of organizations are sending lobbyists to the legislature, some are increasing the number of their lobbyists, and a few are moving their headquarters from Louisville to Frankfort.

Some organizations have tried to play a role in leadership contests, and they are likely to make greater efforts to influence the selection of committee members. As the committees assume greater importance in decision making, membership on those committees assumes greater importance. In examining the membership of House and Senate committees for the 1980–1984 period, we find a number of examples of legislators serving on committees dealing with their specialized interests, thus providing interest groups with obvious allies. The executive directors of the state American Federation of Labor–Congress of Industrial Organizations (AFL-CIO) and the Associated Industries of Kentucky each sat on the House Labor and Industry Committee. Three of the seven members of the Senate Banking and Insurance Committee during this period had strong professional ties to the banking or insurance business. The chair and vice-chair of the Senate Education Committee were, respectively, a school principal and a former university president.

We can illustrate the variety of strategies being employed by looking at examples of diverse interest groups and issues.[9] Labor and business interests frequently take opposite sides on major economic issues in the General Assembly. Labor unions are not numerically strong in Kentucky, but in recent years the state AFL-CIO has become better organized for political action and lobbying under a new state director, Ron Cyrus, an experienced member of the General Assembly. The AFL-CIO and individual unions have been devoting more attention in recent years to legislative elections and to the coordination of lobbying efforts. Business organizations are also giving higher priority to legislative lobbying.

Not surprisingly, legislators do not like to be caught in the middle of conflicts between business and labor; they prefer to vote for bills that represent compromises between these two major groups. Efforts to solve controversial issues through committees or task forces on which the two groups are represented have increased. Such a joint study led to nearly unanimous passage of a bill in 1986 to reform the unemployment insurance system, and also to the establishment of a similar task force to study workers' compensation during the 1986/87 interim.

The horse-racing industry in Kentucky is deeply divided. On the one hand are the major horse breeders and owners, with close ties to several of the major racetracks. Traditionally these groups have sought political influence by supporting candidates for governor, but in 1983 they established the Kentucky Thoroughbred Association (KTA) in order to increase their influence in the legislature. On the other hand are the smaller horse owners and trainers, who have been organized for a longer time as the Horsemen's Benevolent and Protective Association (HBPA). This organization began active lobbying of the General Assembly in 1978 and also began funding legislative candidates earlier than did the KTA. The two organizations disagree on a number of economic issues and on the role the state should play in the horse-racing industry. In addition, each of the state's racetracks has its own interests to protect.

The major goal of the horse industry in 1986 was passage of an omnibus horse-racing bill, designed in part to renew and extend tax credits to racetracks, in order to permit larger purses at the tracks to attract better horses. Because of its more extensive political and lobbying efforts, and the assistance it provided to Don Blandford in his election to the speakership, the HBPA expected to have a major hand in shaping that legislation. But Speaker Blandford insisted that the various groups in the horse industry must reach a compromise on the major issues in the proposed bill and established an informal committee to accomplish that. The resulting compromise was endorsed by the speaker and passed by the General Assembly.

Education interests also field active players in the lobbying game. One source of the KEA's strength is the fact that significant numbers of teachers are found in every county in Kentucky. A second source is its willingness to become actively involved in electoral politics and, most significantly, its recognition of the importance today of legislative elections. As we have noted, the PACs run by KEA and its county affiliates in recent years have made larger donations to legislative candidates than any other group has. In addition they have provided campaign services (such as polls, voter-targeting information, and media advisors) as well as volunteer workers to these candidates.

The KEA's influence on educational policy was demonstrated during the 1984 regular session and 1985 special session, when the General Assembly wrestled with a package of reforms initiated by the governor, and a tax bill to pay for these reforms. After a deadlock during the 1984 session, in 1985 the General Assembly passed both a reform package and a tax increase. Between the two sessions the governor's educational package was substantially revised, largely as a result of efforts by a small group of legislators on the House Education Committee who had close ties to the KEA. Their revisions, particularly those regarding salary structure, made the package much more acceptable to the KEA, which then worked hard for its passage in 1985.

Another major educational interest group, the Prichard Committee (named after Edward Prichard, its original chair), operates quite differently. It is composed of leading citizens, rather than professional educators; its strategy is to recommend reforms, based on extensive research, and to mobilize public support for its recommendations. The General Assembly's 1990 session adopted a sweeping reform of the state's educational system, including financing, organization and governance, and curriculum. It was responding to pressure from the Kentucky Supreme Court, which had declared the existing school system unconstitutional, and to pressure from public opinion and the media for reform. The Prichard Committee not only helped to create a climate of opinion supportive of educational reform but also developed many of the specific proposals for reform and innovation that were adopted in 1990.

A variety of health organizations have assumed growing importance in the legislature because health issues have become more important, and the escalating costs of health care are creating serious problems for state government. While these groups share many common concerns, economic pressures and competition lead them to take opposite sides of some issues. In the 1986 session several prominent legislators tried to gain passage of a comprehensive health-care bill, designed primarily to meet the needs of those persons not adequately covered by insurance. Although the bill had the support of the Kentucky Hospital Association (KHA), it was opposed by the Humana chain of hospitals (which is based in Kentucky), Blue Cross–Blue Shield, and the Association of Health Care Facilities (representing the well-organized nursing-home industry), as well as by several business organizations. One sponsor of the proposal, Sen. Benny Ray Bailey, eventually succeeded in developing a compromise version of the bill, with changes in the funding mechanism, that was acceptable to the major interests; this measure was passed in the 1990 session.

The most divisive health issue in the 1990 legislative session concerned a challenge by the Humana hospital chain to the certificate-of-need program, under which hospitals were required to get state approval for new and expanded facilities and major equipment. With great difficulty, Humana succeeded in winning legislative approval for changes in the requirements that would permit it to carry out a major expansion of its facilities in Louisville. Most of the other hospitals in the state, fearing greater competition from Humana, were opposed. But Humana was able to mobilize strong support from the Jefferson County (Louisville) delegation, in part because of its threat to move out of Louisville if its proposal were rejected. In the health field, as in other areas, an interest group or corporation that is able significantly to affect the state's economy has a major advantage in legislative battles.

Interest Groups in the Administrative Arena

During the legislative session interest groups try to get bills passed, amended, or defeated, but after legislation affecting an interest group has been enacted the group often tries to influence the implementation of the law. Lobbying on legislative issues is no longer directed primarily at the governor, but as political issues grow more complex, interest groups must pay increasing attention to administrative decision making. Groups may try to influence the selection of administrators, bring informal pressure on agencies, or participate in formal hearings when administrative regulations are promulgated.

Little research has been done in Kentucky on such interest group activities, except with regard to legislative oversight of administrative regulations. Since 1972 a legislative subcommittee has reviewed administrative regulations, held hearings on controversial ones, and made recommendations for changes to the originating agency.

The procedure has given interest groups a formal opportunity to raise objections and recommend changes in administrative regulations at both the executive and legislative levels. On the relatively infrequent occasions when interest groups choose to criticize administrative regulations, they are often able to win some support from the legislative subcommittee, which in turn is often successful in winning modifications from the executive. Among the groups most often seeking change in administrative regulations are coal, oil, and gas operators concerned with environmental regulations; other business organizations; nursing homes and some other health groups; and public employees' organizations concerned with state personnel regulations. Legislators appear to be particularly responsive to complaints that proposed regulations will be damaging to business interests in the state.

Interest Groups and the Courts

When interest groups lose battles in the legislative arena they sometimes seek to reverse the outcome by taking their case to the courts. A group that fails to prevent enactment of legislation can try to prove that it is unconstitutional. A group that fails to get legislation passed can sometimes find a way to accomplish its objectives judicially. There is nothing unusual or distinctive about interest group efforts in the courts in Kentucky, and no comprehensive research has been done on the topic, but a few examples will illustrate how important the courts can be in settling conflicts among interest groups.

Usually, organizations that are trying to get increased spending for particular objectives must accomplish their goals in the legislative rather than the judicial arena, but occasionally there are exceptions to this rule. In the late 1970s organized educational interests that were seeking to increase local spending for education believed that they were handicapped by unrealistically low assessments on which the property tax was based. They took their case to the courts and won a short-lived victory when the Kentucky Court of Appeals determined that the state constitution required that property be assessed at 100 percent of fair market value. But groups opposing such tax increases persuaded the General Assembly to pass a tax-rollback law, requiring that local tax rates be lowered so that revenue would not increase, and permitting rates to be increased annually by only a small percentage unless voters approved a higher rate.

In 1985 a group of school superintendents representing sixty-six of the poorest school districts was organized to ask the state courts to require a higher and more equitable level of state spending for education. They argued that the spending levels failed to meet the state constitutional requirement that the General Assembly "provide for an efficient system of common schools throughout the State." In 1988 a state circuit judge ruled that Kentucky's system of financing public schools was unconstitutional and placed responsibility on the legislature to provide better funding of education. In June 1989 the Kentucky Supreme Court upheld that decision and broadened its scope, declaring that the entire system of primary and secondary education was unconstitutional. This led directly to the sweeping reforms of the state's educational system in the 1990 General Assembly, described above. It is worth noting that the "interest group" that turned to the courts for help was an organization of local officials—the school superintendents.

Industry has also turned to the courts. Kentucky law permits the use of "broad form deeds" under which companies that own mineral rights may mine materials such as coal even though this activity— particularly strip-mining—damages the land owned by another person. Organized interests have failed in their efforts to get the Kentucky courts to declare broad form deeds invalid, while coal interests have successfully challenged the constitutionality of laws designed to modify or abolish the broad form deed. The issue was resolved in 1988 when the voters approved a constitutional amendment that had the effect of reversing the court's decision and drastically limiting the impact of broad form deeds.

Some organizations have succeeded in winning from the courts what they could not win from the legislature. During the 1970s organizations of religious schools tried unsuccessfully to get the General Assembly to repeal legislation regulating such schools. Then these groups turned to the courts and won a decision that legislation regulating religious schools violated the state constitution. Similarly, a few years ago opponents of a retail liquor price-fixing law failed to gain its repeal but succeeded in persuading the Kentucky Supreme Court to declare it unconstitutional.

Assessing the Power of Interest Groups

What are the most powerful interest groups in Kentucky, the ones best able to gain their objectives, to pass the bills they favor and defeat those they oppose? There is no simple, precise answer to that question.

In her 1980 study, which ranked the most significant pressure groups in each state, Morehouse included the following for Kentucky: coal companies; liquor interests; tobacco interests; KEA; rural electric cooperatives; and the Jockey Club. The list appears both incomplete and out of date, particularly the reference to the Jockey Club, which flourished in the 1920s but has had little influence since then.[10]

Perhaps the best way to estimate the strength of interest groups is to ask legislators, who must deal with them on a continuing basis. Jack Bizzel, who conducted surveys of Kentucky legislators after the 1980, 1982, and 1984 sessions, in each case asked them to list the most powerful or influential interest groups in each session. He then ranked the ten most frequently listed groups in each session.[11] If we combine these rankings, we find six groups in the top ten in all three sessions: Kentucky Farm Bureau; Kentucky AFL-CIO; KEA; Kentucky Chamber of Commerce; Kentucky Bankers Association (KBA); and Kentucky Medical Association.

In order to evaluate interest groups in Kentucky, we will divide them into several major categories, rather than trying to compare groups that differ greatly in their size and the scope of their agenda. First are the groups that represent large numbers of persons or businesses and usually take stands on a wide range of issues, such as the Farm Bureau, the AFL-CIO, and the Chamber of Commerce. These groups were ranked first, second, and fourth by the legislators. It is noteworthy that while the Farm Bureau has been consistently ranked first, some legislators believe it is now declining in influence. Each of these groups is strong enough so that it can often prevent passage of legislation that it perceives seriously damages its interests. Moreover, when major bills affect the interests of several of these groups, some kind of compromise is usually necessary to gain passage of legislation.

A second category of groups that we might anticipate as important are those representing particular economic interests that are especially important in Kentucky, such as the tobacco, liquor, coal, and horse industries. For several reasons, none of these groups is quite so influential in the state as we might expect. Most legislative issues involving tobacco are settled at the national rather than the state level. The influence of the liquor industry in Kentucky is balanced by the strong prohibitionist sentiment found in the rural, Bible Belt counties; and most of the legislative issues, such as Sunday liquor sales in larger cities, are of marginal importance. The coal industry is vitally important to Kentucky, and the legislature frequently grapples with issues affecting coal—the severance tax, a possible tax on unmined minerals, weight limits for coal trucks, regulation of strip-mining, and compensation for black lung disease, for example. The Kentucky Coal Association is the most important interest group representing coal operators, but divisions and conflicting interests within the industry have weakened its political effectiveness. The horse industry is even more sharply divided, with different organizations representing the breeders and larger owners on the one hand and smaller owners and trainers on the other, and with each of the racetracks having its own special interests.

A third category consists of those groups representing interests with major political or economic power, or both, groups that are likely to have an interest in major pieces of legislation in every session of the General Assembly. The most powerful of these, according to legislators, is the KEA. It is powerful because teachers are a significant force in every county in the state, and because they are more politically organized and active than most groups. Another important group, the KBA, is influential because of the economic and political power of its member banks. However, several years ago, when the KBA split on a major banking bill, its effectiveness was seriously eroded. Some of the other most powerful interest groups in Kentucky are those in the health field, and their influence has grown as health issues have assumed higher priority on the legislative agenda.

In recent sessions the legislators most frequently named the Kentucky Medical Association, but several other groups have become very active in recent years, including the KHA, the Humana hospitals (which do not belong to the KHA), Blue Cross–Blue Shield, and the organization representing nursing homes.

A fourth category comprises groups that represent narrower, more specialized interests, or groups that become active in lobbying only intermittently, as specific issues arise in a particular legislative session. Examples include the state dental association and groups representing optometrists, social workers, and chiropractors, as well as individual businesses.

A fifth category of interest groups comprises those representing particular units of government, such as cities or counties, or universities. Recently legislators have emphasized the relative effectiveness of lobbying efforts by political leaders from the major cities, while being less impressed by the effectiveness of the Kentucky Municipal League. In the area of higher education, each of the state universities tends to have a group of legislative supporters from its own geographic area. For several years the universities have been engaged in struggles for budgetary priority and for authority to operate particular graduate and professional schools, a struggle that has weakened higher education. Prior to the 1986 session the various higher-education interests agreed to work more closely together. This cooperation helps to explain a breakthrough in funding for higher education in the 1986 session, although its effect was diminished by budget cuts, in the following biennium, resulting from revenue shortfalls.

Conclusion

Two major trends have been occurring in Kentucky that help to explain the current role of interest groups in its political system. One of these trends is political pluralism—the proliferation of organized interests that are represented in Frankfort. Kentucky government and politics are no longer dominated by two or three special interests (coal, horse racing, liquor, or agriculture). Some of the traditionally strong interests, such as the coal and horse industries, have been weakened by division into more-specialized and often conflicting interests.

But there are several more-important reasons for this new pluralism. The economy of the state is becoming more complex and varied, and Kentucky is gradually becoming more urbanized. The state government now deals with a wider variety of issues (partly because of program cutbacks in Washington), and the interests affected by the issues must make their views known in Frankfort. Some of the major issues facing the state are complex ones on which a large variety of specific interests form shifting and often conflicting coalitions—issues such as the costs of medical care, the environmental impact of extractive industries, and restructuring the tax laws.

The proliferation of interests represented in Frankfort is also caused by the second major trend in the state: the shift in power from the governor to the legislature. That trend is not necessarily irreversible, but it is highly unlikely that the General Assembly will ever be as subservient to the governor as it was as recently as the 1970s. The political system is now much more open. Instead of decisions being made in the governor's office with the participation of a few interests, there are now extensive legislative hearings in which all pertinent groups are represented, and the corridors of the State Capitol are crowded with lobbyists seeking out legislators.

In practice the newly independent General Assembly is still evolving. Critics, including some legislators, believe that the committees are too often dominated by members identified with a special interest, and that, even when this is not the case, the committees have not shown enough courage in resisting group pressures. There are differences of opinion about the strategies that legislative leaders should follow to counter some of these pressures. We have noted that the legislators, and their leaders, often follow the strategy of insisting that conflicting interest groups work out compromises, a strategy that minimizes the cross-pressures the legislature must face.

In the years ahead the trends of the recent past are likely to continue. Kentucky's economy will grow more varied, and interest groups will proliferate. The state will face more-complex issues and more-difficult choices of spending priorities, with decision making made more complex by conflicting demands of interest groups. Future governors may play a stronger role than the most recent ones have. The General Assembly will become more professional, with better staffing and more-experienced members devoting more time to the job; and it may develop better techniques for dealing with the demands that interest groups make on the state.

3

TENNESSEE

NEW CHALLENGES FOR THE FARM, LIQUOR, AND BIG BUSINESS LOBBIES

David H. Folz and Patricia K. Freeman

In many respects, Tennessee is a composite of several of the important factors that have shaped the New South and that still limit achievement of its potential. It is a state of great geographical diversity, long-standing political tradition, and considerable economic change in recent years. The Volunteer State is a place of paradox where tradition and change, progress and retrenchment, and innovation and regression drive the economic, political, and social evolution. Its citizens are individualistic and mainly conservative; however, from increasing economic diversity and political change, new groups have emerged to challenge traditionally influential interests. The nature of the evolving pattern of interest group power in Tennessee is our focus here.

Gradually, the old stereotypes of a state populated by moonshiners, hillbillies, and old folks who sit on the porch and sip sour mash are eroding in the wake of trendsetting educational reforms and a string of successes in economic development that include major investments by both Japanese (Nissan) and U.S. (General Motor's Saturn) automobile makers. Tennessee also has made some progress in capturing its share of high-technology development by capitalizing on the science and engineering expertise of the Oak Ridge National Labs, the Tennessee Valley Authority (TVA), and the University of Tennessee at Knoxville. However, stubborn pockets of poverty, unemployment, and illiteracy remain despite the state's investments in education and job growth. Agribusiness is still the most important economic sector, and almost half of the state's land area is farmed. Production agriculture, farm supply, and food processing and distribution account for one-fourth of the state's payroll and employment base. The Tennessee Farm Bureau was the single most powerful interest group in the state prior to the redistricting required by *Baker v. Carr* (1962), which finally broke the rural arm lock on the General Assembly. Despite more-equitable representation of urban and suburban populations, the agricultural interests promoted by the Farm Bureau are still among the most influential in Tennessee.

Tennessee extends from the Great Smoky Mountains National Park in the east to the City of Memphis and the Mississippi River in the west. Its partisan loyalties mirror its geographical relief. Conservative Republicans traditionally win state legislative and congressional races in mountainous East Tennessee. The upland counties of West Tennessee and the suburban communities of Memphis are other Republican areas of strength. Democratic strongholds include Middle Tennessee, Nashville, and most of West Tennessee including the heterogeneous City of Memphis. Democrats traditionally have dominated both the executive and legislative branches.

In this century the state's black voters, most of whom reside in the urban areas of Memphis, Nashville, and Chattanooga, have been consistent supporters of the Democratic party. At a time when most blacks were disenfranchised in the South, black voting continued in Tennessee and especially in Memphis where the support of black voters was important to the longevity of the Crump machine in the years preceding World War II. Shelby County blacks, many now led by the Ford brothers' political machine, continue to play a prominent role in the Democratic party's electoral strategies.

Recently, Tennessee has become more politically competitive for statewide elective offices and in presidential elections.[1] Republican presidential candidates carried the state in every race since 1968 with the exception of Jimmy Carter's victory in 1976. Republicans captured the governorship in 1970 and again in 1978 and 1982. A coalition of East Tennessee and suburban Memphis Republicans, combined with Democrats disenchanted with their party's candidate, and a large number of independent voters were the basis for Republican electoral success. In general, the hallmark of both parties is political conservatism.

Solid Democratic majorities still exist in both houses of the General Assembly, where the respective speakers enjoy considerable power over the political agenda and committee appointments. Each of the speakers is in the vortex of virtually all interest group lobbying. Former House Speaker Ned McWherter's election as governor in 1986 and 1990 resulted in a noticeable decline in the intensity of interest group lobbying of the speakers as attention shifted to the office of the Democratic governor, who wields considerable control over virtually all legislative matters in the early 1990s.

Tennessee's largely traditionalistic political culture and its citizen's historical dislike of big government perpetuate the importance of wealthy, socially prominent families in the state's politics and continue a low-tax and low-service climate especially favorable to the powerful farm, banking, insurance, and liquor interests. The historically low levels of voter turnout do little to upset the influence of these interests. Tennessee remains one of the few states without a state income tax, despite Governor McWherter's 1991 proposal to adopt one. Public pressure for higher-quality state services seems to be growing in response to elements from a moralistic culture concentrated in the eastern part of the state and from new migrants from the Northeast and upper Midwest.

In our survey of state legislators, the respondents indicated that the six most pressing issues facing Tennessee, ranked in order of priority, are: (1) improving the educational system; (2) economic development; (3) health-care services; (4) crime and corrections; (5) unemployment; and (6) controlling substance abuse.[2] These policy priorities, together with the political and economic changes that have occurred in the last twenty years, suggest that the influence of the dominant interests should diminish. More-extensive legislative staff support and legislative independence from the governor, growing economic diversification and urbanization, and more political competition are factors that may upset the balance of interests and diminish the power and influence of interest groups.[3]

The implications of these forces of change are significant for interest groups. As competition for state resources becomes keener, the skills, resources, and personal rapport of veteran lobbyists become more important—especially as more responsibility for funding programs and services devolves to state officials because of cutbacks in federal aid. Clearly, the pressure group system in Tennessee, which Morehouse classified as strong, and, more specifically, the business interests that traditionally have dominated it, will be tested as more groups and new types of lobbyists enter the political fray to protect or advance their interests.[4]

Registration and Reporting
Requirements for Lobbyists: The Rules of the Game

Tennessee's conservative, largely traditionalistic political culture is reflected in the minimal regulatory intervention into the customary modes of interest group lobbying. The Regulation and Disclosure Act of 1975, as amended in 1985 and 1989, requires lobbyists to register and to report gifts and political contributions to officials in the three branches of state government. However, these disclosure requirements are easily circumvented, so that examination of the annual reports made by registered lobbyists reveals little of the actual pattern of who gets what, how, and why.

The Tennessee Code Annotated (TCA 3-6-102[12]) defines lobbying as "communicating directly or soliciting others to communicate with any official in the legislative or executive branch with the purpose of influencing any legislative or administrative action." Likewise, a lobbyist is any person who communicates "directly or indirectly with any official in the executive or legislative branches with the purpose of influencing any legislative or administrative action" (TCA 3-6-102 [13]). Anyone who spends more than $200 during any legislative session for the purpose of influencing any legislative or administrative action is also defined by statute as a lobbyist. An individual "acting solely on his own behalf" (TCA 3-6-102 [13] [B]) who does not spend more than $200 (other than for political contributions) is specifically exempt from the registration provisions. All lobbyists except those representing state agencies or educational institutions are required to pay an annual filing fee of $25.

Public officials in the executive or judicial branches as well as representatives of state educational institutions who engage in lobbying activities directed at the legislative branch are specifically included in the definition of lobbyist. The act contains a loophole: a person need not register with the Secretary of State "if he is a public official performing the duties of his office" (TCA 3-6-102[8]). In practice this provision means that officials of state and local governments do not have to register as lobbyists. Because of the exemptions for individuals acting in their own behalf and for state and local officials, the number of registered lobbyists does not reflect the actual extent of lobbying activity. Lobbying by local governments of executive agencies and the governor's office, for instance, is not reported, and neither is the extent of lobbying by individuals or public officials that is targeted to the legislative or judicial arenas. Consequently, registered interests represent only a partial picture of the spectrum of interests important in public policy-making.

Annual disclosure of all gifts and political contributions made by lobbyists to legislative and executive officials is required at the end of each legislative session. "Gifts" to legislators are defined as "a payment, honorarium, subscription, loan, advance, forbearance, rendering or deposit of money or service" of $50 or more (TCA 3-6-104[d]). Such gifts to executive officials must be reported if they are $25 or more in value. Political contributions of more than $100 given to any public official and his or her staff or family also must be reported annually.

The legislators' gift-reporting limit was raised from $25 to $50 in 1985 at the request of several lobbyists who found it difficult to entertain in Nashville establishments while spending less than $25 on each legislator. As a result, few lobbyists' disclosure forms report any gifts to legislative officials. Even before the spending limit was raised, only one state senator, much to his consternation, discovered that he was the recipient of a lobbyist's gift in 1984. "That's incredible, unthinkable and unacceptable," Sen. Ben Longly told reporters when informed about the results of a review of all disclosure forms.[5] The senator believed that he was not the only legislator who ate, in the company of a lobbyist, a dinner that cost more than $25: "I have every confidence . . . the cost of a full dinner at a leading restaurant in Nashville is going to be over $25."[6] At the favorite legislative watering holes, such as the Capitol Hill Club, the senator's estimate is indeed a conservative one. Tom "The Golden Goose" Hensley, a liquor lobbyist with a reputation for picking up tabs, explains that "the entertaining of lawmakers is really an exercise in budgeting. . . . if you split tabs it makes it easier on everyone's budget."[7] This refers to the time-honored practice of two or three lobbyists picking up the dinner tab so that the cost per lawmaker does not exceed the reporting threshold.

In the wake of influence-peddling and vote-buying scandals in the 1989 session, a bill to strengthen reporting requirements and increase monitoring of lobbyists' activities was finally passed, after being stripped of most of its provisions. This law requires lobbyists to disclose expenditures on legislators that exceed $50 in one week or $500 in one year. Lobbyists are also prohibited from paying legislators' hotel bills or from giving them credit cards. Receptions hosted by lobbyists to which all members of the General Assembly receive invitations are exempt from the financial disclosure requirements.

The disclosure forms do not reveal the extent of actual political contributions to legislative campaign war chests. Only a few of the 340 reports by lobbyists indicate political contributions of more than $100. The interests represented by lobbyists may contribute unlimited amounts to lawmakers through the more than 250 registered PACs. While it is difficult for the press and public to link the specific political contributions by lobbyists to individual legislators, interest group representatives have no need to make such connections obvious to legislative recipients. The intensely personal level of the politics of lobbying in Tennessee insures that such political contributions are approved by the legislators before they are made. In fact, many such contributions are actively solicited by many legislators in what the Tennessee media refer to as "shakedowns" of the State Capitol lobbyists: $500 per ticket fund-raisers held both during and after legislative sessions.

PACs in Tennessee are required to register with the secretary of state, but there are no limits on the amounts they can contribute to candidates for public office. The state's campaign disclosure laws require that candidates submit a list of the sources and amounts of all contributions of more than $100. If candidates accept contributions from groups headquartered out of state, the disclosure forms must indicate the original sources of all contributions of $1,000 or more to the organization or PAC. This enables interested persons to discover the actual sources of contributions to the PACs that spend money in state election campaigns. PACs are also required to submit quarterly reports on the amounts of their contributions to public officials, but no summary data are compiled by the staff in the secretary of state's office.

The Triumph of Economic Interests

Many interest groups flourish in Tennessee. Growing economic diversification, weak party organizations and factionalism, and increasing competition for the state's highest office have contributed to the slow but steady growth in the number of interests operating in Nashville. In 1987, 340 lobbyists, representing 262 separate interests, registered with the secretary of state.[8] As indicated on Table 3.1, the three categories of interest groups with the largest number of lobbyists and organizations are business and industry, education, and the health-related professions and industry. Among the most important unregistered interests are state agencies and city and county governments. The estimated number of unregistered lobbyists, of all types, is over one hundred. In 1980 three hundred lobbyists were registered to operate in the General Assembly. Most of the increase in the number of registered lobbyists between 1980 and 1987 occurred in the health, education, and business categories.

Business and Manufacturing Interests

As in most other states, the largest proportion of lobbyists in Tennessee represents business and manufacturing interests. More than three-fifths (62.4%) of all interest groups and over half (56%) of all registered lobbyists are connected with business enterprises. Virtually all of the state's major corporations employ at least one, and frequently three or more, full-time lobbyists.

Figuring prominently in Tennessee's recent industrial recruitment

Table 3.1 Distribution of Interests and Registered Lobbyists in Tennessee, 1987

	Number of Interests	Number of Registered Lobbyists
Agriculture	5	4
Banking	15	14
Business and industry	58	50
Education	8	57
Health-related professions and industry	32	40
Insurance	15	25
Law/legal professions	9	11
Liquor/beer	4	6
Local governments	9	19
Private sector unions	11	9
Public employees' associations	4	7
Real estate and construction	14	11
State agencies	3	3
Transportation	6	6
Utilities, oil, gas, and electric cooperatives	29	46
Other	40	32
Totals	262	340

Compiled from data supplied by the Office of the Tennessee Secretary of State, Division of Elections.

successes are Nissan Motor Manufacturing Company and the General Motors Saturn Corporation. These interests successfully secured a substantial state investment in infrastructure and training programs to support plant operations. Many smaller business firms also retain professional lobbying services, and many are represented by state-level associations organized around a particular interest. These associations span the range from general business climate (e.g., the Tennessee Manufacturers' and Taxpayers' Association [TMTA] and the Tennessee Business Roundtable) to specific business interests (such as the Tennessee Malt Beverage Association, the Licensed Beverage Wholesalers of Tennessee, and the Tennessee Retail Federation).

Banking interests do well in almost every legislative session. They have been able to defeat with some regularity proposals to lower the maximum interest rates for credit card accounts and to reform banking laws such as those governing holding companies. Nonetheless, there is more competition among and challenge of traditionally powerful business interests.

The 1986 session of the General Assembly, for example, featured a clash of the titans with the powerful Tennessee Farm Bureau and the TMTA allied against a coalition of health-care providers led by the Nashville-based Hospital Corporation of America, the world's largest private provider of health-care services. At issue was a bill sponsored by health providers to require mandatory coverage for mental health care, alcoholism treatment, and drug dependency care for all Tennessee workers with group health insurance. The Farm Bureau and the TMTA managed to prevail. This close, hard-fought battle is notable for two reasons: It signifies the continuing weakness of labor interests, which played only a minor role in the lobbying process despite the fact that the bill was highly germane to employee benefits; and it indicates the growing political influence of the health-care industry in Tennessee.

Lobbying battles with unpredictable outcomes normally involve competing economic interests. Nevertheless, disputes between business and other interests such as labor, consumers, or environmental groups are occurring with increasing frequency. In 1989, for instance, the Tennessee Association of Business succeeded in repealing local governments' veto power over hazardous-waste disposal sites. This victory was possible, however, only after intense negotiations and considerable compromise with environmentalists.

The Health-Care Industry

Health-care interests have grown substantially in number, and the competition for scarce health-care dollars has become more fierce. Health-related interests are 20 percent of interest groups and 12 percent of all registered lobbyists. Increasingly, these interests are listed in the winner's column in major legislative battles. In 1986 the nursing-home industry triumphed by stopping any meaningful reform of state nursing-home regulation and quashing attempts to impose stiffer civil penalties for violations of existing standards. In 1989 hospital groups were able to stave off attempts to impose a gross-receipts tax on them to help fund the costs of health care for indigents.

The Educational Lobby

Educational lobbyists in Tennessee account for approximately 17 percent of all registered lobbyists but represent only 3 percent of all interest groups. Of these, the Tennessee Education Association (TEA) is the largest in both membership (39,000) and lobbyists (27). Morehouse considered this lobby, specifically the TEA, among the most influential, yet its record of success is not as impressive as its reputation purports. The Lamar Alexander administration's landmark Comprehensive Education Reform Act of 1984 contained many provisions to which TEA objected, including mandatory teacher evaluations, a career-ladder system of advancement, and pay based on performance. The TEA's most significant weakness appears to be its inability to win the battle for public opinion when opposed by a determined, articulate governor. In 1989, for instance, it was unable to arouse sufficient public or legislative interest to press Governor McWherter to abide by his promised increase in teachers' salaries.

Agribusiness

Organized agribusiness interests in Tennessee are few in number but figure prominently among the politically powerful. Despite a declining farm population and increasing economic diversification, agriculture is still the single most important sector of the state's economy. The Tennessee Farm Bureau represents the largest and most powerful agribusiness interests. It provides a wide range of services to members, including insurance, sale of agricultural input products such as chemicals, feed, and seed, and also serves as a marketing and purchasing agent. The Farm Bureau has close ties with the banking, credit, insurance, and real estate lobbies and has a remarkable history of success on most issues that concern it.

Tennessee's political history is replete with examples of the Farm Bureau's political influence. The structure of the state's classified property tax system is largely a product of the Farm Bureau's domination of the state constitutional convention in 1971.[9] Tax advantages for gasohol (made from corn), the content of legislation establishing minimum auto liability insurance limits, the treatment of property in the state's inheritance taxes, the extent of tort reform and the lack of reform in the state's General Sessions Courts are all testimony to the power exercised by the Farm Bureau lobby in the legislature.

Generally, there are relatively few floor battles between the Farm Bureau and other groups. The rural roots and farming background of many lawmakers enhance legislative sensitivity to agribusiness interests. Only the most contentious issues, involving conflict with other economic interests or with the governor in tandem with public-interest groups, escape the committee system to reach a full floor battle. Because of the economic importance of agriculture and the Farm Bureau's extensive lobbying resources, agribusiness lobbyists find a very receptive legislative audience that is predisposed to agree with them ideologically.[10]

Governmental Lobbies

Throughout the first two-thirds of this century Tennessee's governor reigned supreme in state politics. After *Baker* and the 1970 census the state redrew its electoral district boundaries for the first time since 1901. A new legislative complexion emerged that served as a catalyst for resurgence in that body's political power. Nonetheless, the office of governor remains a very powerful one.

Attention to more-sophisticated legislative liaison operations is one of the prerequisites to effective governance for the modern chief executive. These liaison operations were especially salient for two-term Republican Governor Alexander in his interaction with the Democratic-dominated state House and Senate. Major reforms in education and state corrections, and sizable investments in economic development and transportation improvements, were the fruits of his lobbying victories.

The governor's office is a popular target for lobbyists seeking to advance or protect their interests. In fact, on election in 1986 Democratic Gov. Ned McWherter established a system of "regional governors" across the state, with cabinet-level pay and status, to serve as conduits to the governor's executive power and legislative agenda.

State agencies and departments are increasingly active in lobbying activities both as promoters of departmental interests and as targets of lobbying by other groups. The Department of Health and Environment and the Department of Revenue are among the most active in legislative lobbying. The popularly elected Public Service Commission also is an important lobbying force on legislative issues germane to its jurisdiction.

Lobbying activities focused on the executive branch agencies generally follow three avenues of appeal: contacts with agency directors or departmental commissioners; communications with the governor's personal staff or "regional governors"; or case presentations made to one or more of the citizens' advisory boards that meet periodically with agency leaders. The most effective route to influence on policy set by the executive branch is usually through the governor's personal staff.

Local governments' interests are represented by the Tennessee Municipal League (TML), the Tennessee County Services Association (TCSA), and a number of cities that retain their own independent lobbyists. Almost 6 percent of the registered lobbyists represent local governments' interests. Morehouse identified the TML and the TCSA as among the most influential groups in Tennessee.[11] The results of surveys conducted in connection with this study confirm that the TML is still among the most influential interest groups.

"Organized" Labor

Because Tennessee is a "right-to-work" state, organized labor has been a very weak pressure group. The AFL-CIO Labor Council, the Teamsters, the United Mine Workers, and several other unions have registered lobbyists. The weak organizational base of these groups has never provided the resources to combat the more highly organized and well-funded corporate interests. Only 14 percent of the nonagricultural work force were union members in 1983, compared to a national average of 22.2 percent. In a major defeat for the United Auto Workers, employees at the Nissan plant in Smyrna rejected union organization by a two-to-one margin in July 1989.

Unlike private sector labor groups, the Tennessee State Employees Association (TSEA), formed in 1977 to lobby for improved pay and benefits for state employees, has grown in membership and political influence in the General Assembly. It survived attempts by Governor Alexander to discontinue dues collections through payroll deductions, and has compiled impressive victories in the legislature. Almost annually the TSEA manages to enhance employees' pay or benefits beyond any increase initially suggested by the governor or Assembly.

This portrait of the major interests in Tennessee's pressure group system underscores the power of economic interests. However, the situation is not monolithic. The established economic and political order in Tennessee is frequently challenged by ad hoc alliances focused on specific issues. Grass-roots citizens' advocacy groups, the governor and state departments, and intergovernmental pressures occasionally play very important roles in the lobbying process.

A case in point is the tumultuous two-year battle to pass mandatory seat-belt legislation. Led by lobbyists for the national auto makers, including General Motors Traffic Safety Now, the Motor Vehicle Manufacturer Association, the Tennessee Safety Belt Coalition (a citizens' group), and the governor, mandatory seat-belt legislation was finally pushed through the Assembly despite opposition among most voters and the party leaders of both House and Senate.

The increasing necessity of compromise and an intensity of conflict characterize Tennessee's contemporary pressure group system.

Teachers, the health-care industry, and state employees have joined the ranks of the lobbying powers. Consumer, environmental, and public-interest lobbies enjoy only somewhat greater legislative success than they have in the past, but their success usually depends on support from the governor and alliances with other interest groups. Business interests remain the dominant lobbying forces in the State Capitol. Overall, the growth of Tennessee's interest groups has not mirrored the phenomenal increase of special interests in Washington, D.C.

Lobbyists and Techniques of Influence

The exact distribution of lobbyists, by type, changes with each session of the General Assembly. Single-issue volunteer lobbyists descend upon and then quickly withdraw from the legislative arena once their issue is presented or resolved. With each passing legislative session, there seems to be a larger number of contract lobbyists with multiple clients. Increasingly, former legislators and top public officials join public relations or law firms and engage in contract lobbying, or they secure employment as in-house lobbyists with organizations related to their area of policy expertise. Of the 132 legislators in 1977, for instance, more than a dozen are now lobbyists. Many of these "hired guns" have attained a stature that rivals the reputation of the law firm of Bass, Berry, and Sims, or the lobbying firm of Smith and Johnson Government Relations. A new generation of highly skilled technical experts with established links to the "old boy" legislative network seems to be emerging to compete with the older-style, "single-shot" lobbyists who represent one interest full-time. The latter are not necessarily being replaced; rather, both types now constitute the elite in the business of lobbying in Nashville.

Veteran lobbyists are trusted by seasoned and freshman lawmakers alike for their knowledge, expertise, and skill in the legislative process. As the state Senate minority leader pointed out, "I find them helpful in providing information on the positions of the groups they represent. I find most are accurate and honest. If they misrepresent the facts, they won't be around for very long."[12] For veteran lawmakers, the linkage with the lobbying elite is based on years of personal friendship, shared expertise or values, and a long-term pattern of mutual support. For less-experienced legislators, these lobbyists are a valuable source of information about how the General Assembly works and a means for accelerating the socialization process involving legislative customs, personalities, and power.[13]

Regardless of their years of experience, many legislators use veteran lobbyists as an extension of their staff resources. Trusted lobbyists serve as sources of information, a means to influence other legislators, consultants on strategy for moving legislation, and mediators for negotiating conflicts among competing interests. The political power of the lobbying elite seems to stem more from its financial resources, contacts, access, and network of personal or professional relationships among legislators than from just the size of the group it represents or its past record of success in influencing all issues of interest to that group.[14] As one veteran lobbyist explains, "the individual is more important than anything else. The individual talks to members of the Senate and House and is more sensitive to their needs than anybody else."[15]

On average, registered lobbyists have 10.6 years of working experience. Our survey of the sixty-one lobbyists retained by the major state interest group associations indicates that each represents an average of 4,005 group members. When asked how receptive legislators were to the lobbyists' ideas on proposed legislation that affected the interest group, 53.6 percent of the lobbyists responding stated that legislators are "always receptive," and 46.4 percent responded that legislators are at least "somewhat" receptive.[16]

To explore the nature and techniques of lobbying in more depth, legislative staff members who work for the standing committees that conduct business throughout the year were questioned extensively about their perceptions of lobbying in the legislative process. Staff members were asked about the nature, importance, and frequency of lobbying techniques and the importance of group characteristics in determining the influence that interest groups have in the legislative process. Based on the responses of the seven out of eighteen staff members who completed our mail questionnaire, lobbying is conducted more openly than it used to be. All respondents agreed that interest groups provide more campaign assistance to legislators than in the past. Most of the legislative staff respondents disagree that lobbying involves more technical assistance than pressure tactics; they believe that lobbyists use both with equal frequency.

The influence techniques used most frequently, according to the legislative staff, include testifying at hearings, doing favors for legislators, and alerting lawmakers to the effects of legislation. Asked to rate the relative importance of several factors for group influence, the majority of the staff respondents considered the group's financial resources, ability to give campaign assistance, the reliability of information given to legislators, and the personal friendships between legislators and interest group representatives "very important" in determining the interest group's influence in the General Assembly. Factors considered "important" by most of the staff include the lobbyist's reputation, group size, ability to get out the vote on an issue, and the group's past record of lobbying success.

A profile of the effective lobbyist in Tennessee, constructed on the basis of these responses, consists of the following: experience in the legislative process; ability to capitalize on a trusting personal relationship and a legislator's professional ties to group interests; capability to supply legislators with reliable information; and adroitness at channeling money and other types of support to legislators during election campaigns. The effective lobbyist is also skilled in distributing favors, testifying at legislative committee hearings, and informing key legislators about the effects (both positive and negative) of proposed legislation. There is nothing particularly secret or sinister about how lobbyists conduct their business. The legislative staff considers lobbyists to be basically honest and reliable participants in the legislative process.

Not surprisingly, the lobbyists considered to be the most reputable and respected in the legislature are those that represent the traditionally powerful interest groups. Prominent among these are Tom Hensley, who represents the Licensed Beverage Wholesalers, and former Lt. Gov. Frank Gorrell, who represents several banking, building, and corporate interests such as International Business Machines (IBM) and Browning-Ferris Industries. As finance chairman for Governor McWherter's 1990 reelection campaign, Gorrell's prestige among Democratic legislators is further enhanced. Other lobbyists of reputed effectiveness include John Lyell of the Tennessee Bar Association; Betty Anderson, who represents Nissan, McDonald's, and the Pharmaceutical Manufacturing Association; and George Benton of the Tennessee Soft Drink Association, to name a few.

Are these lobbyists influential because of their interest group's resources and political power, or are the traditionally influential groups so powerful because of the expertise, skill, and connections of the lobbyists? Based on our analysis of the state lobbying process, group resources are a necessary but not a sufficient basis for influencing the outcome of legislation. The expanding corps of veteran lobbyists in Nashville has repeatedly secured victory on many important issues on which the odds, and often preliminary legislative and public sentiment, appeared to be contrary to the group's wishes. We suspect that these successes are partially a result of the changing composition of and more-sophisticated techniques used by the veteran lobbyists. Obviously, a systematic analysis of the record of wins and losses over the last fifteen or twenty years would yield the best measure of lobbying success on issues of importance to the group. However, such a comprehensive analysis is beyond the scope of our study. Based on a review of several key issues decided by the General Assembly since 1980 and the survey responses by the legislative staff, our conclusion is that the skill, experience, reputation, and personal network of contacts possessed by many veteran lobbyists play a very important, if not critical, role in an interest group's lobbying success.

Patterns of Interest Group Power

Morehouse depicted Tennessee as a state with a strong pressure group system.[17] Considering the changes in economic diversification, urbanization, interregional migration, political competition, and the professionalism of the state legislature, one would expect the strength of interest groups to diminish. However, countervailing forces may work to strengthen the state pressure group system even in states experiencing these changes. Withdrawal of federal intergovernmental aid encourages a greater centralization of decision making in state capitals. The decline in federal domestic spending and policy innovation creates a "funding and policy gap" between interest groups' demands and governments' service delivery. As a result, state lawmakers are pressed to be more active and assertive in policy leadership. Centralization of fiscal and programmatic authority follows states' assumption of more responsibility for social, health, and economic problems—including those associated with local governments.[18] Since groups tend to be most active where the money is to be spent, the greater centralization of decision making for resource allocations may work to the advantage of those lobbies that are already entrenched and influential in state capitals.[19] It may also promote the formation of a more active, stronger pressure group system, an outcome suggested by the analytic framework developed by the editors in Chapter 1. The increasing legislative dependence upon PAC contributions, combined with the lobbying elite's extensive network of contacts and favors, may perpetuate the historical pattern of strong influence from interest groups on issues that concern them.

To explore the pattern of interest group power in Tennessee, state legislators, legislative staff, the capital press corps, and the lobbyists representing the major state associations were asked to rate the influence of various interest groups and to assess how their influence may have changed since the respondents began their respective careers in state politics. In a questionnaire (conducted by mail during December 1986–January 1987) individuals in each of these four groups were asked to rate the influence of twenty-two groups believed to be among the most active in state politics in the 1986 session of the General Assembly. They were also asked in an open-ended question to indicate the three interest groups they considered to be the most influential. Finally, those surveyed were asked to assess how the influence of the twenty-two groups has changed since the respondents first started working in their jobs.

A majority of legislators who responded rate most groups as having at least a moderate level of influence. A majority rate the Tennessee Farm Bureau and the TEA as having a high level of influence, and more than 40 percent of legislators also believe that the Automotive Association, representing auto makers and dealers, has a high level of influence.

With few exceptions, the lobbyist, legislative staff, and press corps respondents think that most groups have a high level of influence in the General Assembly. Most of the respondents from these three groups agree that the Banker's Association, the liquor lobby, the Farm Bureau, and the TEA have a high level of influence. None of these respondents rated these four interests as having no influence.

In general, there was considerable agreement among the four groups of respondents that most of the interests listed have at least a moderate level of influence, and many have a high level of influence. For those interests traditionally believed to be the most influential, such as the Banker's Association, the Licensed Beverage Wholesalers, the Tennessee Malt Beverage Association, the Insurors of Tennessee, the TMTA, and the TML, a large proportion of the lobbyists, legislative staff, and press corps respondents agree that these groups continue to exercise a high level of influence. These opinions represent only a "snapshot" of group power during one session of the General Assembly, but in our observation little has transpired since the survey was administered to dissuade us of its descriptive accuracy for the early 1990s.

To investigate trends in group influence, respondents with more than one term of office or two years of working experience were asked to assess how interest group influence has changed during their career. Interestingly, there is even greater convergence of opinion among the four groups of respondents with regard to how interest group influence has evolved. A majority of each responding group believes that most of the interest groups have retained about their same level of influence. Legislators think that the TEA, in particular, has gained influence.

Considering the convergence of opinion among all respondents, we conclude that most of the groups considered to be influential historically have maintained or enhanced that influence. Groups not traditionally considered to be influential that apparently have gained the most influence over time include the Tennessee Business Roundtable, the Tennessee Bar Association, and the Tennessee State Employees Association.

Legislators, lobbyists, legislative staff, and the capital press corps were also asked to identify, in an open-ended question, the three groups that they considered to be the most powerful and influential in the capital. The rankings of interests based on the survey responses are indicated in Table. 3.2. The traditionally powerful lobby-

Table 3.2 Influential Interest Groups in Tennessee by Respondents' Rankings, 1987

	Legislative	Lobbyists	Legislative Staff	Press Corps
Tennessee Farm Bureau	1	1	—	3
Tennessee Education Association	2	4	3	4
Banker's Association	3	3	4	1
Licensed Beverage Wholesalers of Tennessee	4	2	1	2
Tennessee Municipal League	5	7	—	5
Tennessee Automotive Association	6	5	—	5
Tennessee Road Builders Association	7	—	—	—
Tennessee State Employees Association	8	—	—	—
Tennessee Trial Lawyers	9	8	—	5
Tennessee Bar Association	10	7	4	—
Tennessee Malt Beverage Association	10	—	2	—
Tennessee Press Association	10	—	4	—
Tennessee Manufacturers' and Taxpayers' Association	—	6	3	—
Tennessee Medical Association	—	7	—	—
Tennessee Business Roundtable	—	—	4	—
Tennessee Health Care Association	—	—	4	—
Insurors of Tennessee	—	—	4	—

Note: The group rankings for each interest are based on the frequency with which respondents listed the interest among the three most influential in Tennessee. Data in Tables 3.2 and 3.3 were gathered through a mailed survey in December 1986–January 1987. Response rates were: legislators, 46.2 percent (N = 61); lobbyists, 47.5 percent (N = 29); legislative staff, 38.8 percent (N = 7); and press corps, 61.1 percent (N = 11).

ing elite figures prominently in the top choices of all four groups. The Farm Bureau, banking, liquor, and educational lobbies appear in all of the lists. Likewise, the TML appears in three of the four lists (the exception being the legislative staff list).

In contrast to the Morehouse study, we found interests new to the elite among powerful lobbies appearing in at least three of the four respondents' lists, including the Tennessee Automotive Association, the Tennessee Bar Association, and the Tennessee Trial Lawyers Association. Other newcomers to the ranks of the most influential are the Tennessee Press Association, the Tennessee State Employees Association, the Tennessee Medical Association, and the Tennessee Health Care Association.

Apparently, legislators and staff were impressed by the influence of the Tennessee Press Association in defeating in the House, during 1986, a bill backed by the state's law enforcement officers to restrict public access to police records. Considering its increasing importance in the state's economy, it is not surprising to find the automotive industry at the top of several lists. An impressive lobbying campaign for a mandatory seat-belt law, against a tenacious opposition, is among that interest's growing number of victories. The emergent power and influence of the Trial Lawyers and Tennessee Bar associations may be the product of several lobbying victories in which the lawyers teamed up with other interests to gain most of what they wanted. The limits placed on privatization of the state's prison system are an example. The state legislators also were impressed with the lobbying expertise of the Tennessee State Employees Association, which represents a growing proportion of state employees.

The group that apparently has declined in influence, according to the opinion of all except legislators, is the Tennessee County Services Association, a technical advisory group that lobbies for county government and often works closely with the TML. Surprisingly, the TMTA did not make the list of either legislators or reporters. However, these groups are still highly rated by lobbyists and the legislative staff. A summary ranking of the twelve most influential interest groups is provided in Table 3.3.

In sum, there appear to be no really big losers among the traditionally powerful lobbies but rather the addition of new winners, as Tennessee increasingly resembles what Zeigler termed the "triumph of many interests."[20] Many of the traditionally powerful interests have retained their influence, but other groups, armed with veteran lobbyists in their own employ, have arrived to contend for influence in Tennessee politics.

Table 3.3   Summary Ranking of the Twelve Most Influential
Interest Groups in Tennessee, 1987

1	Tennessee Farm Bureau
2	Licensed Beverage Wholesalers of Tennessee
3	Bankers' Association
4	Tennessee Education Association
5	Tennessee Automotive Association
6	Tennessee Municipal League
7	Tennessee Bar Association
8	Tennessee Trial Lawyers Association
9	Tennessee Malt Beverage Association
10	Tennessee Press Association
11	Tennessee Road Builders Association
12	Tennessee State Employees Association

Note: Overall rank was calculated by summing each group's rank as given by legislators and at least two other responding groups, then ordering the interests based on the mean rank. The same procedure was used to find mean rank based on legislators' and one other responding group's ranking. Finally, the Road Builders and Tennessee State Employees associations were added, based on legislators' ranking. This method gives legislators' rankings more weight than those of the other categories of respondents.

Conclusion

Amid the trends of growing legislative professionalism and independence from an executive that essentially controlled the political agenda as recently as the 1960s, interest group influence in Tennessee could be expected to decline. However, program cutbacks in Washington have devolved more policy-making and resource-allocating decisions to state officials. This trend, in conjunction with relatively weak political parties in Tennessee and the growing importance of financial contributions by PACs, has intensified the competition among interests and raised the stakes in the lobbying contest. To avoid diminished influence, once independently powerful business lobbies are more likely to form coalitions on a number of issues to combat the more sophisticated lobbying tactics of competing groups.

While lobbying has become more complex, and traditional interest groups are less assured of success than in the past, it appears that the new pluralism in Tennessee has expanded the circle of winners rather than weakened the overall influence of interest groups in the legislative process. The resurgence of the Assembly's policy-making role invites more interest group activism. The factionalism and weak organization of the parties creates a leadership vacuum that experienced lobbyists help to fill. Whether continual support by professional staff, stronger party organization, or greater economic diversification will diminish interest groups' influence in the General Assembly in the future is problematic. The analytic framework developed by the editors (see Chapter 1) suggests that these changes may weaken interest group influence. The well-financed, experienced lobbyists for business and agricultural interests in Tennessee are dug in firmly, however, ready to take on any newcomers. These groups find a receptive audience among politically conservative legislators who have mostly rural roots and business or farm backgrounds. It is a strong linkage built on tradition and political culture that is likely to endure until challenged by strong executive leadership, more-extensive party competition, greater turnover in legislative seats, or continued economic change.

4

VIRGINIA

A NEW LOOK FOR THE
"POLITICAL MUSEUM PIECE"

John T. Whelan

In his classic work *Southern Politics*, Key observed in the late 1940s that "of all the American states, Virginia can lay claim to the most thorough control by an oligarchy."[1] At the time, the state was governed by the Democratic party organization of Harry F. Byrd, Sr. For nearly forty years, 1926–1965, Byrd, first from the governor's office and then from the U.S. Senate, led a machine unrivaled among the states for its "durability and power."[2] The basis of the machine's success was the control it exercised over a small electorate, kept restricted by the poll tax and other means; yet its makeup also reflected a political culture that accorded considerable deference to the governing role of the social and economic elite. For Key, Virginia's politics resembled a "political museum piece."[3]

Much has changed since the Byrd era. Electorally, the Republican party has emerged as a competitive force, and candidates of both parties contest for public support in an electorate significantly expanded by the nullification of the poll tax and enactment of the 1965 Voting Rights Act.[4] Once the home of the Byrd organization's policies of "massive resistance" to integration of public schools, Virginia in 1989 elected the country's first black governor, L. Douglas Wilder. Although hardly a national leader, Virginia has increased its commitment to public services, no longer ranking at the bottom of the states for spending on education, welfare, and other programs. During the last decade and a half every branch of state government has undergone modernization as the leaders of those institutions have sought to cope with their enlarged governing mission.

Underlying these political changes have been transformations in the state's population and economy. Whereas the Byrd organization flourished in a rural, small-town agricultural setting, Virginia's contemporary state government functions primarily in an urban, industrial environment. The change is most evident in the "urban corridor" stretching from the Washington suburbs in Northern Virginia, south to the Richmond capital area, and then east to the Norfolk–Virginia Beach–Newport News metropolitan area, spanning Hampton Roads. Overall, the corridor contains approximately 60 percent of the state's population and the majority of its economic development.

It also embraces the region—Northern Virginia—that illustrates most dramatically the changing face of state politics. The Byrd organization was weak in this part of the state, facing opposition to its policies on race relations and public services. Slighted during the Byrd era, Northern Virginia has emerged as a formidable force in statehouse politics. It is now the state's largest, most affluent, and fastest-growing region in population and economic development. Its competitive electoral politics make it a pivotal area in statewide elections, and its affluence is increasingly being tapped by candidates, helping erode the traditional dominance of Richmond's "Main Street" in financing campaigns.

Yet for all the changes afoot in the New Dominion, there are also powerful forces of continuity at work. Despite the emergence of the Republicans as a competitive force in federal elections and in contests for the offices of governor, lieutenant governor, and attorney general, the Democrats remain dominant in elections for the General Assembly. And since state judges are elected by the Assembly and more precisely by the Democratic party caucuses (party members are bound to vote for their caucus's nominees), Democrats retain a major say over the makeup of the state judiciary. Institutionally, the General Assembly remains one of the most stable state legislative bodies in the country; its strong committee system features continuity in committee membership and leadership predicated on seniority, characteristics more typical of the U.S. Congress than of most state legislatures. Conservative principles figure prominently in the state's political culture, as do its historical traditions. "Virginia reveres her glorious past and looks to that past as much as to the future," notes political scientist Larry Sabato.[5] And finally, although the state has experienced impressive economic growth, the pattern has been uneven, mainly concentrated in the urban corridor. Less affected have been areas such as Southside Virginia, once the key base of the Byrd organization and still more like the Deep South than any other part of the state, and Southwest Virginia, site of the state's coal-mining operations. In short, to understand Virginia politics one needs to appreciate the interplay between the old and the new, a point that will be evident as we explore the makeup, operations, and power of the state's interest groups.

Virginia's Interest Group Community

The community of interests active in Virginia's state government is large, diverse, and growing. As indicated in Table 4.1, 401 groups had lobbyists registered with the secretary of the commonwealth during the 1984 General Assembly session.[6] Since these registrations are a major source of information on the makeup of the interest group community, a few comments are in order about the legal provisions governing registration.

The Code of Virginia (Ch. 2.1, S 30-28.1) defines lobbying as "promoting, advocating or opposing" any legislative matter during the period between November 15 and the adjournment of the session, or during the immediately prior to each special session. A lobbyist is any person who is employed or retained to lobby or any person who has expended or will expend in excess of $100, exclusive of personal living and travel expenses related to lobbying. The law requires that lobbyists register before lobbying in Richmond or within five days if lobbying occurs outside Richmond. Also, lobbyists and their employers must file a joint report on their lobbying expenditures or payments within sixty days after the Assembly adjourns.

The Virginia lobbying law is weak. The Office of the Secretary of the Commonwealth lacks the authority and the resources to investigate the reports submitted to it. Moreover, there are significant ex-

Table 4.1 Types of Interest Groups with Registered Lobbyists, 1984 General Assembly Session

	Number	Percentage of Total Registered Groups
Business groups	259	64.6
Occupational and professional groups (excluding educational, public employees', and public officials' groups)	55	13.7
Unions (excluding educational unions)	10	2.5
Public employees' and public officials' groups (excluding educational groups)	10	2.5
Agricultural groups	8	2.0
Educational groups	15	3.7
Religious groups	5	1.2
Public-interest/advocacy/cause groups	32	8.0
Miscellaneous	7	1.8
Total	401	100.0

Source: Office of the Secretary of the Commonwealth of Virginia.

emptions written into the law. Much of the period between sessions, a time of increasing legislative and interest group activity, is not covered. And even for the covered period lobbyists are not required to identify the legislators they were attempting to influence. Additionally, officials of local and state governments are exempted from the registration and reporting process, although heads of state agencies and boards must furnish the secretary of the commonwealth with a list of "official spokesmen" who will represent their organization in the Assembly. Also exempted are private citizens who volunteer their services in a lobbying effort, large numbers of whom have been mobilized in recent years on issues such as the Equal Rights Amendment, drunk driving, and abortion. Despite these shortcomings, the registration lists provide a good starting point from which to describe the makeup of the interest group community.

Business

Historically, the business community has enjoyed a strong position in Virginia government. As shown in Table 4.1, it constituted nearly two-thirds of the groups registered in 1984. Reflecting the diverse and balanced nature of the state's economy, no one set of business interests dominated. Businesses involved in services, manufacturing, retail and wholesale trade, construction, finance, transportation, communication, public utilities, and mining were represented. Even more numerous were the general and specialized business associations. Examples of the former include the Virginia Chamber of Commerce, the Virginia Manufacturers Association, and the Virginia Retail Merchants Association. Most, however, had a narrower base, focusing on one aspect of the economy, such as the Virginia Automobile Dealers Association, the Virginia Bankers Association, and the Virginia Homebuilders Association. Given their numbers and their resources, one would expect that any listing of the most influential groups in Virginia would be heavily business-oriented, including such groups as the railroads, banks, truckers, manufacturers, retailers, utilities, and builders.

Overall, the business lobby has experienced a good deal of growth in the last two decades. A case in point: about a half-dozen utility interest groups were regularly represented at the State Capitol in the early 1970s, a more tranquil period for utilities, predating, for example, the Organization of Petroleum Exporting Countries' 1973 oil embargo and subsequent consumer protests over rising utility rates. By 1984 the utility interests had more than tripled. Indeed, that year Virginia Power, the state's largest electric utility, was involved in an unsuccessful effort to secure Assembly approval for a coal slurry pipeline and deployed a lobbying force larger than the entire utility lobbying force of the early 1970s.

Occupations and Professions

While the registration list included such occupational groups as lawyers, engineers, building contractors, and realtors, the health-related occupations were most numerous. Various medical, dental, and nursing associations were registered, as were representatives from the allied health community, such as physical therapists and dental hygienists. Ironically, in a conservative state where the virtues of the free marketplace are so often espoused, the occupational groups, the second-largest set of registered interests (13.7%), have over the last two decades increasingly sought government regulation (e.g., in efforts to secure licensure requirements). It is also an area marked by "turf battles" between professions, with the General Assembly being asked to settle differences. The long-standing feud between optometrists and ophthalmologists over the diagnostic and therapeutic use of drugs by optometrists typifies such disputes.

Unions and Public Employees

The AFL-CIO, some of its affiliated operating unions, and the United Mine Workers were registered; however, in this "right-to-work" state, organized labor historically has been a weak force. Labor's political standing is symptomatic of its weak organizational base; only 11.5 percent of Virginia's manufacturing work force in 1984 was unionized, ranking Virginia approximately in the bottom quartile of states.[7] Nor are groups of public employees, lacking the right to bargain collectively, a strong force. The major exception, of which more will be said later, is the Virginia Education Association (VEA).

Agriculture

Farm issues do not figure prominently in Virginia state politics, nor do farm organizations, which constituted only 2 percent of the registered groups. The registration figures understate farm group representation, however, because the Virginia Farm Bureau and the Virginia Agribusiness Council, two major agricultural groups, are federations, made up of numerous organizations. There are also agriculture-related interests in a number of the other categories; for example, the Virginia Veterinary Medicine Association in the category of occupations and professions. Still, Virginia has long since evolved from the days when a governor could proclaim, as William Tuck did in 1945, that "our farms constitute the bedrock of the State's progress. . . . It is important for Virginia to remain an agriculture state."[8]

Education

Consuming the largest part of the state budget, education is an area rife with group activity. Since officials representing state and local governmental entities are largely exempted from the lobby law's registration and reporting provisions, one has to go beyond the secretary of the commonwealth's records to appreciate the makeup of the educational lobby.

It is clear that education is a sizable and growing force. For instance, the higher-education field has seen the emergence of newer state universities, such as James Madison, George Mason, Old Dominion, and Virginia Commonwealth, to challenge the dominance of traditional institutions such as the University of Virginia and Virginia Polytechnic. Furthermore, both these new and the traditional four-year schools have been joined in the competition for educational resources by the system of community colleges that emerged in the 1960s. In the realm of public schools, the growing role of the teachers (predominantly the VEA) has helped spur an expanded capital effort by individual school systems, particularly from the larger, urban jurisdictions, and by such related associations as the Virginia Association of School Board Officials.

Religious and Public Interests

The groups considered thus far have been organized around some common economic interest or source of livelihood. Yet there are other groups, such as religious, public-interest, and advocacy organizations, that are cause-based and not economically oriented; or if they do pursue economic goals, it is usually on behalf of others less able to do so. These groups run the gamut, consisting of church interests; environmentalists; consumers; sportsmen; civil rights and civil liberty advocates; those working on behalf of victimized children, the handicapped, and the poor; or people involved in causes such as abortion/antiabortion and campaigns against drunk driving. Additionally, there are groups committed to promoting better government, such as the League of Women Voters and Common Cause. These categories embrace a diverse and growing range of interests (9.2% of the registrants), reflecting the politicization of issues and the growth of citizen-oriented politics in the commonwealth. Such groups draw a good deal of public attention because they tend to be involved in controversial or newsworthy issues. Visibility, however, is not synonymous with influence. The Religious Right, for example, is active in the state, Virginia being the home of the Rev. Pat Robertson's Christian Broadcasting Network and the Rev. Jerry Falwell's Liberty Foundation (formerly the Moral Majority). Yet those forces appear to have fared better nationally than in Virginia's political process.[9] Since many of the groups in the religious and public-interest categories depend on volunteers, the official registration lists do not fully reflect the scope of their lobbying activity.

Black civil rights groups are an exception. The National Association for the Advancement of Colored People (NAACP) and several other civil rights groups can be found in the registrations. Yet the significant expansion in black participation that has occurred in Virginia since the 1960s has been felt principally in the electoral process, especially in the Democratic party, and not in the interest group processes of the legislative and executive branches. And while black civil rights groups have been active in the courts, the American Civil Liberties Union (ACLU) has spearheaded the most notable civil rights litigation in the 1980s, suing approximately twenty localities under the Voting Rights Act for allegedly diluting black voting rights.

Governmental Lobby

State and local governmental interests, largely unregistered yet a growing capital lobbying force, constitute the major gap in the interests categorized in Table 4.1 Nowhere is this more evident than in the legislative arena, as the governor and agencies conduct extensive legislative liaison operations. The office of governor is strong in Virginia, and recent governors have moved to strengthen their position in the Assembly. For example, starting with Gov. John N. Dalton in 1978, Virginia governors have instituted a legislative clearance system, requiring agencies to clear legislative proposals with the governor's office. Also, staff has been added to that office, the governor's cabinet system has been strengthened, and centralized control agencies, such as the Department of Planning and Budget, have been upgraded to support the governor.

Governmental interests also manifest themselves along intergovernmental lines as local governments bolster their statehouse presence. Such major cities as Richmond, Norfolk, and Virginia Beach, and large urban counties such as Fairfax in Northern Virginia and Henrico in the Richmond area, have mounted their own lobbying operations, supplementing the traditional efforts of the Virginia Municipal League and the Virginia Association of Counties.

Nationwide, intergovernmental relations increasingly have taken on a horizontal dimension, featuring interstate relations, a pattern that also includes a group aspect. In Virginia, officials are part of a growing national network of professional associations that are linked "together in a web of information exchange, policy promulgation, and political lobbying."[10] For example, a study of Virginia's leading regulatory agency, the State Corporation Commission (SCC), found national and regional associations of state regulatory officials an important source of policy information for Virginia regulators.[11] The relevance of such professional channels of communication is not lost on private-interest groups. For example, major business interests, including ones from Virginia, have been active in the annual meetings of the National Conference of State Legislatures.

In summary, statehouse interest groups constitute a sizable force, one that has grown larger and more diverse over the last several decades. Still, for all the changes, there is much that is familiar; most notably, the business community remains the dominant set of interests represented at the Capitol.

Lobbyists

"One striking difference between state and national lobbyists is that few state lobbyists are lawyers," observed Zeigler and van Dalen.[12] Yet in Virginia 29 percent (188) of the registered lobbyists during the 1984 session had a legal background.[13] That percentage would probably be higher for the full-time lobbyists; indeed, in certain issue-areas that have a high administrative law component (such as banking, insurance, and alcoholic beverages), lawyers made up a majority of the registered agents. It appears that lawyer-lobbyists used to play an even greater role in Virginia. For example, they accounted for three-fourths of the registered lobbyists during the 1948 session.[14] Lawyers have been important historically in Virginia politics; over the years the General Assembly has had one of the highest incidence of lawyer-legislators in the country (46% in 1986).

Lawyers are usually contract lobbyists, hired on a retainer basis by groups, and are much less likely to be in-house employees of the groups for whom they lobby. In 1984, for example, 65 percent of the registered lawyers reported they were retained, while only 9 percent of the nonlawyers indicated such a work relationship. Not surprisingly, the Richmond-area lobbyists were in the best position to capitalize on lobbying opportunities. This was particularly the case with the retained lawyers, nearly three-quarters of whom were from the capital area. Most notable in this regard were lawyers from four major Richmond law firms: Hunton and Williams; McGuire, Woods and Battle; Mays and Valentine; and Christian, Barton, and Epps. Together, lawyers from these firms were 40 percent (49 out of 123) of the retained lawyers. There are indications that these firms once made up an even larger part of the lobbying corps.[15] Regardless, their lobbying clientele continues to be well stocked with blue-chip business interests.

Notwithstanding the significant lobbying role played by lawyers, nonlawyers far outnumbered them (71% of the registrants). In sharp contrast to the lawyers, nonlawyers were mainly in-house lobbyists. While their employment status differed from that of lawyers, they represented mainly the same kind of interests. For example, 69 percent of the lawyers and 66 percent of the nonlawyers represented exclusively businesses or business associations. The nonlawyers included some of the most influential interests and lobbyists—for example, Virginia Power and its chief lobbyist, E. L. Crump, and the Virginia League of Savings Institutions and its main lobbyist, Mark W. Sauers. Underscoring the lobbying resources that key business interests can deploy, both organizations also had major law firms on retainer; Virginia Power used Hunton and Williams and the League had Thomas and Fiske, a Northern Virginia firm.

However, the group that had the largest number of registered lobbyists at work—employed or otherwise—was the VEA. The teachers' group registered forty-two persons in 1984; a core group of seven worked the Capitol full-time during the session, supplemented by registered field workers and volunteers from around the state—a far cry from the group's one-to-two-person operation of the early 1970s.

Whether they are lawyers or not, a core of veteran lobbyists has amassed a good deal of stability and influence, underscoring the importance of experience in Virginia lobbying. That apparently is not always the case in other states, for, as Zeigler and van Dalen wrote, "like legislative skills, lobbying skills develop with experience and practice; like state legislators, relatively few lobbyists possess such experience."[16] Yet in Virginia not only do key legislators have a good deal of experience but so too do their lobbying counterparts. The dean of the lobbying corps, E. H. Williams, known as Judge, has been lobbying for more than thirty years, representing mainly the Virginia Trucking Association. Overall, 29 percent of the lobbyists registered in 1974 were also registered ten years later. In a 1981 series on statehouse lobbying, Dale Eisman, then Capitol correspondent of the *Richmond Times-Dispatch*, profiled ten of "Virginia's most effective lobbyists."[17] Surely it was a veteran group. Nine were registered lobbyists, eight of whom were not only lobbying in 1984 but had also been on the scene ten years before, seven as lobbyists and one, Garry DeBruhl, as a legislator. DeBruhl left the Assembly in 1978 and started a successful lobbying career.

DeBruhl's case illustrates that the so-called revolving doors between government and the businesses that do work with government operate in Virginia, too. The Virginia traffic through those doors has featured some distinguished figures, as evidenced by the inclusion in the 1984 registration of a former governor, John Dalton, a former attorney general, Anthony Troy, and at least fifteen former legislators. Dalton, now deceased, was a partner in the Richmond law firm of McGuire, Woods and Battle, while Troy is a partner in the Richmond firm of Mays and Valentine. Since 1984 the major Richmond law firms have recruited a number of other key officials. For example, Hunton and Williams, the largest law firm in the Southeast and the former firm of retired U.S. Supreme Court Justice Lewis Powell, had former Gov. Charles S. Robb in its ranks before he was elected to the U.S. Senate in 1988, and two years later it landed Gov. Gerald L. Baliles when he left office.

As in most states, ex-legislators in Virginia do not constitute a large lobbying group; probably less than half of the fifteen former lawmakers who registered in 1984 were heavily involved in lobbying. However, two of them, Garry DeBruhl and Judge Williams, made Eisman's list of the most effective lobbyists. When Williams stepped down as the truckers' head lobbyist, he was replaced by L. Ray Ashworth, also a former legislator.

Legislative staff positions can provide another spawning ground for state lobbyists; the most notable case is that of William G. Thomas, also a member of Eisman's top-ten list. Yet the state agencies provide the biggest training ground for lobbyists, as exemplified by the office of the attorney general. Besides former Atty. Gen. Anthony Troy, at least ten other registered lobbyists in 1984 worked at that office before going into private practice.

Developing and retaining experienced representation has been a problem for less-established interest groups, particularly in the religious and public-interest categories. However, in a conservative state such as Virginia, the ACLU presents an interesting example, having emerged in the 1980s as an effective force in statehouse politics. One of its most notable efforts occurred in the 1981/82 struggle over redistricting for the House of Delegates, a year-long saga that saw the ACLU repeatedly challenge Assembly-drawn plans and end up playing a leading role in crafting the single-member legislative district plan under which House members are now elected.

In Judy Goldberg, the ACLU had a skilful legislative lobbyist who had been lobbying in the Assembly since 1974, an unusual length of experience for a lobbyist operating in the religious/public-interest area. Such groups tend to have a fragile organizational base, evidencing a good deal of turnover in staff. For example, Common Cause, which was very active in the mid- to late 1970s, has been less so since Goldberg left the organization for the ACLU in 1980. Since then Common Cause has had at least three legislative directors. The consumer movement was without a full-time lobbyist during the 1984 and 1985 sessions.[18] And to bring things full circle, Goldberg left the Virginia Chapter of the ACLU in late 1985 to join the organization's national office in Washington. Five years later, the Virginia ACLU had not regained the effective legislative presence it had under Goldberg.

Women and blacks have recently begun making inroads as lobbyists. In the case of women an approximate number can be determined by checking the first names of the registrants. Doing so reveals that lobbying is still very much a man's world, but women were approximately 20 percent of the registered lobbyists in 1984, having doubled their number in six years. Law, a traditional pathway into Virginia lobbying, has begun to open up to women. Twenty-three females representing 12 percent of the lawyer-lobbyists were registered; this is about the proportion of women in the Virginia State Bar.[19] As a sign of the times, the Virginia Women Attorneys Association has been registered. But if female lobbyists constitute a growing presence at the Assembly, only a few of them could date their lobbying experience back ten years.

In summary, the lobbying corps, like the community of interests it represents, has become larger and more diverse in its makeup, reflecting a broadening of the pathways into Virginia politics. Despite such changes, there are some enduring features in the makeup of the lobbying corps, notably the continued importance of lawyers, particularly from the major Richmond law firms, and experience. And significantly, well-established interests, particularly in the business and occupational-professional categories, are in the best position to tap such lobbyists.

A Changing Environment and Changing Tactics

Just as the makeup of the interest group community and the lobbying corps has changed, so too has the environment in which they operate. Three significant political and governmental changes over the last two decades bear special mention: changes in the state government's calendar; the cast of statehouse participants; and the ground rules under which they operate. As a consequence of such changes, lobbying has become a more challenging undertaking for traditional interests, requiring a greater commitment of time and more political and technical expertise.

By the early 1970s the lobbying calendar was being transformed, with lobbying becoming an annual, if not year-round, activity. The adoption of the revised constitution in 1970 ushered in annual legislative sessions. While such sessions are the most demanding time for lobbyists, the period between sessions requires increased attention as the Assembly expands its interim activities, conducting studies and investigations.

Regardless of what the Assembly does between sessions, interest groups increasingly use this period to prepare for the session, organizing their membership, developing legislative agenda, and lobbying relevant participants, including legislators, agency officials, other group leaders, and news media figures. "My theory of lobbying is you win the battles before the legislature even starts," remarked lawyer-lobbyist William G. Thomas.[20] Then, too, for many interest group representatives the Assembly is not the only arena of state government requiring attention. The growth of state agencies and their programs expanded the administrative policy-making process and also the involvement of interest groups, a point we will return to in the last section of this chapter.

Besides a revamped calendar, lobbyists and other capital participants need a new scorecard to keep track of the revised lineup of statehouse participants. The larger, more diverse lobbying corps mirrors personnel changes occurring elsewhere in the political process. In the private realm the 1970s saw the state news media expand their capital coverage, particularly during the Assembly sessions.

In the governmental realm population change over the past several decades, and legislative redistricting, helped change the complexion of the Assembly as the rural membership lost ground to the growing numbers of urban and suburban legislators. To be sure, the governor was still the most powerful figure in the legislative process, and majority party leaders and committee chairs remained an influential set of participants. But gone were the days when a relatively few figures, representing the leadership of the Byrd organization, dominated the process. The 1970s was also a decade of modernization in state government, and, among other changes, professional staffing was upgraded in the legislative, executive, and regulatory realms. Consequently lobbyists and other statehouse figures had a larger and more pluralistic set of political participants with whom to deal.

Interest groups trying to influence state government also found the ground rules changing. The modernization of state government, particularly improvements in staffing and facilities, prompted a more sophisticated approach to problems of public policy. A case in point is the creation of the Joint Legislative Audit and Review Commission in 1973 and the development of its professional staff, which increased the Assembly's capability for evaluating state agencies and their programs. In the process interest groups that had a stake in those programs were also challenged and thus forced to respond in a more technical fashion than was the case before. For example, groups were drawn into complex debates over the methodology to be used in determining the proper allocation of costs between different users of Virginia's highway system or the costs of fully funding the constitutionally mandated standards of quality for public education.[21]

Whereas in the Byrd era, politics was conducted in fairly restricted circles, the last several decades have seen that process substantially enlarged, requiring interest group practitioners to be increasingly involved in the public arenas that influence government. Electorally, Virginia experienced increased party competition and public participation, but it also saw campaign costs escalate, with interest groups playing a larger role in funding. However, in state elections PACs have been less important in Virginia than in some other southern states, as Virginia election laws neither prohibit corporations and other groups from contributing directly to candidates nor set limits on the amount of money individuals and groups can contribute to campaigns.

Groups have also stepped up constituency or grass-roots activities to supplement their State Capitol efforts. Some well-established interests, such as the retail merchants, truckers, homebuilders, and the state's major universities, have been known for their ability to mobilize grass-roots support on behalf of legislative positions. Others have developed or are trying to develop that capability. Teachers clearly fall into the former category. During legislative sessions the VEA mounts the most visible grass-roots effort, daily bringing to the Capitol teams of teachers from around the state. The VEA's effort begins long before the session and includes workshops for its local leaders, lobbying simulations for rank-and-file members in which performances are videotaped and critiqued, and legislative contact teams, keeping in touch with legislators throughout the year.

Not surprisingly, in an increasingly media-oriented age, statehouse participants have become more conscious of public relations. Lobbyists have always been good sources for reporters, and lobbyists and the groups they represent have figured prominently in news accounts of the state government's activities. Yet in the last decade or so, as press coverage has increased and the press corps has become more assertive, interest groups and their lobbyists have had more opportunities to influence and be influenced by the news media. That trend was perhaps most noticeable when lobbyists and interest groups became the target of critical press accounts; yet not to be overlooked were interest groups' efforts to cultivate press coverage in the hope of mobilizing support, undercutting opposition, or both. Such efforts included press conferences, staged rallies, appearances by newsworthy figures at public hearings, and packaged information for reporters and editorial writers.

In summary, capital lobbying has become more demanding for traditional interests, requiring substantially more time and sophistication. Yet the process of "demystification" that Jeffrey Berry observed at the national level has also taken place in Virginia as more segments of the state's society have learned how to organize and operate interest groups.[22] While that process is most evident in the religious and public-interest categories, it is by no means limited to those types of interests.

Still, there remains a good deal of continuity in interest group operations. In the legislative realm, for instance, a core group of experienced lobbyists is at work, the best of whom exhibit qualities long associated with effective lobbying: knowledge of the issues and procedures; adeptness in making their case; a knack of knowing when and how to strike a compromise; and a network of connections with fellow lobbyists, agency officials, and legislators. Veteran lobbyists are well aware that friendly, well-positioned legislators make the best lobbyists vis-à-vis their colleagues. Finally, interest group operations, mirroring the state's political culture, continue to be a relatively clean pursuit—integrity in public service was a distinguishing feature of the Byrd machine operations.

Power

In the comparative literature on state government, Virginia has been consistently depicted as having a moderately strong interest group system, the only southern state not ranked in the strong category.[23] That stable portrait is striking in light of the changes that have occurred in the commonwealth, some of which (increased economic development, urbanization, political party competition, and governmental professionalism), as noted in Chapter 14, were thought to diminish interest group strength. However, to explore systematically Virginia's stable ranking would require drawing up a sample of issues that cut across the different areas of state governmental policy-making, including issues that are raised and those that are avoided (the other, or hidden, agenda), constructing case studies to examine those issues, and drawing inferences about the strength of various forces, governmental and nongovernmental, that influence policies. Obviously, such an undertaking is beyond our scope here. However, enough material is available to raise questions about Virginia's ranking in the literature, and more fundamentally, about the utility of a ranking system in discussing interest groups in a state undergoing considerable change.

Writing during the Byrd era, Belle Zeller (1954) and Harmon Zeigler (1965) based their moderate rankings on questionnaires completed by experts on state politics.[24] Yet with the benefit of hindsight, it appears that such a ranking understated interest group strength, particularly for interests that were allied with the Byrd machine (e.g., the business community). Historically, those interests have enjoyed a special place in Virginia politics. Indeed, Key, writing at the height of the Byrd era, observed that the machine enjoys the enthusiastic and almost undivided support of the business community and of the well-to-do generally, a goodly number of whom are fugitives from the New York state income tax. Organization spokesmen in Congress look out for the interests of business, and the state government, although well managed, manifests a continuing interest in the well-being of the well-to-do. The quid pro quo for support of the organization is said to be taxation favorable to corporations, an anti-labor policy, and restraint in the expansion of services, such as education, public health, and welfare.[25]

J. Harvie Wilkinson III, in his classic work on Byrd, took exception to that passage, noting that corporate leaders were never key machine figures, nor did they enjoy excessive tax privileges. On the other hand, he did not challenge the notion that a mutually supportive relationship generally prevailed between business and the machine.[26]

O'Toole and Montjoy's study of the SCC, the powerful independent state regulatory agency, is instructive on this point.[27] Nearly all the business matters in which the Byrd machine had an interest, such as banking, insurance, public utilities, and intrastate transportation, but not highways, fell under the jurisdiction of the SCC, giving the agency the broadest jurisdiction of any state regulatory body in the country. Relations between the SCC, governors, legislators, and the business community were friendly and supportive. The commissioners and key agency staff were Byrd organization loyalists, and underlying those political ties was a similarity in outlook. O'Toole and Montjoy summarized the relationship that prevailed between the SCC and regulated interests: "A debate about whether the SCC has been a supporter of business or a judicious servant of the Commonwealth ignores the more important point. For most of the participants, these roles were identical."[28]

Ironically, in 1959 the business elites broke with the Byrd machine over massive resistance to racial integration that had led to school closings. Concerned that this resistance was hurting Virginia, particularly its economic development, the business elites played a key role behind the scenes in reversing the policy.[29] In short, well-established interests, particularly in the business community, played a more influential role than the moderate interest group ranking would suggest.

Morehouse (1981) developed the most recent ranking of interest group strength in the states, one also used by Zeigler (1983).[30] Once again Virginia is placed in the moderately strong category, based on a review of four regional works; however, only two cover the post-Byrd era. More fundamentally, the posting of a particular ranking suggests a static conception of policy-making that can be misleading in a state undergoing considerable change. Consider, for example, state regulation of major economic interests. O'Toole and Montjoy's study of contemporary decision making at the SCC, particularly in the areas of insurance and public utilities, found that regulated interests (e.g., Virginia Power) still had a decided advantage in the resources that any group would need to influence the agency—"access and information."[31] Besides being well positioned to make their case before the SCC, the major regulated interests were similarly situated elsewhere in the governmental process to influence decisions on the SCC. Virginia Power, for example, having previously relied on external counsel from Hunton and Williams, developed during the 1970s an in-house governmental relations department, headed by one of the Assembly's most respected lobbyists, E. L. Crump. Besides deploying those two sources of representation, the company established a political action committee and a grass-roots lobbying operation.

Yet, for all their influence, the regulated interests were not the only force affecting the SCC regulatory process, one that had undergone considerable change from the earlier period. The business community was no longer so united; disputes over utility rates found Virginia Power and other utilities squaring off against major industrial users. Consumer interests were now represented, joined by the Division of Consumer Counsel that had been established at the attorney general's office. The SCC itself had undergone modernization. Staff and facilities had been upgraded, putting the commission on a stronger analytical footing vis-à-vis regulated interests, and procedures had been formalized to insure greater fairness in the proceedings. O'Toole and Montjoy concluded that the SCC, as it headed into the 1980s, was a more "complex organization," its decisions influenced by a "multitude of factors" that are "variable in their potency from case to case and over time."[32]

That pattern was less evident in the environmental field, where major economic interests have had a decided advantage in a conservative state government eager to promote economic development. Whereas economic regulation falls mainly under the SCC's jurisdiction, environmental regulation has been divided among a number of agencies that are smaller and do not have legal, technical, or political resources comparable to the SCC's.

In the regulation of air pollution, for instance, business has long exercised a strong influence on the deliberations of the State Air Pollution Control Board. An unusual public demonstration of that fact occurred in 1984 when the board, under a new chair, proposed amendments to the state air control plan that would have toughened state regulations and made Virginia a regional leader in this field. However, the board, a low-profile state agency not known for an aggressive regulatory posture, ran into a phalanx of opposition from regulated interests: the Virginia Manufacturers Association; the Virginia Chamber of Commerce; the Virginia Farm Bureau; and an assortment of businesses and business associations involved in such things as manufacturing, construction, mining, transportation, public utilities, and lumbering/forestry, plus some government agencies and legislators. Environmental interests were barely visible, making up only three of the one hundred groups that participated in the public hearings held around the state. In the aftermath of the stormy public-hearing process the board "went back basically to the drawing board and started over again," said John M. Daniel, assistant executive director for enforcement, deleting or relaxing the contested proposals.[33]

Yet in other areas environmental interests have begun to fare better. In the early to mid-1980s a grass-roots environmental coalition played a key role in the Assembly, blocking uranium mining in Virginia. Governor Baliles, more committed to environmental affairs than were his predecessors, won the Assembly's approval in 1986 of a reorganization plan establishing a cabinet-level secretary of natural resources, a move long opposed by regulated interests. (Environmentalists had felt at a disadvantage under the old cabinet arrangements because environmental affairs fell under the commerce secretariat.) The Chesapeake Bay Foundation and other public-interest groups have been active in water-pollution problems, especially with regard to the bay, helping enact in 1988 the Chesapeake Bay Preservation Act, giving Virginia a greater role in local land-use decisions affecting the bay. In short, in at least some important areas of environmental policy-making it was no longer politics as usual.

Even in such a seemingly settled area as labor-management affairs there can be more going on than first meets the eye in this economically conservative, promanagement state. In contemporary state government some of the most important labor-management issues have arisen not in the private sector but in the public sector between state and local governments and employees' organizations. And while in Virginia organized labor has historically been a weak force, in at least one part of the public sector organized labor (particularly the VEA) has emerged as a force to be reckoned with in state politics.

Since the mid-1970s the VEA has revamped and upgraded its headquarters and field staff, and expanded dramatically its presence in the electoral process and in legislative and executive decision-making circles. Besides fielding the largest registered lobbying force, its chief lobbyist, Richard Pulley, was named in 1981 one of the ten most effective lobbyists.[34] The year before, the VEA scored an impressive victory, playing a critical role in defeating a retirement plan backed by the governor and leading legislators that would have reduced retirement benefits for public employees. Since then the VEA has played a major role in helping boost state funding for public education and in particular for teachers' salaries.

Despite a concerted effort, however, the VEA has been unsuccessful in achieving one of its top goals, the restoration of collective-bargaining rights.[35] As is the case in most states, Virginia law prohibits public employees' striking. However, with the exception of public-transportation workers, the code is silent on the question of collective bargaining for public employees. By 1976 approximately 30,000 public employees in Virginia were covered by collective-bargaining agreements with local governments. Of these employees, approximately 20,000 were teachers represented by the VEA. That year Gov. Mills Godwin directed the attorney general to file a lawsuit challenging agreements with public employees in Arlington, a

Northern Virginia locality. Although a lower court upheld the agreements, the Virginia Supreme Court in 1977 unanimously reversed that decision, finding that the Assembly had not expressly granted localities that authority.[36]

While the VEA has repeatedly failed in its efforts to secure some form of collective-bargaining legislation, a related development has been unfolding in policy-making affecting public schools. The VEA has sought to gain through the state legislature, with varying degrees of success, those kinds of provisions (e.g., salary, benefits, and work conditions) that are negotiated locally in collective-bargaining agreements.[37] Indeed, such provisions were negotiated in certain Virginia localities before the 1977 state supreme court ruling. That setback demonstrated the importance of the state governmental arena and helped spur the VEA's development of a larger and more sophisticated statehouse operation.

In summary, this review of state policy-making suggests two problems with the moderate ranking that Virginia interest groups have been assigned in the comparative literature of the last thirty years. In the first place, such a ranking understates the strength of well-connected interests during the Byrd era. Second, the designation of one ranking masks the more dynamic nature of contemporary state policy-making and the variable role that interest groups play in different issue-areas and even in the same issue-area over time.

Conclusion

Virginia, Key's "political museum piece," has undergone considerable change since the decline of the Byrd machine, not the least of which has occurred in the interest group realm. Specifically, statehouse interest groups and lobbyists, constituting a supplementary system of representation, have increased in number and become more diverse in their makeup—a trend that parallels the expanding scope of participation in the state's electoral process. Both are significant developments in a state known for its elitist political culture. Operationally, statehouse representation has become a more demanding undertaking for traditional interests, requiring a greater commitment of time and more political and technical expertise. And yet a process of demystification has also been evident as more segments of Virginia society have learned how to organize and operate in state governmental circles. Then, too, the modernization of state government and related political developments have made for a more dynamic state policy-making process in which power and interest group fortunes are more variable than used to be the case.

Notwithstanding the important changes that have occurred, Virginia is also a state where the forces of continuity remain strong. Traditional, well-established interests are still very evident in the larger, more pluralistic interest group community, more often than not represented by veteran lobbyists, whether in-house lobbyists or ones drawn from major Richmond-based associations and law firms. And for all the increased sophistication in interest group operations, time-tested practices are still very much a part of effective statehouse operations. Finally, traditional interest group powers, although less assured of success than in the past, are still best positioned to advance their interests or, better still, defend the status quo, usually a tactically advantageous position, made stronger in a state where traditions die hard.

5

NORTH CAROLINA

INTEREST GROUPS IN A STATE
IN TRANSITION

Jack D. Fleer

When Bill Holman goes to work he dresses differently than other persons who practice his profession. He wears a blue suit, a yellow shirt, and a tie depicting a fish—a walleyed pike, to be precise. Most of his cohorts wear gray pin-striped suits, white shirts, and dotted ties. They carry briefcases containing numerous documents. Holman stands out in the halls of the General Assembly not only in his attire, but in his message and in his effectiveness. As a lobbyist for the Conservation Council of North Carolina and the state chapter of the Sierra Club, Holman was recognized as one of the most influential lobbyists in the 1985/86, 1987/88, and 1989/90 sessions.[1] As the principal environmental lobbyist in North Carolina, Holman symbolizes important changes in the state's politics and in interest group activity. The changes have occurred in and are a product of the political, social, and economic context, the number and variety of interests represented, the techniques used by groups, and the influence of groups in the state's politics.[2] These changes have contributed to the transition of North Carolina, a state of developing political pluralism.

Politically, North Carolina is changing from a modified one-party system in which Democrats have won almost all offices on the state and local levels. The transition began in 1972 when a Republican governor was elected for the first time in this century, and voters also elected a Republican U.S. senator and supported Richard

Nixon, the Republican candidate for president. However, the limits of the transition are shown in the fact that Democratic candidates continue to win almost all statewide executive offices and to win substantial majorities in both houses of the state legislature. In the general election of 1988 the Democrats' share of state House and Senate membership was decreased by gains in the Republican delegation; at the same time Democrats lost the governorship for only the third time in this century and the position of lieutenant governor for the first time. Nonetheless, in the 1989/90 General Assembly, Democrats held thirty-seven of fifty seats in the Senate and seventy-four of 120 seats in the House—about two-thirds of the seats in each chamber.[3]

In North Carolina the legislative branch is perceived as being very powerful. Indeed, the election of a Republican governor in 1984 and 1988 may well have enhanced this perception. The Assembly's power comes in part from its being the only state legislature in the nation whose decisions cannot be vetoed by the governor. The Assembly has a well-established committee system and uses interim study committees extensively. In the 1980s the high degree of stability among legislative leaders (especially the House speaker and the Senate president, who is also lieutenant governor) contributed to a centralization of power in each of those bodies, especially the House of Representatives. From 1981 through 1988 the speaker of the House served an unprecedented four terms in that position, acquiring a power base that accrues from experience and continuity. Additionally, more committee chairs served successive terms, especially on major committees such as Appropriations and Ways and Means.[4]

The General Assembly meets for a regular session of approximately seven months in odd-numbered years and for a short session of four to six weeks in even-numbered years. The regular session has a general agenda, while the short session has a more restricted agenda focusing on adjustments in the biennial budget. The Assembly continues to emphasize its character as a "citizens' legislature," with most members being part-time and serving brief terms. While the institutional research staff has been improved, individual staffs are small except for those of committee chairs.

The executive branch of state government underwent a streamlining in 1971 and is now composed of eight departments headed by elected officials and ten departments headed by secretaries appointed by and serving at the pleasure of the governor. Appointment powers are among the major components of the governor's arsenal. Additional power comes through the governor's role as director of the budget. In 1977 the right to two successive gubernatorial terms was approved.[5]

Economically, North Carolina is also in transition. The state's economy was formerly dominated by three manufacturing industries—textiles, tobacco, and furniture. These industries were tied very closely to the state's agricultural and rural nature. Workers engaged in these enterprises did not need a high degree of skill and education and thus did not command high wages. Until recently these industries were labor-intensive. As recently as 1970 more than half of all manufacturing employment in the state was concentrated in the big three. Historically, North Carolina has had the lowest percentage of unionized workers and the lowest wages for manufacturing employees in the nation. This low-income, poorly trained, land-based employment was scattered around a state whose population was located on the farm and in numerous small towns.[6]

In the past two decades not only have the big three declined in significance, but the manufacturing sector itself is less prominent in the state employment picture. And rural and metropolitan areas have grown apart to such an extent that some observers see a dual economy of booming, economically diversified cities and depressed, stagnant rural areas. The transition is fueled by efforts of recent governors, especially James B. Hunt, to attract new high-tech industry to the state and by the rise of the service sector. One focus of the first effort was the development of microelectronics centers and the mechanization of traditional industries such as textiles. The greater transition comes from the growth of trade, government, and service employment. Since 1960 the number of jobs in the state's service sector has more than tripled. In 1960 trade, government, and service employment accounted for approximately 43 percent of the nonagricultural employment. By the mid-1980s more than one-half (53%) of the state's employment was in these three areas. This development in North Carolina reflects national trends.[7] In addition, financial institutions and real estate construction and development provide numerous jobs. These changes are reflected in the system of interest representation and in the state's policy agenda by, for example, more-varied business groups and increased presence of professional and environmental groups.

Allocations in the state budget also have great impact on the representation of interests. State government provides approximately three-fourths of the funds for elementary and secondary education.[8] In the 1989/90 budget 30 percent of state expenditures were for public school education. Another 17 percent of funds went to higher education including community colleges. Thus nearly one-half of the state budget is allocated for this single service.[9] Government as a portion of the state's economy has been growing, as evidenced by expenditures and employment by government. Between 1970 and 1982 general revenue expenditures by state and local governments in North Carolina grew from $2.7 billion to $8.4 billion. In 1985 government absorbed 11.6 percent of the gross state product. In 1980/81 North Carolina ranked eighth among the fifty states in state percentage financing of total state and local general expenditures from its own revenue sources.[10] Meanwhile government (federal, state, and local) employees increased from 218,000 to 414,000. While local governments are undoubtedly the largest public employers, employing approximately 60 percent of all public workers including public school teachers, state government is also a major employer.[11] Thus city, county, and state employees and interests press the state government for policy decisions and funds.

In summary, North Carolina is in transition from a one-party-dominant state to a politically competitive state, although the Democrats continue to have the advantage for most offices. The state's economy is moving from one dominated by a few low-skilled manufacturing industries into one in which manufacturing continues as important but service and government employment is expanded. The state has a large population (the tenth largest in the nation), but that population is scattered quite broadly in numerous small and medium-sized towns and in rural areas. Charlotte, the largest city in the state, has a population of approximately 400,000. These developments have produced new sources of political, social, and economic pluralism. Such pluralism is a breeding ground for political conflict, giving rise to more-varied and intense interest group representation and activity.

Regulation of Lobbying and Its Administration

Lobbying regulation for North Carolina is set forth in Article 9A, Chapter 120 of the General Statutes of North Carolina, originally written in 1933. Under this law "every person who is employed or retained as a legislative agent shall register." A legislative agent is defined as "any person who is employed or retained, with compensation, by another person to give facts or arguments to any member of the General Assembly during any regular or special session thereof upon or concerning any bill, resolution, amendment, report or claim pending or to be introduced." Registration is with the secretary of state and is required for each session of the General Assembly and for each employer or retainer for whom a person works as an agent. Each member of the General Assembly is provided a list of all registered legislative agents within twenty days after the opening of each session. Lists are updated as new registrations occur.

After the General Assembly adjourns, each legislative agent and each employer must file a report of expenses for transportation, lodging, entertainment, food, any item worth more than $25, and "contributions made, paid, incurred, or promised, directly or indirectly." The employer also must report the compensation paid a legislative agent except in the case that the agent is a "full time employee of or is annually retained by the reporting employer."

The statutory requirements are not applicable to an individual citizen who expresses a personal opinion on a matter before the legislature, to an elected or appointed national, state, or local governmental employee when acting in an official capacity, to representatives of news media when performing their duties, or to members of the General Assembly. However, since 1975 the law has required all persons who are "authorized official legislative liaison" personnel representing the governor, members of the Council of State, and heads of departments, agencies, and institutions of the state government to register with the secretary of state.

Violations of this law are misdemeanors subject to punishment by fine or imprisonment. Data on apparent violations of the registration law are limited but reveal incidents from 1981 through 1985. During that period reported infractions include only one case of an unregistered agent, forty-five cases of failure to file report after notice, and forty-five cases of failure to pay the late-filing fee. However, the Office of the Secretary of State does not audit reports or have other investigative powers that could provide a more complete assessment of the level of compliance with the law.[12]

The focus of this law is on lobbying directed at the legislative branch of state government. Persons who attempt to influence policymakers in the executive or judiciary are not covered; nor does the law require that expenses incurred in actions directed at these branches be reported.

Article 10 of the General Statutes requires the registration of persons or organizations "who or which [are] principally engaged in the activity or business of influencing public opinion and/or legislation in" North Carolina.[13] Few registrations occur under this statute, undoubtedly because the statement applies to persons or organizations "principally engaged" in such influence.

A major change in interest group activity in North Carolina is the dramatic and steady increase in the number of registered agents, as

Table 5.1 Registration of Legislative Agents, 1969–1989

	Number of Registrants	Number of Persons	Number of Groups
1969	151	138	140
1977	323	294	222
1979	453	—	—
1981	505	—	—
1983	584	—	—
1985	666	411	369
1987	805	457	451
1989	848	467	453

Source: Office of the Secretary of State, North Carolina.

shown in Table 5.1. In the 1989 General Assembly 848 registrations of legislative agents were reported by the Office of the Secretary of State. As indicated, the number of registrants and the number of persons are different. The difference is due to the fact that some persons register to represent more than one organization or interest during the session. Multiple representation is a common feature of lobbying. For example, in 1989 Samuel Johnson, who was rated the most effective lobbyist in the session, was listed as agent for nineteen diverse groups, from the North Carolina Automobile Dealers Association to Waste Management, Incorporated. Also, many organizations or firms have multiple agents. In 1989 the North Carolina Bankers Association had eight agents registered. However, most persons represent only one interest, and most interests have only a single representative.

In Table 5.2 data on types of organizations that have had legislative agents registered in recent years are provided. Classifications indicate that most registrants are working on behalf of business interests, a rather typical finding in studies of interest groups among the states and in the national government. The definition of business interests used here is comprehensive and includes corporations, banking, utilities, and retail merchants, to name just a few. Other major interests frequently represented include professional and trade associations, education, and health care (doctors, hospitals, etc.). Labor interests are few but include both traditional and new-style groups such as associations of state and local employees, including teachers.

Looking at the pattern over the past decade, the diversity of interest group representation has not changed significantly but has increased. However, by the late 1980s new groups had emerged in environmental and citizens' affairs. Additionally, education and governmental employees' groups have an increased presence. The enlarged role of black citizens in state politics is not reflected among the registered legislative agents. However, since 1969 the Black Legislative Caucus has been a growing influence in the General Assembly.[14] Despite increases in the number of legislative agents registered, those interests represented most frequently in 1977 continue to be most frequently represented in 1985.

Table 5.2 Classification of Interests Represented

	Year of Registration		
	1969	1977	1985
Business	58	115	182
Corporations	(20)[a]	(28)	(65)
Utilities	(6)	(10)	(25)
Banking, finance	(9)	(15)	(24)
Insurance	(14)	(27)	(28)
Trade associations	34	32	48
Professional associations	5	8	16
Agriculture	5	8	16
Environment	1	1	6
Citizens' groups	3	9	17
Labor	7	3	4
Education	3	8	13
Employees of governmental units	4	10	15
Medicine, health care	13	18	29
Miscellaneous, unclassified	11	10	41

[a] This and other parenthetical numbers are interests within the subcategory.

Source: Office of the Secretary of State, North Carolina

The other major category of interest group represented before the General Assembly comes through official legislative liaison personnel from executive departments, agencies, and institutions. A December 1990 directory from the Office of the Secretary of State lists 288 persons serving in such capacity. Among them are twelve individuals listed as representing the governor's office and forty-eight representing various components of the Department of Economic and Community Development. Frequently, the persons listed include the secretary of the department, as in the cases of Labor and the State Treasurer.

Techniques of Interest Group Influence

Some techniques used by interest groups to influence policy have been practiced for decades. In addition, new means of influence have been developed in recent years and are being used with much fervor. Of particular interest is the emergence of PACs as funding sources for state campaigns. In a recent survey both legislators and lobbyists were asked to indicate which tactics are most effective.[15] The two groups agreed that the most important is a skilful, personal appeal to legislators. This choice highlights the significance of the lobbyist who represents a particular group in the halls of the General Assembly. While differing on levels of importance of several techniques, both sets of respondents indicated that other useful means include presenting testimony before legislative committees, assisting in drafting bills for introduction, forming coalitions with another group or groups, and mobilizing public opinion through letter writing, the media, or both avenues. Legislators differed from lobbyists in that the latter said supporting legislators in elections was an effective lobbying technique. While legislators generally did not select that option, 95 percent stated that they did receive financial support from groups in election campaigns.

Interest groups certainly see election support as a means of influencing public policies and policymakers. While PACs have existed for quite some time, they have emerged with new prominence in the past two decades, and their presence and numbers have increased dramatically in recent years.[16] In North Carolina PACs are regulated through registration and financial disclosure statements filed with the Office of Campaign Reporting of the State Board of Elections.[17] Committees are required to file periodic reports listing contributions, loans, and expenditures. Political committees' contributions to any candidate or other committee are limited to no more than $4,000 per election. Total expenditures by PACs are not limited. Reasonable administrative support by the parent organization of a PAC is permissible and must be disclosed in an annual report. The number of nonparty PACs registered with the State Board of Elections has increased from twenty-nine in 1974 to 270 in 1989.

The staff of the *Charlotte Observer* conducted a comprehensive examination of PACs and state legislative politics covering the 1984,

1986, and 1988 elections. We will depend heavily on those findings of financial activity in North Carolina House and Senate campaigns. As Ken Eudy states, the *Observer* staff "found a recurring connection between political contributions and legislative activity. The most active contributors . . . were people or groups whose financial interests are the most heavily lobbied in the General Assembly."[18]

In 1986 and 1988, according to Eudy, more than half the money contributed by nonpartisan PACs came from eleven groups including MEDPAC (North Carolina Medical Society), North Carolina Academy of Trial Lawyers PAC, North Carolina Realtors Association PAC, Duke Power Employees State PAC, and Carolina Power and Light Company PAC. Other major groups were committees for Southern Bell, NC Power, Jefferson Pilot (Insurance) PAC, and the North Carolina Association of Educators.

Among the major conclusions of the *Observer*'s study are its findings that

- 95 percent of legislative candidates received contributions from PACs
- PACs were the largest single source of identifiable contributions to state legislative candidates, contributing almost $1 of every $4 raised
- PACs gave substantially more to incumbent and winning candidates than to challengers and losers
- PACs contributed to candidates of both parties running for the same seat as well as candidates who run unopposed

Each of these factors may well provide the contributing organizations with significant leverage in the legislative process.[19]

Eudy concludes: "The more heavily a business and industry is regulated by the state, the more likely were contributions to legislative campaigns."[20] More than half the contributions to winners that were identified came from persons and organizations in a few businesses or professions[21] (see Table 5.3).

The North Carolina Center for Public Policy Research examined the role of PACs' contributions to the North Carolina governor's contest in 1984,[22] finding that the role of PACs in that race was much less than in the state legislative races in the same year. Ap-

Table 5.3 Source and Dollar Amount of PAC Contributions to North Carolina Legislative Campaigns

	1986	1988
Health care	273,309	285,429
Utilities	150,160	250,493
Legal	187,711	231,889
Building and real estate	149,275	188,116
Trade	183,075	173,773
Manufacturing	85,920	134,827
Insurance	77,150	122,184
Banking	53,271	74,091
Agriculture	—	46,219
Transportation	—	23,065

Adapted from Jim Morrill, "Lobbyists Escalate 'Arms Race,'" *Charlotte Observer*, April 9, 1989, A1, 8.

proximately 3 percent of funding was contributed by PACs out of slightly more than $11 million reported as contributions. An analysis of PAC giving is provided in Table 5.4. PAC contributions played a minor role in providing funds for the gubernatorial candidates as compared with the proportion of contributions by PACs to state legislative candidates. The top five PACs in the governor's race include a variety of groups but represent two major interests—business and the medical profession. The five PACs were North Carolina Chiropractic PAC, contributing $25,000; First Union Bank Employees PAC, $17,175; MEDPAC, $13,250; Jefferson Pilot (Insurance) PAC, $11,900; and Carolina Power and Light Company PAC, $11,500. The interests are similar to those which played a major part in funding state legislative races.[23]

A complementary study conducted by the *North Carolina Independent* reveals that contributions from individuals to the campaigns of the two party nominees for governor reflect interest group bias toward particular candidates. James Martin, the Republican nominee and victor, received major contributions from business interests within the state. The *Independent* concluded that "what is striking . . . is the unprecedented degree to which North Carolina's top business leaders, Republicans and Democrats alike, rallied behind his campaign." The authors note a high correlation between Martin's major contributors and the officers and directors of the North Carolina Citizens for Business and Industry, a major interest group and advocate for business in the state. The Democratic nominee, Rufus Edmisten, received most of his large donations from lawyers, including attorneys in the attorney general's office (which Edmisten headed), and from employees of state government.[24] These contrasts in sources of major contributions reveal the way in which individuals who are associated with particular interests can supplement the work of PACs and organized interests.

Additional research is needed on the PACs' role as a means of interest group influence in state politics. However, a review of research on their role in North Carolina indicates that PACs are significant participants, especially in state legislative politics. PACs have come to be a major weapon in interest groups' arsenal. For groups that have the resources, PACs can enhance their influence in shaping public policies.

Lobbyists also provide gifts to legislators in order to create goodwill and to promote their causes. In recent sessions members of the General Assembly snacked on cookies from RJR Nabisco, refreshed

Table 5.4 PAC Contributions to the 1984 North Carolina Gubernatorial Race

Candidate	Number of Contributing PACs	Total Contributions (in Dollars)	Average Contributions (in Dollars)
Martin	44	88,490	2,011
Edmisten	27	47,238	1,750
Knox	34	40,460	1,190
Faircloth	11	24,026	2,184
Green	34	40,750	1,199
Gilmore	9	14,742	1,638
Ingram	5	12,100	2,420

Adapted from North Carolina Center for Public Policy Research, "The 1983–84 Govenor's Race Contribution Analysis" (n.d., manuscript).

themselves with Pepsi-Cola, and attended numerous breakfasts and receptions sponsored by such organizations as the North Carolina Association of Life Underwriters and the Raleigh Chamber of Commerce, to name just two. They attended Durham Bulls baseball games and North Carolina School of the Arts concerts. While these and other gifts are forms of promotion, they do raise questions about securing access and influence. But as one legislator stated, "if a legislator can be bought off by a soda and a few crackers, the state's in real trouble."[25]

Assessing Interest Group Influence

The findings from a 1986 survey, conducted by the author, of members of the General Assembly and of legislative agents registered with the secretary of state provide answers to several questions: What are the most important groups in North Carolina? What makes groups and their agents effective in influencing public policies in the state? How important are interest groups in general in North Carolina politics?[26]

Respondents were asked to list the five most influential interest groups in the state at election time and the five most influential interest groups during the 1985/86 session of the legislature. The questions were open-ended, and thus various phrasings of the influential groups were received. Responses were coded into categories of interests. Numerous groups were mentioned, but a few were mentioned frequently (see Table 5.5 for a summary of responses from legislators and from lobbyists). The most frequently mentioned influential group comprises educational interests and teachers. Almost three-fourths of the respondents listed public school teachers, educators, or, more specifically, one of the organized educational groups—the North Carolina Association of Educators (NCAE)—as among the most influential groups. In three of the four categories of responses, the NCAE was mentioned more frequently than any other. Only among the lobbyist respondents was education not rated first.

The second most frequently mentioned interest category is business, including listings for industry, corporations, chambers of

Table 5.5 Five Most Influential Groups in North Carolina

At Election Time		During Session	
Legislators	**Lobbyists**	**Legislators**	**Lobbyists**
Education	Education	Education	Banking
State employees	Business	Banking	Business
Business	Banking	Business	Education
Doctors	State employees	State employees	Insurance
Lawyers	Insurance/Doctors[a]	Local Governments/Lawyers[a]	Lawyers

[a] Tied ranking.

commerce, and, more specifically, the North Carolina Citizens for Business and Industry (NCCBI), a major business organization in the state. Approximately one-half of the respondents rated business interests among the most influential groups in North Carolina both at election time and during the legislative session. The next most frequently mentioned interest category is a subcategory of business—banking and bankers. Three of the four sets of responses include this category among the top five; only legislators rating influential groups at election time did not include banks. Overall, about 40 percent of the respondents rated banks among the influential.

No other interest category was listed among the top five in all four categories of responses. However, the fourth most frequently mentioned influential group are state employees; more specifically, the State Employees Association of North Carolina, rated among the top five in three of the four categories of responses. Lawyers, including the North Carolina State Bar and the North Carolina Academy of Trial Lawyers, two specific organizations of lawyers, were mentioned in three categories.

While respondents were not asked to explain the influence of particular groups, they were asked to list characteristics of interest groups that make them influential in the legislative session. In other words, what makes an interest group and its lobbyists effective? How can personal representatives of groups be influential in the legislature? Survey respondents gave a wide variety of responses. However, the following were most often mentioned by legislators: knowledge of the subject and credibility; nature and frequency of contacts, general visibility and access; character of presentation of information, including positive and personal appeal; and relationship with constituents, especially registered voters. Also mentioned were "rapport with leadership" and providing campaign support.

The North Carolina Center for Public Policy Research, which conducted surveys during several sessions of the General Assembly, provides another perspective on effective lobbying. The center asked legislators, legislative agents, and news correspondents to name the most influential lobbyists in each session. In addition to Johnson and Holman, who were mentioned earlier, that list includes J. Allen Adams, Zebulon Alley, and J. Ruffin Bailey. Adams, Alley, and Bailey each represent numerous clients, including the Arts Advocates of North Carolina, Seatbelts for Safety, Kaiser Foundation Health Plan of North Carolina, and the North Carolina Beer Wholesalers Association.

Consistently, the lobbyists most frequently named as most effective were former members of the state legislature and practicing attorneys. In 1985/86 all of the top five, and ten of the top twenty, were former legislators; in 1989 six of the top ten were ex-lawmakers.[27] "Good legislators who quit the General Assembly after a few sessions don't just fade away. They become lobbyists, cultivate old friendship ties, and make a lot of money."[28]

These findings have led some commentators to renew the debate on whether effectiveness depends on legislative experience and legal training. Ran Coble, director of the center, has stated that good lobbyists, many of whom served as legislators, can better plead a case because they know the legislative process and when and how information can be most effectively presented. Additionally, he says, they "know the players [and] what each individual legislator cares about."[29] Past service, although it can be beneficial, does not guarantee the requisite knowledge and sensitivity. As one of the top five lobbyists commented, "I haven't noticed anybody bowing down or falling over just because I've been in the legislature."[30] This debate prompted a member of the legislature who served as cochair of the Legislative Ethics and Lobbying Committee to prepare a bill requiring former state officials to wait five years before becoming professional legislative lobbyists.

Another legislator has remarked that the effectiveness of a lobbyist derives in part from his or her clients and cause. Explaining the success of a top lobbyist, the legislator concluded: "He represents those who have power, so he has power. Anybody with his lists of clients, and the resources and clout they bring with them, would do well in the General Assembly. I doubt [he] would be effective if he were lobbying for Legal Services."[31] Other factors that might help explain the influence of groups and their representatives include the size of a group, its membership composition, their geographical distribution, and previous and current political activity.

Comparing the results of the 1986 survey with those of approximately two decades ago provides historical perspective on the influ-

Table 5.6 Comparison of Interest Group Rankings

1966		1986	
Legislators	Lobbyists	Legislators	Lobbyists
Electricity (public)	Trucking	Education	Education
Education	Education	State employees	Business
Trucking	Governmental units	Business	Banking
Electricity (private)	Agriculture	Lawyers	State employees
Utilities[a]	Labor and public employees	Doctors/banking[b]	Insurance/doctors[b]

[a] Excluding electricity.
[b] Tied ranking.

Sources: Rankings for 1966 are from Harmon Zeigler and Michael Baer, *Lobbying: Interaction and Influence in American State Legislatures* (Belmont, Calif.: Wadsworth, 1969), pp. 32-33. Rankings for 1986 are from the author's survey.

ence of groups in North Carolina. (See Table 5.6 for a comparison of the 1986 survey with findings of a survey of lobbyists and legislators conducted in 1966 by Zeigler and Baer.) Comparison is made difficult by the use of different categories of interests. However, recognizing these differences, some conclusions can be reached. In both surveys educational interests are prominent, with the possibility that their prominence has increased from being the second most important group to being the most influential. Zeigler and Baer mention a wide range of business interests that their respondents rated as influential. However, most of these particular business interests were not given specific attention in the 1986 survey. In particular, utilities, including public and private electricity, were much less frequently mentioned in 1986. Additionally, trucking interests were mentioned often by respondents twenty years ago, but are not among the top groups in the 1986 survey. In their place is the more generalized interest category of business. Banking and bankers, rated tenth by lobbyists in the 1966 survey, had risen to third in 1986. Explanations of these changes in ratings of influential groups include changes in the employment structure of the state, as discussed earlier, emergence of the service sector in the state's economy, and the improved organizational representation of interests, including emergence of NCAE and NCCBI.

Assessing Interest Groups' Overall Strength

The 1986 survey provided legislative and interest group respondents several opportunities to give general assessments of the role of interest groups in the political process. General assessments are difficult to make because of the variety of groups and the numerous policy decisions in which lobbyists and legislators relate. But it is possible and useful to have participants' overall evaluations (see Tables 5.7 and 5.8 for data on general assessments of group influence). When asked to select a single statement to describe group influence, both legislators and lobbyists select what could be considered as positive assessments. In Table 5.7 we see that approximately three-fourths of the lobbyists and two-fifths of the legislators rate interest group influence as crucial or very important

Table 5.7 Ratings of Overall Interest Group Influence by Percentage of Responses

	Legislators	Lobbyists
Crucial	9	24
Very important	32	48
Important	44	22
Of little importance	4	0
Insignificant	0	0
No answer	11	6

in policy-making. No lobbyist and only two legislators indicated they regarded interest group influence as minimal.

Both lobbyists and legislators show broad support for the view that interest group influence is necessary and valuable or sometimes useful in political decision making (see Table 5.8). However, a significant minority does find interest group influence contrary to the public interest. While it is important to remember that these options are not logically exclusive, the respondents' choices were exclusive, thus revealing fundamental beliefs.

A second major conclusion is that lobbyists, not surprisingly, evaluate their role and influence more positively than do legislators. In responses to both survey questions, lobbyists selected the most fa-

Table 5.8 Ratings of Interest Group Activity by Percentage of Responses

	Legislators	Lobbyists
Necessary and valuable	41	58
Sometimes useful	30	25
Reduces rationality	0	2
Ineffectual and unnecessary	0	0
Contrary to public interest	15	11
No answer	13	4

Table 5.9 Ranking of Policymakers' Relative Influence
(by Percentage)

	Legislators	Lobbyists
General Assembly	1	1
Interest groups	2	2
Governor and staff	3	3
Media	4	4[a]
Governmental departments	5	4[a]
Judiciary	6	6

[a] Among lobbyists, media and governmental departments tied in rank.

vorable responses more frequently than did legislators. This undoubtedly reflects the different perception of each group regarding
its contribution to policy-making, plus the vested interests of lobbyists.

An evaluation of interest group influence within North Carolina's
political system was obtained by asking legislators and lobbyists to
rank various forces in policy-making (see Table 5.9 for data placing
interest groups in perspective). For both legislators and lobbyists, the
most important influence on policy decisions among those listed is
the General Assembly. Based on a composite of total score, most-
frequent rating, and average rating, the state legislature ranks a clear
first. Several respondents volunteered that not the entire legislature
but the leaders (speaker and lieutenant governor) or the "six power
brokers" of the General Assembly were the major influence in legislative policy decisions.

Interest groups were ranked as the second most important influence, followed closely by the governor and his staff. Several
respondents commented that if the governor were not a Republican
that office and its occupant would be a greater influence. In a state
where Democrats have had a virtual monopoly on executive and
legislative leadership and power, the second Republican governor of
the century is seen at a disadvantage in shaping public policy. Indeed
in 1985–1989 some observers of Governor Martin's relationship
with the General Assembly concluded that he did not attempt to

provide strong legislative leadership.[32] With more experience and a larger party delegation, a Republican governor could be a greater influence. Apparently the void has been filled by interest group power. What the relative influence of the governor and interest groups would be if a Democrat were to return as chief executive is unknown.

Among other agents, the media ranked fourth; government departments and agencies fifth; and the judiciary sixth. However, among lobbyists, the media and governmental agencies tied at fourth.

The several general assessments of the role and influence of interest groups in North Carolina government and policy-making suggest that such groups are perceived as important and positive participants in the process. While it is clear from earlier analyses that influence varies greatly among groups, with the policy under consideration, and from year to year, the significance of interest groups as a whole is confirmed by the 1986 survey results.

The Overall Impact of Interest Groups

An assessment of the role of interest groups in state politics must include consideration of their general strength in shaping public policy. In North Carolina are interest groups on the whole strong, moderate, or weak? Over the past three decades several efforts to answer this question have reached widely different conclusions. Zeller in 1954 and Morehouse in 1981 reported that North Carolina was a strong pressure group state.[33] Wahlke and colleagues in 1962 and Zeigler and Baer in 1969 concluded that "lobbyists exert little pressure" and that North Carolina was a "weak lobby state."[34] These different conclusions may be attributed to actual changes in the dynamics of the interest group–decision makers relationship or to differences in the measures used to assess interest group strength, or to both factors. We will examine a variety of explanations that have been given to assess the strength of interest groups in order to understand their applicability to the current strength of interest group activity in North Carolina.

Two elements of interest groups' environment in North Carolina that have remained fairly steady are associated with weak interest groups and help describe the character and development of the state's political system. Zeigler and Baer posit the notion that North Carolina has an old, established political system in which the rules of the game are fixed to limit interest group influence. Classifying North Carolina as having a "traditionalist political culture" characterized by a "paternalistic and elitist"[35] power structure correlates with this idea. Each of these features infuses the political system with a legacy of restricting the activity and influence of groups in the dynamics of political decision making. While that legacy is subject to challenges and changes, it remains a component that weakens the legitimacy and impact of groups in state politics.

Another category of factors is the level of economic and social complexity that characterizes a state. Zeigler, for example, says that "the strong interest group states typically do not have complex economies" and societies.[36] Morehouse reinforces that view when she suggests that strong pressure group states, such as she classified North Carolina at the time of her study, are dominated by a single or a few economic interests.[37] While North Carolina did have an economy and society strongly dominated by agriculture and related activities in tobacco, textiles, and furniture, changes have been occurring, as our earlier discussion of an economy in transition indicates. Additionally, the figures showing growth in the number of interest groups with registered agents and the increased diversity of those groups and agents suggest a growing complexity in the state's group representation. Even while the category of business representatives remains large, the greater variety of interests within that category reflects an increased complexity in North Carolina's economy and society.

Greater complexity also derives from changes in the capacity of political parties to provide interest representation in North Carolina. These changes have come with greater competition between the two major parties, increased internal party cohesion, and improved organizational strength of the two parties. As discussed earlier, in recent years the Democratic party has been faced with a more effective opposition from the Republican party, which has won statewide offices, such as the governorship and a U.S. Senate seat, and more seats in the state legislature. While the Republican party has some way to go to challenge the Democrats as the majority party in North Carolina, its situation has improved. As the two parties' relative positions change, the incentive to "circle the wagons" to gain strength against the opposition is clear. Internal discipline has been improved. Finally, state parties have improved their organizational capacity through, for example, better financing, more professional personnel, and better campaign coordination.[38] Improved parties in North Carolina provide more-effective restraints on interest group influence.

Finally, greater professionalism in state legislative and executive politics has developed in North Carolina, and this, too, restricts interest group influence. The North Carolina Assembly has increased its professional personnel, reducing the need and inclination to depend upon outside sources for information and direction. Greater continuity and experience in representation come from modest reductions in turnover among legislators.[39] These developments, however, occurred against a background of continued emphasis on an amateur or citizens' legislature. Executive professionalism has also increased as the governor's office has added more highly skilled personnel, and the state's major departments have been reorganized. However, the office of the governor in North Carolina remains relatively weak in formal powers, a condition undermined by the current occupant's being a member of the minority party. Zeigler argues that weak governors are related to strong lobbies.[40]

This review of factors associated with the strength of interest groups reflects conflicting developments, some pointing to weak interest groups and others suggesting that interest group influence is strong. On balance, however, the evidence supports a conclusion that social, economic, and political conditions in North Carolina limit interest groups to being moderate and complementary influences on public policy.

6

FLORIDA

THE CHANGING PATTERNS OF POWER

Anne E. Kelley and Ella L. Taylor

As Florida's booming growth rate continues and its economy becomes more diversified, political pluralism increases. The rapidly expanding population is marked by an older citizenry, more professionals in medicine and health care, and an increase in active minorities, particularly Hispanics in South Florida. Along with the increase of people has come economic diversity marked by service industries such as high-tech, financial, and consumer businesses. These changes have created many more demands on government for regulation and services and have nurtured an increased number of interest groups and PACs and a new breed of lobbyist.

The most outstanding demographic change is in the age structure. Senior citizens constitute over 18 percent of the state's population and one in every four Florida voters. Not only does Florida have the oldest population of any state, it also has the largest proportion of population over sixty-five years old. Within that category, the number of persons seventy-five and over is increasing at the fastest rate. Politically, the social-security generation has had an impact on the state government's current policy relating to medical and health-care costs.

Power Structure

As Florida began to diversify, new interest groups appeared on the scene, challenging the "old guard." The state's power structure is going through a metamorphosis—a shift from the personality cult or individual power brokers to the corporate age, with corporations and their executives associated in industrial development.[1] Florida is no longer dominated by a few powerful individuals such as the late Ed Ball, who headed the billion dollar Alfred I. duPont industries in the state; the late Chester Ferguson of Lykes Brothers Meat Company of Tampa; the late Ben Hill Griffin in agribusiness; and William Henry Dial, the Orlando banker who was instrumental in luring Disney World to the area. In addition, such traditionally strong groups as the phosphate, citrus, horse-racing, and liquor industries have been challenged by many new, specialized groups. A good illustration is the phosphate industry, which previously enjoyed a well-established position among the interest groups but now seems to have been ousted from its once high power position by the increasing strength of environmental groups and "clean" industries.

Florida's weak political parties and fragmented governmental systems make options available to interest groups. The lack of a developed two-party system, a governor who depends upon moral suasion and a decentralized executive system, and other variables such as its strong Legislature compound fragmentation in the political system.

In the Sunshine State the two parties are in transition. The Democrats are still stronger, but the Republicans are approaching parity, and the party system increasingly resembles a competitive two-party system.[2] The Republicans are contesting statewide elections successfully and are competing for legislative seats and local offices, particularly in more-populous and rapidly growing areas. However, organizationally the two parties are weak. Restrictive public policy, party factionalism, and lack of competition have inhibited the development of traditional strong party organizations and party cohesion in the legislative policy-making process. Even the once dominant multifactional Democratic party falls short of the classical system of party organization. Without a party system to provide cues and information, interest groups are given motivation to furnish whatever information is needed by citizens and policymakers.

Florida's plural executive system, dependent upon gubernatorial moral suasion, plus the structure of the executive branch, exerts an impact on interest groups' activities and methods. Each cabinet member is elected statewide, with the right to endless tenure, whereas the governor is limited to two terms. The cabinet, with the governor presiding, serves as a collegial decision- and policy-making board for several state agencies and functions. The situation creates special constituencies for each of the six cabinet members and the governor; it also increases the potential for interest group influence in policy-making. Moreover, the executive structure with its twenty-five departments, its host of independent boards and commissions, and its numerous select agencies controlled by the governor or members of the cabinet provides many incentives for groups to organize.

The balance of power between the legislative and executive branches changed in the late 1960s. A shift from biennial sessions to annual sessions and initiation of professional committee staffing empowered legislators who were previously forced to delegate much of their authority to executive agencies and other units outside the legislative branch.

Power within the Legislature, a bicameral body with forty senators and 120 representatives, shifted from rural conservative leaders to a new generation of progressive Democrats mainly from large metropolitan areas. Traditionally a disproportionate amount of power was held by the so-called Pork Chop Gang, conservative Democrats from rural North Florida and the Panhandle. This tightly organized conservative bloc wielded influence in many areas of public policy for decades. Illustrative of hidden power was the late Sen. Scott Dilworth Clarke, who served in the Legislature for forty years. He was a Democrat from rural Jefferson County in North Florida, which had a population of fewer than 10,000.[3] Senator Clarke rarely spoke for more than a few seconds on any bill, usually limiting his comments to "good bill, good bill," or "bad bill, bad bill." Many legislators with little or no knowledge about the contents of the measure would go along with his advice. As former Gov. Reubin Askew once remarked, "it boiled down to things being passed or defeated by who wanted them and who was against them rather than on the merits of the bill."[4]

A marked change in the Legislature followed reapportionment in 1982. About one-third of the new membership were progressives or moderates from urban areas. The election of progressives to leadership positions modified the schism between the liberal House and conservative Senate. Casey Gluckman, environmental lobbyist in the late 1980s, summed up the alterations when she remarked: "Lobbyists joke that you used to go down to the Senate just to kill things, so we just didn't have to go down until May [the end of the session]. There was a dramatic difference this year."[5] In addition the Legislature had begun staffing legislative committees with year-round professionals such as analysts, researchers, lawyers, and accountants, who enable legislators to function more effectively. Lobbying altered its character to meet the needs of a professionally staffed legislative body.

Registration of Interest Groups and Lobbyists

In Florida registration of lobbies began in 1955.[6] All persons, except legislators and authorized staff, who seek directly or indirectly to encourage the passage, defeat, or modification of any legislation must register as lobbyists. No major changes occurred in the rules until 1976, when a constitutional amendment was passed prohibiting a member of the Legislature from lobbying for two years after the expiration of his or her term. Also, lobbyists must file periodic reports listing all lobbying expenditures and their sources, except personal expenses for lodging, meals, and travel, or fees for services.

Any lobbyist who violates any of the various rules or laws, or who fails to file expense-disclosure reports, can be reprimanded, censured, or prohibited from lobbying for all or any part of the legislative session during which the violation occurs (Chs. 11.045 and 11.061, 1978, of the Florida Statutes). The House Ethics and Elections Committee was charged with overseeing compliance with disclosure; however, there exists no regular review of the reports to ensure compliance. Only one lobbyist has been formally censured for comments imputing malicious motives to a senator.[7]

There are obvious weaknesses in these laws. First, persons who merely appear before a legislator or committee to express support for or opposition to any legislation are not required to register as lobbyists. Second, grass-roots or hometown lobbying is not covered. Third, the "willfulness" provision in the law (i.e., a lobbyist shall not knowingly and wilfully falsify, conceal, or cover up any trick, material fact, and so forth) is very difficult to prove. For example, in 1974 the election of the presiding officers of the Legislature was reportedly decided by big banking interests.[8] Big banking, desiring a branch-banking bill, selected Rep. Don Tucker (Democrat from Crawfordville) as the next speaker of the House, since he was sympathetic to the banking measure. Former Rep. Kenneth L. MacKay (Democrat from Ocala), who was opposed to branch banking, was defeated for the post. Likewise, big banking wished Sen. Lew Brantley (Democrat from Jacksonville) to be Senate president instead of Sen. Bob Saunders (Democrat from Gainesville), the president-designate. Lobbyists for big banking called in their chits (based on campaign contributions) from a number of senators, and Brantley was elected.

Finally, under the existing laws lobbyists are required to disclose only all lobbying expenditures and sources of such funds. They are not required to report salaries or whether their salaries or fees are based on successfully passing or defeating specific legislation. It was reported that former House Speaker Donald Tucker had half a million dollars riding on a piece of legislation.[9] Seminole Harness Raceway paid him a $40,000 retainer during the legislative session to lobby for legislation permitting a racetrack to convert from harness to dog racing. If the bill passed Tucker was to receive an additional $460,000. The bill passed.

Thus the laws are not very meaningful in disclosing the amount or nature of money spent to influence legislation. The former clerk of the House, who served as clerk for twenty years, believes the chief value of registering lobbyists is to identify them.

Interest Groups

The number and diversity of registered interest groups in Florida has vastly expanded. The total number increased from 1,069 in 1970 to 2,828 in 1990—a 164 percent increase in two decades. They can be broadly classified into at least twenty-three distinct interest-area categories based on registration data filed with the clerk of the Florida House of Representatives, as shown by the listing in Table 6.1. The top five categories listed make up 57 percent of the interest group arena.

The largest number of groups registered include business and trade, state and local governments, public interest/citizens' groups, and health care. In recent years the increased numbers of business and trade groups manifest a response to the expanded scope of governmental activities and greater competition among business and emerging groups. Some of the hundreds of business groups include Associated Industries of Florida (4,000 businesses), gas and oil, the Chamber of Commerce, Martin Marietta Aerospace, and IBM.

As government has expanded, so has the number of governmental agencies, boards, and commissions seeking to influence public policy. In state government the Departments of Education, Transportation, and Corrections, and the governor's office were the most prolific. A myriad of units within the judicial branch attempt to affect policies relating to administration of justice, pressing for reduction of caseloads, additional court personnel and courts, and increased salaries and retirement benefits, among other measures.

The enormous growth in activity of state governmental interest groups is related not only to the drastically changing role of government in Florida's life but also to delivery of more social services to more segments of the population. The shift of power from the federal to state governments during the Reagan administration, and cutbacks in Washington, forced many more programmatic decisions in Tallahassee. County and city governments have accelerated their group activities as needed revenues to build and to maintain infrastructure such as roads, schools, highways, and water and waste systems, and to provide fire and police protection have put an added strain on local governments' capabilities. In recent years traditional city governments were joined by county governments seeking more financial support for these expanding needs.

Expansions in health-care, public-interest, and social-issue groups are new phenomena in interest group politics in Florida. Since Florida has the largest elderly population in the nation, there has been a proliferation of health-care groups representing physicians, nurses, hospitals, mental health workers, and the pharmaceutical industry. Likewise, public-interest groups—Good Government (League of

Women Voters and Common Cause), Native Americans, women, alcohol and drug rehabilitation proponents, for example—have increased their attempts to influence public policy. Finally, social-issue groups have extended their presence in the interest group arena. New groups and associations include such diverse concerns as abused children, animal rights, human services, and unemployment; and there is even a group of voting motorists.

Women's groups and lobbyists might be expected to have made greater inroads into the lobbying group system considering that females constitute 52 percent of the population. Women constituted 35 percent of the total number of lobbyists in the 1988–1990 reporting period. In the mid-1970s Kelley found women's groups ranked low among the total groups registered to lobby.[10] However, as Stowers pointed out in her study, female groups have a direct impact on certain issues that are important to them.[11] For example, recently the pro-abortion-rights issue evidenced women's strength by rallying close to five hundred lobbyists to help defeat major changes in Florida's abortion-rights legislation. Also, MADD aided in strengthening the sanctions against driving while intoxicated.

We also expected blacks to have extended their political influence considering the expansion in black political participation in Florida over the last twenty-five years. About 13 percent of Florida's population are black; they constitute 10.8 percent of the voting-age population and 9.9 percent of registered voters.[12] The number of elected black officials has multiplied over the years; most are mayors (19) or members of municipal governing bodies (116). However, black participation and election to public office have not affected black interest group activities, which appear amorphous. "There is not a single, strong, statewide black political organization, although several politically oriented black groups exist."[13] Nor has any apparent attempt been made to create real solidarity among blacks. The oldest and best-known groups are the NAACP and the National Urban League, which represent two segments of the black community. Several civil rights organizations such as the Congress of Racial Equality (CORE), Florida Progressive Voter League, and Voter Education Project were active during the 1960s and 1970s. Occasionally ad hoc black interest groups appear on the local scene and effectively promote issues and programs of interest to them. An undetermined

Table 6.1 Registered Interest Groups and Total Representation of Lobbies, by Group Category, 1988–1990

	Number in Interest Group Category	Total Representation[a]	Approximate Percentage of Total	
			Group Representation	Lobby Representation
Business and trade	622	1,366	22.0	15.9
Public interest/citizens' groups	277	524	9.8	6.1
Health care	275	698	9.7	8.1
Local government associations	248	715	8.8	8.3
Education[b]	193	514	6.8	6.0
Social-issue groups	145	243	5.2	2.8
Labor unions, including teachers	113	703	4.0	8.2
State departments, boards, and commissions	109	1,006	3.9	11.7
Insurance companies or associations	108	263	3.8	3.1
Tourism/recreation, food/lodging, etc.	96	232	3.4	2.7
Transportation	89	244	3.1	2.8
Builders, contractors, developers	73	120	2.6	1.4
Environmentalists	72	183	2.5	2.1
Communications/broadcasting/cable/TV, etc.	72	180	2.5	2.1
Banking/finance	71	167	2.5	1.9

Real estate interests	66	204	2.3	2.4
Agriculture	48	90	1.7	1.0
Fuel (gas and oil)	42	90	1.5	1.0
Utilities (public, private)	37	132	1.3	1.5
Courts/attorneys	36	117	1.3	1.4
Women's groups	24	555	0.9	6.4
Religion	11	15	0.4	0.2
Self (individual citizens)	1	248	0.0	2.9
Total	2,828	8,609	100.0	100.0

[a] Total representation refers to the total number of individual lobbyists representing a category. As some lobbyists work for more than one employer or agency, it was felt that this figure was more descriptive of actual representation in a rapidly changing lobbying community.

[b] Education includes universities and colleges (public/private): 58 groups, 188 lobbyists; elementary and secondary: 82 groups, 237 lobbyists; and miscellaneous—vocational, school boards, etc.: 53 groups, 89 lobbyists.

Source: Compiled from John B. Phelps, *Lobbying in Florida* (Tallahassee: Florida Legislature, Office of Clerk, 1990), 1–51.

number of blacks have been members of predominantly white interest groups such as veterans', labor, and teachers' organizations. But
very few black interest groups or black lobbyists are listed in the
official lobbying registers.

"Few observers assess organized labor or its leaders to be strong in
Florida."[14] Partial explanations include the facts that organized labor is conditioned by "right-to-work" provisions in the state's constitution, by statutory constraints, and by fragmentation of the
labor movement. Union members, excluding farm workers, constitute only about 10 percent of the total work force. Labor unions
are more prominent in the public sector of Florida's economy than
in the private sector.[15] The largest unionized groups among public
employees are the Florida Teachers Profession–National Education
Association (FTP-NEA) and the American Federation of State,
County and Municipal Employees (AFSCME). Even though teachers
have a large contingent in Tallahassee, they have been somewhat
less effective than the private/business organizations, as evidenced
by the level of support for education. In the private sector, the AFL-
CIO, International Machinists Association, and the Teamsters have
registered regularly. The major impact of unionized labor involves
contributions in political campaigns and elections.

Individual citizens registered as an interest group are listed as Self
in Table 6.1. These private citizens lobby on their own behalf and
regularly attend legislative sessions in large numbers. They bear
their own expenses to push causes in which they have a deep personal interest. Legislators tend to take citizen lobbyists quite seriously, recognizing their commitment and deep concern about
an issue. An example of such a citizen lobbyist was Nell Foster
"Bloomer Girl" Rogers, a self-styled people's lobbyist who stalked
The Capitol's corridors for thirty-seven years.[16] Armed with the belief that knowledge is power, Rogers always had in-depth knowledge
of pending bills, especially those that might impinge upon the rights
of "ordinary folks." Her diligence prompted former Gov. Ruebin
Askew to remark that "she studied the bills and when she spoke
legislators listened." The Bloomer Girl, who was widely respected,
got her nickname from her unusual attire—knickers, corduroy
shirt, and a broad-brimmed hat.

Political Action Committees

A recent phenomenon is the rise of PACs, which act as an arm of special-interest groups and associations, legally entitled to raise and to contribute funds to favored candidates (mostly incumbents) or political parties.[17] We found that special-interest lobbyists controlled the flow of PAC money from special-interest groups they represented to various political campaigns. Overwhelming majorities of both lobbyists (97.2%) and legislators (97.4%) we consulted agreed that lobbyists definitely play a significant role in PAC campaign contributions to legislators.[18]

Although groups defined as PACs are found nowhere in the Florida Statutes, in 1973 the Legislature recognized (in Ch. 106.11 [5]) two forms of politically interested groups—political committees and committees of continuous existence. These two types of committees are not linked to political parties or candidates. A political committee is legally defined as any group of two or more persons whose primary or incidental purpose is to raise and to spend money in support of or opposition to any candidate, issue, or political party, and anticipates receiving contributions or making expenditures in an aggregate amount exceeding $500 during a calendar year. A committee of continuous existence is a relatively permanent, ongoing committee with a dues-paying membership.

The increased financing of legislative campaigns by PACs has been accompanied by a sharp rise in the number of corporate and other PACs, especially ideological ones. PAC contributions have steadily increased, from $1.1 million in 1976 to $10 million in 1987, an 809 percent gain in little over a decade.[19] In the mid-1980s ten of the most powerful interest groups gave over half of the total campaign contributions through PACs; corporate PACs alone accounted for 26 percent of the total.[20] Financing legislative campaigns through large contributions to PACs rather than to parties has heightened the influence of PACs at the expense of political parties.

A new PAC strategy is involvement in financing judicial campaigns. Courts have traditionally been targets of special-interest groups. In general, strategies used to influence judges include amicus curiae (friend of the court) briefs, test cases, and personal contact with judges. It is difficult to determine accurately what groups are spending how much money on whom because there is an absence of comprehensive research on judicial races. But campaign contributions to Florida Supreme Court justices indicate significant increases in relatively uncompetitive races. For instance, in 1974, $88,235 was contributed; two years later the sum was $363,147.[21]

When the law regulating PACs took effect in 1973 fifty-six PACs existed; by the late 1980s the number stood at more than fifteen hundred. According to the Division of Elections, some of these PACs are essentially staff organizations with little or no membership and none of the traditional ties to their members—a factor that raises serious questions about their representativeness.

Limiting aggregate amounts that legislators can receive from PAC contributions is frequently debated. Attempts in the Legislature to set limits have been unsuccessful. Although Florida Statutes do limit the amount of contributions a candidate may receive from individual PACs and corporations per election, the statutes do not limit "independent" expenditures by PACs to further a candidate's election as long as the campaign activity is not coordinated in any way with an official campaign (Ch. 106.11 [5]). Independent and uncoordinated expenditures are also controversial.

Lobbyists

The lobbying community in Tallahassee expanded from 872 in 1970, to 8,609 by 1990—an almost 900 percent increase.[22] The latest number may be slightly high, as more than one interest group may hire the same lobbyists. Thus some lobbyists get counted twice or more.

According to Hrebenar and Thomas, lobbyists can be classified into five types: contract and in-house lobbyists, government lobbyists or legislative liaisons, citizens or volunteers, and private individuals.[23] We found that of the 8,609 registered lobbyists representing 2,828 interest groups in 1988–1990, about seventy-five were full-time contract lobbyists.[24] This number is misleading because many businesses and industries employ numerous lobbyists for specialized tasks on a fee basis, or on part-time contracts.

In-house lobbyists or persons who are employees of organizations and business represent such groups as business, health-care, oil and gas interests, and labor unions including teachers. Particular groups include such prominent businesses as Winn-Dixie Food Stores, IBM, the Florida Medical Association, Florida Power and Light, Gulf Power Corporation, Florida Bankers Association, Real Estate, and AFL-CIO. These in-house lobbyists constituted about 26 percent of the total lobbying community.

Government lobbyists or legislative liaisons constitute about 20 percent of registered lobbyists. As indicated in Table 6.1, some 1,721 lobbyists registered as representatives of 357 groups in the various levels of government. At the local level, counties outdistanced cities in numbers of lobbyists. Government's lobbying of government is a permanent feature of state lobbying activity, as various agencies have a great stake in appropriations and other legislative actions. Most state and local governmental departments and agencies, and the governor's office, have legislative liaisons to assist their lobbying efforts.

Citizens or volunteer lobbyists or those who represent citizens' and community organizations on an ad hoc and unpaid basis usually represent one narrow interest. Frequently these lobbyists are well-educated, highly skilled, and issue-oriented. They can be found urging the passage of various social programs and "public" interests, from the environment and health care to civil rights for women, to issues concerning minorities and the handicapped. Although it is difficult to determine their numbers, this category of lobbyists constitutes about 12 percent of the lobbying community and does make its presence felt. A case in point: the Good Government lobbyists of the League of Women Voters and Common Cause have been influential in campaign-finance laws. Environmentalists' strength was manifested in growth management and planning laws, and in protection of Florida's coastlines against oil spills, as well as protection of endangered animals.

The expansive power of interest groups and their lobbyists has evolved from the rapidly changing population, economic growth of the state, growth of professionalism, and more acceptance of interest groups. The problems and issues besetting Florida have become more complex, calling for more specialization and professionalism.

Now lobbyists are highly skilled technicians, better educated and higher paid than in the past. In our survey most (62.2%) of the lobbyists identified their principal occupation as lobbying. They were mostly college educated (70.3%), young (30–50 years of age), and some have incomes of over $100,000 yearly. These new, highly skilled, knowledgeable information brokers are rapidly replacing many traditional "good ol' boy" lobbyists.

The expansion of professional legislative staff on standing committees and numerous subcommittees has led to more interest group representation and more sophistication in lobbyists' attempts to influence the drafting of highly technical legislation. More people must be consulted and a higher quality of technical and political information presented to legislative staff. Over 89 percent of the legislators we consulted reported that they relied heavily on advice of their committee staff in making policy decisions.

The shift in interest group tactics in legislative lobbying can be seen with startling clarity in committee hearings. When the Legislature met biennially, with its short sessions and crowded calendars, committee meetings tended to be perfunctory. It was commonplace for lobbyists to make personal contacts with individual committee members before committee meetings. These personal contacts supplemented and often replaced the need for formal appearances before committees. The changing balance of power between the executive and legislative branches correlated with an increase in the frequency and length of committee hearings. Presently lobbyists' testimony before committees is a major tactic for lobbying, requiring highly sophisticated technical expertise.

The Strength of Interest Groups

We believe that a systematic understanding of the strength of individual interest groups and individual lobbyists can be attained by an examination of legislators' and lobbyists' perceptions of the lobbying community.[25] The validity of this assessment is based on the fact that almost two-thirds (63.6%) of the interest groups surveyed indicated that they use the Legislature primarily to influence and to gain access to lawmakers. Over 15 percent indicated legislative campaigns were also very important.

Our assessment of legislators' and lobbyists' perception of influence is drawn from the results of a survey mailed in the summer of 1986 to all legislators (160) and a selected group of influential lobbyists (62). Initially, twenty-five lobbyists were chosen based on reputation in the media. In turn, this procedure led to another thirty-seven lobbyists who were named by legislators and lobbyists as influential. This approach—based on reputation—seemed most appropriate for determining the strength of individual interest groups as well.[26] The survey covered many aspects of the respondents' opinions and their perceptions of influential actors in the legislative process.

We asked legislators and lobbyists to rank-order interest groups on a four-point scale ranging from very influential to not at all influential. The most influential groups in rank order are those concerning realtors; business; trial lawyers; insurance; the governor's office; education; the phosphate industry; land development; medical/health care; and agriculture. The high ranking of insurance can be partially explained by the dominance of insurance rates in the 1986 legislative session.

The types of groups regarded as powerful in the states are usually given as business, labor, farm, education, and government, in that order. Not only did we find business and related groups as most influential, but we also discovered that environmentalist, senior citizens', and communications interests are considered strong as well.

Assessment of the most influential lobbyists was likewise measured along a four-point scale ranging from very influential to not at all influential. Again, the assessment was by both legislators and lobbyists themselves. The results indicate that there is a close correlation between the rating of powerful interest groups and the rating of their representatives. A profile of individual lobbyist's strength is shown in Table 6.2. Lobbyists representing realtors, insurance, business, utilities, health care, construction, and the environment top the list.

In strong interest group states, such as Florida, business interests dominate. Our data clearly support this finding, particularly for

Table 6.2 Legislators' and Lobbyists' Choice of Most Influential
Interest Group and Lobbyists

	Percentage
Interest Group	
Associated Industries	61.9
Florida Association of Realtors	52.2
Homebuilders and Contractors Association	34.1
Florida Bankers Association	32.1
Florida Trial Lawyers	31.9
Florida Association of Insurance	31.6
Office of the Governor	30.9
Florida Chamber of Commerce	29.5
Florida Power and Light	29.4
Florida Medical Association	24.3
Lobbyists and Interests[a]	
Harry Landrum (realtors, insurance)	70.6
Jon Shebel (Associated Industries)	63.9
Wade Hopping (utilities)	46.3
Ken Plante (hospitals)	42.9
Ralph Haben (health care)	42.1
Kinney Harley (builders)	35.4
William G. McCue, Jr. (insurance)	32.5
Richard McFarlain (Florida Bar)	28.4
Earl Henderson (utilities)	28.1
David Gluckman (environment)	25.8

[a] Where more than one interest is listed, the group most prominently associated
with the lobbyist's name was used for survey purposes.

service-oriented businesses. Many business contract lobbyists constitute a stable corps of professionals. Corps members may have one
or many clients on a continual basis. The reputed top contract lobbyists in our survey each represent between one and twelve client

groups, the average being 5.4 clients (see Table 6.3). A number of these influentials can be found in the powerful Breakfast Club, one of the oldest continuing legislative traditions. Currently the club has twenty-two lobbyists representing large business and commercial interests. Glen P. Woodard, a senior member representing Winn-Dixie, was quoted as saying: "We're rough, tough, irascible money making bastards. We take a strong stand on issues we care about."[27] The club meets primarily to plan strategy for coping with legislative action in various committees and subcommittees within the two chambers.

In recent years the business community's power status has been tested. During the 1980s the Legislature passed at least two bills increasing business taxes. Although both bills were repealed, their mere passage suggests a slippage in business's hold on power.

In an attempt to assess lobbying effectiveness, we began by concentrating on the communication model of interaction between legislators and lobbyists. To be effective, lobbyists have to interact with legislators regularly and frequently.[28] We asked both legislators and lobbyists how many lobbying contacts (of any kind) occurred per week during the legislative session. A vast majority of legislators and lobbyists contact each other more than twenty times per week during and after legislative sessions.

Examining the nature of the interaction, we found that 88.7 percent of Florida legislators see informational communications as the major form of interaction. In contrast, 47.2 percent of lobbyists perceive persuasion of legislative opinions as their prime form of communications. Thus the nature of interaction is viewed decidedly differently: Legislators are more likely to see lobbyists as service agents than as opinion manipulators. This pattern is consistent with that in other states.[29]

At least one determinant of lobbying effectiveness is the extent to which legislators accept lobbyists as legitimate sources of information. On a four-point scale ranging from "all of the time" to "none of the time," legislators overwhelmingly (80%) find the information received from lobbyists helpful at least most of the time. Accordingly, a powerful source of strength of interest groups in Florida is legislators' acceptance of information provided by lobbyists, espe-

Table 6.3 Florida's Top Ten Contract Lobbyists and Their Clients

	Number of Clients	Names of Clients
Kinney Harley	1	Florida Home Builders Association
Earl Henderson	1	Gulf Power Corporation
William G. McCue, Jr.	1	Florida Insurance Agents Association
Jon Shebel	2	Associated Industries of Florida
		Florida Business Forum
David Gluckman	3	Sierra Club
		Audubon Society
		University Boulevard Coalition
Richard McFarlain	4	Merrill Lynch Stockholders
		Citicorp
		The Florida Bar
		Renewable Fuels Association
Ralph Haben	10	Professional Diving Instructors
		Wine Institute
		American Medical International
		South Florida Water Management District
		Standard Oil Corporation
		Car Audio Specialists Association
		Hospital Management Association
		Fairfield Communities, Inc.
		Florida Power and Light
		All Seasons Resorts, Inc.
Harry Landrum	10	Outdoor Advertising Association
		American Insurance Association
		Florida Optometric Association
		Florida Realtors Association
		Florida Respiratory Association
		Florida Premium Finance Association
		Florida Insurance Council, Inc.
		Florida Surety Agents Association
		Blue Cross-Blue Shield
		National Kidney Foundation

	Number of Clients	Names of Clients
Ken Plante	10	Florida Psychological Association
		Humana Hospital
		Orange County
		Southland Corporation
		State and Federal Associates, Inc.
		Transgulf Pipelines
		Rinker Materials Corporation
		Florida Association Pest Control
		Telesat Cablevision Inc.
		Toyota Distributors SE
Wade Hopping	12	Orange County Expressway Authority
		Stardial Investment Company
		Lost Tree Village Corporation
		Florida Electrical Power
		Florida Industry Council
		Mobil Oil Corporation
		CF Industries, Inc.
		Central Florida Gas Corporation
		ITT Development Commission
		Hollywood, Inc.
		Jupiter Islands
		Island Dunes

Source: Compiled from Allen Morris, *Lobbying in Florida* (Tallahassee: Florida Legislature, Office of the Clerk, 1986), 75, 82, 85, 90, 95, 116, 133–134, 160, 185.

cially when an issue arises about which highly technical information is needed. All of the legislators in the survey agree that provision of reliable information was the most important service expected from lobbyists in the Legislature. Forty-seven percent of the legislators and 28.6 percent of the lobbyists feel that "basis research" is an influential lobbying technique.

Looking at lobbying effectiveness from a slightly different perspective, we assumed that legislators' seeking out lobbyists for information indicates their acceptance of the legitimacy of interest groups. We questioned both legislators and lobbyists about the acceptability of being seen socially with each other. Over 96 percent of the legislators and 97 percent of the lobbyists responded that socializing was acceptable.

Assessing interest group influence as a singular variable acting on legislative decision making is difficult. As Patterson explains, "many confounding influences are at work in legislative decision-making."[30] It is likely that interest group influences may be felt through the effect of a legislator's constituency; committee staff's influence may reflect decisions of interest groups or of specialists in executive agencies; or sources of influence may be interrelated and multifactorial by the nature of lawmaking. However, as an aid in the general assessment of influence, particularly of interest groups, Uslander and Weber's model of sources legislators consulted in making decisions was expanded to include Florida politics.[31]

In general, Florida legislators receive influences from many interacting forces both within and outside the Legislature. Our findings indicate that legislators consult sources mainly within the legislative body, such as friends and committee staff, in making decisions (see Table 6.4). Political parties' leaders outside the Legislature ranked lower as a consulting source, reflecting Florida's weak party system. Outside of the legislative arena, legislators give priority to longtime supporters and friends and community leaders for cues in making decisions. These people have more direct contact with legislators as well as "built-in" trust and confidence. Unlike Uslander and Weber, we did not find that interest groups rank high, although many groups are considered quite influential in lawmaking. Perhaps the gap in mutual expectations between legislators and lobbyists, mentioned above, may account for their low consultation rating. Specialists in the executive agencies were also expected to rank as prominent; their influence may be conveyed to legislators through committee staff. The rating of the governor's office does not reflect its esteem as a lobbying organization.

It was expected that legislators with employment other than the Legislature would place greater emphasis on consulting influences outside the Legislature. Our findings did not substantiate this ex-

Table 6.4 Most Influential Sources Guiding Legislators' Decisions

	Percentages[a]
Inside Sources[b]	
Friends in Legislature	93.4
Committee staff	89.2
Own-party legislators from same or nearby district	86.5
Legislative office staff	76.4
Legislative party leaders	76.0
Committee chair	72.2
Legislators from both parties, from same or nearby district	66.7
Outside Sources[b]	
Constituents	97.3
Community leaders	92.1
Longtime supporters and friends	90.9
Interest groups	86.5
Specialist in the executive agency	67.6
Office of the governor	48.6
Party leaders outside the Legislature	16.4

[a] Percentages are based upon survey responses to a four-point scale ranging from very influential to not at all influential. The percentages combine the scores of scale points coded "very" and "somewhat" influential.

[b] Categories of inside and outside sources are based on those found in Eric M. Uslander and Ronald E. Weber, *Patterns of Decision Making in State Legislatures* (New York: Praeger, 1977).

pectation. With the exception of friends in the Legislature and long-time supporters and friends, we found that part-time legislators do not differ substantially in the sources consulted in making legislative decisions from legislators with no outside employment. Part-time legislators do appear to place more emphasis on longtime supporters and friends than do full-time legislators. Fifty-two percent of part-timers as opposed to 24 percent of full-timers rank this group as very influential. Also, part-time legislators (90%) find friends in the Legislature less important than do full-time legislators (100%).

Changing Methods, Approaches, and Tactics

Major technological developments in information processing have transformed lobbying tactics. One recent article stated: "Inside Tallahassee a new team is playing for power. An unlikely army of special interest lobbyists forms a permanent, unelected government where legal beagles and technocrats call the shots."[32] An example of the use of these new techniques is provided by the Associated Industries of Florida, one of the most powerful business lobbies in The Capitol. The four thousand–member group has revitalized its lobbying services by introducing modern technological hardware and a healthy measure of public relations. It engages simultaneously in face-to-face lobbying, public opinion–polling information, brochures, graphics, and campaign advice. Business programs are sent out across the state from its own television studio. In addition, it is armed with targeted polling data, computerized mailing lists, and its own PAC. On the spur of the moment the Associated Industries of Florida can mount a computer-based direct mail campaign to stir up grass-roots support for selected political candidates and issues. Its lobbyists are legal experts and technocrats equipped to deal aggressively with complex state issues.

To be influential, a lobbyist today must provide more than social entertainment, although effective lobbying still requires some. David Gluckman, a lawyer and lobbyist for the Audubon Society, best summed up the new lobbying world when he said: "You can no longer cut it just by taking these guys to dinner, saying you need their support and leaving it at that. That's why a lot of the people in Florida who used to be good lobbyists are now dinosaurs." Presently, "good lobbyists have a lot more influence than most individual legislators," says Jay Landers, Jr., who spent ten years in government before becoming a lobbyist.[33]

The top lobbyists' network is made up of highly educated legal experts and technocrats with backgrounds that make them able to deal with complex issues. The majority (52.4%) of Florida lobbyists have six to ten years of experience working with the Legislature. Well over half (62.2%) classify their principal occupation as lobbyist. An overwhelming majority (94.6%) have at least a college degree, and over 70 percent have postgraduate degrees.

Occasionally, legislators will turn over highly specialized legislative bills to competing lobbyists and allow them to work out a compromise among themselves. The Legislature will then approve the bill almost verbatim. A clear example was the wetlands legislation of 1984.[34] A group of highly respected lobbyists met in the speaker's office and hammered out the bill paragraph by paragraph without a single legislator present.

Another aspect of interest group strategy is site selection to gain access to and influence decision makers. We asked lobbyists to designate, on a four-point scale ranging from very influential to not at all influential, those agencies, locations, and activities that were favorable sites to achieve interest groups' goals. As shown in Table 6.5, lobbyists see the Legislature as the most important site for gaining influence and access to lawmakers. In rank order, legislative campaigns, the governor's office, executive campaigns, media campaigns, and executive agencies were considered good sites for influence peddling. Judicial action and judicial campaigns are at a much lower level. At the bottom of the list are democratic reform devices such as the initiative, referendum, and recall.

Next we asked the respondents to name the sites used most often. Once again at the top of the list was the Legislature (63.6%), followed by legislative campaigns (15.2%), media campaigns (9.1%), and a combination of the rest (9.1%). The Legislature far outdistances all other sites for gaining access and influence in decision making in public policy. The ranking of mass-media or public relations campaigns is understandable because of the expense in reaching the ten media markets in Florida.

In examining the role interest groups play in the Legislature and in policy-making, our major concern was to assess the tactics of the groups. Our study indicates, on a six-point scale ranging from "strongly agree" to "strongly disagree," that both legislators and lobbyists overwhelmingly agree that the Legislature works better with interest groups. Second, they agree that the job of the legislator is to work out compromises among conflicting interests. Third, they

Table 6.5 Sites for Successful Interest Group Influence
(by Percentage of Ranking)

Agency/Activity	Very Important	Somewhat Important	Not Very Important	Not at All Important
Legislature	85.7	11.4	2.9	0.0
Legislative races	79.4	8.8	11.8	0.0
Governor's office	40.0	48.6	11.4	0.0
Executive races	35.3	44.1	14.7	5.9
Media campaigns	25.7	57.1	14.3	2.9
Executive agencies	17.1	62.9	17.1	2.9
Initiative	9.1	9.1	24.2	57.6
Judicial process	8.8	17.6	44.1	29.4
Executive Boards and Commissions	8.6	51.4	34.3	5.7
Judicial races	3.0	9.1	24.2	63.6
Recall	0.0	0.0	13.3	86.7
Referenda	0.0	9.1	21.2	69.7

both disagree that interest groups have too much power in the Florida Legislature, but differ on whether lobbyists have too much power. A majority (53.8%) of legislators feel that lobbyists have too much power, whereas a larger majority (75.7%) of the lobbyists disagree.

The power of political parties is central to assessing interest group strength. Many legislators (54.7%) believe that interest groups have lessened the power of political parties in public policy; 47 percent of the lobbyists agreed. The lack of clear difference between legislators and lobbyists on this issue seems to confirm the weakness of Florida's party system.

What is essential for effective lobbying in Florida? Both legislators and lobbyists agree that frequent contact with policymakers is crucial. But agreement ends there; legislators rank knowledge of government and familiarity with policymakers as only slightly less important than frequent contact, whereas lobbyists rank lobbying experience second most important but considerably less important than frequent contact.

Thus, based upon our findings, effective lobbying techniques in the Florida Legislature include frequent contact with policymakers, ranging from twenty or more times per week during the session to five or fewer times per week outside the session; provision of reliable information; skill in legislative matters; familiarity with policymakers; and lobbying experience.

Conclusion

In recent years Florida has been referred to as a bellwether state—a state at the forefront of social innovation. "By carefully watching what is happening now in Florida, we stand to learn a wealth of information about the problems and opportunities the whole nation will face in the future."[35] The problems and opportunities Florida faces involve transition in its power structure in the wake of an increasingly pluralistic society. State government must be assertive because of rapid economic and social changes and cutbacks in federal programs. Is it true that Florida is still ruled by one of the strongest interest group systems in the nation, as stated by Morehouse and by Zeigler and van Dalen? In her study of state government, parties, and interest groups, Morehouse classifies Florida as one of twenty-two states with strong pressure groups.[36] She lists as influential Associated Industries, utilities (e.g., Florida Power Corporation and Florida Power and Light), the Farm Bureau, bankers, liquor interests, chain stores, racetracks, and the Phosphate Council. Our study revealed a much different list. State and local governments, public-interest and citizens' groups, health-care, education, and special-issue groups emerged as influential, while utilities, bankers, the liquor industry, chain stores, and racing interests had lost influence. One other study, conducted by Gannett News, shows a very similar listing to ours, with the exception of utilities, banking, and environmental groups. Florida can still be classified as a strong interest group state. As the Florida economy has become service-oriented, such groups as those concerned with health care, public interest, and social issues have emerged as strong competitors in Tallahassee with the traditional well-established interests.

Over the last few decades some megatrends have occurred. One of these is political pluralism—the number of interest groups and lobbyists increased significantly. Growth of interest groups with relatively narrow single issues, from abortion and drunk driving to environmental concerns, has accelerated. The second major trend is that the dominance of state government by a few well-established powerful actors has been replaced by a pluralistic model of interest groups partially brought about by the state's diversifying economy and demographics.

From our examination of registered interest groups and lobbyists, and from data collected in our survey, we conclude that some discernible trends are likely to continue. Interactions between legislators and lobby–interest groups based on mutual acceptance and benefits will accelerate. Lobbying is less of an "evil." Professionalism is a permanent feature of state government. The practice of government employees' and employees' unions' lobbying state government is a permanent part of the lobbying scene, for they have a vested interest in lobbying for their programs and jobs. Paralleling increases in Florida's aged population and enactment of programs that benefit it will be more interest groups making demands on state government rather than local and federal governments. Our comparison of legislators' and lobbyists' perception of political parties suggests political parties play a weak role in the legislative process. Yet the rapid growth in numbers of Republican legislators being elected to the once dominantly Democratic Legislature argues for the rise of more party cohesion and diminishing opportunities for interest groups to exercise influence. Moreover, and ironically, the fragmented nature of the executive branch is likely to provide the governor's office wide opportunities for more influence in public policy. Positive action by the governor is seen as a way to counteract this fragmentation, resulting in governors' playing a stronger role in policy-making. PACs are far exceeding political parties in campaign financing—a task traditionally performed by parties. Since PACs have tended to give large contributions to incumbents, competitive elections are becoming less the norm. The expanded scope of PAC participation in the state's electoral process will not change until Florida's campaign-finance laws are modified.

Perhaps acting as a countervailing force, political parties in Florida are evolving into a two-party system. Among the state's grassroots activists (precinct committeemen and committeewomen), party labels are being made relevant through party realignment.[37] If this behavior occurs among other party activists, such as the party-in-government, and in the electorate, the evolution will produce a two-party system. Strong, cohesive parties could help balance power in the state's increasingly pluralistic and interest group–dominated society.

7

TEXAS

THE TRANSFORMATION FROM PERSONAL TO INFORMATIONAL LOBBYING

Keith E. Hamm and Charles W. Wiggins

An examination of the role played by interest groups in Texas politics is essential for an adequate understanding of the state's political system. Certainly groups play an important role as policy initiators and campaign supporters and financiers in many states; but the power that they exert could hardly be more significant than that wielded by their counterparts in the Lone Star State. Various historical, socioeconomic, and political circumstances have made interest groups a definite force to be reckoned with in Texas politics.

The Socioeconomic and Political Environment

As emphasized by Thomas in Chapter 1, a state's interest group structure is usually strongly linked to its socioeconomic development. Although Texas continues to have a cowboy image in the minds of many outsiders, today the typical Texan is a business-person from Houston, the Dallas–Fort Worth metroplex, or San Antonio, dressed in a three-piece suit. In recent decades Texas has become urban, with approximately 80 percent of its over 15 million residents living in and around cities. Most of these urban residents reside in the twenty-eight metropolitan areas (Texas has more than any other state) scattered across the vast reaches of rolling hills and prairie. The size of the overall population and the great distances between population centers generate special problems for candidates for statewide office; they must raise large sums of money to support what have come to be mainly electronic campaigns in Texas's numerous media markets.

During the 1970s and early 1980s Texas experienced a significant population expansion, over 27 percent, stimulated mainly by the economic boom in the oil and gas industry. State and local governments strained to provide needed public services. However, with the major drop in oil and gas prices of the mid-1980s, population growth decreased significantly. Public officials gained at least a brief respite in the need to expand public facilities and services but felt some stress as a result of reductions in important oil and gas revenues.

Although the situation is changing, limited diversity of ethnic groups and nationalities has characterized Texas over the years. Today, slightly less than 66 percent of the state's residents are Anglos. Blacks, most of whom reside in urban areas of the eastern region of the state, constitute approximately 12 percent of the population; Hispanics contribute over 22 percent. Although many members of the Hispanic population reside in large urban communities dispersed around the state, they are especially concentrated in the southern region, close to the Rio Grande, where they make up around 90 percent of the populations of several counties. Hispanic population growth today exceeds that of other elements of society, to the extent that several Texas demographers have predicted that minorities (i.e., Hispanics and blacks) will exceed Anglos in numbers shortly after the turn of the century.

Economically, Texas remains the primary oil and gas–producing state in the United States, as well as the nation's leading refiner of gasoline and producer of petrochemical products. Although energy production remains the chief component of the state's economy, a marked degree of economic diversification has occurred in recent decades. For example, the mid-1980s decline in oil and gas prices had a lesser impact on the Dallas–Fort Worth metroplex, given important developments in the electronic, aviation, and related industries in that region. On the other hand, Houston, Texas's largest metropolitan community, is still very dependent on the health and vitality of the oil and gas industry and was especially hard-hit by the major recession in this natural-resource industry. Chapter 11 bankruptcy law replaced oil and gas law as the specialty of many Houston law firms.

Since the end of Reconstruction in the mid-1870s, Texas has had a one party–dominant party system, a situation that has facilitated an important role for interest groups within the state's political system. Thus, the critical battles for public offices have occurred within the context of Democratic primary election campaigns. For the most part, these campaigns have been based upon personality appeals—a major feature of the Texas cultural landscape—as opposed to programmatic proposals to solve major economic and especially social problems that are perceived as confronting the state. From 1874 until 1978, when Republican Bill Clements was elected, Democratic nominees were victorious in every gubernatorial campaign. Although the U.S. Senate victory of Republican John Tower in 1961 signaled some increase in Republican minority strength, Democrats retained their grip on the bulk of national, state, and local offices.

Although Clements's 1978 victory resulted partially from a bad split in the Democratic party, it also reflected major demographic and political changes of recent decades: the in-migration of "Yankee" Republicans to urban centers; and the "bolting" of native (especially younger) Democrats from the party ticket stimulated initially by national party issues.[1] Although the GOP has made inroads at gubernatorial and congressional levels, Republicans remain very weak with regard to other statewide offices, the legislative branch (6 to 25 in the State Senate and 56 to 94 in the State House in 1987), and especially at the county level.

Neither chamber of the Legislature is organized along partisan lines. No partisan leadership positions, such as majority leader, have been established, and party caucuses are not normally held. The Democratic speaker of the House is normally elected by a bipartisan coalition, or team, that includes at least a few Republicans who usually are awarded key committee chairs and assignments.

The general absence of a party-based issue orientation in Texas extends to the party as an organization. Party organizations are quite weak. Although they hold caucuses and conventions in election years, and adopt platforms, attendance is low and officials rarely attempt to implement their organization's policies and platforms.

Overall, the absence of strong party organizations, inside or outside of Texas government, facilitates a strong interest group presence and influence.

Structurally, the organization of Texas state government also facilitates the influence of interest groups, a point emphasized by Thomas in Chapter 1 (see Table 1.1, Factors 4 and 5). A product of the immediate post-Reconstruction era, Texas has what might best be described as a decentralized decision-making structure. Executive power, for example, is parceled out among several popularly elected state officials (such as treasurer, land commissioner, comptroller of public accounts, and attorney general). Numerous state departments and agencies are governed by part-time boards and commissions whose members are appointed for overlapping terms; but it is usually the boards or commissions, and not the governor, who appoint the top full-time administrators of their departments.

Culturally, Texas can be described as having a combination of traditionalistic and individualistic political cultures.[2] The early, more traditionalistic Texas settlers were from the southern region of the United States and brought with them plantation economies when they settled in the eastern region of the state. The second pre–Civil War immigrant wave, heavily made up of individuals from more-liberal Germanic backgrounds, brought with them individualistic values. Although both types of cultures contained some inherent contradictions, a cultural synthesis evolved containing key elements of both. Historical factors unique to Texas—the fight for independence from Mexico, existence as an independent nation, involvement on the side of the Confederacy in the Civil War, and so on—produced a high degree of cultural cohesion.

In many ways the Texas political culture is unique. Among its key components are, first, its strong elitist tendencies, although the resource base of this elitism has shifted from the agricultural to the business-industrial sectors of the state economy. Today's Texas elite, or establishment, is made up of the captains of the major economic enterprises in the state. Although they may not personally interact with one another on a regular basis, they do share the common view that Texas governmental programs should emphasize economic development. This corporate-welfare orientation has thwarted any serious legislative consideration of a corporate income tax.

The second major component of the Texas political culture is personalistic politics. Political campaigns and major debates in the Legislature are frequently cast in personal terms as opposed to the presentation of rational arguments to buttress one's position. "Good ol' Texas bull" is also frequently inserted into such debates. In addition, the Texas electorate has been very vulnerable to the demogogic appeals of such politicians as James E. "Pa" Ferguson and W. Lee "Pappy" O'Daniel.

The third key component of Texas culture is its liking for limited, conservative government. According to this ethos, governments exist solely for the promotion of economic development. Governmental regulation of business as well as the provision of programs and services to the less fortunate are in many ways an anathema to this culture. Thus, on a per capita basis, Texas usually ranks quite low on most measures of state and local spending, especially in the areas of welfare and public health.

The Legal Environment

Little regulation of lobbying occurred in Texas for a hundred years or so after Reconstruction. Although a 1907 statute prohibited "efforts to influence legislation 'by means other than appeal to reason' and provided that persons guilty of lobbying were subject to fines and imprisonment," it was not enforced.[3] A 1957 law shifted emphasis from prohibition to publicity by requiring lobbyists to register and disclose certain information about their activities.[4] However, the law contained significant loopholes and therefore was not effective.[5] In response to the major Sharpstown Scandal, a more stringent law was passed in 1973, with significant amendments added in 1983.

In some ways the law is very encompassing. "Lobbying" pertains to efforts to influence not only the Legislature, but also the executive branch. The act is applicable throughout the year; it does not apply just to the period when the Legislature is in session. Individuals who register as lobbyists must indicate who their employer is, provide a breakdown of expenditures (but not any information on compensation), and list the types of bills or regulations about which they are concerned. Individuals are required to register if they meet one of three criteria: (1) individuals who lobby as a regular part of their job, excluding individuals working for the government; (2) individuals who receive more than $200 in any one calendar quarter as pay for lobbying; and (3) individuals whose outlay for any gifts, awards, or entertainment in order to influence legislation exceeds $200 in any calendar quarter.[6]

From the perspective of a very general definition of lobbying, a major limitation of this law is that it bypasses those individuals who spend a large part of their time lobbying for entities of state government. Thus, the numerous lobbyists for state universities or major state agencies are overlooked. When one attends hearings on the state's appropriations bill, the extent of this unofficial lobbying activity becomes obvious. Another difficulty appears in the definition of who must register. The number of lobbyists registered has decreased from about twenty-four hundred in 1977 to around eight or nine hundred in 1985.[7] Has the number of lobbyists actually decreased? No; rather, informed speculation indicates that two different trends are occurring: Lawyer-lobbyists are not registering (they claim they are representing clients, not lobbying); and if teams of lobbyists have been assembled, only the chief lobbyist is registering, since only he or she handles the money.[8]

Interest groups also attempt to influence legislative decision making indirectly through their role in elections. Aside from endorsements, a major activity is their support of candidates through campaign contributions. In Texas, corporations or labor unions, in attempting to aid or to defeat a ballot measure (not candidates), may contribute their own funds to a PAC only if the PAC exists exclusively to support or oppose the particular measure; otherwise, it is against the law.[9] However, employees, members, or families of the corporations, unions, and associations may form a PAC and make individual voluntary donations. As in the majority of states, no restrictions exist in Texas as to the amount of money a PAC may give to candidates or the amount that candidates may receive.[10]

PACs must register, and designate a campaign treasurer, with the appropriate filing authority (e.g., a PAC concerned with a state or district office or measure would file with the secretary of state) before accepting any contributions or making any election-related expenditures. PACs are considered either general-purpose (i.e., supporting or opposing measures or candidates indefinite in identity) or special-purpose (i.e., supporting or opposing specific, identifiable measures or candidates).

PACs in Texas, if not directly assisting an officeholder, are required to file contribution and expenditure statements in election years on either the first of each month or the thirtieth and seventh days before and thirtieth day after the primary or general election, and a summary statement on January 15 following the election year. In a nonelection year the only report is due on January 15 following that year. These statements include the name and address of each person contributing more than $50 ($10 for general-purpose PACs filing monthly), plus the date and amount of the contribution. For expenditures, the name and address of each person to whom any aggregate amount of more than $50 ($10 for general-purpose committees filing monthly) was given must be indicated, plus the amount, date, and reason for the expenditure. Contributions may not be made from thirty days before the beginning of the biennial session to the final adjournment. Recent changes in the law make it more difficult for the coordinators of a PAC to hide their role in the organization, since now a general-purpose committee must "report the name of each corporation, labor organization, or other association that directly establishes, administers, or controls the political action committee."[11]

The Group and Lobbyist Universe in Texas

What types of interest groups lobby legislators and administrators in Austin? A partial answer may be found in the information presented in Table 7.1, which was compiled six weeks into the 1987 session (i.e., late February 1987). The overall picture is one of diversity, both in terms of the scope of the organizations and the types of economic and noneconomic interests represented. As might be expected, business interest groups predominate, constituting almost 65 percent of the groups represented. Not only are there the general business organizations (e.g., Texas Association of Business) and the typical statewide trade associations (e.g., Texas Association of Builders, Texas Realtors' Association), but 56.7 percent of the 517 entities registered in this category are single companies (e.g., Adolph Coors, Monsanto Company, Transamerica, Foley's). Several business interests, while perhaps belonging to one or more major trade associations, still find it necessary to have one or more lobbyists registered to protect the interests of their individual companies. While we have no comparable data for ten-to-fifteen years ago, we conjecture that the growth in business lobbying may be due, in part, to the proliferation of this type of individual company representation.

As to specific business sectors, slightly more than 25 percent of the overall total of 796 registered groups consists of a combination of financial/insurance (e.g., Texas Association of Life Underwriters, Texas Life Insurance Association, Texas Bankers Association, Texas Savings and Loan Association) and energy/chemical interests (e.g., the major producer group, Texas Mid-Continent Oil and Gas Association; the major independent oil company organization, Texas Independent Producers and Royalty Owners Association; and Texas Chemical Council). However, in these two industries, almost two-thirds of the entities registered are single companies (e.g., Republic Bank, Texaco, Lone Star Gas).

Perhaps surprisingly, the somewhat amorphous category of non-economic interest groups accounts for the second-largest number of both interest group and lobbyist registrations. More than three-quarters of these organizations appear to be statewide. They cover the gamut from general ideological groups (e.g., Young Conservatives of Texas) and public-participation groups (e.g., Texas League of Women Voters) to specific single-issue groups (e.g., Texas Women for Pari-Mutual Betting). Interestingly, while black interest groups tend to play a prominent role in local politics, especially in Houston, their presence and impact at the state level is much more limited.

The remaining 19 percent of the registered groups is divided among four general categories. Professional groups constitute 7 percent, led by health-care providers (e.g., Texas Medical Association, Texas Dental Association, Texas Chiropractic Association). Most professional groups are statewide associations, except for, mainly, major individual law firms (e.g., Baker and Botts of Houston). Only about one in twenty groups involves private and public employees (e.g., AFL-CIO, Texas Classroom Teacher Association), and a few of these are local (e.g., Houston Police Officers Association). Organiza-

Table 7.1 Distribution of Texas Interest Groups and Lobbyists, February 1
by Type and Scope of Activity

	Groups (Percentage)	Lobbyists (Percentage)	Groups (Number)	Lobbyi (Numb
Business	64.9	63.0	517	969
Financial/insurance	17.0	11.4	135	176
Energy/chemicals	8.2	9.0	65	139
Building/construction	2.2	2.7	18	41
Transportation	4.8	6.0	38	93
Utilities/telecommunications	4.9	7.7	39	119
Real estate/apartments/hotels	0.9	1.8	7	27
Alcohol-related	1.5	1.1	12	17
Aerospace/steel and iron/high tech	2.0	2.3	16	35
General	0.6	0.5	5	8
Miscellaneous commercial	20.2	18.0	161	276
Miscellaneous manufacturing	2.6	2.5	21	38
Professions	7.0	9.8	56	151
Attorneys	1.6	2.7	13	42
Health care-related	2.9	4.7	23	71
Architects/engineers/CPAs/surveyors	0.8	1.4	6	22
Miscellaneous	1.8	1.0	14	16
Employees	5.3	6.2	42	95
Private sector	2.0	1.4	16	21
Public sector				
Education	1.4	3.3	11	51
Local government	1.4	1.0	11	15
Miscellaneous	0.5	0.5	4	8
Agriculture/ranching/forestry	2.5	2.2	20	34
Noneconomic	16.0	13.7	127	210
General	2.1	3.4	17	52
Specific-issue				
Nationality/ethnicity	0.1	0.1	1	1
Education	3.0	2.2	24	34
Taxation	0.3	0.3	2	4
Morality				
(e.g., gambling, abortion)	0.5	0.4	4	7
Conservation/natural resources	1.4	1.2	11	19
Miscellaneous	8.6	6.1	68	93
Local Government/special district	4.3	5.1	34	79
Total	100.0	100.0	796	1,538

Source: Lobbyist registration records, Office of the Secretary of State, Texas.

Statewide		Regional/Local		Single Company	
Number of Groups	Number of Lobbyists	Number of Groups	Number of Lobbyists	Number of Groups	Number of Lobbyists
09	371	15	26	293	572
81	73	1	1	53	102
14	30	—	—	51	109
11	29	1	1	6	11
20	57	2	4	16	32
6	18	4	7	29	94
4	17	1	5	2	5
7	10	2	2	3	5
2	6	—	—	14	29
5	8	—	—	—	—
55	111	4	6	102	159
4	12	—	—	17	26
46	132	1	11	9	18
4	24	—	—	9	18
23	71	—	—	—	—
6	22	—	—	—	—
13	15	1	11	—	—
35	75	7	20	—	—
15	20	1	1	—	—
9	39	2	12	—	—
7	18	4	7	—	—
4	8	—	—	—	—
16	25	1	4	3	5
99	160	28	50	—	—
12	36	5	16	—	—
1	1	—	—	—	—
14	20	10	14	—	—
2	4	—	—	—	—
4	7	—	—	—	—
7	13	2	6	—	—
57	79	11	14	—	—
9	28	25	51	—	—
14	791	77	152	305	595

tions of local government, including those representing general-purpose municipal governments (e.g., Texas Municipal League), school districts (Texas Association of School Boards), and other special districts (Texas Public Community Junior College Association) are one in twenty-five of the total groups registered. In this category the majority of the entities are single local governments (e.g., City of Houston). Given the ranching and agricultural base of the older Texas economy, it is interesting to note that organizations associated with these sectors represent the smallest percentage of groups, about one in forty of those registered (examples include the Texas Farm Bureau and the Texas and Southwestern Cattle Raisers Association).

Lobbyists: Types and Trends

The overall distribution of lobbyists fairly well parallels the overall distribution of interest groups by type (i.e., business, professional, etc.) and scope (i.e., statewide versus local or single company). In addition, 38.7 percent of the 796 groups retained two or more lobbyists, with sixty-six organizations each having five or more lobbyists registered with the secretary of state. At least early in the 1987 session no single interest group or company could match Southwestern Bell Telephone in 1979, which had sixty of its executives registered as lobbyists (three full-time), "more than all the state's labor and consumer groups combined."[12] However, the organizations or companies with the five highest number of lobbyists registered include two statewide business associations (Texas Motor Transportation Association with 13, and the Texas Association of Realtors with 11, a single company (AT&T with 18), and two professional organizations (Texas Trial Lawyers with 17, and the Texas Medical Society with 11).

What generalizations can be made regarding the characteristics of Texas lobbyists in the late 1980s? Two major changes are worth noting. First, while no empirical data exist to provide a comparison across the last fifteen years, the impression is that there is now a greater number of lobbyists in Texas, as in other southern states, who are contract lobbyists (or "hired guns"), lobbying for numerous groups simultaneously and sometimes for only one bill (cf. Table 14.5). However, roughly four in five contract lobbyists in Texas work for no more than one client, as shown in Table 7.2. In terms of multiple representation, slightly less than 10 percent of the lobbyists have two to four clients, another 5.3 percent have five to eight, and the remaining thirty-three lobbyists (4.1%) have nine or more retainers, with the highest number being twenty-seven. Several former legislators, while not an overly large percentage of the total lobbying pool, tend to become contract lobbyists as opposed to full-time, permanent employees of the organizations they represent (i.e., in-house lobbyists). For example, at least fifteen of the seventy-five lobbyists who have five or more clients are former state legislators (those serving between 1969 and 1986). Former Speakers Billy Clayton and Rayford Price, and former state Representatives or state Senators Jerry "Nub" Donaldson, Ed Howard, Bill Messer, Lynn Nabers, Neal "Buddy" Jones, and A. R. "Babe" Schwartz fall into this category. In

Table 7.2 Number of Clients per Registered Lobbyist, as of February 26, 1987

Number of Clients Represented	Number of Lobbyists	Percentage
1	629	79.7
2	52	6.6
3	22	2.8
4	11	1.4
5–8	42	5.3
9–12	15	1.9
13–16	7	0.9
17–20	8	1.0
21–27	3	0.4
Total	789	100.0

Source: Lobbyist registration records, Office of the Secretary of State, Texas.

addition, Jack Gullahorn and Rusty Kelly, former assistants to the House speaker, represent ten and nineteen clients, respectively. However, not all of the most successful lobbyists are those with multiple clients. A recent writer on five of Texas's top lobbyists mentioned two who were employed by a single client.[13]

The second trend involves changes in the composition of the lobbying force. Women, blacks, and Mexican-Americans are "now playing an increasing role as lobbyists."[14] There were 150 women and thirty-nine Mexican-Americans registered as lobbyists in February 1987, with fourteen of these being Mexican-American women. More impressively, 17.3 percent of contract lobbyists with five or more clients were women. In part, this increased role is linked to the fact that interest groups now assemble a team of lobbyists to negotiate the political process. Individual lobbyists are assigned specific legislators based on a host of criteria—"common interests, ethnic minority, personality types and regional backgrounds."[15]

Interest Group Tactics

Elections and Political Action Committees

The growth of PACs in Texas politics has been phenomenal. As of December 1986, 1,920 PACs were registered with the Texas secretary of state's office. However, not all of these PACs were necessarily related to interest groups. In fact, by our count, active PACs that may be tied to interest groups numbered only 970. The remaining PACs were candidate or party PACs (665); inactive (without a campaign treasurer, or terminated) or formed after the November 1986 elections (250); or inadequately documented (35).

In Table 7.3 the active nonparty/noncandidate PACs are categorized by scope and type. Overall, only 27.8 percent of the PACs are statewide organizations. The largest number of PACs are regional or local (e.g., South Texas Transpac or the Dallas Firefighters Public Safety Committee). Slightly more than 30 percent of the PACs are either single-company PACs (e.g., Browning-Ferris Industries PAC) or single professional office PACs (e.g., H&G PAC of the Hutcheson and Grundy Law Firm).

These PACs are also classified into one of four major PAC types: business; professions; public and private sector employees, in which the PACs are not affiliated directly with the company (e.g., Amarillo Central Labor Council COPE PAC); and noneconomically oriented entities. This last type of PAC includes general statewide ideological and issue-oriented PACs (e.g., Coalition of Conservative Texans, League of Women Voters), local citizens' groups (e.g., Citizens for a Better San Marcos), and single-cause groups (e.g., Texas Right to Life Committee and Children's Rights Through Informed Efforts).

The majority of PACs in 1986 can be classified as representing different business interests, with financial/insurance PACs being the largest category. In this energy-rich state, specific energy/chemical PACs are also quite prominent. Public-interest, social-issue, and good-government PACs form the second-largest category. Interestingly, almost 80 percent of the general PACs in this category typically encompass only a single county or city (e.g., League of Women Voters of Arlington), while a majority of the specific-issue PACs are statewide in scope (Sierra Club Committee on Political Education-Tx.). PACs representing professionals constitute another 13.7 percent, with attorneys accounting for over 50 percent of this category. However, we should be cautious about concluding that these prominent PACs represent attorneys themselves. In some cases, and it is difficult to determine the exact number, given law firms may not be using their own money. Rather, they are using funds deposited by the clients for whom they lobby. As a consequence, even though the PAC may be listed as a law firm, it really may represent a much larger set of interests. The smallest of the four major types of PACs are those affiliated with private and public sector employees' groups. Most in this category are regional or local PACs, and employees of educational entities and other local governmental bodies (e.g., firefighters and police) are the most numerous of those so represented.

PAC money is definitely increasing in Texas state legislative elections. From its study, Common Cause indicated that money from PACs had increased from 26.5 percent of all contributions to Texas House members in 1983 to 49.8 percent in 1985.[16] In the 1986 elections PACs were found to have given at least $4.7 million to the 182 state lawmakers, or roughly 61 percent of all money raised by Speaker of the House Gib Lewis, Lt. Gov. Bill Hobby (presiding of-

Table 7.3 Distribution of Active PACs in Texas in 1986, by Type and Scope of Activity (Excluding Political Party and Candidate PACs)

	Percentage	Number	Statewide	Regional/Local	Single Company
Business	48.6	472	113	115	244
Financial/insurance	14.6	142	13	15	114
Energy/chemicals	5.4	52	45	0	7
Building/construction	4.6	45	9	28	8
Transportation	3.6	35	7	21	7
Utilities/telecommunications	2.8	27	5	0	22
Real Estate/apartments/hotels	2.6	25	4	16	5
Alcohol-related	1.4	14	6	7	1
Aerospace/steel and iron/high technology	1.4	14	1	0	13
General	0.8	8	8	0	0
Miscellaneous commercial	10.1	98	49	20	29
Miscellaneous manufacturing	1.2	12	4	8	0
Professions	13.7	133	40	40	53
Attorneys	7.2	70	5	23	42
Health care–related	3.1	30	20	9	1
Architects/engineers/CPAs/surveyors	2.4	23	9	4	10
Miscellaneous	1.0	10	6	4	0
Employees	12.4	120	31	89	
Private sector	3.7	36	8	28	
Public sector	8.7	84	23	61	
Education		50	9	41	
Local government		26	6	20	
Miscellaneous		8	8	0	

	%				
Agriculture/ranching/forestry	2.2	21	18	1	2
Noneconomic	23.1	224	76	148	
General	12.4	120	23	97	
Specific issue	10.7	104	53	51	
Nationality/ethnicity	1.3	13	12	1	
Education	1.8	17	6	11	
Taxation	0.9	9	3	6	
Morality (i.e., gambling, abortion)	0.7	7	6	1	
Conservation/natural resources	1.3	13	10	3	
Miscellaneous	4.7	45	16	29	
Total		970	278 (28.7%)	393 (40.5%)	299 (30.8%)

Source: PAC disclosure records, Office of the Secretary of State, Texas.

ficer of the Texas Senate), state representatives, and state senators.[17] Yet significant differences exist among legislators in their reliance on PAC money, with the range being from 0 to 96 percent. Interestingly, Speaker Lewis received 96 percent of his $653,407 in campaign contributions from PACs, while Lieutenant Governor Hobby's PAC receipts accounted for only 37 percent of his contributions.[18]

What guides the PACs in their allocation of monies? Two basic theories regarding PAC allocation decisions appear in the political science literature.[19] In the first theory PACs are seen to allocate their campaign resources to candidates in competitive races and to those most compatible with the policy objectives or the broad ideological concerns of the PAC. The second theory hypothesizes that candidates' issue positions are flexible; thus, even in uncompetitive races contributions are made in the hope that, once elected, the winning legislator will grant access to lobbyists representing the relevant interest group. The expectation is that the legislator will be more likely to accede to the interest group's or PAC's request because funds had been supplied. Since an extraordinarily large percentage (usually in excess of 90 percent) of incumbents are reelected, most PAC contributions are directed toward them. Incumbents holding key positions within the Legislature (e.g., speaker, committee chair) are especially favored.

Most academic research[20] has focused on the role of PACs in Washington, D.C., and in campaigns for the U.S. Congress, with only marginal consideration given to state elections.[21] No major empirical study exists regarding the strategies pursued by PACs in Texas. However, in this chapter we will compare and contrast the strategies of two "heavy hitters" in Texas politics—the Texas Trial Lawyers' PAC (Lawyers Involved For Texas) and the Texas Medical Society's PAC (Texas Medical PAC). As shown in Table 7.4, the Texas Medical Society, while giving the largest amount (62.2%) of its money to Texas state legislative candidates, also provides money to other state candidates as well as to national office seekers and the national medical PAC. In contrast, the Texas Trial Lawyers, aside from a few donations to state political parties, focus exclusively on state legislative races. Surprisingly, both PACs allocated over 40 percent of their contributions in state legislative races to candidates for open seats. The Texas Medical Society appears to be following a

Table 7.4 Percentage Breakdown of Campaign Contributions Made by Two Texas PACs (August 1985 to November 1986)

Recipients	Texas Medical PAC	Texas Trial Lawyers PAC
National PACs	19.4	
U.S. congressional candidates	0.5	
State political parties		1.7
Statewide offices		
Governor/lieutenant governor	4.3	
Supreme Court	11.4	
Other Texas PACs	2.2	
State legislative races	62.2	98.3
Incumbents[a]		
Democrats	32.1	45.1
Republicans	22.8	3.0
Challengers		
Democrats	0.7	7.0
Republicans	0.3	2.0
Open seats		
Democrats	41.4	42.7
Republicans	2.7	0.2
Total	100.0	100.0
	($1,013,936)	($509,700)

[a] Texas Medical PAC contributed funds to seventy-six of the 106 Democratic incumbents, and to fifty of the fifty-five incumbent Republicans. Texas Trial Lawyers PAC funded seventy-five incumbent Democrats and nine Republican incumbents. Fifteen incumbent state senators who were not then running for office also received funds.

Source: PAC disclosure records, Office of the Secretary of State, Texas.

strategy geared more to gaining access, in that it gave money to 72 percent of the Democratic incumbents and to 90.9 percent of the Republican incumbents. In addition, it tended subsequently to support candidates who defeated the PAC's preferred candidate. On the other hand, the Trial Lawyers were more discriminating in their support, providing funds to only 70.7 and 16.4 percent of the Democratic and Republican incumbents, respectively. In addition, the Trial Lawyers were more likely to support challengers to sitting legislators, although still with only a small percentage of the total funds expended.[22]

In summary, PACs in Texas play a significant and increasing role in the funding of elections, particularly those of legislative candidates. Unfortunately, no data exist to suggest the precise effect that all this money may have on the policy process.

Legislative Lobbying: Old and New Tactics

A wide variety of techniques are employed by Texas lobbyists and interest groups in their efforts to influence legislative decision making.[23] The traditional lobbying orientation in Austin frequently emphasized "booze, bribes, and women" according to some veteran statehouse observers. For example, it was not at all unusual several years ago to see a lobbyist in Austin regularly frequent a local barbeque restaurant with a large group of lawmakers and their guests for an evening of beer, ribs, and storytelling. At the State Capitol itself the conventional tactic was for lobbyists to buttonhole lawmakers in the cloakrooms and hallways (most legislators had no offices at the time) in order to present personal arguments in support of their employer's positions on questions of public policy.

Indications are that this traditional lobbying orientation has been deemphasized in recent years, although new lobbying forms, or tactics, have not completely replaced it. Entertainment is still an important aspect of the Austin lobbying environment, especially for the more prosperous groups (business, trade, and professional) that can afford it. The site of food-and-drink parties has tended to shift from barbeque restaurants to posher and more sedate private clubs, such as the Headliners. Direct bribery appears to be on the wane; the last conviction of a lawmaker occurred in the early 1970s as the result of the Sharpstown Scandal. As for making women "available" to interested male lawmakers, a veteran lobbyist reported in 1981 that "I got hit up for the first time this session by a member wanting me to get him a woman. I told him that I have trouble enough getting my own dates."[24]

More-prevalent lobbying techniques now are those involving grass-roots public relations campaigns, more-systematic informational reports, and presession campaign contributions. Although campaign contributions were discussed earlier, it should be emphasized again that some groups (business, trade, and professional) are better able to utilize this technique than others (consumer, environmental, public cause, etc.). For example, Texas physicians and attorneys have well-organized and well-endowed PACs, while other groups with limited resources, such as the Texas Civil Liberties Union, Texas Consumer Association, and Citizens United for the Reform of the Errants (a prison-reform group) do not have enough resources even to form a PAC.

Grass-roots public relations lobbying, originated by consumer and labor groups, has also become a more common weapon in the arsenal of Texas lobbying groups. This tactic normally involves coalition building and strategy making on a major issue, plus the gathering of information and data addressing the issue. These activities usually commence at least several months prior to the convening of a legislative session. This tactic was employed successfully in 1981 by financial institutions (banks, personal loan companies, etc.) to obtain legislation increasing the maximum interest rates that could be charged customers. A prominent media consultant was employed to assist with strategy, advertisements were scheduled with local media, and a speakers' group was organized to travel the state to visit with local newspaper editors, as well as members of the local business community. The primary purpose of such campaigns, of course, is to make it easier for some lawmakers to vote for a particular bill by building support for it in their districts.

In addition to bringing many lobbyists, especially those representing business interests, out of the State Capitol's cloakrooms and Austin clubs, public relations campaigns have added a new expense to lobbying. As one veteran lobbyist indicated in 1981, "it's not cheap traveling the state holding press conferences. . . . Nor is it cheap to have consultants like George Christian [former press secretary to President Lyndon B. Johnson]."[25]

Several observers have noted the recent informational emphasis in lobbying activities. For example, one characterizes a new breed of lobbyists, "armed with the latest electronic gadgetry[,] edging out the back-slapping, whiskey-drinking influence peddler. In the modern legislative battle, the winning edge now comes with sophisticated studies, public opinion polls, and computerized mailings."[26] This is not to say that the old-time lobbyist is extinct, "but increasingly, special interests . . . are favoring the microchip over the martini to out-maneuver the opposition."[27]

Administrative Lobbying

Interest groups and state agencies interact quite often in Texas. Roughly two in three state administrators surveyed in 1982 indicated that interest group–initiated contact with the agency was either very frequent or frequent, while the corresponding figure for administrator-initiated contacts was over 50 percent.[28] Why do these two political participants seek each other out? Interestingly, there appears to be a certain symmetry to their actions. In Texas, administrators cite the most frequent purpose of interest group–initiated contacts as gaining information on agency programs, while the agency heads' second most frequent reason for initiating contact was to gain information on the effects of the unit's programs from the perspective of the affected interest groups. Also, while administrators sought out groups to solicit input on proposed regulations, interest groups were seen as trying to influence rules and regulations.[29]

The linkage between interest groups and the relevant Texas state agency is often enhanced by the appointment or election of state administrators. In the same 1982 survey of state administrators there was little indication of interest groups' attempting to influence personnel decisions or of agencies' soliciting suggestions from groups to fill vacancies.[30] On the other hand, several commentators have suggested that while an affected industry may not always secure the appointment or election of its designated candidate, those who oppose the industry are rarely selected. A clear-cut example is the powerful Railroad Commission, which has control over Texas's oil and gas policy. Initial selection to this popularly elected board is often by appointment after a member resigns before the expiration of his or her term. And, according to one study, "in the last twenty years, governors have never appointed a person to the Railroad Commission who was generally hostile to the industry, but neither have they picked individuals who were dictated, or even suggested by, the industry."[31] And when elections are held, the industry's candidate uses the twenty-to-one advantage in campaign contributions to increase his or her identification with the typical Texas voter, and thus win the low-visibility contest because of better name recognition.[32] Other cases of industry influence in the selection process also exist: "For example, over the last three decades the Texas Good Roads Association has sponsored virtually all of the eventual appointments to the three-person commission that heads the Department of Highways and Public Transportation."[33] However, this type of control is not guaranteed across all state agencies. For example, Agriculture Commissioner Jim Hightower was elected in 1982 and 1986 by the voters, even though organized segments of the agricultural community were not favorably disposed toward him.

What impacts do organized interest groups have on state administrative policy? The argument is frequently made that in a given policy area the affected major interest groups, the governmental agency responsible for implementing the policy, and the relevant legislative committees form "cozy triangles" in which policy is formulated, adopted, and administered.[34] Policy changes advocated by the governor, top legislative leaders, the media, and other interested citizens are often resisted by these small groups of participants. For example, in discussing the operation of the influential Railroad Commission, Prindle contends that, "in general, it is not too great an exaggeration to say that what has existed in Texas for nearly fifty years is not public regulation of the petroleum industry but regulation of the industry as a whole, under public auspices, by the independent portion of that industry."[35] In fact, in 1971 two major oil industry groups, the Texas Independent Producers and Royalty Owners Association and the American Association of Oil Well Drilling Contractors, placed an advertisement in the *Texas Almanac* whose headline was "Since 1891 The Texas Railroad Commission Has Served The Oil Industry."[36] There is some evidence, however, that suggests that the iron triangle may not be as cozy as sometimes thought. In one study, interest groups in Texas were ranked only thirtieth among the fifty states in terms of influence on state agencies.[37]

Also, the environment of a state agency is not simply made up of one or two interested groups; more than 70 percent of the state administrators questioned in the 1982 study indicated that four or more groups paid close attention to their unit's programs and operations. When asked about the interest group's orientation toward the state unit, the dominant response (65%) was that the orientation was highly variable.[38] The author, in discussing the situation in eight states, including Texas, contended that, "hence, there is some reason to suspect that all is not sweetness and light as far as agency–interest group relations are concerned."[39]

Unfortunately, not enough in-depth studies have been conducted to provide a firm generalization on the extent to which the cozy triangle exists across a wide variety of Texas state agencies.

Interest Group Power Structure

Given the Texas political system's lack of party competition and cohesion, the state's weak party organizations, its highly fragmented governmental structure, and its traditionalistic and individualistic political culture, interest groups have played a very influential role over the years. The exact nature of the interest group power structure appears to have changed, however. The initial phase of this structure can be characterized as the alliance of dominant interests. Given the agricultural nature of the Texas economy, cotton growers and cattle raisers were the major partners in this alliance. Shortly after the turn of the century, with the discovery of oil at Spindletop in southwest Texas, oil producers joined this alliance.

More recently the Texas group power structure has taken on a "triumph of many interests pattern," or one similar to that in California.[40] The emergence of this pattern is consistent with Texas's increasing urbanization, as well as the diversification of its economy. Although groups overall are still very powerful, no group or small combination of groups appears consistently to call the shots on state policy questions.

Within this structure, what groups are perceived to wield the most influence? An April 21, 1983, survey by *Texas State Government Newsletter* of veteran state lawmakers sheds light on this question. Groups mentioned most frequently as most effective at lobbying were the trial lawyers, doctors, realtors, and teachers. The Texas Trial Lawyers Association was cited for its ability to initiate phone calls and contacts from lawyers in legislative districts, donate campaign money, and provide research assistance, staff help, and expert witnesses, as key sources of its influence. Medical doctors, or the Texas Medical Association, were cited for their homework on policy questions affecting members, plus their ability to get doctors back home involved in legislative issues, as bases for their effectiveness. Similar views were expressed about both the Texas Realtors Association and Texas State Teachers Association, although the alleged employment of threatening, intimidating, and obnoxious lobbying tactics earned the teachers' group at least a few negative assessments. Also nominated by many lawmakers for a top effectiveness position were Texas Motor Truck Association, Texas AFL-CIO, Independent Oil and Gas Producers Association, Texas Chemical Council, Texas Association of Business, and the Texas Savings and Loan Association. The numerous nominations for most-effective lobby groups lend support to our view that the Texas interest group power structure is no longer as monolithic as it once was and does not consist of only a handful of key economic enterprises.

Interest groups in Texas are seen to be important influences in the governmental process.[41] In fact, to some observers, "comparatively, interest groups are probably more important in the Texas legislative process than they are in the U.S. Congress or most state legislatures."[42] To what extent is this portrayal accurate?

Case studies abound relating the impact that groups may have.[43] However, for our purposes, a different methodology is used. A 15 percent random sample of bills introduced during the 1983 Texas Legislature was selected. Data were acquired on interest group activities for each bill. The major data source were lobbyists' monthly activity statements filed with the Texas secretary of state. These statements, aside from having lobbyists disclose the amount of money spent for different categories of expenses, contain a listing of proposed legislation, including a statement of the registrant's position, on which the registrant communicated directly with members of the legislative or executive branch. In addition, committee hearings, witness affirmation cards, and organizational newsletters were scrutinized for information as to different interest groups' positions on the 577 pieces of legislation. Telephone calls were made to several lobbyists to clarify positions. In the analysis that follows, any lobbying by specific state agencies, including Texas state universities and colleges, is excluded. The focus is on organizations outside the official state governmental system.

The major results of our study are summarized in Tables 7.5, 7.6, and 7.7. As shown in Table 7.5, about one in four bills introduced into the 1983 Texas Legislature did not attract the active attention of any interest group. On the other hand, five or more groups expressed a preference, as proponents or opponents, on slightly more

Table 7. 5 Number of Interest Groups Taking a Position on Individual Bills, 1983 Texas Legislative Session

Number of Groups	Number of Bills	Percentage
0	147	25.5
1	134	23.2
2	77	13.3
3	49	8.5
4	43	7.5
5–6	44	7.6
7–9	38	6.6
Over 10	45	7.8
Total	577	100.0

Mean number of groups per bill	3.2	
Mean number of groups per bill with at least one group taking a pro/con stand	4.4	

Sources: Lobbyist registration records, Office of the Secretary of State, Texas; committee hearing summaries; and mail and phone communications with representatives of Texas interest groups.

Table 7.6 Interest Group Involvement by Type of Sector, 1983
(in Percentages)

	Involvement	
	Overall[a] (N = 577)	Adjusted[b] (N = 430)
Business	41.4	55.6
Local government	32.8	44.0
Non-economic	25.1	34.0
Farm/ranch	1.9	2.6
Public employees	9.9	13.3
Professional	15.8	21.2
Labor	4.6	6.3

[a] Overall involvement includes the percentage of sample bills on which each sector participated.

[b] Adjusted involvement includes the percentage of sample bills with at least one group from the sector participating on which any sector participated.

Sources: Lobbyist registration records, Office of the Secretary of State, Texas; committee hearing summaries; and mail and phone communications with representatives of Texas interest groups.

than one in five bills. Among those bills on which at least one group took an active position (430), the phenomenon of countervailing forces squaring off against one another in the legislative arena occurred in only 38.1 percent of cases. In the majority of these 430 cases the tendency was for all the interested parties to support the proposed legislation. For the remaining 10.2 percent of bills all the active groups opposed the legislation.

As shown in Table 7.6, a wide spectrum of participants are involved, reflecting Texas's economic diversity. No interest sector is active on a majority of the random sample of bills, although if those bills on which no group took a pro or con position are removed from the sample, then the business sector is shown as being active on 55.6 percent. Interestingly, while two of the recently cited active participants in state legislative lobbying—local governmental organizations and noneconomic interest groups—account for only 4.3 and 16 percent of the total number of registered interest groups, they are

Table 7.7   Success of Texas Interest Groups in Conflict/Agreement
with Other Influence Agents, 1983 (in Percentages)

Other Influence Agents	In Conflict	Not Involved	In Agreement
Governor's office			
Success	23.5 (17)[a]		96.2 (133)[a]
		35.6 (247)[b]	
Gain/loss	-12.1[c]		+60.6[c]
Majority leadership			
Success	25.0 (4)[a,d]		73.0 (37)[a]
		66.1 (545)[b]	
Gain/loss	-41.1[c]		+6.9[c]

[a]   The total number of situations in which groups and other influence agents took conflicting or the same positions is shown in parentheses.

[b]   Situations in which groups' positions were balanced or in which there was no group involvement are excluded.

[c]   Percentage change figures represent the success of groups when in conflict or agreement with other influence agents minus their success when the other influence agent was not involved in the situation.

[d]   Note the low number of situations in this cell.

Sources: Lobbyist registration records, Office of the Secretary of State, Texas; committee hearing summaries; mail and phone communications with interest group representatives; and interviews with legislative staff liaison personnel in gubernatorial and legislative leaders' offices.

actively involved in roughly one-third and one-fourth of the entire sample of legislation, respectively. Professional and public employees' associations are also moderately active, while farm/ranch associations and labor groups restrict the number of bills on which they take a stand.

Do the various classifications of Texas interest groups tend to support or oppose proposed legislation? While there might be a class of organizations that try to hold the line and oppose most proposed measures relevant to their goals, this is not true for the major classificatory groupings in our study. This imbalance in terms of the ratio of support to opposition is most definitely the case for local government (the ratio being almost 3:1), public employees (more than 4:1), labor (3.5:1), and noneconomic interest groups and professions (more than 2:1 for each type). The smallest ratio is for the business community, but even it exceeds 1.15.

How successful are interest groups? Our data indicate that around 55 percent of the time the position taken by the majority of interest groups prevails. Our working hypothesis was that the probability of passage should increase as the interest group pattern changed from all opposition to all support. The data bear out this conjecture in that there is a statistically significant increase in success rate as one moves from the all-groups-opposed category through increasing interest group support, culminating in the all-groups-support category. However, results also indicate that interest groups in Texas are more successful at defeating legislation than at passing it, since, even in the all-groups-support category, only 49.1 percent of the legislation is adopted.

A final question relates to the relative strength of interest groups versus political party leaders. The data in Table 7.7 indicate the significant effect that party leaders may have on the fortunes of interest groups. When a majority of groups involved in measures take a position opposite to that taken by the governor or legislative leaders (lieutenant governor or speaker), their ability to influence legislative outcomes is reduced. This is particularly true when they go head-to-head with the presiding officers of the Legislature, although it should be emphasized that there are only a small number of cases in which such conflict occurs. On the other hand, interest group success tends to increase when group positions are consistent with the governor's or legislative leaders'. In these situations agreement with the state's chief executive appears to have the larger impact. Overall, our conclusion here is that the positions taken by the governor or legislative leaders in relation to interest groups can have a major bearing on the latter's influence.

Conclusion

The interest group system in Texas contains elements of both stability and change. As is true in other southern states (see Chapter

14), change has characterized the structure of the system, as Texas has moved from a rural and agricultural economy to an urban and manufacturing/service-based economy. The number of interest groups has multiplied, thus creating a much more diverse interest group structure. Rural-based groups, such as the Farm Bureau and various commodity groups, were much less successful in recent legislative sessions than they had been a decade or two ago.

Money remains a major resource available to at least the more prosperous groups, but its use has shifted away from the bestowing of more-personal, or individual, benefits upon lawmakers to PAC contributions and well-organized, grass-roots–oriented public relations campaigns. Lobbying of lawmakers has shifted from a major emphasis on personal argumentation to information-based communications.

Groups will probably continue to play a major role in policy-making, given the traditional weaknesses of the party organizations and the lack of meaningful two-party competition. Reapportionment of the Texas Legislature in 1991 may alter this pattern, depending mainly upon the balance of party forces in the Legislature at the time and the nature of possible constraints imposed by federal courts.

Finally, for the most part, interest groups will probably continue to play a major role in the policy decisions of administrative agencies. The highly decentralized structure of the executive branch will allow interest group representatives relatively easy access. Given the lack of any reform effort on the horizon, any changes in relations between lobbyists and state administrators will be mostly unobtrusive.

8

ARKANSAS

THE POLITICS OF INEQUALITY

Arthur English and John J. Carroll

Many of Arkansas' most powerful interests operate from office buildings on the streets radiating out from the State Capitol in Little Rock. The Arkansas Poultry Federation has set up shop in the popularly labeled "Chicken House," a few minutes down the street from the General Assembly. Here poultry growers and legislators chat over cheese and bologna during informal hospitality hours after the legislature has finished for the day. Not far away are the state's powerful utilities—Arkansas Power and Light (AP&L) and the Arkansas Louisiana Gas Company (ARKLA). The labor unions, the State Chamber of Commerce, Associated Industries, the pharmacists, and even the Grocers' Association are just down the street, an easy walk to the center of political power.

In the winter and early spring in odd-numbered years when the legislature is in session, the office buildings disgorge their lobbyists, who descend on the statehouse to add their voices to the debate over the public's business. The professional lobbyists are often well-dressed lawyers and executives who greet legislators by their first names. Lobbyists and legislators transact considerable portions of their business in the Capitol's white marble corridors because House members lack their own offices and Senate offices are above the chamber and out of the flow. Lobbyists can be seen waiting outside the House or Senate chamber for a brief word with a legislator, or huddled in extended conversation with legislators and committee staff. Sometimes the discussions adjourn to Buster's, a favorite lunchtime and evening watering hole, located in the old train station, a five-minute walk from the Capitol.

In the legislative hearing rooms, younger and sometimes casually dressed representatives of the citizens' lobbies, such as Arkansas Community Organization for Reform Now (ACORN) and Common Cause, may be giving testimony. And groups of constituents, bused in, most commonly, for a tour, but sometimes to lobby, may demand attention from legislators as well. The skilled, professional lobbyists representing traditional economic interests—utilities, banks, labor—have easy and convenient access; but the citizens' groups and their lobbyists must sometimes be reckoned with as well, for they can make a powerful noise, and officeholders are uncomfortable when these groups are aroused.

Arkansas politics and its interest group system are undergoing significant change; they are becoming more pluralistic as the number and variety of organized interests increases; they are preoccupied now with economic development, rather than race; and they are free of the long-standing contest with Mississippi and Alabama for the title of Great American Backwater—the South has moved into the national mainstream and Arkansas has moved with it. But while change floods in, much of what characterized the old Arkansas still characterizes the new—the old conflict between entrenched economic interests and their populist challengers is still a distinguishing feature of Arkansas politics and its interest group system.[1]

Politics Arkansas-Style

Arkansas politics is structured by the hard realities of economic inequality. With 22 percent of the state's population below the federal poverty line, inequality of wealth is a well-understood and often accepted part of Arkansas life. Even so, the state is endowed with substantial natural resources—timber, water, and rich farmland—for those with the financial ability to exploit them.

Modernization came late to Arkansas and was restricted to its more accessible parts, those not cut off by the Ouachita and Ozark mountains, which were natural barriers to commerce. Because agriculture, the state's mainstay, was labor-intensive and the state was off the beaten track, a skilled manufacturing labor force was slow to develop. In consequence, Arkansas' economy has not supported a large middle class; instead, there have been a few rich individuals and many poor folk. By several measures the state's economic health deteriorated during the 1980s. The gap in per capita income compared to the national average increased from $3,000 in 1984 to $4,700 in 1989; and while the jobless rate is usually only a point or two above the national level, this understates the very high rates of unemployment in rural counties outside the Little Rock metropolitan area.[2]

Inequalities of wealth have had enormous influence on the Arkansas political tradition, which has seen a continuing struggle between the defenders of entrenched interests and their populist critics. After the Civil War, the Bourbons—a probusiness, antitax coalition composed of merchants, landowners, and their heirs—dominated Arkansas politics.[3] The Bourbons used their economic power and social prominence to control the political system and to keep the lower classes, particularly blacks, in check. Until the 1960s the Bourbon tradition was sustained by the white primary, the state poll tax, and a plantation orientation toward progress.

The 1874 constitution, which is still in force, framed a government that was particularly appropriate to the protection of entrenched economic and social interests. This constitution created a part-time, fragmented governmental structure of limited powers, which made it difficult to reform the system. The governor was elected for a two-year term, and the General Assembly convened for just sixty days. The governor shared executive power with a full slate of constitutional officers: lieutenant governor; attorney general; treasurer; land commissioner; and state auditor. After adoption of Amendment 19 in 1935, the state constitution required that all state taxes (the sales tax excepted) be enacted by a three-fourths majority of the General Assembly. This has made it difficult for Arkansas to raise revenue, and nearly impossible to increase corporate taxes.

An influential countertradition, populism, has been associated with a succession of colorful figures who have come to power by attacking the Bourbons and their vested interests. This tradition appeals to grass-roots resentment against faceless corporations and self-serving politicians and bureaucrats, who are blamed for the problems of the common man.

In the 1930s Joseph T. Robinson and Hattie Caraway carried the populist banner against big business and the utilities. Caraway, the first female U.S. senator elected in her own right, brought in the Kingfish himself, Huey Long, to campaign on her behalf.[4] But sometimes the backdoor dealings of the self-proclaimed populists were far different from their public face. Robinson, for example, was the U.S. Senate majority leader during the New Deal and one of Franklin Roosevelt's strongest supporters. Yet when FDR approached him about Arkansas' participation in the public power project that was later realized as the TVA—an offer that power-poor Arkansas could hardly refuse—Robinson vetoed the idea because his law partner represented AP&L, whose interests were inconsistent with those of inexpensive public power.

When Sid McMath was elected governor in 1948 he gave the populist tradition a progressive twist. McMath was a Truman Democrat who believed that government should play a positive role in education, highway construction, health, and rural power, and act as a moderating influence on race relations.[5] By 1952, when McMath was brought down by a scandal in the Highway Department, he had built a constituency for the idea that state government should address the problems associated with inequality of wealth.

Like the rest of the South, Arkansas was strongly Democratic. Prior to Winthrop Rockefeller's election in 1966, no Republican had been governor since Reconstruction, and the legislature never had more than a sprinkling of Republicans, a situation that still prevails. But the paucity of Republicans is not a function of deep affection for the Democratic party. Tradition, the New Deal, and the politics of race made, and kept, Arkansas Democratic. But the new campaign technology and weak party organizations have produced a new politics of personality and image to which a now-volatile electorate reacts.[6] The unpredictability of Arkansas voters is most clearly demonstrated by the 1968 elections when the state supported segregationist and American party nominee George Wallace for president, Democrat and internationalist J. William Fulbright for the U.S. Senate, and Republican and racially moderate Winthrop Rockefeller for governor. This unpredictability—or independence—has continued as Arkansans have elected a mixture of conservatives and liberals, Democrats and Republicans to gubernatorial and congressional seats. The state's voters seem more attuned to the individual styles of its politicians than to its political parties.[7]

The old theme of populism versus entrenched interests endures. Since the 1970s, for example, the utilities have been a favorite target of Democratic state attorneys general who have vaulted themselves into contention for the governorship by challenging increases of utility rates. The specter of $200-a-month electric bills, not unusual during a hotter than normal summer, can galvanize antiutility sentiment quickly. In reaction, the utilities have established a strong political presence to defend themselves from charges that they seek to raise rates without much concern for the public welfare. The politics of utility regulation also centers on appointments to the Public Service Commission, the chief regulatory agency for utilities. Gov. Frank White, a Republican who defeated Bill Clinton in 1980, was reported to have sent possible appointees for interviews with AP&L's top executives before he formally nominated them. Clinton, campaigning successfully to regain the governorship in 1982, promised to appoint commissioners with strong consumer credentials.

The Variety of Interest Groups

Stable, well-financed economic organizations are the most commonly represented groups within Arkansas' variety of interests. Business, which accounts for approximately half of all interests with registered lobbyists, includes groups, organizations, and firms from every important sector of the state's economy, including banks and finance, insurance, oil and gas, utilities, and timber; umbrella organizations such as the State Chamber of Commerce and the Associated Industries of Arkansas; and a variety of corporations engaged in enterprises as diverse as railroading, aluminum, horse racing, beverages, tobacco, and chemicals (see Table 8.1)

Unions and employees' groups are also an important feature of the interest group system, with sixteen such groups exemplified by the AFL-CIO, the Teamsters, and the State Employees' Association.

Table 8.1 Interest Group Categories and Number of Registered
Lobbyists, 1985

	Number of Organizations	Number of Lobbyists	Ratio of Lobbyists to Organizations
Utilities	21	102	4.86
Business/industrial	45	52	1.16
Unions and employee groups	16	29	1.81
Professional	11	23	2.09
Government	15	20	1.33
Banks and finance	15	17	1.13
Health	15	16	1.06
Oil and gas	12	15	1.25
Insurance	13	15	1.15
Feminist	3	12	4.00
Agriculture	8	10	1.25
Liquor and soft drinks	12	10	0.83
Timber	7	9	1.21
Religion	4	6	1.50
Newspapers and press	6	6	1.00
Water	4	5	1.25
Environment	4	5	1.25
Railroads	3	3	1.00

Source: Reports filed with the clerk to the House and the secretary to Senate, 1985.

Farmers are organized into eight separate groups; while governmental organizations, such as county sheriffs, school administrators, and the Association of Arkansas Counties, are also numerous.

Nonprofit and citizens' groups make up a relatively small but growing proportion of the interests with registered representatives. Cooperative rural utilities, religious organizations, and medical groups, such as hospitals and physicians' associations, are the most commonly represented form of nonprofit organizations; while environmentalists and feminists typify the citizens' lobbies organized to work for positions on public policy. Some groups, particularly those at the bottom of the economic or social scale, do not appear on the list at all. The unemployed, the homeless, persons on welfare, renters, and homosexuals, among others, have not had specialized lobbyists to argue their causes before the Assembly.

Characteristics of Arkansas Lobbyists

The number of lobbyists an organization fields is closely related to its organizational structure. The large number of utility lobbyists is a function of the grass-roots lobbying networks of the electric cooperatives of rural Arkansas. Of the 102 registered utility lobbyists, eighty-five are affiliated with the cooperatives, while the two largest commercial utilities, AP&L and ARKLA, have just five and two lobbyists, respectively. Women's groups are also organized as grass-roots lobbies, and because there are few such groups in Arkansas their active membership results in an unusually high ratio of lobbyists to organizations. Typically, organizations are represented by one or two registered lobbyists, as demonstrated by financial institutions, industrial groups, railroads, and oil and gas interests, as well as the unions and medical and professional lobbies.

The part-time nature of the Assembly is reflected in the fact that only 15 percent of lobbyists rely on lobbying for their primary source of income.[8] Of those who do not derive the bulk of their income from lobbying, 48 percent said they were not paid for lobbying; and of those who were paid, the majority were attorneys, association directors, or retirees. These data underscore the fact that most Arkansas lobbyists are either in-house lobbyists (organization, group, or business employees) who lobby as part of their job when the Assembly is in session, or they are part-time contract lobbyists hired by a group to advocate its interests. In either guise, they do not fit the mold of the full-time, paid lobbyists who abound in Washington, D.C., and some of the larger states where professionalized legislatures with well-institutionalized patterns of interaction are in session most of the year.

Arkansas lobbyists share the characteristics of the Arkansas es-

Table 8.2 Characteristics of Arkansas Lobbyists, 1986 (in Percentages)

Male	85
Female	15
Under 30	2
30–39	27
40–49	22
50–59	20
60 or older	28
High school graduate	15
Some college	10
College graduate	32
Graduate school	43
Democrat	62
Republican	15
Independent	24

tablishment: They tend to be male, middle-aged, well-educated Democrats (see Table 8.2). This is not a surprise when one considers the larger political system of which lobbyists are a part. The Arkansas General Assembly, for example, is a middle-aged, well-educated, and Democratic domain in which only ten women served in the 1989/90 session. Lobbyists tend to be older than the state's adult population, and the experience, information, and other skills required of them reflect the important stakes that interest groups seek to protect or to secure. Sixty-two percent of lobbyists report that they are Democrats, 24 percent are independents, and only 15 percent are Republicans; the General Assembly is 95 percent Democratic.[9] Arkansas lobbyists also fit the stereotype that political elites have more formal education than the average citizen: Seventy-five percent of lobbyists report a college or graduate degree.

Lobbying Styles and Tactics

While the theory of the pluralist struggle holds that good public policy is forged from the contest of interests, Arkansas legislators and lobbyists understand that the contest is rarely equal and the outcomes are sometimes unfair. Almost 60 percent of both lobbyists and legislators believe that opposing interests are not evenly matched in resources and influence (see Table 8.3). Furthermore, almost three-fourths of lobbyists and over two-thirds of legislators who responded to our survey believe that interest groups sometimes convince public officials to support legislation that is harmful to the public interest. This is a frank appraisal by the participants that the state's interest group process often does not reflect the broader needs of the Arkansas public.

We noted earlier that the interest group system in Arkansas parallels the culture of economic and political disparity, and the populist challenge to that inequality. It is a system in which professional lobbyists and well-entrenched special interests have the upper hand, but in which outsiders, those lacking political resources and established contacts with decision makers, can sometimes write their

Table 8.3 Attitudes of Legislators and Lobbyists to the Interest Group Process (in Percentages)

	Lobbyists			Legislators		
	Agree	Disagree	Unsure	Agree	Disagree	Unsure
It is rare for opposing interest groups to be evenly matched in influences and resources on a particular issue.	57	22	22	59	31	10
Sometimes lobbyists and interest groups convince public officials to support legislation that is not in the public interest.	73	10	16	69	19	12

policy preferences into law. An interest group system of this type is one in which all sorts of groups move, but powerful institutionalized groups employing professional, well-connected lobbyists are at a decided advantage. The utilities provide an excellent example: The chief lobbyist for AP&L is a former speaker of the House who is personally known to virtually every prominent officeholder in the state; ARKLA's director of public relations ran the Little Rock office of U.S. Sen. David Pryor and founded the Political Animals, an informal group of political insiders who meet twice a month to talk politics.

In one part of our survey, lobbyists and legislators were asked which three lobbying tactics were most commonly used, and which one they considered the single most effective tactic (see Table 8.4).[10] The most commonly used techniques were testifying at hearings, personal presentations to legislators, contacts through an influential person, campaign contributions, entertaining, letter-writing campaigns, and releasing policy studies. As we see on Table 8.4, several techniques commonly used in other states, especially formal or indirect methods, are not viewed as very effective lobbying tactics in Arkansas. The state's interest group system very much emphasizes access to and personal contact with political decision makers. Lobbyists and legislators alike cite the ritual of going on record at public hearings, but neither group believes this is an effective lobbying tactic. On the other hand, three-quarters of legislators and lobbyists believe that a face-to-face presentation by a lobbyist or an influential person is the single most effective technique. Public relations campaigns, press conferences, political protests, and letter-writing campaigns are seen as ineffective, and sometimes improper, lobbying tactics. Interestingly, these are techniques most likely to be used by groups operating through activist memberships, such as good-government groups and groups that are outsiders to the system.

However, it would be an exaggeration to claim that access to political elites is the exclusive monopoly of institutionally powerful groups. Some groups that are relatively unorganized or use unconventional lobbying techniques, such as religious organizations and good-government groups, have launched successful campaigns. For example, midwives successfully campaigned to legalize their profession because they were willing to employ a multifaceted lobbying

Table 8.4 Most Commonly Used and Most Effective Lobbying Tactics (by Percentages of Legislators and Lobbyists Listing Tactic)

	Three Most Commonly Used Tactics		Single Most Effective Tactic	
	Legislators	Lobbyists	Legislators	Lobbyists
Testifying at hearings	73	69	9	14
Personal presentations	70	71	48	56
Contact through influentials	54	75	24	21
Campaign contributions	37	23	6	4
Entertaining	20	29	1	0
Letter-writing campaigns	18	8	0	0
Releasing policy studies	14	8	0	0
Public relations campaigns	6	4	0	0
Publicizing voting records	5	2	0	0
Press conferences	4	6	0	0
Political protests	0	0	0	0

strategy that took maximum advantage of their resources. Their spokesperson, Carolyn Vogler, belied the stereotype of the midwife as an uneducated "granny" who delivers babies for the rural poor when a doctor cannot be found. Instead, she conveyed the image of an intelligent, caring person who is extremely knowledgeable about her craft. She brought her message, carefully documented with public health statistics, to the press, which portrayed her in populist terms as a modern Joan of Arc struggling against an intransigent Arkansas medical establishment. In an unusual strategy, the midwives used their access to a friendly legislator to suspend the legislative rules so that Vogler and two of her allies could address a session of the House. Passage of a compromise bill, which legalized midwifery in six counties, gave the midwives their primary goal—legitimization of their right to practice.[11]

Most mass-based groups have neither the skill nor the political imagination of the midwives. These groups start with enormous liabilities they are often unable to overcome. Furthermore, organizations that will not play by the accepted rules of the game may find that government decision makers are inclined to dismiss their efforts as coercive and give only perfunctory attention to their claims.

While entrenched, well-institutionalized interests are regular participants in the policy-making process, groups like the midwives tend to be active or inactive, or come into existence, as the public policy agenda shifts. For these groups, the most crucial tactical choice is the threshold decision to enter the interest group struggle. With this decision, interest groups both respond to and help form the policy agenda.

For example, ERArkansas was organized to advocate the ratification of the Equal Rights Amendment (ERA) in the 1981 session, just before the federal extension of the ratification period lapsed. When the time limit expired, so did ERArkansas. Family, Life and God (FLAG) was organized primarily to work against adoption of ERA. Again, as the threat passed the organization declined until there were no FLAG lobbyists registered for the 1985 session. The fluidity of interests is also seen in the organization of a new group, Women Involved in Farm Economics (WIFE), during the 1985 session, to support the embattled farmer. And in the 1989 session, after competition from racetracks in neighboring states had significantly cut into profits, lobbyists for Oaklawn Racetrack established a presence to lobby the General Assembly and the governor for a longer racing season.

The phenomena of one-session groups is not limited to organizations lobbying the flamboyant causes of the contemporary social agenda. The Arkansas Rural Water Association emerged during the 1983 legislative session because a comprehensive water bill affecting access was before the Assembly. The Fraternal Order of Police and the Arkansas Association of Retired Persons were active in the 1985 session because of their interests in pension rights. And prior to the 1989 session the Arkansas Fairness Council, a coalition of progressive groups, and the governor sought a constitutional amendment to lower the required legislative majority from three-fourths to three-fifths to pass new taxes. Had this strategy been successful it would have made it much easier for the 1989 Assembly to impose taxes on corporations and wealthier groups. But the amendment was easily defeated by a clever media campaign orchestrated by business groups articulating the theme that adoption of the amendment would raise everybody's taxes.

Groups share a belief that lobbying must be personal and pragmatic to be successful, but the ability to lobby effectively varies with the kinds of resources a group brings to the process. Some groups use their grass-roots membership to effective advantage. During the midwifery debate the Arkansas Medical Association was taken by surprise by the easy passage of a bill in the Senate permitting the practice. The association regrouped its forces in the House by asking doctors to call their representatives and lobby against the bill. As a result, the Senate version was defeated on the House floor.

Populist groups generally lack the quality of access developed by business and utility lobbies, and employ somewhat different tactics. They may form coalitions such as the previously noted Arkansas Fairness Council, which has long lobbied to remove the sales tax on groceries. This coalition, including the NAACP, the AEA, the Urban League, the AFL-CIO, the Women's Political Caucus, the National Organization of Women, and ACORN, uses press conferences to publicize its views and to place public pressure on decision makers. Similarly, the Urban League, with financial support from the progressive Winthrop Rockefeller Foundation, issued a report at a 1987 press conference starkly revealing the educational, income, and employment disparities between Arkansas blacks and whites. This strategy had some success when the report's findings were widely disseminated, and the issue of black inequality assumed a higher place on the state's political agenda. Groups with limited resources for lobbying or those with a poor image in the Assembly are sometimes forced to resort to legal remedies to overturn legislation they could not successfully oppose in the legislature. A 1981 law mandating that schoolchildren be taught "creation science" on an equal basis with evolutionary theory quickly passed the Assembly and was signed into law by Governor White. The law was declared unconstitutional by a federal court after the Arkansas affiliate of the ACLU challenged the law in what came to be known among ACLU lawyers as the Great Banana Trial.

Government-based groups have their own special advantages. The constitutionally independent Fish and Game Commission, for example, claims to speak for the thousands of sportsmen and women in Arkansas. In 1984 the commission gathered enough signatures to place a constitutional amendment on the ballot that would have increased the sales tax by one-eighth of a percent, the revenues to be earmarked for Fish and Game use. The tax was strongly opposed on the grounds that many citizens would not benefit from the revenue, and the money could be spent at the complete discretion of the commission. Nonetheless, although the amendment failed, it attracted 45 percent of the vote.

The governor actively lobbies the Assembly, where he claims to speak for a statewide constituency that is of great consequence to legislators, who watch public opinion carefully. During the 1982 struggle over teacher testing most legislators supported the governor's initiatives because they knew from their constituents that the program was popular at home. On the other hand, an intense lobbying campaign carried to the floor of the 1987 legislature by the governor's staff could not rescue a quarter-cent increase in the sales tax. Governor Clinton worked the Capitol corridors himself, talking to representatives one on one, but legislators resisted his arguments on the grounds that their constituents were opposed. A similar situation occurred during the 1989 Assembly when Clinton's higher-education tax package was defeated by legislators under intense pressure from constituents.

In many ways the most powerful governmental lobbyists, with the exception of the governor, are Assembly members who directly represent interests with which they are occupationally connected.[12] A House member has been director of Industry Relations for the Arkansas Poultry Federation since 1967. When he retired after the 1989 session the federation dipped into its legislative well to find a senior member of the Senate to take the job. Other legislators are connected with groups influential enough to have an informal inside lobbyist. One legislator is executive vice-president of the Oil Marketers Association, and yet another is president of a regional ARKLA company.

In 1986, 11 percent of lawmakers were farmers by vocation, 19 percent were realtors and insurance agents, and 21 percent were attorneys. These groups exercise power from within as well as from outside the legislature. The Assembly's core of farmers and ranchers has combined with a strong American Farm Bureau lobby to maintain special tax treatment for agricultural equipment purchases. Legislation to build a new office complex near the Capitol, which would have saved the government rental fees for office space, was introduced in 1985 by a former speaker of the House, a senior legislator of considerable prestige. Not only did he incur the wrath of the Arkansas Realtors Association, but he felt a considerable coolness from his realtor-insurance colleagues as well.

The Recent Surge in Lobby, Campaign, and Ethics Regulation

For many years interest groups in the state of Arkansas were largely free of regulation, which gave them considerable latitude in their lobbying and campaign efforts. Lobbyists were required only to file a one-page registration form with the General Assembly indicating the organization for which they lobbied and the type of legislation on which they would be active. In the 1987 legislative session efforts on behalf of a comprehensive ethics law failed to pass the Assembly despite a strong campaign by Governor Clinton, who mobilized good-government groups and public opinion behind the proposal.

With the political climate responsive to reform, an initiated act sponsored by Common Cause defining and regulating relations between government and lobbyists passed with 62 percent of the vote in the 1988 general election. Spurred on by this success, Common Cause in coalition with other good-government groups passed a law, Act 719, in the 1989 Assembly requiring the public disclosure of groups organized to oppose or support initiated or referred ballot questions. The effect of this law is to make invisible campaigns against ballot measures—particularly progressive ones—much more difficult, because the public will be able to identify a campaign with the interests sponsoring it.

In the summer of 1989 a good-government coalition consisting of Common Cause, the League of Women Voters, the Arkansas Association of Retired People, Arkansas Impact (church groups), and several progressive legislators began to hold hearings throughout the state in preparation for an initiated act on campaign reform. Calling themselves the Campaign Ethics Committee, they succeeded in obtaining the more than 55,000 signatures needed to place the act on the 1990 general election ballot. The ballot measure passed in the November 1990 general election.

The new climate for ethics is having a strong effect on the Arkansas interest group system. The act initiated in 1988 and its 1989 amendments require lobbyists to report any expense over $25 and any gift over $100 incurred or given while the lobbyist is engaged in lobbying. Special-event expenses for public officials must also be reported aggregately by date, and there are provisions requiring public officials to report sources of income and any possible conflict of interest when a board on which they sit is regulated by the state or does business with the state. The 1990 campaign-reform act reduced the amount of money individuals can contribute to a campaign from $1,500 to $1,000 and limited the amount of money a PAC can receive from any source to $200 annually. In addition, after the election candidates have to relinquish any unspent funds raised during the campaign, either by paying them into the state treasury or by returning contributions to the sources from which they received them.

It is clear from these reforms that public officials and lobbyists no longer work in a political market unimpeded by regulation. Indeed, the reforms have irked many legislators who have criticized them for their red tape and their incursions into what they perceive as private business. They have argued that the new regulations will cloak public service with a blanket of suspicion, causing officials and those contemplating a political career to spurn public service. Whatever the perception, the new legislation makes it easier for the media and public watchdog organizations to follow the paper trails of public officials and lobbyists. And it may encourage more challenges to incumbents who have long championed established interests, as well as inject more pluralism and parity into Arkansas' interest group system.

Interest Group Power

Interest groups are especially powerful in Arkansas because they dominate functions that in some states are performed by political parties. Groups help finance political campaigns, provide campaign volunteers, channel information to their advocates in the Assembly, and even provide "private patronage" for the constituents of supportive legislators. In 1949 Key saw Arkansas as having a "friends-and-neighbors" style within its one-party system, an observation equally true today.[13] This is a system well suited to the entrenched economic interests whose lobbyists capitalize on their personal contacts and friendships with political elites.

Weak parties have meant strong interest groups in Arkansas.[14] Both state party organizations are forbidden by their rules to endorse or support any candidate in primaries or runoffs, which forces candidates (including the unofficial party favorites) to distance themselves from the party and to seek support from groups not bound by the pledge of neutrality.[15] The state Democratic party, located in the capital city, the best-heeled and largest party organization in Arkansas, is limited by law to a $2,500 contribution per candidate in an election and is often able to field only a handful of campaign workers. Operating under these limitations, it is not able to exercise much influence over party candidates. In contrast, the Arkansas Education Association (AEA) has provided phone-bank volunteers in all seventy-five counties to help get out the vote. It is common during the campaign season to see AEA leaders strolling to the campaign headquarters of an anointed politician for a strategy meeting. Similarly, while Arkansas' Republican party must often advertise in its party newspaper to drum up candidates, business interests help fill the vacuum by playing a strong role in recruiting candidates, as they did in 1980 when the Republican candidate for governor, a bank executive, was encouraged to run by promises of financial support.

State legislators and registered lobbyists are among those best positioned to judge which groups are the most powerful within this strong interest group system.[16] We have ranked each interest group by the number of legislators and lobbyists who nominated it as among "the most powerful lobbies in Arkansas." The results support the perception of the systems' being heavily weighted toward entrenched economic and political interests. The utilities (67 nominations), the AEA and the banks (each with 36 nominations), the Farm Bureau (29), the state Highway Department (28), the Poultry Federation (26), the Chamber of Commerce (24), and railroads (21) were the eight most frequently mentioned groups. Labor, insurance, and lawyers' groups all received between ten and nineteen nominations. Groups receiving less than ten nominations were the Arkansas Medical Association, the timber industry, the Arkansas Association of Counties, nursing-home operators, and truckers.

AP&L is the most powerful lobby among the utility groups, and may well be the most powerful single lobby in Arkansas. In the 1987 General Assembly AP&L showed its muscle on at least three occasions. A bill to facilitate the acquisition of power plants by municipalities was opposed by AP&L and defeated. A bill to allow a state takeover of AP&L should its share of an idle out-of-state nuclear plant (Middle South Utility's Grand Gulf) reach $1 billion never emerged from committee. After the smoke had cleared, and despite public clamor, the utility received a substantial rate hike to pick up part of its costs from what had come to be known as the Grand Goof Fiasco. And AP&L lobbied what came to be known as the Scott Trotter bill through the Assembly to stall the career of its populist opponent, the head of Ratepayers Fight Back and executive director of Common Cause. This precisely tailored bill would have required any person running for attorney general to be a lawyer with at least six years' experience. Trotter had just graduated from law school. Governor Clinton eventually vetoed the measure, noting it would have disqualified two of the last three attorneys general, including himself, from running. Given the utilities' success as a regulated industry in a state with strong populist learnings, it is not surprising that they are judged most effective in protecting their interests.

During the 1980s legislators probably had more dealings with the second-ranked group, the AEA, than with any other. In the late 1970s the AEA brought before the Assembly an extensive legislative package dealing with fair dismissal and hearing procedures, a package that passed virtually intact. A survey of state legislators after the 1979/80 session found that the AEA was ranked the most powerful group in the state.[17] The tide shifted in 1982 when Bill Clinton regained the governorship on a platform of teacher and student testing for primary and secondary schools. His program required teachers to pass skills examinations in math and reading by 1987 or lose their certification. The AEA attacked the tests as insulting to the profession and invalid methodologically. Nonetheless, the program passed over their bitter objections. During the 1985 legislative session the AEA sought repeal of the teacher-testing law, proposing that evaluations be performed by educational professionals in the teachers' own schools. Its campaign was unsuccessful. Despite this, AEA's ubiquitousness—its headquarters are only a hundred yards from the Capitol, its membership base is statewide, and its issues highly visible—maintained the association's powerful reputation among legislators and lobbyists.

Banks are powerful lobbies in Arkansas because they have the financial resources to advocate forcefully and persistently, as demonstrated by their prolonged campaign to amend the 10 percent usury provision in the state constitution. For decades the limit has given banks and financial institutions ample loan flexibility, but the advent of double-digit inflation caused capital to flow from Arkansas banks into states with higher interest rates. Squeezed between the high cost of new money and the usury limitation, they made several unsuccessful and unpopular attempts to amend this provision during the 1970s.[18] At their low point in 1974 they were defeated by a six-to-one margin in a general referendum. In 1982 the banks finally found a successful advertising strategy, which emphasized job creation. While the connection between raising the usury limit and jobs was never precisely explained, they carried the day when a constitutional amendment passed to raise consumer rates to a maximum of 17 percent and allow business loans to float with the federal discount rate. Financial institutions in Arkansas also have been involved in candidate recruitment. Stephens Brothers, the largest investment banking firm off Wall Street, run by two political kingmakers, Jack and Witt Stephens, has offered candidates financial support to run and financial security should they lose.

The fourth-ranked Farm Bureau was formed in 1934 to represent then-unrepresented farmers, and has drawn much of its strength from its grass-roots organization in the counties, which can quickly mobilize their constituencies. When rumors circulated in Little

Rock that legislators might repeal the sales-tax exemption on farm machinery, the county farm bureaus stopped the idea dead in its tracks. As one lobbyist observed, the most visible example of the Farm Bureau's power is that there is no state department of agriculture—the implication being that policy is made at the bureau.

The Highway Department may be the most powerful governmental lobby in Arkansas with the exception of the governor. Like the Farm Bureau, it has a rural constituency, concerned about the upkeep of 61,500 miles of country roads. The department is a favorite of legislators whose constituents—farmers, truckers, and poultry companies—depend on a good road system for their livelihood. The department's governing authority, the Highway Commission, has the constitutional autonomy to make policy with a minimum of interference from the legislative and executive branches. Highway commissioners, although appointed by the governor, serve ten-year terms and are responsible for selecting the executive director of the commission. The executive director, while theoretically accountable to the commission, has in reality been the most influential person in the Highway Department and one of the most powerful men in the state, in part because of his friendship with senior legislators. This combination of constituency support, constitutional independence, insulation from the daily wear and tear of executive-legislative politics, and the cult of personality has made the Highway Department a powerful player in Arkansas' political system.

The interest groups that lobbyists and legislators left off their lists are as interesting as those they included because these unmentioned groups reflect the great disparities of income and power within the state. The less visible, less powerful, or underrepresented interests include groups such as the NAACP and ACORN, which represent persons who lack economic resources and social status. Also missing are groups such as those involved in the ERA campaign, whose concrete legislative goals have been more transitory than the aims of the banks and utilities.[19]

No good-government or populist groups are mentioned as significant players in the system. The League of Women Voters, which may play a more active role in local than state politics, was mentioned by only one lobbyist and not at all by legislators. Common Cause, which maintains a chapter of eight hundred members in the state, received no mentions, but our survey took place before its success in getting ethics legislation written into law. ACORN, a regional umbrella organization for lower-income community groups started in Little Rock in the late 1960s, received only two mentions from lobbyists and none from legislators. Even so, ACORN has developed considerable visibility in Arkansas, and now boasts a membership of several thousand and its own radio station. No civil rights or civil liberties organizations were mentioned. Neither the Urban League (about 2,000 members), the NAACP (7,500–10,000 members statewide), nor the ACLU (about 800 members statewide) appears on the list, which is indicative of their lack of clout in the legislative system. The NAACP's absence is indeed ironic, for no group in this century has had a greater impact on southern and Arkansas politics. Through its strategy of litigation, the NAACP, operating through its national office and its state affiliates, has restructured the patterns of daily life in the South.

Religious groups are also considered less powerful than economic groups, even though a high percentage of Arkansans (57%) consider themselves member of Christian churches.[20] Religious groups have a history of political mobilization when they believe specific issues threaten their economic interests or value systems. In 1983 a bill requiring the inspection of religious day-care centers by the state was fiercely opposed by the churches. They bused their congregations into Little Rock to lobby legislators and demonstrate at the Capitol. The bill ultimately passed, but in a considerably weakened form. In 1986 church groups were again active, this time in support of an antiabortion amendment that would have made it state policy to protect unborn life. Religious groups obtained more than 80,000 signatures (10% of the vote in the preceding gubernatorial election) to place the amendment on the ballot. The amendment lost by the narrowest of margins—by only five hundred of the 636,520 votes cast. This church campaign combined the well-tested populist techniques of the initiative and referendum with sophisticated modern tools such as voter targeting and professional advertising. These techniques paid off in the 1988 general election when a similarly worded amendment was adopted 398,107 to 368,117. A year earlier the Baptist churches were able to dilute a bill that would have extended the horse-racing season by including a fall meet. The success of that campaign, which emphasized letter writing and demonstrations, illustrates that church groups with active grass-roots organizations are difficult to resist, even though they may not be seen as powerful by legislators and lobbyists, who are more favorably disposed to status quo groups that play an insider's game.

Legislators and lobbyists were also asked whether they believed that the power of each major group has been increasing, decreasing, or remained the same. For each group, the percentage of respondents who believed its power was decreasing was subtracted from the percentage who believed its power was increasing. The result is an index that reflects the consensus of opinion on whether power has shifted toward or away from each group (see Table 8.5). Those groups that are already distinguished by their central role in Arkansas' economic and political structure are reputed to be increasing their power. Business and corporate groups, the utilities, banks and financial institutions control much of Arkansas' wealth and occupy the center of its economic life. Even though they are intermittently under siege by populist citizens' groups, corporate control over the state's natural resources, over its capital, its jobs, and the production of energy, makes them a formidable force. AP&L and ARKLA, for example, are constantly under attack, but they have weathered every storm and seem always to emerge a little ahead of where they were before. The new emphasis on economic development, which has fostered efforts to develop partnerships between government and business, has reinforced attitudes among Arkansas' political leaders that strong working relationships with corporate groups are essential.

A second group of interests whose collective power is thought to be rising is the state governmental players. The governor and the Highway Commission are viewed as increasingly powerful, perhaps because their governmental authority places them in close working relationships with other elites. Bill Clinton has been the state's governor, or Democratic candidate for governor, since 1978. His long tenure in office has allowed him to devise effective legislative programs and appoint majorities to virtually every state regulatory board and commission. The Highway Commission continues to be powerful because it puts contracts on state roads up for bids; this means jobs for businesses, and road improvements for legislators to tout to their constituents.

Table 8.5 Index of Shifts in Power of Interest Groups as Perceived by
Legislators and Lobbyists

	Increase or Decrease
Executive branch	+59
Business and corporate groups	+53
Highway Commission	+47
Utilities	+41
Banks and financial institutions	+41
ARKLA	+28
Insurance groups	+25
AP&L	+21
State employees	+25
Arkansas Bar Association	+14
Farm organizations	+12
Timber industry	+10
Arkansas Medical Association	+ 7
Good-government groups	0
County governments	0
Municipal governments	- 1
Antiabortion groups	- 4
Environmental groups	-19
Railroads	-23
AEA	-46
Feminist groups	-50
ACORN	-58
ACLU	-60
Labor	-66

Falling in the middle of the index are groups whose power has
remained stable or has increased or decreased moderately. These organizations include the timber industry, good-government groups
generally, county and local governments, truckers, farm organizations, antiabortion groups, doctors, and lawyers. Finding farmers
and prolife advocates among these groups is surprising given the im-

portance of agriculture to the state's economy and the visibility of the prolife issue. But this can be explained by the changing economic agenda in Arkansas and the way that groups advocating a single issue are viewed by politicos. Farmers in Arkansas and the nation endured difficult times in the 1980s and seemed unable to effect a remedy from the government. Therefore, the Arkansas Farm Bureau, a normally powerful group with a strong grass-roots constituency, is perceived as declining. At the same time the stable rating of antiabortion groups is a consequence of the controversial nature of the abortion issue and the confrontational tactics of those groups involved in it.

The lower third of the index is occupied by organizations believed to be losing power dramatically. Some of these groups have lost power because of national economic and political trends. Labor, for example, has always had an active lobby in the Capitol despite the fact that a "right-to-work" law is enshrined in the state constitution. In studies conducted in 1967 and 1978–1980, legislators rated labor as one of two most influential lobbies in the Capitol; while business interests were evaluated as prominent but not dominant.[21] But times and political agendas change. The strong antiunion stance of Republican administrations coupled with tough economic times for industries with large union memberships have weakened labor substantially, a condition captured by the rock-bottom position accorded to it by our respondents.[22] Railroads are another previously powerful interest that has lost power because of national economic and political trends, including cheaper gasoline and deregulation of competing airlines and truckers.

The rankings in Table 8.5 speak directly to the inherent inequality of the interest group system. Labor's loss in status is reflected in a rise in the power of business and financial groups. The AEA's steep fall is complemented by the increasing power of the governor, who undermined its reputation by passing the teacher-testing law over its intense opposition. But groups that achieve greater influence at the expense of others may suffer the same consequences if they are unable to live up to the power perceptions accorded them. According to interviews with members of the 1989 General Assembly, the governor's influence has declined significantly because of his inability to pass progressive tax-reform legislation over the strong opposition of business and corporate groups.[23] These data also support the conclusion, evident from Table 8.5, that the organizations that are consistently powerful in Arkansas' interest group system are those with the resources to employ skilled, sometimes slick, insider lobbyists who utilize face-to-face lobbying styles based on informal contacts with decision makers, while groups like ACORN and the ACLU, which are outside this network, are thought to be losing power, even though they began with very little.

Conclusion

Interest groups in Arkansas work within a fragmented political system characterized by weak parties and multiple centers of power.[24] Powerful individuals in the public and private sectors, such as the governor, the Stephens brothers, senior legislators, and influential businessmen, dominate the system through their ability to influence the state's economy and to make deals with other decision makers. But the power of these interests is put to the test by Arkansas' love for populist politics. The banks long labored under a 10 percent usury limit, which they found difficult to dislodge from the state constitution. The utilities are under constant attack by ratepayers and the politicians who take up their cause. Liberals in bib overalls, such as Dale Bumpers, are elected to public office alongside such more-conservative populists as Orval Faubus and Congressman Tommy Robinson. This is a system of partially countervailing power, in which the rich and powerful are sometimes defeated by seemingly weaker interests, by "a little girl and country legislator," as the head of one powerful group lamented after his struggle over midwifery.

In Arkansas there are effectively two worlds within which interest groups move. The first is the world of the utility, the corporation, the trade group, the bank, and the union, where one or more paid lobbyists provide professional representation and operate as insiders within the system. In this world the preferred tactics are a personal chat with the legislator, a campaign contribution, and a lobbying effort largely unconnected with the group's mass membership. It is a world in which the familiar players with quality access almost always win. Yet it is also one in which powerful groups suddenly find themselves in positions of weakness, as the AEA did on the teacher-testing issue, and as a newly reelected governor did when he pushed a 0.25 percent increase in the sales tax.

The second world is that of the public-interest lobby, the feminist, religious, or civil rights group, the organization that operates through its membership in letter-writing campaigns, press conferences, political protests, high-intensity presentations, and the gritty grass-roots work of collecting signatures to place an initiated act before the people. This is the world of populist and activist politics and one of protest techniques that are disdained by insiders. But these groups must sometimes be reckoned with because they are capable of capturing the moment and rallying public sentiment. And while they may not win most of the time, they do win some of the time, and provide a measure of balance to a system dominated by well-entrenched interests in which familiarity with political decision makers is the key to access and influence.

PART II

THE DEEP SOUTH

9

SOUTH CAROLINA

THE RISE OF THE NEW SOUTH

Robert E. Botsch

In South Carolina, in the 1990s, nearly all politics is interest group politics. If anything, the role of interest groups is even stronger in a polity that has long been considered a strong interest group state. However, the dominant interests in state politics are in a process of transition in South Carolina, where the New South forces of industrialization and economic development are winning against more-traditional powers. The wheeler-dealer tactics used by some groups have given way to more-professional modes of behavior. Scandal is hastening this change. In the summer of 1990 a Federal Bureau of Investigation (FBI) sting operation uncovered widespread vote buying in the General Assembly. This negative national attention focused a spotlight on a whole range of unethical relationships between interests and state government. Reforms are sure to come. But they may alter behavioral styles without diminishing the rising power of the more modern and sophisticated interests.

When Key looked at politics in South Carolina just after World War II, he saw the epitome of the ills of one-party politics and multifactionalism. All serious class-based political questions were crushed under the weight of racial politics. The end result was issueless politics revolving around ever-changing personalities and factions that had no realistic programs to address the state's severe economic and social problems. This clearly favored those who benefited from a cheap and docile labor force, both in the fields and in the mills.[1] The organization of political power in South Carolina reinforced the protection of the status quo. The few formal powers given to the governor made that office one of the weakest in the nation and rendered its occupant impotent to bring about any significant change, even on those rare instances when governors were inclined to want to do so. The Assembly dominated the state, and the rural eastern low-country areas dominated the Assembly. Local low-country white elites found it relatively easy to send their own kind back to the legislature year after year because most of the low-country population, the blacks, were excluded from political participation.

What Key called "banker-planter-lawyer-bourbon rings," or coalitions of these low-country elites, not only ran the state through their seniority and numbers in the Assembly, but they also ran local politics.[2] Virtually every county expenditure had to be approved by the legislature. These local bills and the yearly "supply bill," that was in effect the county budget, could be passed only if they had the support of the county delegation, which was led by the single senator who represented each county. Thus, the real barons, in what could be described as an almost feudal system of counties, were the senators.[3]

The best-known and enduring of these coalitions was called the Barnwell Ring, because most of its leaders came from rural low-country Barnwell County.[4] In an oral interview in 1982 Sol Blatt, the last surviving member of the Barnwell Ring, described the political philosophy that held the group together and determined the state's social programs—a philosophy that gave only lip service to South Carolina's enormous human needs: "The good thing about that combination was that we believed in good government, good, stable government, and a balanced budget. So far as state-wide measures were concerned, we fit in the key to accomplish that purpose of government, which is to serve its people at the least dollars that could be spent."[5]

Textiles, South Carolina's other powerful interest, was based in the up-country, where there was swiftly moving water to provide power, and failing small farms to provide a large, willing white work force. Up-country interests often opposed low-country interests on questions of patronage, state construction projects, moral issues such as liquor referenda, and gubernatorial selection in the Democratic primary (reflecting sectional pride). However, elites from both sections formed alliances on class-based economic issues such as labor legislation.[6]

Those who reexamined South Carolina in the 1960s and 1970s found both continuity and change.[7] The governor was still relatively weak. The powerful legislature was still dominated by rural barons who were quite conservative. Textile interests used their power to discourage new industries' coming into the state, which might raise pay scales and possibly bring in labor unions.[8] The rural-textiles alliance promoted only those programs that supported its narrow self-interests.[9] The alliance generally opposed increased expenditures for education, or supported only modest new programs. It made sure that South Carolina's taxes remained comparatively low, and that costs of kindergartens and technical schools fell mainly on the poor in the form of sales taxes.[10]

But the 1970s also saw the beginning of change—the enactment of some mildly progressive yet significant social programs. Political leaders in the Assembly and executive branch were able to act a little less conservatively for two reasons. Extremely conservative cotton-based agricultural interests were declining, and economic diversification was beginning to erode the power of textiles.[11]

These changes were related to two other forces of change: the end of one-party politics; and the inclusion of blacks in state politics.[12] The emerging Republican party appealed to lower-class whites who refused to share the Democratic party with blacks. The GOP also appealed to extremely conservative business leaders and to industrial newcomers who carried with them a Republican identification along with fiscal conservatism and moderate social progressivism. Democrats appealed to the remaining white working classes, blacks, local officials who had long-standing patronage ties to the party, the small community of white academics and liberals, the weak labor movement, and more-progressive development-oriented business interests.[13]

Both parties were organizationally weak, and neither advocated any dramatic policy shifts. They posed no challenge to the interests that were powerful. Although the Barnwell Ring was passing from the scene, the most significant interests were still those noted by

Key—rural low-country planters, bankers, and lawyers, along with textile interests.[14] At the same time a host of new interests were emerging, and some older ones were changing their orientation. Utilities, rapidly expanding to meet the power requirements of a developing economy, built close political ties to the still dominant state Senate.[15] Interests associated with tourism and resort development were beginning to have an impact at the state level. They sometimes came into conflict with industrial development interests. For example, on Hilton Head Island the developers joined environmental groups and local fishermen to stop the building of an industrial chemical plant on the coast. They overcame the support the plant had from the governor and most of the rest of South Carolina's political establishment.[16]

This picture is essentially the same as that given by Morehouse, who listed South Carolina as a strong interest group state with the dominant interests being planters, textiles, a utility, and banks. Her data sources were also from the 1970s.[17]

An overview of state politics as we move into the last decade of the century reveals some continuity, but more change along the lines noted by those who looked at South Carolina in the 1970s. The flavor of the state's politics is still conservative, and power is perhaps even more fragmented. But political power is certainly no longer rural-based, and it is much less local in its orientation. The planters and traditional agricultural interests have almost completely passed from the political scene. Moreover, the economic decline of textiles that was first noted in the 1960s has accelerated and is reflected in the decline of the industry's relative political power.[18]

Court decisions of the 1960s on reapportionment have slowly led to the end of rural domination in the Assembly. The decisions eroded the concept of local rule by county delegations, as district lines no longer conformed to county lines. Counties and cities were granted limited home rule that has been slowly expanding as they organize themselves politically to press for more local autonomy and power.

Party competition increased throughout the 1980s to the point where the Republican governor and Republican legislators (one-third of the Assembly in 1990) are worrying about intraparty communication and unity. However, geographical patterns of competition relegate electoral competition to smaller towns and working-class suburbs. Democrats dominate rural areas and central cities, and Republicans dominate the growing, affluent suburbs. Levels of partisan competition and organization are still not strong enough to replace interests as South Carolina's most significant political-structuring factor. Lamis notes that who the business community supports for governor is more important than party in deciding who will win.[19]

Executive power was increased by allowing a gubernatorial second term as of 1982. Nevertheless, the governor's institutional powers are still too weak to compete effectively with interests, many of which have built symbiotic relationships with the Assembly and the semiautonomous boards and agencies that cover South Carolina's governmental landscape.

In sum, the passing of the planters and the weakening of traditional interests have resulted in the creation of a power vacuum in which interest group politics seems to provide the only viable means of structure. Until political parties become strong enough to provide an alternative force for political aggregation, this will likely remain the central theme of South Carolina politics.

Interests and Groups Active in the Palmetto State

A very wide range of interests and interest groups are active in South Carolina politics. We will focus mainly on those specific groups that are more important, although there are dozens of less-notable and much less powerful groups, such as the Retail Fireworks Dealers Association and the Podiatry Association.

The dominant flavor of interest group politics and South Carolina politics is business. By every measure employed, interests within the business lobby are quite powerful. Manufacturing interests are the most important economically, although they lost ground to service interests throughout the 1980s. In 1986 South Carolina was the second most industrialized state in the nation, following just behind North Carolina, with almost one in four jobs in the manufacturing sector.[20]

Within manufacturing interests, the textiles industry is still by far the most important, with about 40 percent of all industrial employment. No other single industry claims more than 10 percent of the industrial work force.[21] One of the most important and politically active textile firms is Milliken and Company, headed by Roger Milliken, a very conservative businessman who has been financially quite generous to Republican candidates. His is the largest single privately owned business in the state, with annual sales of over $1 billion.[22]

However, the relative importance of both manufacturing and textiles is diminishing. During the 1970s and 1980s manufacturing employment was growing at a much slower pace than wholesale/retail trade. By the late 1980s employment between the two sectors differed by only a few percentage points. At the same time textile jobs were leaving the state by the thousands each year.[23] In the first half of 1990 South Carolina lost over three thousand jobs in textiles and in the closely associated apparel industry.[24] The voice of textile interests can no longer drown out all other voices that are straining to be heard within a more diversified business sector.

The state's changing economy has brought about significant changes in the economic character and political power of two other politically powerful interests, banks and utilities. During the 1980s the assets of banks in the state grew faster than the national average, while the number of banks headquartered in South Carolina actually dropped, a reflection of mergers across state lines.[25] Employment in the financial sector nearly doubled its share of the state's jobs between 1960 and the late 1980s.[26] From an interest group perspective, this means that banks carry relatively more clout and are less likely to be controlled by local elites.

South Carolina's utilities have long been politically active and are also growing in economic importance as the state develops. Among the utilities are South Carolina Electric and Gas, Carolina Power and Light, Duke Power, the Public Service Authority (popularly known as Santee Cooper, South Carolina's version of the TVA), and a very politically active electric cooperative system. Of particular importance here is the strong nuclear orientation in the utility industry. A third of the state's electricity is nuclear-generated (as compared to about 10% nationally).[27] Utilities can also be expected to be more supportive of industrial development today than in the past, when they were so closely tied to antidevelopment rural and textile interests.

The fast-growing tourist industry is also becoming a significant part of the economy. It accounts for nearly 6 percent of South Carolina's employment, a higher percentage than in any neighboring state.[28] Organized interest groups associated with tourism include the Hotel and Motel Association, the Restaurant Association, several beverage groups, and many developers and resorts.

The conflict between resort developers and industrial developers that began in the 1960s continues into the 1990s. Resort developers have opposed industrial location in coastal areas because it undermines the image they are trying to project and raises the cost of labor. Recently the resort industry has been criticized as creating a new plantation system in the coastal region. Poor blacks are employed in low-wage service jobs as maids and grounds keepers. They are driven inland as resorts and retirement communities buy land and drive up property taxes to provide services to wealthy retirees. With no alternative employment opportunities, these people live in economic apartheid. They ride buses for hours to reach their menial jobs, passing through the guarded gates of resort communities with names like Sea Pines Plantation.[29]

Other important business interests include insurance, consumer loan companies, retail merchants, transportation (including railroads and the trucking industry as well as auto dealers), industrial waste–disposal firms (such as Chem-Nuclear, which is fighting an ongoing battle to retain its rights to bury low-level nuclear wastes in the state), and the Chamber of Commerce. Although these other business interests do not get all they want from the Assembly, they usually succeed in defensive actions; for example, railroads prevented passage of legislation that would have forced them to pay for safer railroad crossings.

As business retains its power, many of the interests within the health-care lobby have become more politically active. Nursing homes, along with many other health-care groups such as the Mental Health Association, are often organized around state regulatory agencies. The South Carolina Medical Association increased its political activities at the state level, attempting to reduce the cost of malpractice insurance through tort reform, a battle that brought it head to head with the lawyers. Chiropractors have been struggling to gain equal recognition as valid providers of health care.

The structure of government brings governmental groups onto the lobbying scene. South Carolina's executive branch is best described as highly decentralized and fragmented. All ten major executive officers are elected independently of each other. In addition, the initial state budget is drawn up by an entity called the Budget and Control Board, on which the governor has but one vote, just as do two other executive branch members and two legislative leaders. Moreover, the governor shares with the Assembly powers of appointment to regulatory boards and commissions. All this invites each department and agency to participate in a free-for-all in lobbying for its budget.

There are many important groups that are organized around the more than two hundred semiautonomous regulatory boards and commissions listed in the *1989 South Carolina Legislative Manual*. One of the more important is the South Carolina Bar, which has associated with it the Trial Lawyers Association and the PAC formed by lawyers in the state.

Many less significant groups are also active, such as barbers and beauticians. When South Carolina considered abolishing or combining the two boards that regulate the licensing of barbers and cosmetologists, both boards were able quickly to mount a campaign to block the proposal. They were helped by the two groups they were presumably regulating.[30]

Municipal and county governments are formally organized into the South Carolina Municipal Association and the South Carolina Association of Counties. The South Carolina School Boards Association played a very active role in pushing for the Educational Improvement Act, the state's most significant effort to increase school funding. South Carolina's nearly three hundred special-purpose districts are politically organized and have been highly effective in preventing more–general purpose governments from reducing their powers.

Another important set of government interests concerns higher education, an interest that is riddled with turf and funding battles. The groups here include two major universities—the University of

South Carolina (USC, a system of nine semiindependent campuses) and Clemson (which unsuccessfully fought the establishment of a second engineering school on USC's Columbia campus)—the Medical University of South Carolina in Charleston (which unsuccessfully opposed the establishment of a second medical school on USC's Columbia campus), six nonsystem public colleges and universities, the governing boards for each of these, the State Commission on Higher Education (which at least in theory provides enlightened coherence to all these institutions), technical colleges, and the State Board for Technical and Comprehensive Education (which outlobbied the universities in getting two-year associate-degree programs approved, sometimes at campuses within a few miles of existing two- and four-year state universities).

Agricultural interests are declining. Whether we are talking about small up-country dirt farmers, who were once rallied by populist governors, or elite low-country planters, who withstood those challenges, agriculture must be placed near the bottom of the list of currently powerful interests in South Carolina. Agriculture's decline can be seen in both demographics and politics. In the early 1960s there were almost 90,000 farms in South Carolina.[31] By mid-1990 only 24,500 remained. Current estimates are that the number is declining at a rate of a thousand a year.[32]

The situation has eroded to the point that farmers feel they are unable to block legislation that undermines their most vital concerns. One farmer who was a legislative candidate complained that the "agriculture department is not standing up for the farmers. The Farm Bureau is not standing up for them. Even the rural caucus [in the legislature] is not standing up to be counted."[33]

The ethos of southern farmers may make it more difficult for them to function effectively in the modern political world. Explaining this declining influence, a county extension agent said that farmers are unable to agree on anything with each other or even with themselves. In one moment they blame the government for their woes and in the next they demand more government assistance. Farmers also have a sense of rugged individualism that creates a reluctance to give up any individual discretion to any organization, even if that organization is their only means for effective political action.[34]

Labor, too, suffers from fragmentation and a lack of cohesion. Together with North Carolina, South Carolina has about the least
unionized labor force in the nation. Only a little more than 5 percent of the private work force is organized. In the public sector a
little over 16 percent of state and local workers are unionized, compared to nearly 50 percent of all state and local workers nationally.
Within this relatively small group of organized workers, teachers are
probably the most significant group in terms of numbers; a third of
them are organized as the South Carolina Education Association.[35]
The association played a significant role in the successful 1984 drive
to bring teachers' salaries up to the southeastern average. Although
the Communications Workers of America and the AFL-CIO both
have registered lobbyists in the state, their importance is negligible.

A variety of environmental groups exist in the state, such as the
South Carolina Chapter of the National Audubon Society and the
Palmetto Alliance, an antinuclear group. But few, if any, are very
powerful. Perhaps the most noteworthy is the Energy Research
Foundation, a group funded mainly by Springs Mill textile heiress
Francis Close Hart. This group has targeted South Carolina's nuclear
industry and succeeded in helping to halt the construction of a nu-
clear reprocessing plant.[36]

Finally, a wide variety of ideologically oriented groups also exist in
South Carolina. However, few can be considered powerful. Among
them are the Legal Services Association, the League of Women
Voters, pro- and antiabortion groups, the Brown Lung Association,
the ACLU of South Carolina, the Carolina Alliance for Fair Employment, South Carolina Common Cause, and the state branch of the
NAACP, which is certainly the most important in this category.[37]

Interest Group Tactics

Interests and interest groups in South Carolina engage in the full
range of political tactics used elsewhere. Here we will consider several types of activity along with empirical evidence and examples to
illustrate how these activities relate to policy outcomes.

Campaign Activities

Interest groups are the single most dominant force in campaign financing of legislative elections in this strong legislative state (see Table 9.1). Interest groups of all varieties account for at least 30 percent of the money spent in House and Senate races. This is a very conservative estimate for two reasons: Much of the money counted as loans and never repaid could also be considered interest group money; and many contributions listed as coming from individuals in fact come from lobbyists and company heads. Unless the researcher knows all these people by name, the money cannot be separated from purely individual citizens' contributions. Moreover, as the FBI's 1990 sting operation revealed, lobbyists give legislators a significant amount of money in the form of cash, some of which is never reported.

If we consider just those who actually win legislative elections, we can see an even greater importance. In 1983/84, the last time all reported contributions were comprehensively analyzed, the average incumbent House member received 83 percent of his or her campaign expenditures from interest groups.[38] The average senator elected in 1984 received 36 percent of his or her campaign expenditures from interest groups. Put quite simply, interest groups give the bulk of their money to candidates who are likely to be successful—incumbents, Democrats, and strong challengers, in that order.[39]

If we look at the kinds of interests that are most important in campaign finance (see Table 9.2), we see a picture of business dominance within the interests represented. This reflects an economy that is diversifying and becoming more service-oriented. In both the House and Senate elections in these two years, the same interests cluster at the top of the table, and most are business groups. Banks, lawyers, real estate, auto and truck dealers, and utilities are among the leaders. Textiles is still among the leaders in campaign finance but is certainly no longer alone at the top.

Banks have emerged as the single most important contributor. Legislative candidates are not the only candidates in South Carolina that value the importance of banks. In the 1986 governor's race the supporters of Republican Carroll Campbell publicly rejoiced when they received the endorsement of "Hootie" Johnson, the chair of the

Table 9.1 Major Sources of Legislative Campaign Funds

	1981/82 House Campaigns		1983/84 Senate Campaigns	
	Amount (in Dollars)	Percentage	Amount (in Dollars)	Percentage
Candidates personal funds, small contributions, and loans	657,269	53.8	1,164,636	49.6
Business interest groups, PACs, and corporations	271,553	22.2	458,409	19.5
Large contributions from individual citizens	145,487	11.9	422,326	18.0
Health-care interests and professions	63,400	5.2	88,534	3.8
Party organizations	31,071	2.5	60,456	2.6
Professional organizations (e.g., lawyers)	19,950	1.6	64,300	2.7
Large contributions from relatives and family	17,080	1.4	41,979	1.8
Ideological interests and PACs	11,332	0.9	31,478	1.3
Labor interests and PACs	4,150	0.3	10,250	0.4
Agricultural interests	500	0.04	2,850	0.12
Total	1,221,992	99.8	2,345,217	99.8

Source: Candidate-expenditure reports filed with the South Carolina House and Senate Ethics Committees.

Note: Unlike in most other states and at the national level, in South Carolina there is no prohibition of direct political contributions by corporations and labor groups. Therefore, interest group contributions include money from interest groups themselves, PACs, and also directly from businesses, corporations, and labor groups. PACs are also not required to use a title that describes the nature of their interest. All this makes the accounting process very difficult.

Table 9.2 Largest Interest Group Contributors in South Carolina Legislative Elections

	1982 House Elections			1984 Senate Elections	
	Amount (in Dollars)	Category		Amount (in Dollars)	Category
Banks	39,250	Business	Lawyers	62,600	Professional
Utilities[a]	30,200	Business	Banks	58,475	Business
Textiles	27,000	Business	Real estate	36,865	Business
Real estate	21,900	Business	Textiles	35,886	Business
Auto and truck dealers	20,750	Business	Auto and truck dealers	31,950	Business
Doctors	20,125	Health	Hospitals	31,109	Health
Lawyers	18,250	Professional	Utilities[a]	30,950	Business
Insurance	17,150	Business	Doctors	27,300	Health
Hospitals	17,100	Health	Advertising and public-relations firms	20,220	Business
Gas and oil distributors	12,175	Business	Optometrists	17,100	Health
Savings and loan	10,300	Business	Insurance	16,625	Business
Construction	9,525	Business	Trucking companies	15,700	Business
Major oil companies	8,000	Business	Construction	12,050	Business
Liquor and beer distributors	7,900	Business	Major oil companies	10,600	Business
Dentists	7,800	Health	Forest and paper	10,200	Business

[a] Does not include telephone companies.

Source: Candidate expenditure reports filed with the South Carolina House and Serate Ethics Committees.

board of one of the state's largest banks. Disappointed Democrats responded by announcing names of their own supporters within the banking community, describing one as "not having as high a profile as Hootie Johnson, but he's got a bigger bank."[40]

Health-care professions have also emerged as an important category of interests in campaign finance. These professions have come under government regulation; and the rise in health-care costs has increased public concerns and money available for political use. As a result, these professions, along with private for-profit hospitals that are springing up all over the state, have begun to organize themselves for political action. As part of its battle for tort reform, the South Carolina Medical Association (SCMA) announced plans to target contributions carefully. The SCMA president said that "we are really keeping a tally sheet on our legislators. If they are voting for us or against us, we know about it. If they are taking a walk, we know about it."[41]

The most important revelation of Table 9.2's data may be who is not represented. The traditional opponent of business, organized labor, is almost entirely out of the picture. Other than textiles, there was no manufacturing interest that was prominent enough to stand out alone. Newer, narrow ideological interests may have generated a great deal of press nationally, but they have not made a significant dent in legislative campaign financing in South Carolina. Perhaps the most significant omission from the top contributing interests is agriculture.

Legislative Lobbying

In 1974 the law regarding registration of lobbyists was amended to strengthen reporting requirements. Ironically, the amendments were signed by then–Speaker of the House Rex Carter, who later became one of the most powerful lobbyists in the state. The law requires lobbyists to register with the secretary of state's office and file a yearly spending report showing the money disbursed in trying to influence legislation, broken down into broad categories such as lodging, food, entertainment, postage, and salary.

These requirements are quite weak and have not been enforced.

For years Common Cause of South Carolina campaigned—rather unsuccessfully—to strengthen these rules. Common Cause wants to require that lobbyists disclose the source of their income, itemize expenditures in more detail, and identify the recipients; to require that state agencies file reports on their lobbying expenses and activities; to increase penalties for violations; and to centralize responsibility for enforcement and record keeping. With the 1990 FBI sting operation that caught a number of legislators accepting cash gifts from lobbyists in exchange for promised votes, it is likely that a first order of business will be to tighten requirements in 1991.

Spending totals (shown in Table 9.3) indicate that lobbying is a growth industry in South Carolina, although the average lobbyist is still likely to work only part-time. However, professionals who work as contract lobbyists are becoming much more common. In 1989 the top four lobbyists in terms of salaries (all over $100,000) were all

Table 9.3 Number of Registered Lobbyists in South Carolina in Selected Years, 1974–1989

	Number Registered	Reported Expenditures (in Dollars)	Expenditures per Lobbyist (in Dollars)
1974	121	135,000	1,116
1984	255	976,385	3,828
1985[a]	299	1,481,378	4,954
1986	316	1,575,198	4,985
1989	290[b]	3,800,000	13,103

[a] Part of the increase from 1984 to 1985 may be due to a state attorney general's opinion that lobbyists should include in expenditures their salaries received for lobbying. However, state officials were still reporting in 1986 that not all lobbyists are reporting all expenses or all salaries. See David F. Kern, "Tort Reform Effort Tops Lobbying Tab," *The State*, July 29, 1986, 1, 18-A.

[b] The number of lobbyists and their reported spending are given as approximations. See Cindi Ross Scoppe, "Give and Take at the State House," *The State*, August 12, 1990, 1, 6-A.

Source: Reports filed with the South Carolina Secretary of State.

contract lobbyists who worked for a total of over fifty different clients.[42]

If we look at lobbyist spending on legislative entertainment in 1990, we see a pattern that is consistent with a diversifying set of interests and groups. While textiles was in first place (spending more than $37,000), the next five were the South Carolina Chamber of Commerce, a waste-disposal firm, the South Carolina Beer Association, Michelin Tire Corporation, and the Association of Realtors.[43]

The behavior patterns of lobbyists fit two dramatically different styles, the wheeler-dealer style and the professional provider of information. Wheeler-dealers are reported to have engaged in practices ranging from the usual dinners and cocktail parties to running open tabs for legislators at night clubs, loaning credit cards for trips, and offering money for votes.[44] Some unethical legislators have exploited the situation by threatening to hold bills hostage until they get campaign contributions, or by purposely introducing bills that are harmful to a group and withdrawing them after a contribution is made.[45]

Legislators benefit from attending social functions sponsored by interest groups because of the information lobbyists can provide. One House member we interviewed exclaimed that "I thought I could operate as a representative without going to those cocktail parties given by lobbyists. I finally attended one and learned when MY bill was scheduled for hearings—from a LOBBYIST!" With the publicity surrounding the uncovering of all these practices in 1990, it is likely that behaviors will be constrained by additional laws and common sense. However, lobbyists will continue to use their most powerful weapon, information. The most effective lobbyists already operate in this way. A prominent committee chair explained that lobbyists "do a lot of research and data-gathering that you can't do, which can be very beneficial." Jerry Beasley, lobbyist for the Textile Manufacturers Association, will continue to provide information. He just may not be able to invite the entire legislature to a beach resort for the weekend, as he has done in the past.[46]

One of the best ways to gain influence in the Assembly is through direct representation of members of an interest. A comparison of the occupational self-identifications of members of the legislature in the early 1970s with those of the late 1980s (as listed in the *Legislative Manuals*) reveals changes consistent with what we have already seen. In the early 1970s the Assembly was dominated by lawyers and businessmen, followed by planter/farmers (who were significant in terms of numbers and political positions, and alliances with other powerful rural low-country legislators). By 1990 one would have to revise that description, saying that the body is slightly more diversified, with businessmen being the most numerous, followed closely by lawyers and then by a fairly wide variety of small groups including educators, farmers, and a few who call themselves career legislators. The greatest relative decline is among farmers, who have lost about half of their representation.

Another way of attempting to measure the relative power of interests in lobbying the legislature is the reputational approach. The most recent (1982) study taking this approach surveyed all members of the South Carolina Assembly. They were asked a number of questions about their relationship with interests.[47] One of the more important questions was who they thought were the most powerful groups in the state. On Table 9.4 the frequency and percentage for each type of response is listed by major lobby, along with some of the more frequent particular interests and groups within each lobby. Although the diverse general business lobby is most frequently mentioned, utilities and banks are the single interests that are most often thought to be powerful. Textiles is no higher than third among the specific business interests mentioned by legislators. Labor, with the familiar exception of teachers, is again missing from the scene, and agriculture is almost relegated to the miscellaneous category.

Interest groups are so central to South Carolina's legislative process that they serve both as an important source of legislation and as significant actors in negotiating passage. For example, in 1986 the General Assembly passed a landlord-tenant act that was originally proposed at the urging of the South Carolina Legal Services Association. Opposition to the bill was formed around the South Carolina Association of Realtors. The compromises necessary for passage were worked out with a great deal of help from these two interest groups. An officer in the realtors' group described the process in terms that indicate the centrality of the groups' roles: "While land-

Table 9.4 Interests Perceived to be Powerful by South Carolina
Legislators

	Frequency		Percentage	
General business	115		33	
Chamber of Commerce		27		8
Textiles		25		7
Insurance		20		6
Transportation		11		3
Auto dealers		6		2
Financial	61		17	
Banks		42		12
Savings and loans		19		5
Utilities	49		14	
Government	38		11	
State agencies		19		5
State employees		11		3
Local governments		7		2
Education	37		11	
Higher education		26		7
Public school teachers		11		3
Miscellaneous	21		6	
ERA (pro and con)		11		3
Lawyers		3		1
Medical	18		5	
Farm	12		3	
Total	351		100	

Note: The response rate to the survey was 41.5 percent. Percentages are rounded to
the nearest one percent.

lords and tenants are clearly parties with adversary interests, each
side recognized early on that reform was needed. We began negotiations at an early stage to develop a statute that would be acceptable
to both sides."[48]

Given the chief executive's relatively weak constitutional powers and the weakness of party as an aggregating force in the Assembly, the governor must act as an effective lobbyist to be successful in gaining passage of legislative programs. Gov. Richard W. Riley, who retired at the end of his second term in January 1987, illustrated this point, providing a model of successful lobbying that gained him considerable national attention. His successful campaign to secure a one-cent sales tax increase for the purpose of better funding public education surprised many political observers. His other remarkable lobbying successes with the legislature and the public include the passage of a constitutional amendment allowing the governor to serve a second four-year term—from which Governor Riley directly benefited. He also successfully lobbied for several innovations in health-care services for the poor and elderly that the *New York Times* called "notable for the South."[49]

Lobbying the Administration

As in other states, lobbying the administrative branch is increasing in importance as government becomes more involved in regulation. For example, the South Carolina Chapter of the National Audubon Society began its push for more restrictions on beach construction with a presentation to members of the South Carolina Coastal Council. It included a slide show titled "Coastal Follies" demonstrating the negative results of existing policies.[50]

Litigation

Interest groups in South Carolina also utilize the courts, especially groups that are too weak to gain effective access to the legislative or administrative arena. The South Carolina Brown Lung Association made fairly effective use of both state and federal courts in bringing about changes in South Carolina's workers' compensation system so that it was easier for textile workers disabled by lung problems to file and collect claims.[51] However, more-powerful groups also use the courts. For example, the State Chamber of Commerce sued the General Assembly to stop the practice of "bobtailing" nonbudgetary riders to the state budget bill. This practice made it easier for the legislature to pass some controversial legislation that the chamber opposed, such as a 1985 bill that allowed State Employees Association members to have their organizational dues deducted from their paychecks.[52]

Grass-Roots Lobbying

Nearly all organized interests in South Carolina understand the importance of public relations and spend time and money in this area when they cannot realize their goals through quieter actions. A favorite public relations theme is to use the threat of lost jobs when attacking or defending state policies.

One of the most highly publicized and controversial public relations efforts of the 1980s was mounted by the State Chamber of Commerce in late 1985. The effort centered around an eleven-month study that was advertised as "what could be the most comprehensive audit of South Carolina's economy ever conducted."[53] Most of the comparisons made with five other states in the Southeast were not controversial. However, the three areas that were given most play in news conferences and following newspaper stories involved state taxes, the number of state employees, and the size of the state debt. The chamber's political agenda, as revealed by statements of its president, was to create an atmosphere to press for lowering commercial property taxes. Governor Riley responded with his own public relations campaign in which he charged that the statistics were biased and harmed South Carolina's "efforts to promote economic development."[54]

A second example involves a grass-roots citizens' group that employed primarily grass-roots techniques to achieve remarkable success in a relatively short period of time.[55] CAVE (Citizens Against Violent CrimE) was started in early 1984 by the father of a victim, who within two years had built an organization of 45,000 members. They were consulted in drafting major parts of the Omnibus Crime Bill of 1985, which was passed and which toughened penalties for violent crimes. CAVE also prompted successful letter-writing campaigns to the State Parole Board asking that specific inmates be denied parole.

Conclusion

The ultimate test of who is politically powerful in South Carolina rests on the substance of policy output. In the past, when the state was dominated by textiles and agricultural interests, that output could be characterized as fiscally conservative and antidevelopment. By 1990 it was becoming clear that while the climate is still fiscally conservative, the state has become decidedly prodevelopment, with a more modern industrial emphasis.

We can see two industrial subcultures locked in battle.[56] The older, traditional industrial interests that rely on cheap, docile labor are slowly dying. Nevertheless, they continue to slow programs that would educate and train South Carolina's work force. They oppose improvements in human-welfare services on the grounds of fiscal conservatism. They sometimes join with resort interests and environmentalists in policy networks to block new industry. The newer, more modern technical and industrial interests (including some textile companies that have gone high-tech) fit the description of Black and Black's "entrepreneurial individualists." They see the business of state government as promoting business.[57] They support more spending on education and training and even some social-welfare programs. They are winning because they are surviving economic change. An excellent example of how fast the Assembly can move to help industrial development took place in January 1986. In one day both houses of the legislature moved a bill through that gave Mack Trucks, Incorporated, an additional $3 million in state tax breaks to relocate a manufacturing plant into South Carolina.[58]

The emphasis on development is indirectly helping interests that have long held little power. Blacks have not been successful in lowering the Confederate battle flag from over the State House and have not won a statewide office. But by the late 1980s they had members in the Senate and had benefited from a variety of state programs aimed at targeting development in the rural areas where many blacks live.[59] They also have a new fair-housing law designed to spruce up the state's image in attracting new industry.

As South Carolina moves toward the year 2000, struggling to develop existing businesses and attract new ones, and as the economy becomes more diversified and more service-oriented, we can expect this trend toward increasing diversity among important interests to continue. With a moderate climate, a relatively low cost of living, and an already active tourist industry, we can expect the state to attract a larger retirement community from an aging national population. This will strengthen the resort sector and the other interests that provide services to the elderly, such as the health-care industry. Increased affluence will increase the base of support for preservationist and environmentalist groups. They will oppose almost all development that compromises South Carolina's natural landscape and small-town character that so many people find attractive. We can expect to see more conflicts among a wider variety of groups over the direction, location, and pace of development in the state.

In 1989 a coalition of relatively progressive and diverse businesses and industries formed an interest group called South Carolina 2000. Its policy agenda, which grew out of the Commission on the Future of South Carolina, placed a heavy emphasis on education, planned land use, protection of the environment, promotion of the arts, and centralizing government power to pursue those policies. This coalition has deliberately and wisely chosen an interest group strategy in this strong interest group state.

10

GEORGIA

BUSINESS AS USUAL

Eleanor C. Main, Lee Epstein, and Debra L. Elovich

"Consensus politics" describes the recent Georgia political scene.[1] General agreement on the rules of the game and the scope of government has developed from a political history filled with contradictions: the archetypical southern demagog Eugene Talmadge; the symbolic leader of the civil rights movement, Martin Luther King, Jr.; the tremendous political and social clout of the South's cultural capital, Atlanta; the state's unofficial nickname, Empire State of the South; and the rural poverty of the state's Black Belt counties. Georgia, like the images and pictures it evokes, is indeed a melange of differing political strains and interests. For many decades these differences, particularly those between urban and rural and between black and white, tended to dominate state politics. However, there has been a gradual, yet dramatic, shift from what V. O. Key described back in the late 1940s as the politics of "rustics."[2]

Organized interests do not operate in a vacuum. Groups seeking to influence the course of policy in Georgia are no exception. Two sets of environmental considerations are paramount: the state's sociopolitical culture; and the interactions among its political institutions.

Georgia's changing demographics and its active pursuit of modernization and economic development have spurred an alignment of interests. After years of conflict, urban and rural dwellers, blacks and whites often share the interests of the business elite. Formerly opposing coalitions now rally around a common goal: the economic well-being of the state. The growth of the economy gave impetus to the acceptance of the breakdown of the biracial society. Consensus politics developed as the "self-interest of the business elite merge[d] with blacks and working-class whites in the broad quest for modernization and economic development."[3] The business elite was quick to understand that protracted and bitter strife would hinder development. For these leaders, the "main concern . . . was neither white supremacy nor social equality, nor any other moral/ethical issue; it was economic well-being."[4] The primacy of economic development has led to the emergence of a "public ideology that stressed the role of state government in promoting economic growth."[5] An important correlate in the public ideology is the limited role of the state government in other areas. Although the state's role extends to creating a climate in which businesses can thrive, the scope of state government is ideally limited in other areas. Georgians "expect to get little from government and expect to pay little for what they do get. They also prefer the status quo to trying something new."[6]

We have defined the power of an individual interest group as the ability to achieve its goals as it defines them, and as perceived by the various people directly involved in and who observe the public policy–making process. Although numerous analytical strategies exist, we chose to use a variation of the traditional "power study" approach. Scholars who employ Hunter's reputational approach conduct "snow-balling" interviews with elites.[7] "Knowledgeables" identify those who wield power. Our lists of elites include persons based on their positions within the executive, legislative, and judicial branches. We conducted in-depth interviews with these elites, who were asked, as part of the interview process, to identify whom they considered to be key lobbyists. We then interviewed twenty-seven lobbyists. Using a semistructured interview schedule, we asked all respondents to name the most powerful groups, describe the strategies and tactics of these groups, and assess why they were powerful. We were particularly curious about how interest groups worked within the executive, the legislature, the judiciary, and political campaigns. We kept separate lists of influential groups named by elites for each institution. The knowledgeables included persons from the governor's office and the offices of the leaders of the House and the Senate as well as members of the legislative bodies. Others interviewed were from the executive departments and the judicial agencies. Many lobbyists were interviewed from a cross section of groups as well as those specifically named by others as being particularly effective.[8]

However, we did not conduct our study in the absence of specific expectations. Previous work suggests that states in which one party dominates, that have an unequal distribution of wealth, and that lack a diverse postindustrial economy give rise to strong interest groups. These characteristics place Georgia in the class of states with strong interest groups, with business groups ranking among the most powerful.[9] In contrast, other groups do not have the same level of resources and/or visibility. Stability of interest groups is also a major trait in such states.

The Interest Group Environment

Sociopolitical Culture

Although Georgia's sociopolitical culture has changed rapidly over the past decades, geography, race, and the predominance of the Democratic party still affect politics. With the demise of the county-unit system, urban interests became increasingly prominent in Georgia politics.[10] By 1990 two-thirds of Georgia's population was in metropolitan areas, and these large urban centers dominated the economy.[11]

Two factors tend to mitigate the effect of this urban-rural disparity. First, the suburbs have grown faster than the state's urban population: for example, between 1960 and 1990 the city of Atlanta lost 21 percent of its population, while its immediate suburban counties expanded by an average of 119 percent.[12] Second, politicians have sought to minimize the rural-urban split, warning that divisiveness undermines the best interests of the state as a whole. They fear that a dichotomy between urban "haves" and rural "have nots" will upset Georgia's political and economic agendas. Gov. Joe Frank Harris characterized this split as "insidious[ly] . . . attempting to drive a wedge, to divide our people, to pit one section of our state against another."[13] Political leaders articulate the ethos of the Georgia of the 1980s and the 1990s as follows: The interest groups in the state have to work together to achieve the overriding goal of economic development. To this end, historical divisions in the state can no longer be encouraged or even tolerated.

The role of a second sociopolitical factor, race, has also changed in Georgia. The black vote is no longer monolithic in most Democratic primaries.[14] Yet throughout Georgia the black vote and black candidates are still a powerful political force. In 1990 there were 483 black officeholders in the state, the third highest number in the nation.[15] While it holds less than 10 percent of legislative seats, the Black Caucus has gained power as other legislators consult it about a wide range of issues. Moreover, candidates for public office know that they cannot campaign successfully by attacking blacks. In fact, Democrats actively seek their support, and black voters and rural whites often form a "night and day alliance."[16] The politics of race—pitting whites against blacks—has "gone with the wind."[17]

In the 1990 primary campaign, when Andrew Young attempted to become the first black candidate for governor, there was virtually no mention of race by any of the candidates. Young's candidacy was very much in the tradition of the recent gubernatorial candidates: He ran as a consensus candidate, campaigning among rural whites as well as urban blacks. Mayor Young campaigned on economic development, promising that his business "would be to bring business to South Georgia, money to South Georgia."[18]

Finally, in spite of recent encroachments by the Republican party, Georgia remains a "bastion of Democratic strength."[19] Republican strength, however, has emerged in contests for federal offices. Except for supporting the presidential candidacy of its native son, Jimmy Carter, in 1976 and 1980, Georgia has registered in the Republican column in every presidential election since 1964. The Republicans won their first statewide victory since Reconstruction in 1980, when Mack Mattingly was elected to the U.S. Senate; but it was short-lived. In 1986 Wyche Fowler, at the time the "liberal" incumbent congressman representing Atlanta and some of its suburbs, reunited the coalition of black, urban, and some rural white voters to win back the seat for the Democrats. Notably, Fowler was "very different from other consensus Democrats, who had rural roots and yet developed a following in the urban areas."[20]

The Republicans are just beginning to develop a farm system of local officeholders to train and run for higher office. Although there are more than two hundred Republican officeholders in the state, they still remain a distinct minority in the General Assembly.[21] This is particularly significant because legislative seats have become a stepping-stone to higher state office—five of the last six governors served in the state legislature. Therefore, Georgia is far from a two-party state.[22] And Georgia politics is still "characterized more by the interaction of interest groups than by political parties."[23]

Institutional Climate

An array of institutional powers also shapes the environment in which interest groups operate. The powers of Georgia's governor make the executive branch an appealing target for organized pressures. In particular, the governor sets the budget and has a line-item veto; and he may succeed himself to a second term. The old bifactional Democratic politics is no longer evident; and the political atmosphere is less volatile. Modern Georgia governors have generally been "adaptives."[24] They have supported increased public spending for public education but have avoided class politics while championing economic development.

The Assembly, too, provides an attractive target for interest groups because power is extremely centralized, resting in the hands of the speaker of the House and the lieutenant governor, who also serves as the president of the Senate. Intense rivalries exist between the House and the Senate and between the presiding officers. Lobbyists must pay attention to both chambers as well as to individual members of the Assembly who hold considerable power because of leadership positions or political skill. Because of its size, the House is more hierarchical in structure. In contrast, the Senate has a few individuals who can deliver votes on almost any issue. The complete domination by the Democrats renders party votes meaningless. Coalitions are fluid. Interest groups can wield enormous power in this setting.

The presence or absence of legal restraints conditions the activities of interest groups. Prior to the 1981 Extraordinary Session for Constitutional Revision, the Georgia Constitution (Art. I,

Sec. II, ¶xii) declared lobbying "to be a crime." Now according to Title 28-7 of the Official Code of Georgia Annotated, lobbying is defined as an activity by those having actual contact with legislators.[25] Lobbyists, or "registered agents," are required by law to register with the secretary of state.[26] Georgia has no reporting requirements for lobbyists, such as financial gifts, expenditures, or compensation by categories or employees. Therefore, no reviews are conducted of reports or complaints; the secretary of state merely compiles a list of registered agents (see Table 10.1 for registered interest groups and individuals by category).

Most state agencies or departments have legislative liaisons who provide assistance to legislators or legislative staff. These liaisons are particularly visible throughout the legislative session, testifying before committees and assisting in the drafting of legislation. During the interim they often help legislators with any constituent problems or assist interim study committees. The appearance and use of the agency lobbyist is a relatively new phenomenon in Georgia that has evolved with the shift in rural "good ol' boy" politics to the complex and technical nature of an evolving state government.

Major Characteristics of Interest Group Activity

Targeting the Executive and Legislative Branches

Interest groups often form client relationships with individual agencies and exert their primary influence through them. However, because of the powers of the Georgia governor, elites more often stressed the relationship between interest groups and the executive. Our respondents usually described the relationship among the interest group, the departments, and the executive as a facilitating one.

Similarly, successful legislative lobbying in Georgia depends upon visibility and credibility, with much of the work done between legislative sessions. Lobbyists warn that "if you have not made your contacts and lined up your initial support before the session, you can't walk in there and hope to win."[27] However, interest group representatives are ever-present during the session; lobbyists gather in the hallways, watching television monitors and sending in messages to

Table 10.1 Registered Interest Groups and Registered Agents by Category, 1990

	Number
Banks, banking, finance	29
Business, business associations	283
Medical, health industry	42
Professional associations, unions	212
Medical, health associations	38
Social issues	182
Medical, health issues	42
Utilities	30
Registered agents	186
Government	13
Total	1,059

Source: Reports on file in the Office of the Georgia Secretary of State.

legislators. Many of the groups hold receptions and dinners during the session.

Our interviews revealed that though lobbyists know some of their more visible lobbyist counterparts in other policy areas, they were far more knowledgeable about those who operated in their own sphere. Business groups are especially adept at forming coalitions. Regardless of the issue, lobbyists are emphatic that their best weapon is grass-roots organization. Many of the groups have sophisticated techniques for keeping their constituents informed and for mobilizing them. The Medical Association of Georgia, for example, has the names of three or four doctors who know each legislator personally. Georgia Power has identified not only its own employees but also local businessmen who can contact a legislator on its behalf. Such strategies, lobbyists claim, constitute the most important way to affect executive and legislative decision making. In contrast, testimony before a legislative committee is mostly a formality, having little effect on the legislative process.

The Dominance of Business Interests

Business is the most influential sector of organized group activity because every governor in the past two decades has given priority to economic development.[28] In light of this, no governor can (or would want to) avoid Georgia's most important businesses: the major Atlanta banks; Delta Airlines; Coca-Cola; and Georgia Power.

Georgia governors are like other "Southern governors [who] have become the de facto executive directors of the state chambers of commerce."[29] The relationship between such businesses and governors is largely symbiotic: Governors are likely to ask these industries to support their "red carpet" tours through the state, the purpose of which is to attract new businesses to Georgia. Moreover, all these companies contribute to the governor's expenses whether he is marketing the state to businesses or entertaining other governors at the annual meeting of the National Governors Association. Georgia Power has developed and collected sophisticated information on all the communities it serves (including descriptions of the population, the businesses, the labor force, utility services, schools, and so forth), which it shares with the Department of Industry and Trade.

This synergy is particularly well-illustrated by Georgia's educational policy. Along with economic development, governors have stressed consistently the need for improvement in the public education system. Gov. Joe Frank Harris described education as the "linchpin between Georgia's past and present. . . . Education and economic development are the cornerstones of my administration."[30] For years, the state has had high illiteracy rates, low teacher pay, and a high pupil-dropout rate. During the Busbee administration (1975–1983) part-time kindergarten was phased in statewide; in 1984 Governor Harris appointed a blue-ribbon Educational Review Commission, composed of educators, businessmen, and local community leaders. Some sources maintain that the governor was prodded into action by business leaders who reminded him of campaign promises. Governor Harris, whose style was to orchestrate behind the scenes before placing his prestige on the line, had the business community sell his Quality Basic Education Program throughout the state. The Business Council of Georgia enlisted its members in the local chambers of commerce to press their local legislators to vote for the governor's program.

Business interests are an integral part of the Georgia Assembly. Legislative service is a part-time occupation.[31] The vast majority of members are employed elsewhere: Three-fifths of the members of the General Assembly are engaged in business occupations, while only 16 percent are lawyers (the next single largest occupational group).[32] Reinforcing the generally probusiness atmosphere of Georgia government, legislators often sit on committees that examine legislation in which they have an occupational interest. For example, the fourteen-member House Insurance Committee includes four insurance agents, one former agent, and an insurance company's general counsel. Some legislators argue that professionals in a certain area can often provide technical expertise that other members of the committee have yet to acquire. They also contend that the expertise of the membership gives the legislators some independence and allows them to weigh carefully the information from organized interests. Georgians, according to one expert, "assume public service may bring opportunities or advantages in private business, and to a certain extent conflicts of interest are tolerated."[33] Each body has a rule stating that members must abstain from voting on a bill if they are "immediately and particularly" interested in the legislation; yet no clear interpretation of this rule exists.

The same business interests that influence the executive branch extend their activity into the legislative branch, and the lobbyists for these individual groups and trade associations are well known. "If you have to waste time introducing yourself to a legislator during the session you've lost 90 percent of your effectiveness," observed one longtime, respected lobbyist. In addition to the previously mentioned groups, the Georgia Poultry Association is considered particularly influential, although of low profile, in the Assembly. The credit for its success is given to its lobbyist and the fact that poultry raising, in which Georgia leads the country, is the only section of agribusiness that is doing well in the state.

Most of the business lobbyists are trying to keep legislation from being passed or are practicing "defensive lobbying." If certain pieces of legislation get to the floor, they may lose. Therefore, the important work has to be done earlier with committee members and with the leaders. Georgia Power, however, prefers to have regulatory legislation come to the General Assembly rather than be submitted to the five-member Public Service Commission (PSC).

Other Interests

Social-issue interest groups are not identified as influential forces in executive or legislative policy-making. Contract lobbyists are more numerous among social-interest groups than any other interests. There is also a large contingent of pro bono lobbyists. Although social-issue groups are visible and some are considered to be experts on their subject matter, they face severe lobbying problems because their requests usually necessitate budgetary increases. As the Georgia Constitution mandates a balanced budget, the competition for even a small increase is intense. Social-issue groups appear to be most effective with their client agencies. The only way for them to succeed is to work closely with the directors of state agencies, who negotiate their budgets with the governor before he presents his budget to the legislature, the staff of the governor's Office of Planning and Budget, and the key legislative members of the appropriations committee.

However, the general view of agency staff, legislative staff, and members of other interest groups is that many social-issue groups regularly sacrifice effectiveness because of their failure to build coalitions and their uneasy working relationships with the agencies. In addition, legislators and representatives of other groups claim that, either for lack of funding or lack of knowledge, the effectiveness of social-issue interest groups is tenuous. They appear "not to have done their homework. You have to lay the groundwork." These groups are also perceived as less willing to compromise and more likely to "threaten" a legislator with lack of support at election time.

Obviously, these indictments do not apply to all groups. Some of the social-issue lobbyists observe that lobbying for part of the budget or for certain clients is inherently more difficult. One lobbyist always tries to identify the most conservative legislator who will lend support so that the issue cannot be identified as liberal. This lobbyist stresses that "it is important to get the whole legislative choir singing from the same hymnbook." Social-issue interest groups also appear to be more successful when they form alliances with professional groups.

The political climate for social-issue groups is improving slowly. Executive staff and legislative chairs appear to encourage consultation and cooperation. For example, the Department of Human Resources (DHR) and the Council on Maternal and Infant Health Care convinced the governor to include $500,000 in his 1986 budget for several neonatal units around the state; the General Assembly concurred. Governor Harris appointed a commission to study child abuse after several legislators, members of DHR staff, and advocates for children's health met with him. In the 1990 legislature a package of bills relating to protection of children was passed. It remains to be seen if the mutually supportive relationship between the executive and the social-issue interest groups will continue to develop when the budget is tighter.

Because of their status, professional associations often sway votes. The Georgia Association of Educators (GAE) is treated with a healthy respect because teachers in the legislators' home districts are numerous and are likely to vote. GAE is continuously lobbying for pay raises as well as educational reforms. In fact, some observers criticize GAE for being more interested in teachers' perquisites than in education. Another influential professional association is the Medical Association of Georgia (MAG). MAG encourages its members to contribute to its PAC and to be involved in local politics. Often pitted against other associations of health professionals, MAG is rated as a formidable opponent, hard to defeat. As does GAE, MAG offers workshops around the state about the legislative process and issues to be dealt with in the upcoming session. However, these two organizations differ in their policy for making political endorsements: GAE has a litmus test of issues, while MAG does not.

During the 1986 legislative session the issue of tort reform was the most visible battle pitting MAG against the Georgia Trial Lawyers Association (GTLA). Much of GTLA's success was due to the fact that Speaker Tom Murphy is a practicing defense attorney. To counter this, MAG had to lobby particularly hard, going so far as to organize a march, fifteen hundred members strong, on the State Capitol, the first time it had resorted to such tactics. Another pro-reform group, the Business Council of Georgia, urged its members to contact legislators while forming a task force on liability insurance. Lawyers, in turn, mounted a $400,000 television, radio, and newspaper advertising campaign. Some compromises were worked out, but adjournment occurred before a final vote. Not surprisingly, business groups took the lead role and kept tort reform a major issue during the 1986 interim session. The lieutenant governor and the speaker both became involved in the drafting of separate pieces of legislation, which resulted in two separate conference committee reports being adopted in 1987 (the Tort Reform Act of 1987 and the Medical Malpractice Reform Act of 1987). Everyone claimed victory: Doctors were granted reduced liability in indigent cases, and lawyers received a cap on damages; the insurance industry remains unscathed.

Governmental Agencies as Effective Interest Groups

After the governor's budget has been presented, executive departments lobby for additional funds and program needs that were not addressed by the chief executive. The success of these efforts depends on the same factors that affect the strength of other interests: constituents' size and status; politically divisible goods; and professionalism.

Using these criteria as benchmarks, the most influential department head was Department of Transportation Commissioner Tom Moreland. His power came in part from a dedicated tax on motor fuel, which gave him great budgetary independence as well as personal control over a precious commodity that most legislators want—roads. He skilfully promoted economic development by allocating his funds to statewide projects while cultivating legislative loyalty by his allocations to local improvements.

The state's Board of Regents also has sway with the General Assembly because legislators are reluctant to be perceived as opposed to higher education. There is a tradition of removing the university system from overt political bargaining since Gov. Eugene Talmadge's actions almost cost its accreditation. Besides its great budgetary leeway (there are no budgetary line-items for the Board of Regents), the governor's liaison with the board is a well-respected veteran who is skilled at smoothing over differences and resolving conflicts.

Traditionally, the Georgia Municipal Association and the Association of County Commissioners, representing most of the elected officials on the local level, have been influential in the General Assembly. However, with the end of federal revenue sharing, they compete for a larger part of the state budget. Moreover, their localized perceptions and demands often ignore broader statewide concerns and needs.

The Judiciary as an Interest and as a Target of Group Activity

While traditional interest group lobbying of the federal judiciary has increased over the past two decades, state judicial commissions dominate court policy-making in Georgia. Our elites agreed that external organized interests and reform groups have had "no influence whatever in the judicial process in Georgia." The only nongovernmental group deemed influential was the State Bar Association, although it was generally considered to have been "an influence for good, but weak." The other influential organizations are governmental bodies: the Council of Superior Court Judges; the Council of Judicial Administrative Districts; the Council of Juvenile Judges; the Council of State Court Judges; the Council of Probate Judges; and the Council of Magistrate Judges.

The Council of Superior Court Judges was rated by all our elites as "the most important group which affects the judicial process in the state." Georgia has always accorded superior court judges "tremendous power" in their own circuits; hence, they have become a group to which policy is not easily dictated. As one of our elites claimed, "if there is to be any change in procedural aspects of the courts, it usually requires strong support of the council." The Council of Juvenile Court Judges is also influential because of the heightened visibility of juvenile problems and increased demand for governmental solutions.

An increasingly important avenue of interest group activity, especially for groups who have met with little success in the legislative and executive branches, is through court challenges and the filing of briefs. Our interviews revealed an outside path of influence: interest group lobbying efforts directed toward the judicial councils. Groups such as MADD, the League of Women Voters, court watchers, and others regularly meet with these councils to apprise them of their activities and request support for their agendas. Our judicial elites could not recall any recent occurrence involving business groups seeking to influence the judiciary.

Interest Groups and Campaigns

Most of the major business interests, professional associations, unions, unregulated utilities (such as the telephone and transportation industries), and social-issue groups have established PACs. One important exception is Georgia Power: As a regulated utility, it is statutorily prohibited from forming a PAC. (See Table 10.2 for a listing of PACs by interest group category.)

Table 10.2   PAC Expenditures by Category, 1986

	Amount (in Dollars)
Banks, banking, finance	509,335
Business, business associations	1,686,477
Medical, health industry	112,346
Professional associations, unions	424,082
Medical, health associations	597,367
Social issues	152,112
Medical, health issues	45,063
Utilities	0
Registered agents	1,500
Government	0
Total	3,528,282

Source: Reports on file in the Office of the Georgia Secretary of State.

Georgia law (Official Code of Georgia Annotated, 21-4 [a] [1]) provides for campaign and financial-disclosure reports. The law states that "any campaign committee which accepts contributions or makes expenditures designed to bring about the nomination or election of a candidate for any office . . . shall file with the [Ethics] commission the required campaign contribution reports."

Campaign and financial reports must disclose the individual sources of contributions or expenditures in excess of $101. The banks, Coca-Cola, Delta, and other businesses routinely contribute to more than one candidate in closely contested races. They also encourage their executives to give individually and to take an active role in campaigning. On Table 10.3 the top twenty PACs for calendar year 1986 are listed, with their expenditures.[34] However, when political parties are included, as in Table 10.4, they rank higher than businesses, professional associations, and banks. Interestingly, one-fourth of the PACs that filed disclosure reports in Georgia were from out of state, evidence of the appeal of Georgia to outside business.

The GAE was the first branch of the National Education Association to form a state PAC. Over the years GAE has used sophisticated techniques to mobilize its members. However, it has been criticized for endorsing candidates too early and too easily. GAE tarnished its image in this "right-to-work" state when it moved toward collective-bargaining demands. Some officials boasted of improving their status with the voters by not giving in to the demands of teachers' special interests. Social-issue PACs, constituting a fairly large category of lobbyists, are the fourth-largest group in expenditures. Their relatively high level of contribution is inconsistent with their ineffectiveness in lobbying the executive, legislative, and judicial branches.

In 1990 the General Assembly amended the Campaign and Financial Disclosure Law (Official Code of Georgia Annotated, 21-5-4–21-5-45) by placing a $3,500 limit per election on individual, corporate, and PAC contributions to candidates for statewide office or the General Assembly. The General Assembly intended this law to become effective on the signature of the governor and to apply to any subsequent 1990 campaign contributions. Citing U.S. Justice Department review of all Georgia election laws, gubernatorial candidate Andrew Young refused to abide by the limits.[35] Other candidates in the gubernatorial primary agreed to comply with the restrictions. All of the candidates had received some large contributions before the deadline, but Young thought his late entry into the race hurt his ability to raise comparable funds.[36]

As in past years, the candidates in most of the 1990 races did not successfully make an issue of the sources of their opponents' contributions. Historically, the influence of special interests in Georgia has seldom been viewed as corrupting the political process.

Table 10.3 Top Twenty PAC Expenditures, 1986 (Excluding Political Parties)

	Amount (in Dollars)
Builders PAC of Georgia Atlanta	219,453
LAW-PAC	203,305
Georgia Medical PAC	180,280
Georgia Health Care Association	162,183
Georgia Realtors PAC	154,419
American Council of Life Insurance	118,119
Metropolitan [Insurance] Employees Political Fund	111,788
Fund for Better Government #2	104,438
Citizens & Southern Georgia Corp. Committee II	98,275
Consumer Credit People for Responsible Government	87,887
Geico	86,156
Trust Company of Georgia Good Government	85,725
Georgia Optometric PAC	68,614
Georgia Dental PAC	68,075
Builders Political Action Committee Savannah	66,262
SOPAC Non-Federal (Standard Oil)	60,435
First Atlanta Fund for Better Government	59,260
Hurt, Richardson, Garner et al.	56,510
Atlanta '88 Committee	55,000
Committee of Auto Retail Dealers of Georgia	51,378

Source: Reports on file in the Office of the Georgia Secretary of State.

Table 10.4   Top Twenty PAC Expenditures, 1986 (Including
Political Parties)

	Amount (in Dollars)
Democratic Party of Dekalb County	357,709
Georgia Republican Party	346,352
Builders PAC of Georgia Atlanta	219,453
LAW-PAC	203,305
Georgia Medical PAC	180,280
Georgia Health Care Association	162,183
Georgia Realtors PAC	154,419
American Council of Life Insurance 3E	118,119
Metropolitan [Insurance] Employees Political Fund	111,788
Fund for Better Government #2	104,438
Citizens & Southern Georgia Corp. Committee II	98,275
Consumer Credit People for Responsible Government	87,887
Geico	86,156
Trust Company of Georgia Good Government	85,725
Gwinnett County Republican Party	84,155
Georgia Optometric PAC	68,614
Georgia Dental PAC	68,075
Builders Political Action Committee Savannah	66,262
Georgia House Democratic Caucus Campaign	62,071
SOPAC Non-Federal (Standard Oil)	60,435

Source: Reports on file in the Office of the Georgia Secretary of State.

Conclusion

For many years "divisiveness" over demographics and race characterized Georgia's political environment. Those old conflicts, however, have largely dissipated. Instead, consensus politics, largely
built around the economic well-being of the state, rules: "Increasingly, the promotion and protection of Georgia interests came to
mean the advancement of corporate capitalist interests."[37] The

state's traditionalistic-individualistic political culture fosters leaders' preeminent concern with economic development.

Well-organized and funded business interests, in particular, have greatly influenced the course of Georgia politics. But business groups must work with political leaders, especially the governor. Businesses, and to a lesser extent trade and professional associations, but not social-issue interest groups, wield power in Georgia. As state government becomes more complex and technical, the expertise of the legislative liaisons of the executive agencies becomes more prominent. Organizations representing the spectrum of social concerns simply have yet to exert much influence on public policy. The cause of change within Georgia politics is difficult to assess. That is, was it business that pressed elected officials to alter the political agenda? Or did politicos come to agreement over Georgia's future first, a policy agenda that would necessarily insure the power and status of business interests within the political process?

Our study indicates that a symbiotic relationship exists between business interests and governmental officials. The latter depend upon business groups to foster and even implement their policies, to provide technical assistance, to act as symbols of Georgia's prosperity, and to contribute to their campaigns. In turn, the governor and legislators avoid policies that would hinder business. Consequently, while other groups have entered the arena, they play a relatively minor role in shaping and securing public policies.

11

ALABAMA

PERSONALITIES AND FACTIONALISM

David L. Martin

For many years Alabama has presented a classic case of Belle Zeller's finding that strong interest groups are found in states with weak party systems.[1] Furthermore, from 1901, when the Alabama Constitution forbad legislators from accepting free railroad passes, to today, Alabamians have been skeptical of lobbyists and interest groups. In four telephone polls conducted between 1980 and 1982, 62 to 70 percent of the respondents agreed with the statement that "state government in Alabama is run for the benefit of a few big interests."[2] Interest groups thrived throughout the 1970s, as the slowly decaying white frame houses visible from the State Capitol steps, where Jefferson Davis took the oath as Confederate president, were demolished and replaced by association headquarters.

Since interest group registration data available in other states are sparse in Alabama, this chapter uses a more qualitative approach for understanding interest groups in this state. The approach involves identifying groups and organizations presently active; examining lobbying styles and the emergence of PACs; consideration of the long-standing tradition of personalized politics in Alabama, which suggests three forms of interest group influence; and discussion of why factionalism (using the 1986 elections as illustrative) produces strong interest group influence in Alabama.

Politics and Government in the Heart of Dixie

In *Southern Politics in State and Nation* even Key was forced to conclude: "In the final analysis, the organizational structure of the amorphous factions of Alabama politics defy general description."[3] After dominating Alabama politics for a quarter-century, Gov. George Wallace retired in January 1987, making state politics more fluid than ever. Over a million Alabamians turned out at the polls in the 1980s, double the number before the extension of civil and voting rights. While the national media marveled at the black support Wallace received in his 1982 comeback to an unprecedented fourth term, Alabama's master politician had counted where the votes were and mended his political fences to become inclusive rather than "segregation forever." With blacks constituting one-quarter of Alabama's population of 4 million, the state has among the highest number of black elected officials in the nation.[4]

Even as the electorate has expanded, Alabama retains what Key characterized as the politics of "friends and neighbors," based on personalities and factions. In 1986 Jim Folsom, Jr., son of the flamboyant governor of the 1940s and 1950s, was elected lieutenant governor, while George Wallace, Jr., gained his first elective office as state treasurer. Chosen president pro tem of the Alabama Senate was Ryan DeGraffenreid, Jr., whose father, a gubernatorial candidate, was killed in a plane crash while campaigning against the elder Wallace. Both the new governor, Guy Hunt, and Lieutenant Governor Folsom were from Cullman County (population 62,000), as was the previous speaker of the House. The speaker was replaced because it was felt undesirable to have all three of the state's top political leaders from the same area. As Key stated, "a powerful localism provides an important ingredient of Alabama factionalism."[5] And with eighteen separately elected executive officials and all 140 members of the Legislature (105 representatives and 35 senators) elected together for four-year terms in both chambers, Alabama has a very fragmented policy-making process that furnishes interest groups many avenues for access.

Regulation of Campaign Finances and Lobbies

Nowhere is the individualism of Alabama politics better illustrated than in the laxity of campaign regulations. Alabama's Corrupt Practices Act, enacted in 1915, provided minimal regulation and only after a declaration of candidacy. Financial disclosure was required fifteen days after a primary election and thirty days after any other (general) election. Traditionally, candidates raised considerable sums before declaring their candidacy and frequently acted as their own campaign committee. A campaign committee might consist of not more than five persons, "but any candidate, if he sees fit to do so," states the Code of Alabama, 1975 (Title 17, Ch. 22, Sec. 10), "may declare himself as the person chosen for such purpose."[6] All contributions over $10 and all expenditures over $5—big money for 1915—were to be listed "in itemized, detailed form" (Sec. 10), but no totals were required! In the 1980s "disclosure" took the form of hundreds of pages of computer printouts after the election. A new Campaign Practices Act passed in late 1988 has, at the time of this writing, yet to be tested in an election.

In contrast to states with a single fair-campaign-practices commission or regulatory body, such as Washington State's Public Disclosure Commission, Alabama has four different agencies responsible for registration, each with differing, minimal disclosure requirements and little power of enforcement. Candidates, or their committees as described above, must file with the secretary of state to obtain an election certificate, as must PACs formed by a business or nonprofit organization incorporated under the laws of Alabama.[7] Anyone wishing to influence the Legislature on more than an "isolated basis" must fill out four-by-six-inch cards with the clerk of the House and the secretary of the Senate. The Senate's lobbyist registration form requests that areas of legislative interest and the "extent of any direct business association or partnership with any current member of the Legislature" be filled in on two lines. The cards are stored in separate file boxes by the clerk and secretary and are kept for the current session only. Directories listing legislators have been published by private groups such as the Alabama Retail Association and *Alabama Magazine.*

The Alabama Ethics Law was passed in 1973 but subsequently weakened by legislative amendments and court decisions. When the Legislature refused to appropriate money to operate the Ethics Commission, Governor Wallace used money from his contingency fund to continue the five-member staff, whose efforts were augmented by unpaid college interns.[8] The current registration requirements for lobbyists (and the wide exceptions) are set out in Table 11.1

Assessing Special Interests' Influence in Alabama Politics

In a state where not even an official tabulation has been kept of the bills vetoed by the governor, it is difficult to measure influence, but three indicators are illustrative.[9]

First, the Alabama Constitution of 1901 is the longest state constitution in the nation. In over five hundred amendments by 1990, many changes have officially incorporated special interests into the fabric of state government. For example, constitutional amendments adopted between 1984 and 1986 included amendment numbers 440, allowing bingo in Mobile; 441, providing health insurance for retired Mobile County employees; 443, conveying state docks property to localities; 449, controlling boll weevil in cotton; 451, creating soil and water conservation commissions; 452, promoting the cattle industry; 453, promoting the grain industry; 454, conveying state docks property; 457, providing money to the Morgan County Sheriff's Reserve; and 458, concerning a truck tax established by the Pike County Commission.

A second measure of special interests' influence on public policy is that Alabama has some forty state boards that regulate entry into and control the practice of a trade or profession. Members of these state boards are invariably chosen by the governor from within the trade or profession to be regulated. A perfect example of this state government–private interest fusion is that the State Board of Health and the State Board of Medical Examiners is, under Title 22, Chapter 2, Section 1 and Title 34, Chapter 24, Section 53 of the Code of Alabama, 1975, ex officio the governing body of the Medical Association of Alabama. And the extent to which this fusion between

Table 11.1 Lobbyist Registration Instructions, Alabama Ethics Commission

WHO MUST REGISTER AS A LOBBYIST?

ANY PERSON WHO FITS THE DEFINITION CONTAINED IN TITLE 36-25-1(7), CODE OF ALABAMA

LOBBYIST. All persons who seek to encourage the passage, defeat or modification of any legislation, except members of the Alabama legislature or any person who, on an isolated basis and without the intent to continue beyond a single day during a session of the Alabama legislature, merely appears before a committee or committees of the legislature in his individual capacity, or on behalf of a corporation, partnership, association or other business entity, with which such person is regularly associated as an employee, officer, member or partner without receiving additional salary or compensation other than reasonable and ordinary travel expenses, to express support of or opposition to any legislation and who shall so declare to a member, members or committee of the legislature with who [sic] he discusses any proposed legislation.

WHO NEED NOT REGISTER AS A LOBBYIST?

(1) Public officials acting in their official capacities and while acting with respect to subjects of their official responsibility, and who make no expenditures for lobbying activities.

(2) Persons who provide professional services in drafting bills or in advising clients and in rendering opinions to Legislators or legislative committees as to the construction and effect of proposed or pending legislation where such professional service is not otherwise connected with legislative action.

(3) Any person whose only participation in lobbying activities shall be in the form of isolated contacts. In this connection, the Constitutional right of every citizen to communicate with members of the Legislature of Alabama and the Executive of Alabama is fully recognized where such communication is made by a citizen acting solely in his individual capacity and not as a person employed by another to make such communication and nothing in these instructions shall be construed so as to limit or restrict the right of any citizen to make such communication.

WHEN IS AN INDIVIDUAL REQUIRED TO REGISTER AS A LOBBYIST?

Within five (5) days AFTER satisfying the requirements in WHO MUST REGISTER AS A LOBBYIST? A new Registration Form must be filed each Calendar Year for each principal represented.

public and private interest in regulating trades and professions can be used to the exclusionary advantage of a private interest and to the detriment of the public good is illustrated by the Mobile barber examiners who once required candidates to be able to shave the lather off a balloon—using a straight-edged razor. These abuses continue unless such barriers attract public attention. The forty licensing boards are also quite free to finance themselves by license fees, independent of state appropriations. This is another area of board activity where abuses often occur. Indeed, the Alabama Examiners of Public Accounts (a state auditing agency) has revealed some of the worst abuses, including instances in which some boards could not account for the license money collected.

A third indicator of interest group influence in Alabama are tax exemptions granted, varying from those given to "certain factories, industries and plants" and various commodities ("tobacco leaf stored in hogsheads") to Elks Clubs and dozens of other organizations, even unto exemptions for "all family portraits" and "ornaments or articles of taste."[10] These tax exemptions total $408 million (two-thirds of the state's general budget), according to the legislator who became the speaker of the House in 1987.[11] Alabama consistently ranks among the ten states lowest in per capita tax burden. The Farm Bureau and the large paper companies that own entire sections of Alabama worked hard for the 1970s "lid bill" on property taxes and "current use" assessment rather than valuation at actual market value. As a result, property taxes in Alabama could be doubled and the state would still have among the lowest in the nation. In the effort to meet the state's financial shortfall during the 1990s, revenue-hungry governmental and educational interests will be pitted against those with large landholdings.

Who Lobbies?

Longitudinal data on the types of interest groups active and on the number and types of lobbyists representing them are notably lacking in Alabama. Hallie Farmer's 1949 classic, *The Legislative Process in Alabama*, for example, makes no mention of interest groups. However, a cross-check of the separate records maintained by Alabama's secretary of state, the secretary of the Senate, the clerk of the House, and the Ethics Commission reveals that during the first half of the 1980s three to four hundred lobbyists were active each year. An examination of the same records for 1986, a typical year in the mid- to late 1980s, identified the groups listed in Table 11.2 as active in lobbying state government. These interest groups are listed by category.

National corporations are the most frequent registrants, but not necessarily with active, full-time lobbyists. These "Fortune 500" companies typically register a regional corporate officer or retain an Alabama lawyer on contract as their representative. The second-largest category comprises public and quasi-public agencies and organizations. Public agencies and their officials must register if they expend money in lobbying. In 1986 this second category embraced fifteen state agencies, a dozen state universities, and the largest cities and counties. The Alabama League of Municipalities, the Association of County Commissions, and the Tax Assessors and Collectors Association represent local officials and local jurisdictions. The municipal league and the county association typically draw up a legislative agenda before each session and also take a position on other bills affecting their governments.

Alabama's business associations include the usual state trade associations, plus two umbrella organizations, the Business Council of Alabama (BCA) and the Alabama Alliance of Business and Industry (AABI). These replaced the state chamber of commerce and the Associated Industries of Alabama, identified by Morehouse in the late 1970s.[12] The BCA lists its interests as "mining, land and land use, taxation, energy and environment, labor relations, unemployment compensation, group insurance and any legislation affecting or pertaining to business or industry, timber products, oil, gas, and others"; in contrast, the AABI simply lists "good government."[13]

Medical and human-services groups include associations of health professionals; hospitals, nursing homes, clinics, and home care providers; Easter Seal, Planned Parenthood, and other service organizations; and the Alabama Funeral Directors.

Alabama is a "right-to-work" state without public sector bargaining rights (teachers and firefighters have rights to "meet and confer"). However, public employees are an important lobbying force, with separate associations for state employees, state troopers, sheriffs, and peace officers, including a Fraternal Order of Police. The limit on military pensions exempted from state income tax was

Table 11.2 Interest Groups Active in Alabama

	Number of Groups	Percentage of Groups	Number of Registered Lobbyists	Percentage of Lobbyists
National corporations	53	18	76	17
Government agencies	40	14	62	14
Alabama businesses	36	12	46	10
Medical/human services	33	11	49	11
Unions/public employees' associations	20	6	36	8
Utilities/services	19	6	26	6
Professions/occupations	18	6	22	5
Financial institutions	17	6	29	6
Insurance	16	5	20	4
Entertainment/beverage	15	5	20	4
Agriculture/environment	12	4	18	4
Education	5	2	31	7
Miscellaneous interests	12	4	16	3
Total	296	100	451	100

Source: Separate registrations with the Alabama Ethics Commission, Alabama secretary of state, clerk of the Alabama House, and secretary of the Alabama Senate, October 1986.

raised in 1985 from $4,700 to $10,000 by dint of the efforts of the National Guard and Retired Officers associations. And state retirement pay is totally exempt from state taxation. The voice of organized labor is A. G. "Ace" Trammell, head of the Alabama Labor Council. Eight national unions also registered representatives.

Competing utility services include South Central Bell and independent telephone operators; Alagasco and other natural gas, propane gas, and pipeline companies; Alabama Power Company, Alabama Electric Cities, and Alabama Rural Electric Association; the railroads, air transport, and river-improvement associations; and the Alabama Towing and Recovery Association. In a recent contest within the utility industry, the Alabama Power Company and the rural electric cooperatives prevailed against the Electric Cities (municipal utilities) that sought to move into their service areas under the "territorial bill" bitterly contested in the 1985 legislative session.

Professional and occupational associations range from those for psychologists to podiatrists. Their influence is such that, compared to other states, Alabama remains rather restrictive on professionals' advertising prices for services.

Financial interests comprise banking, savings and loan, credit unions, mortgage lenders, and consumer finance associations, with individual lobbyists from the largest state bank holding companies and stock brokerage firms. One of the most powerful interest groups until the late 1970s was the Alabama Banking Association, which split over the twin issues of statewide branch banking and interstate regional banking, with the larger institutions forming the Modern Banking Association of Alabama. Branch banking was accomplished by the emergence of four or five statewide bank holding companies, and since July 1987 Alabama banks can merge with banks in neighboring states.

Insurance groups have strongly defended their interests at the State Capitol, to the extent that the U.S. Supreme Court ruled in 1985 that Alabama had violated the Equal Protection Clause by taxing state-based companies far less than others.[14] There are registered lobbyists from each of the major companies, as well as independent agents. Revision of state civil liability laws in the 1980s has energized this group into higher-visibility lobbying than ever, especially through media appearances and campaigning.

Entertainment and beverage interests (including the media and hospitality industries) include such organizations as the state fair and Alabama affiliates of such national organizations as the Distilled Spirits Council, Wine Institute, and Motion Picture Association. The groups in this category pursue a variety of policies. The Alabama Press Association has sought enforcement of laws on open meetings; the Wholesale Beer and Wine Association has lobbied for sales outside of state stores; and the Azalea Racing Club in Mobile and the Alabama Sports Association promote racetracks. Outdoor Advertising has been successful in keeping billboards along Alabama's interstate highways. The vending and mail-order associations are fighting to keep taxes low on their operations. These wide-ranging goals also produce frequent divisions within the entertainment, hospitality, and beverage lobby. For example, owners of cable television systems have fought the right of hotel and motel owners to use satellite dishes.

The state's agricultural lobby is dominated by the Alabama Farmers (ALFA), formerly the Farm Bureau. ALFA's biggest business now is selling insurance. In fact, for selling insurance outside the state, the Alabama organization was ousted from the American Farm Bureau Federation in 1984. This prompted the organization to change its name. The guiding father of the old Farm Bureau was Ed Lowder, who retired and diversified into real estate and banking.[15] Other agricultural lobbies include the Forestry Association, Poultry and Egg Association, and the Horse Foundation. Dealers in farm and power equipment, pest control operatives, and chemical applicators are represented, but there is only a single farmers' production credit association after the decline in agriculture. Most Alabamians view the environment in terms of hunting and fishing, with only the Alabama Wildlife Federation and the Gulf Coast Conservation Association registering representatives of environmental groups.

Educational groups consist of the Alabama Education Association (AEA) and the frequently opposed Association of School Boards and Council for School Administrators and Supervisors. In addition, there is the Private School Association and the Alabama PTA. Although this small number of groups rank low (see Table 11.2), because 75 percent of each Alabama educational dollar comes from the state (a proportion that is among the highest in the nation), and educational trust fund expenditures far exceed the general fund budget, lobbying is constant and intense. Part of the AEA's effectiveness comes from mobilizing its members throughout the state. In 1986 it registered twenty-five lobbyists, more than any other interest group.[16]

Finally, a dozen groups fall into the miscellaneous category, such as the American Legion, Alabama Democratic Conference, Common Cause, State Association of Retired Persons, Friends of Alabama Libraries, and Traffic Safety Now. Besides the Alabama Federation of Business and Professional Women and the League of Women Voters, the Alabama Women's Agenda (prochoice) was opposed by Concerned Women for America (prolife). The Christian Science Committee on Publications registered a representative, as did the Citizen Action Program, a church coalition on moral issues, opposing alcohol, drugs, and gambling.

Lobbyists and Lobbying Styles

There are several salient features of lobbying in Alabama that are similar to those found in medium-sized and small states in the South and throughout the country. These features set Alabama apart from some of the larger states in the nation and from states like Texas and Florida in the South.

First, there are relatively few (under 10) lobbyists who represent more than four clients each. These multiple-client contract lobbyists are likely to be attorneys or former legislators and represent a variety of interests. Thus "Walking Wendell" Mitchell, a former legislator who used this slogan campaigning (unsuccessfully) for the U.S. Congress, runs around Montgomery on behalf of Alabama Crippled Children and Adults, the American Institute of Architects, the State Bar Association, the State Employees Association, First South Production Credit Association, and the Association of Alabama Life Insurance Companies.[17] In 1986 the largest number of clients (11) was listed by the partnership of Fine and Geddie. Registration statements by the firm for that year reveal an appropriately fine diversity of clients (see Table 11.3). Of Joe Fine a longtime Capitol reporter has written: "Former Senate President Pro Tem. Joe Fine of Russellville reigns unofficially as the king of the lobbyists. He was a powerful legislator before he dropped out to run for attorney general in 1978 and did not return to public office after he survived a probe into

Table 11.3 Clients Represented by Fine and Geddie

Alabama Hospital Association

Alabama Chemical Association

Alabama Power Company

Azalea Racing Club, Mobile

First Bank of Childersberg

GTE Sprint

Mutual Savings Life Insurance Company

Outdoor Advertising

Smokeless Tobacco (snuff and chew)

Springhill Memorial Hospital

Traffic Safety Now

Source: Registration statements by Joseph L. Fine and Robert B. Geddie, Jr., October 1986.

alleged corruption in the coal industry. When he is not chatting with his ex-colleagues at their desks, Fine makes himself at home in a chair next to Lt. Gov. Bill Baxley, the presiding officer. It's a wonder he doesn't forget and run the Senate from the microphone as he once did."[18] With such negative media comment, the Alabama preference in a politics of "good ol' boys" is a lobbyist representing a sole principal.

Second, while increasing numbers of lobbyists have registered (see Table 11.2), only about seventy-five are full-time, and most of these are in-house lobbyists. One indicator of this is membership in the Alabama Council of Association Executives (ACAE), an organization representing a large number of in-house lobbyists. The ACAE's membership roster (1986) describes it as "an organization of those professionals who serve as chief executive officers of the state's various business, trade, and professional organizations." The organization emphasizes professional advocacy and was formed in the early 1980s largely in response to media exposés of wheeling and dealing. Members of ACAE are, for the most part, permanent fixtures of Montgomery's lobbying community. In contrast, there are many lobbyists who register for a single legislative session or who are lobbying for one particular bill. These often disappear as quickly as they came. An example was V.O.C.A.L. (Victims of Crime and Leniency) and its lobbyists, a interest group active in the 1983 and 1984 legislative sessions. Once the Governor's Crime Package of bills was passed, this group also passed from the Montgomery scene.

Adding credence to Morehouse's conclusion that "states with strong pressure groups are often states that do not have modern integrated cultures,"[19] Alabama has few of the national public-interest groups. The state League of Women Voters has a Montgomery member as its legislative director; the ACLU has a single staff attorney (female) to handle cases and keep an eye on the Legislature; and Common Cause has Wayne Greenhaw, publisher of *Alabama Magazine* and probably the state's most frequent contributor to the op-ed page of the *New York Times*. Only five individuals were concerned or angry enough (one listed "matters affecting secretaries") to be self-registered on their own behalf.

Third, Alabama lobbying is highly personal: "Good ol' boys" come to Montgomery in three-piece polyester suits, but their roots often extend back to the state's two law schools, and the University of Alabama and Auburn University. Longevity is illustrated by "Mr. Labor of Alabama" Barney Weeks and John Watkins of the League of Municipalities, who both recently retired after a quarter-century as lobbyists. For nearly twenty years spokesmen for education have been Randy Quinn (school boards) and Paul Hubbert (teachers). Reginald Hammer of the Alabama State Bar and John Dorrill, Jr., of the Alabama Farmers are acknowledged masters of their respective spheres. As head of the Association of County Commissions since 1973, O. H. "Buddy" Sharpless has built a new building and considerably increased the association's staff. The ebullient E. H. "Ham" Wilson, who decorated the Cattlemen's Association vehicles with the largest steer horns this side of Texas, retired and then became director of governmental relations for Auburn, the state's land-grant university. His son, E. Hamilton Wilson, Jr., currently represents the Independent Insurance Agents, the National Federation of Independent Business, the Rural Electric Association, and the State Troopers Association, establishing a family tradition that lobbyists can be born, not simply hired.

The personal nature of Alabama lobbying is too often illustrated by such episodes as when the telephone company's relations manager "reached out and touched someone" by providing "the services of a lady of the evening," as the court put it. He was convicted of violating the Alabama Ethics Law—she being considered "a thing of value."[20]

Political Action Committees

If "money is the mother's milk of politics,"[21] PACs have become the surrogate mothers of Alabama politics. Information required by Alabama's 1915 Corrupt Practices Act is not as extensive as lobbyist disclosure under the 1973 ethics law. In 1981 the 1915 act was amended to allow businesses as well as nonprofit corporations to solicit "voluntary contributions to a separate, segregated fund to be utilized for political purposes" (Code of Alabama, 1975, 1982 Suppl., Title 17, Ch. 22, Sec. 3). Consequently, "the 1982 legislative elections were the first in Alabama history to be mainly financed by PACs."[22] In a decade the number of PACs listed in "Political Action Committees Filing Under Alabama Statutes" (compiled by the secretary of state's office) has grown from under ten to 231 on the 1986 list.

While many PACs indicate their affiliation in their title with such creative names as BEEF-PAC (cattlemen), VEND-PAC (Alabama Automatic Merchandising Council), ALATON (truckers), SIX-PAC (beer and wine wholesalers), and Kid-PAC (Alabama Association of School Boards), others are evasive—Citizens for the Truth, for example, or Committee for Good Leadership, with Post Office boxes in Birmingham. Better Alabama Candidacy PAC is a rather uninformative name unless one is aware that its treasurer, Milo Dakin, directs the Alabama Consumer Finance Association—an organization representing loan companies. A number of PACs are created simply for a single campaign, after which they disappear from the secretary of state's files.

Illustrative of PACs in Alabama is one of the first formed and hence best known, AVOTE—Alabama Voice of Teachers for Education.[23] This PAC was formed by the AEA, whose longtime executive secretary, Paul Hubbert, is AVOTE's treasurer. Annual AEA membership dues, plus $6 for the organization's political action arm, are automatically deducted from teachers' paychecks. Between March 1 and June 3, 1986, the period leading up to the June primaries, AVOTE reported expenditures of $415,770. Between the June 3, 1986, primary and the June 24 runoff election, AVOTE spent an additional $130,582, but did not indicate contributions during this period. Expenditures ranged from two $50,000 payments to Lt. Gov. Bill Baxley (running for governor) to $500–5,000 contributions to individual legislators. Most legislative candidates received between $1,000 and $2,500 during the 1986 primary reporting period. Since AEA endorsed a majority of successful candidates during the 1982 and the 1983 special legislative elections, Alabama teachers did receive pay increases during each of the next four years—while other state employees did not. When the media reported Hubbert's giving "thumbs up" or "thumbs down" signals from the visitors' balcony in the Capitol, the House actually adopted a new rule: "Rule 31. When any person sitting in the balcony attempts to attract the attention of any one [sic] on the floor by word, deed or otherwise, or when any person in the balcony makes gestures to attract attention from the floor . . . such person shall be ousted from the balcony."[24]

Analysis of the 1986 legislative elections found a high proportion of PAC money had helped finance successful campaigns.[25] At least, that was the evidence from those who reported PAC contributions; poor enforcement of the reporting provisions leaves the data incomplete. Contributions made by twenty-four specified PACs to the twenty-two of the thirty-five winning senators who reported campaign expenditures averaged $22,407. This means that PAC money constituted over half of the nearly $40,000 average cost of a successful state Senate campaign in 1986. Other PACs undoubtedly contributed additional amounts, pushing the PAC proportion even higher. These twenty-four PACs contributed to the eighty-two representatives reporting an average of $7,272, nearly 40 percent of the almost $19,000 average cost of winning one of the 105 seats in the Alabama House. Media commentators noted how 1986 legislative winners supported by PACs for business, doctors, and insurance interests were appointed to committee chairs for the 1986–1990 legislature.[26]

In June 1990 Hubbert won the Democratic nomination for governor, without resigning his AEA position. The Democratic primary and runoff elections were the most expensive in Alabama's history, with the five major candidates spending a total of over $10 million, most of this raised by interest group PACs. Less than one-third of the Alabamians registered to vote bothered to do so.[27] Hubbert, however, was defeated in the November general election by incumbent Republican Gov. Guy Hunt. Figures on PAC contributions in this election were not available at the time this book went to press. However, judging by spending in the primary and by the increase in PAC money in Alabama elections in recent years, the 1990 general election will no doubt prove to set records in PAC spending and in the total percentages of campaign funds in both the gubernatorial and legislative races.

The Interplay of Factionalism and Interest Group Politics

In a state with strong interest groups countervailing power comes from factionalism. This section examines two sources, personality conflicts and differentiated interests, that produce the kaleidoscopic nature of Alabama politics and act, if sometimes rather crudely, to check and balance the power of what would otherwise be overpoweringly dominant interests.

"Personalization of leadership fractionalizes the electorate":[28] Key's finding about Alabama has endured with the growth of black political power in the state. The Alabama Democratic Conference (ADC), the black political arm of the Alabama Democratic party, has been headed since 1969 by Montgomery city councilman Joe Reed.[29] After the election of Richard Arrington as the first black mayor of Birmingham, the New South Coalition was formed (1985/86) to challenge Reed's domination. Reed had led the black teacher's organization, which was integrated in the late 1960s with the AEA when Paul Hubbert became executive secretary. Reed became number-two man in the AEA, a position he retains. Between March 1 and June 3, 1986, AEA's PAC, AVOTE, gave $19,500 to the ADC and $6,500 directly to the state Democratic party. In the 1986 elections the New South Coalition and the ADC diverged in their endorsements, but in 1987 the alleged loss of black appointments in legislative assignments brought a temporary rapprochement.[30] Thus black personality conflicts and factionalism follow the tradition of Alabama politics observed by Key, with the victories of civil rights substituted for white supremacy as the rallying cry to promote black group solidarity.

While personality splits attract attention during campaigns, differentiated interests maintain factionalism. Traditionally, the Bourbon planters and Birmingham's Big Mule industrialists aligned to keep Alabama a low–property tax state. Since the proportion of Alabama's work force engaged in farming has shrunk from 20 percent in 1950 to less than 3 percent in 1988, it has been difficult for rural interests to retain a political base. In 1986 George McMillan, who campaigned for governor "because if the farmers lose, we all lose," and lieutenant gubernatorial candidate Hinton Mitchem, who advertised he "measures up to Alabama Farm Bureau standards," both lost in the primary election. With the Alabama Farmers (the former Farm Bureau) now mainly engaged in selling insurance, rural interests have less political clout. Nevertheless, the legacy of the "lid bill" on property taxes gives large landholding interests an advantage that may continue in future years.

The 1980s also saw the emergence of a new set of antagonists over tort reform. Legislative changes increasing civil liability pitted trial attorneys and organized labor against insurance companies, hazardous industries (such as mining, steel making, and textile mills), and doctors exposed to malpractice suits. In 1983 Lieutenant Governor Baxley cast a rare tie-breaking vote in the state Senate for more-generous compensation amid cheers from hard hats sitting in the balcony, while dire predictions were made of "a poorer business climate" in Alabama.[31] The AABI and the Business Council declared as their 1986 goal attempting to reverse the triumph of organized labor and trial lawyers scored in the 1982 and 1983 elections.[32]

Feuding interest groups can exhibit all the subtlety of an Alabama mud-wrestling contest, as in a Sunday supplement to the June 19, 1986, *Alabama Journal-Advertiser*, titled "What in the World is Going on in Your School?" It crudely linked the AEA as the state affiliate of the National Education Association with homosexual teachers in Alabama classrooms and to gubernatorial candidate Bill Baxley, depicted as the AEA's puppet. The cartoon illustrated Key's observation that "while all this rebelliousness tends toward the inelegant, it indicates the robustness of Alabama political life."[33]

Effects of Interest Groups on Alabama Politics

The effects of interest groups on politics in Alabama were aptly illustrated in the 1986 elections. With the retirement of Governor Wallace, four prominent Democrats fought it out in the primary: Lt. Gov. Bill Baxley, Att. Gen. Charles Graddick, former (1979–1983)

Gov. Fob James, and former (1979–1983) Lt. Gov. George McMillan. With 940,000 votes cast in the June 4, 1986, Democratic primary, Baxley (with 37%) and Graddick (with 29%) went into the runoff primary three weeks later. Fewer than 30,000 Alabamians voted in the two-candidate Republican primary, nominating Guy Hunt, an Amway distributor and former probate judge who had been badly defeated as the Republican nominee in 1978. As the following quotations suggest, the campaign was perceived in terms of special interests: "Alabama business is trying to buy—literally buy—short-term influence rather than long-term growth" (Marty Connors, executive director of the Alabama Republican party);[34] "Graddick is the candidate of the big boys and the Republicans who want to buy themselves a governor" (Bill Baxley, Democratic gubernatorial candidate);[35] "The ADC and the AEA are going to be diminished quite a bit in their voice in the Legislature if I have anything to do about it" (Charles Graddick, Democratic gubernatorial candidate).[36]

When 931,346 Alabamians voted in the Democratic runoff, Graddick led Baxley by 8,756 votes. Because Alabama does not have registration by party affiliation, a challenge was filed, belatedly joined by Baxley, who said the election was "stolen" from him by illegal Republican crossovers' votes.[37] The summer-long attempt by the Democratic party to decertify Graddick and certify Baxley as their nominee was discussed (or cussed) entirely in terms of special interests. The chair of the Alabama Democratic party, who headed the five-member committee that picked Baxley, is the registered representative of the Norfolk Southern Corporation—leading to jokes about the 1986 nomination being railroaded. Voters reacted in November by electing Guy Hunt as Alabama's first Republican governor in 112 years (Hunt, 696,203 votes; Baxley, 537,163).

In a state where the governor usually controls the Legislature and picks who chairs committees, endorsements of candidates for governor and lieutenant governor are followed with avid interest.[38] Alabama's largest newspaper began its analysis of the June 24, 1986, Democratic runoff election by saying that, "in one sweeping gesture last Tuesday, Alabama voters may have changed the course of state government. Out went key candidates supported by the coalition made up of the teachers' union, other organized labor groups, plaintiffs' trial lawyers, and blacks. In went key candidates backed by conservative business interests."[39]

The vagaries of Alabama's 1986 gubernatorial race kept interest groups scrambling. For example, the Alabama State Employees Association's SEA-PAC was forced to hedge its bets by giving equal amounts to both candidates in the Democratic runoff. The Farm Bureau PAC originally put $50,000 into Graddick's Democratic runoff campaign but, when Baxley was picked as the nominee, declined to support Graddick's write-in effort, switching instead to support the Republican Hunt. Despite $35,000 in cash and $50,000 in in-kind services, including polling,[40] Hunt's rebuff of the Farm Bureau's suggestion as to who should be the new state insurance commissioner led to the group's publicized return of inaugural ball tickets.[41]

Once in office, Alabama officials must attempt to maintain a working coalition of interest groups. For instance, in 1985 municipalities' and counties' efforts to gain a portion of the state's offshore oil royalties were rebuffed by Governor Wallace. In reaction they formed a Local Fair Share Committee to attempt to defeat the Alabama Trust Fund amendment, while a Vote Yes Alabama Committee listed the governor's executive secretary as chair and his legislative liaison as treasurer.[42] As the Alabama Legislature organized in early 1987, the Associated Press began its story: "Lt. Gov. Jim Folsom Jr., whose campaign was bankrolled by groups supporting 'tort reform,' chose state Senate committee chairmen who were backed financially by the same associations."[43] An outraged representative publicly stated he had personally seen lobbyists "actually determining" committee assignments with Alabama House leaders.[44] Thomas and Stewart observe "that interest groups focus on the arena where the money and resources are, which in Alabama is the state government."[45]

Key's conclusion of forty years ago that "factional fluidity and discontinuity probably make a government especially susceptible to individual pressures and especially disposed toward favoritism" continues to be illustrated in Alabama politics.[46] Telephone surveys (1981–1986) by Cotter and Stovall similarly concluded that "political change in Alabama has a distinctive 'short-term force' hue."[47] Personalities, and interest groups and their PACs in combination, will no doubt continue to be the major forces shaping Alabama politics in the short run, and most likely for several decades to come.

12

MISSISSIPPI

AN EXPANDING ARRAY OF INTERESTS

Thomas H. Handy

As late as 1990 the nation's general perception of Mississippi was still one of a bastion of racism, "good ol' boy" politics, and stagnated interest groups.[1] The last of these images, at least, is easy to refute, since Mississippi has experienced the same pattern of change in the number, type, and variety of interest groups as the other states of the nation.[2] In the 1950s "dozens" of interest groups were reported to be lobbying Mississippi's Legislature. The Eagleton Institution's study of the Legislature in 1971 put the number of such groups at "somewhat over a hundred."[3] In June 1990 Mississippi Department of State records showed 289 lobbyists registered to represent 202 interests.

Factors Affecting the
Type and Strength of Mississippi's Interest Groups

The economic and social circumstances of a state are fundamentally important not only in determining the number and variety of a state's interest groups but also, as Zeigler and van Dalen have shown, in determining the strength and influence of those groups.[4]

The nature of five geographic regions dominated the development of Mississippi's economy and its types of interest groups prior to World War II, and their importance continues. Two of these, the large Delta in the northwest and the smaller Prairie on the east side, because of their flat, rich land, became large-scale cotton-farming areas, which led to a large importation of blacks in the last century.

Cotton also grew on family-sized farms in the Hills, the largest geographic region, described by Key as occupying most of the northeastern quadrant of the state and "broadening out almost to the [Mississippi] River in the south and petering out in the pine forest of the coastal plain."[5] Consequently, "up until the 1930s, Mississippi was like one great cotton plantation."[6] Even in 1990 cotton remained the state's largest crop, accounting for about a quarter of all farm income.

The Piney Woods region is synonymous with the coastal plain of southeastern Mississippi. It has long been the state's lumber center, now supplemented by wood pulp, Masonite, and other wood-product interests. A fifteen-to-twenty-mile strip of coastal plain along the Gulf of Mexico forms the Coast region. It has always attracted tourists, some of whom remained. By 1990 it had a cosmopolitan population of over 330,000. Other interest groups in this area are seafood and shipbuilding (including one of the country's premier shipyards).

After World War II three things modified the influence of the geographic regions on Mississippi's economy and its interest groups. One was exploration for oil and natural gas, which developed at such a pace that during the 1960s the state ranked sixth in overall production. As of July 1990 that ranking had dropped to eleventh, but even in that year's legislative session twelve oil and gas interests maintained thirteen lobbyists.

A second and much more important development was a resolve within Mississippi to attain economic diversification. In 1936 this resolve led to the adoption of a Balance Agriculture with Industry (BAWI) program, "Mississippi's enduring contribution to publicly subsidized industrial development."[7] It blossomed in the postwar period and, under the Department of Economic Development, still offers such incentives to industry as local bond issues to raise money for land, buildings, machinery, and equipment, tax exemption for ten years or more, and even public construction of roads and railroad tracks. Because of these incentives, Mississippi has for the last decade been rated among the top ten states in business climate.

Whatever BAWI's shortcomings—an undesirable impact on the tax structure, for example, and the large number of low-paying labor-intensive industries it attracts—it has certainly achieved its primary goal of freeing the state's economy from a near-total dependence on agriculture. By June 1990, 96.8 percent of Mississippi's employed work force was engaged in nonfarm activity;[8] and the state had several strong business groups, a strong manufacturing interest group, a wide range of service groups, and a fair-sized group representing organized labor.

Agriculture showed its resolve to achieve economic diversity when many farmers turned from cotton production to other crops—principally soybeans and rice. Many also turned to farm products other than crops. Chief among these were chickens, other livestock—particularly beef, and pond catfish (a $300 million enterprise by 1988). Although these may all be considered agricultural, there are vast differences in the objectives of the catfish, beef, tree-farming, chicken, and cotton interest groups.

The third postwar change in the state's economy, and thus in interest groups, came with the great increase in the federal government's expenditures. Among these were farm subsidies, defense expenditures, and over five hundred different grant-in-aid projects that, while they naturally affected every state's economy to some extent, had even greater impact on Mississippi's. No one can accurately assess the number of new interests that have emerged because of them, but whatever the causal relationship, by 1990 the accelerated growth of Mississippi's service sector and the increase in the number and activity of its interest groups paralleled that of any other state or the nation as a whole.

Any state's social circumstances give rise to noneconomic interest groups that add another dimension to its interest group arena. Four features of Mississippi's social circumstances make them different from those of most states.

The first of these features is Mississippi's racial composition, and the experiences that whites and blacks have had in dealing with one another. Those experiences have produced attitudes that, while more likely to produce common endeavors than was the case a generation ago, are still susceptible to control by emotions inflamed on the basis of race. With the state's population being 35.2 percent black—the nation's highest—and several black interest groups organized to guard against any proposal or activity they feel might adversely affect the black community, the chance for such inflaming is probably greater in Mississippi than in any other state.

Another distinguishing feature of Mississippi's social environment is poverty. In the mid-1970s researchers Bass and DeVries wrote: "Measured by any index, poverty remains more acute here than in any other state."[9] Obviously poverty means reduced revenues for governmental programs; but it also means public support for conservative policies, since poverty produces a fear that change might be for the worse and perhaps lead to the loss of the little already owned.[10]

The third social factor is ruralism. As late as the 1970s one historian noted that "the fastest growing group in Mississippi's population is the rural nonfarmer."[11] Only by the mid-1980s did over half the state's population come to inhabit municipalities of at least twenty-five hundred people. Rural areas, especially in the Hills and Piney Woods regions, have shown the greatest resistance to laws restricting individual freedom of action. This trait has at times been used by business and other interest groups in their efforts to resist some proposed governmental regulation.

Finally, many Mississippians espouse fundamentalist religious beliefs. Therefore, "when public issues arise that affect the morals of the citizens or that appear to conflict with the scriptural pronouncements of church doctrine, church leaders have not hesitated to take a stand."[12] In 1988 and 1989, in spite of the state's considerable need for new sources of revenue, the Legislature repeatedly defeated measures to allow betting on horse races, gambling ships in state waters, or a state lottery.

The Development of Organized Interests

Exemplifying the sixth factor, Socioeconomic Development, in Table 1.1, once the changes brought on by World War II broke the grip of the one-crop economy, economic interests expanded, developing an array of organizations. So did additional social interests, although in not nearly so great a number.

Some official groups associated with religion, such as Catholic Charities, Christian Science Commission on Publications for Mississippi, Christian Action Commission of the Baptist Convention, and Mississippi Right to Life, are now active in the political arena.

But the majority of religious-interest efforts are carried on informally by groups of church members, individual ministers, or by temporary ministerial alliances formed for specific purposes.[13]

The civil rights movement that broke down so many racial barriers in the 1960s naturally produced a drastic change in the alignment of Mississippi's political parties.[14] But it also brought a great increase in both the activities of groups already established to further black interests and in the number of groups that sprung up for that purpose.[15] Some of the new groups have been transient, arising only briefly to secure better streets in a neighborhood, for example, or to boycott for a black school superintendent or against a planned school consolidation. Others have taken their place alongside organizations such as the NAACP as more-permanent advocates of black interests. These include the state branch of the Rainbow Coalition, Mississippi Association of Black Supervisors, Mississippi Conference of Black Mayors, People United to Save Humanity (PUSH), Magnolia Bar Association, Mississippi State Advisory Committee of the United States Commission on Civil Rights Under Law, and Lawyers Committee for Civil Rights Under Law.[16] In addition, the black senators and black representatives in the Mississippi Legislature, who constitute the Black Caucus, have been given a very wide representation on legislative committees. The caucus meets at least once a week during legislative sessions to discuss pending measures and devise strategies to further black interests. This group constitutes, in effect, a bloc of lobbyists for the black community.

Despite the incidence of poverty in Mississippi,[17] no specific organization has yet been created to combat the problem. However, because of the prevalence of poverty in the black community many of the black interest groups, especially PUSH, have shouldered this cause. Perhaps the most important representative of the poor, however, is the Department of Public Welfare, which can and does fight the appropriations battle, indirectly mobilizing hundreds of its clients to descend on legislators at appropriate times. After the department announced that reductions in funding decreed by the 1986 legislative session would necessitate firing 750 employees and eliminating three hundred vacant positions, with a possible loss of federal funds because of delays in processing applications, it "found" $2.1 million to rehire some 250 discharged employees.[18] But the welfare interest has some powerful rivals in the battle for Mississippi's relatively small revenue.

Since diversification has taken Mississippi's agriculture beyond the limits of the cotton field, it is now represented by many important associations, old and new, including those of cotton, dairy, soybean, tree, and catfish farmers, as well as poultry producers and horticulturists. One agricultural professional claims that if the need arises, practically every legislator in Mississippi can be reached within two or three hours through the network of agricultural interest groups.[19]

Public education has also become a very powerful force. Now that the throes of integration are past, educators are basically united (except for an occasional discordant note involving the consolidation of some districts or the hiring of personnel) in their efforts to influence public policy. In 1990 these interests were thoroughly organized into eight associations represented by eighteen lobbyists.

In higher education, fifteen public junior colleges have their own association. Ties exist between junior college presidents and legislators, and between each college and the several county boards of supervisors who appoint each college's governing board. In the 1986 legislative session the junior college association was sufficiently influential to have obtained a separate governing authority for all junior colleges despite a strong opposing recommendation made in a study by an out-of-state research firm. Among the eight state-supported four-year institutions, the three predominantly black schools prefer to rely more heavily on members of the Black Caucus than on alumni associations for legislative influence. The other five have "representatives," whom they refuse to register or even refer to as lobbyists, and alumni associations that are very active in championing their interests. They are also assisted by the Mississippi Student Network Association.

In business, several fields were temporarily represented by a PAC, the Business and Industry Political Education Committee (BIPEC), in their 1983 and 1987 efforts to elect candidates favorable to their efforts, but the permanent organization representing most businesses is the influential Mississippi Economic Council. Most industrial interests are represented by the equally powerful Mississippi Manufacturing Association, except for the oil and gas groups, which follow independent, although coordinated, paths in promoting their objectives, as do some large concerns such as the First Mississippi Corporation and the Mississippi Chemical Corporation.

One interest group that no longer has the influence it once had is organized labor. In 1971 Claude Ramsey, then AFL-CIO president, could, according to Neal Peirce, say that "we were able to elect a majority of the legislature."[20] In 1986 his successor, Thomas Knight, spoke of reduced union strength (membership being "right at 100,000 members") and marked labor's accomplishments in terms of forestalling efforts to reduce its influence.[21]

Many service groups have also formed associations to further their interests. Insurance has four, while finance has five in addition to the powerful Mississippi Bankers Association. Within the field of public service, state employees, county supervisors, circuit clerks, justice-court judges, constables, and sheriffs all have organizations representing their interests. Seven organizations represent legal interests, and six seek to further those of utilities. In fact, dozens of state-licensed service professions have similar agencies, which could be named alphabetically—architects, barbers, beauticians, chiropractors, dentists, dieticians, and so on. In 1990 there were nineteen professional organizations represented by thirty-one lobbyists in the health field alone.

The tremendous growth in the number and variety of organizations over the last generation has produced a new pattern of interest group politics that influences the course of government. An evaluation of the influence of the most important organized interests in the late 1980s is set out in Table 12.1.

Interests, the Court, and Administrative Agencies

As organized interest groups increased in both number and variety, a proliferation of lobbyists sought to achieve benefits for their groups by any means that promised the desired result. Increasingly, many groups turned to the state judiciary and administrative agencies for the benefits these could offer.

As the ultimate authority on the interpretation of both statutes and the constitution, the Mississippi Supreme Court has more fundamental power than do administrative agencies.[22] But its power is so limited by regulations regarding who can utilize it—and when and how—that its utility for interest groups, while important, is really limited to three types of actions: class action suits; test cases; and amicus curiae briefs.[23]

In Mississippi, class action suits have been much less used as an interest group tactic than in the federal courts. The relatively few of these suits that the state court hears each year come almost entirely from legal services bringing cases in civil rights matters.

The state supreme court's test cases, whether sponsored or not, average only a handful a year. Unlike the U.S. Supreme Court, which can make extensive use of the writ of certiorari to select cases in developing areas of law, the state court is the appellate court, and must take whatever cases come along. However, the Mississippi Trial Lawyers Association has brought some cases in areas such as product liability as well as some intended to see how the state court intends to develop national court rulings as those are applied to various affairs within the state. Test cases have also been brought by services coalitions and such state agencies as the Welfare Department, the State Tax Commission, and the Public Service Commission.

Only gradually over the past half-dozen years have interest groups come to regard the use of amicus briefs as likely to serve their purposes. Again, trial lawyers have been those most active in using this procedure. Two recent (1987) cases of statewide interest involved boards of supervisors' briefs in a suit concerning the fees and collections of a chancery clerk, and the briefs of six senators in a case upholding the lieutenant governor's power under Senate rules to appoint the chair and members of committees.

Although state agencies may seem to be less powerful than the state supreme court because their rules and their interpretations of statute can be overturned by that court, they use their power much more often and over a wider field of situations than does the court. It is, of course, in the nature of administrative agencies to work so closely with affected interests that some become coworkers in a common cause. As a recent national study on politics and state administration puts it, "in general, interest groups and state agencies are allies."[24]

This alliance is even more likely to be formed in Mississippi than in most other states. Instead of an administrative hierarchy of of-

Table 12.1 Influential Organized Interests in Mississippi

Most Influential

1. Mississippi Association of Educators (MAE)

   The MAE represents public school teachers. The MAE, Mississippi Professional Educators, and the Mississippi Federation of Teachers, AFL-CIO, are all part of a cohesive interest group, but MAE is about 70 percent of it. The designation "schoolteachers," "teachers," or "MAE" was ranked first or second in all survey and interview material.

2. Mississippi Bankers Association (MBA)

   The MBA ranked high in legislative effectiveness, although it received only a moderately high ranking as a participant in election campaigns.

3. Mississippi Economic Council (MEC)

   The MEC is the state's chamber of commerce. It was ranked equal with the MBA in 1986 data, but fell in the August 1990 review of rankings.

4. Public utilities

   While Mississippi Power and Light and South Central Bell are the largest of these, utilities have a lower profile and are seen as less effective in election campaign activity than in legislative activity.

5. Mississippi State Medical Association (MSMA)

   When the MSMA teams with other health interests in a legislative effort victory is practically assured, but MSMA is quite influential by itself and is surprisingly active in election campaigns.

6. Industry

   The two major components of industry interest groups are the Mississippi Manufacturing Association (MMA) and the oil and gas companies, but the group also includes such locally important interests as the seafood industry. The August 1990 review of rankings suggests that the MMA has gained influence and now should possibly occupy the third ranking.

Quite Influential

1. Iron Triangles

   The "iron triangles," a somewhat indefinite designation, include those legislator-agency-clientele groupings that consistently succeed in getting most of what they want in the way of new authority and greater financing. This designation would certainly include the Highway Department and related groups, the Agriculture and Commerce Department and related groups (which include the Farm Bureau Federation), the Department of Education and related groups, and, generally the Board of Trustees of State Institutions of Higher Learning, the Department of Wildlife Conservation (from 1990 the Department of Wildlife, Fisheries and Parks), and the Department of Public Welfare (from 1990 the Department of Human Services).

2. Mississippi Trial Lawyers Association

   The lawyers' group has had the advantage of having some 20 to 25 percent of the Legislature in its profession if not its membership. Also, it has been fairly active in past election campaigns and currently seems to be increasing that activity.

3. Insurance companies

   While the insurance industry interest is evidently among the also-rans in election-campaign activity, it seems to have a fair amount of legislative effectiveness.

Noticeably Influential

1. Black interests

   Specific black organizations were absent from the groups listed as having legislative influence on questionnaires returned by legislators. Only the NAACP showed up on those questionnaires as a group involved in election campaigns—with a "moderate influence" ranking. Subsequent interviews produced the conclusion that the Black Caucus (18 members in 1986 and 21 in 1990) had not been thought of as an interest group or as de facto lobbyists for an interest group by many legislators because caucus members were not outsiders trying to influence the Legislature. A judgment as to the effectiveness of the caucus within the Legislature and the NAACP in election campaigns produced this ranking.

2. Mississippi Association of Supervisors

3. Mississippi Municipal Association

   The Mississippi Association of Supervisors and the Municipal Association wield approximately equal influence. The supervisors have the additional influence of operating with the fifteen junior college interest groups in matters affecting these educational institutions.

4. Mississippi AFL-CIO

   Organized labor has fallen considerably in the influence it had a generation ago. While ranked of minimal importance in legislative effectiveness, it receives greater notice for its influence in election campaigns.

Note: These rankings were derived from information contained in three parts of the 1986 questionnaires returned by legislators and that obtained from subsequent interviews with legislative leaders and several politically knowledgeable agency heads. Two senators, two representatives, and three directors of leading departments reviewed these rankings in August 1990. They agreed that with possible minor adjustments the rankings accurately represent the influence groups at that time, except that the MEC had, as noted, fallen considerably in its influence during the last few years because it had aggressively supported some unpopular nonbusiness proposals, and that the industry group, especially the MMA, should probably be moved up to the ranking that the MEC occupies in this table.

fices and bureaus directed by a few major departments, Mississippi has well over a hundred agencies of varying size and design.[25] And as is indicated by the fourth factor of Table 1.1, Integration/Fragmentation of the Policy Process, in such a circumstance each agency is likely to work rather closely with one or more client groups. Actually, in a comparison of the interaction of eight agencies and the interests with which they were involved, Mississippi tied with Connecticut for thirty-fifth place in degree of interaction.[26] One could undoubtedly find (given Mississippi's number of autonomous agencies) examples in this one state of every type of agency-interest relationship existing in the whole nation. As a general rule, however, organized interest groups with attentive advocates certainly establish desired agency-client relationships better than do the less structured or passively represented ones.[27]

Then, too, any interest group may appeal to the Legislature and perhaps obtain a desired modification of a statute administered by an agency. When the tax commission faithfully administered the hard-nosed law requiring sales tax to be imposed on the sale of any item of value, one interest group appealed in vain to the commission for exemption; whereupon the group then found willing sponsors in the Legislature for a quickly enacted bill allowing the Girl Scouts to sell their cookies without collecting the sales tax.

Lobbying Ethics and Regulations

Everyone with any awareness of public affairs is likely to be conscious of what is sometimes referred to as the downside, or underside, of lobbying: what Schlozman and Tierney call the three Bs— "booze, bribes, and broads."[28] The extent of such activities is difficult to quantify. On the one hand, they are probably not nearly so prevalent as the general public seems to suspect. Even so outspoken a critic as former Representative Karl Reisenburg, who in newspaper columns of 1956 and 1958 described social favors offered by interest groups, voiced the opinion that "the few rotten apples in the legislative barrel are proportionally no higher than in any other group."[29] He also acknowledged the public's seeming tendency to think the worst of officeholders: "When a candidate has been elected and taken office, a subtle change takes place in the attitude of the public.

[The legislator] is rarely given credit for a sincere or honest motive."[30]

On the other hand, some indications of possible briberies do exist. One item in a survey conducted for this book asked Mississippi lobbyists to state their greatest frustration.[31] One responded, without amplification: "seeing a very few purchased legislators or officials." Another lobbyist wrote that if a certain interest group "had to list every member that was paying a member of the legislature a lawyer's retainer, or even paying a retainer to his law partner, his wife, son, brother, etc., . . . things would come out you would not believe."

In the questionnaire sent to legislators as part of the same survey, none made reference to any illegal gifts or expenditures.[32] However, in an interview one legislator made an oblique reference to a possible illegal expenditure by an interest group. Another definitely stated that though he did not personally know of any bribery, he understood that two or three legislators could be influenced by fees of one type or another.

Nor can we get around the fact that in 1986 the president pro tempore of the Mississippi Senate was convicted of attempting to obtain $50,000 in exchange for trying to influence the passage of a bill that would have allowed two counties to hold referenda to legalize horse racing and betting. An official of the Racing Association called in the FBI and worked with its agents to develop evidence after the senator had approached him through an intermediary.

Legislation regulating lobbying in Mississippi—providing for, among other things, the registration of both lobbyists and their employers—was enacted in 1916, but implementation was slow. Some decades later, in 1971, an Eagleton Institution report to the Legislature stated that "both pressure groups and members of the legislature have operated as if no such statutes existed."[33] The Eagleton Institution also pointed out that no lobbyist registered until 1924, and that through 1970 only an average of nineteen registered in each biennial session.

The amended law of 1977 (Mississippi Code of 1972, Annotated, Title 5, Ch. 7, Sec. 1) provides that lobbyists hired to influence any member of the Legislature on any matter pending or even possibly slated to come before any legislative committee of either house— and those lobbyists' employers—must register with the secretary of state within fifteen days of such employment and must reregister

each June 1 thereafter as long as the employment lasts. This requirement applies to any person, corporation, firm, government agency,
or association assigned the duty of lobbying as a regular function of
employment. It also applies to such employing and employed entities who make any effort to influence the official actions of any
governing or policy-making body, or their members, or any other
public official in Mississippi.

In addition to registration, the law requires each employer and
lobbyist to file an itemized statement of expenditures each year. Expenditures to be reported under oath include those for phones,
postage, rent, salaries, materials, and "anything of value"—food,
drink, entertainment, or whatever—given in connection with any
matter pending or likely to come before the Legislature or any of its
components. The report must also include the name of any legislator on whom $25 or more was expended on any single occasion.[34]

These records show that the top five spenders in 1985 were the
Mississippi Bankers Association, which disbursed $57,224; Mis-
sissippi Association of Educators, $40,035; Mississippi Consumer
Finance Association, $30,302; American Insurance Association,
$23,499; and Mississippi Power and Light, $22,426.[35] With several
reports incomplete at the end of the June grace period in 1990, the
records show the top five spenders to be the Product Liability Task
Force of Mississippi, $201,921.19; Mississippi Association of Finan-
cial Institutions (Mississippi Bankers Association), $67,661.08; Phil-
lip Morris USA, $60,000; Mississippi Power and Light, $37,992.37
(but with Mississippi Power Company and Electrical Power Association of Mississippi the total would be $80,415.07); and South Cen-
tral Bell, $32,524.51.

The two highest-paid lobbyists of 1985 were the Clifford C.
Thompson law firm, which received $74,455 from its seven clients,
and lawyer Clay C. Cooley, who received $48,927 from twelve cli-
ents. The incomplete 1990 records show the highest-paid lobbyists
were Beth Clay for the Thomas, Price, Alston and Jones law firm,
receiving $165,469.92 from sixteen clients; possibly former Sen.
Ellis Bodron, who received $74,187 from two clients and noted on
his report of two others that they had not been billed yet; Corporate
Relations Management, receiving $99,027.25 from twenty-two cli-
ents; and the Clifford C. Thompson law firm, receiving $81,145.86
from eight clients.

On the basis of news reports and some personal interviews, it seems likely that expenditures, particularly for entertaining legislators, are not always accurately reported. Clients and lobbyists both freely interpret provisions in the absence of any efforts to verify reports (N.B.: research revealed only one lobbyist who has ever found it necessary to list the name of a legislator on whom $25 or more was spent on a single occasion).

When asked to register their opinions of the present lobbying law, half the responding legislators (50.9%) labeled it "about right, fair." Only 8.8 percent found it "pretty strict," and none marked it "far too strict." On the other side of the scale, 28.3 percent of the legislators felt that the law was "not strict enough," and 14 percent thought it "far too lenient."

Naturally, the lobbyists' reactions were very different. While a large majority (88.2%) believed that some regulation of lobbying was needed, an even larger majority (92.3%) felt that the present law was adequate. Moreover, 58.8 percent said they believed that representatives of administrative agencies should register and report as lobbyists, as a strict interpretation of the present law would mandate. No agency representative now follows such a practice.

People Involved in Legislative Influencing

At the time of the survey registered lobbyists in Mississippi numbered 254, of whom fifty-nine were firms and 195 were individuals. Thirty-nine (exactly 20%) were women. Of the unregistered lobbyists, estimated by both legislators and lobbyists to be "at least fifty," a few may have represented some economic or social interests but almost all were held to be what are defined in Chapter 1 as government lobbyists or legislative liaisons. The survey results indicate that most lobbyists in Mississippi are mature individuals. Although their ages ranged from eighteen to seventy-five, only three respondents were under thirty, and almost three-fourths (71.9%) were over forty. The median age was forty-eight. Only 10 percent had not lived in Mississippi before becoming lobbyists. Three-fourths had lived in the state for at least fifteen years, 52 percent for at least a quarter of a century, and 42 percent for at least thirty years. Thus most had a broad base of common understandings and experiences to draw on in dealing with legislators.

The average Mississippi lobbyist is also quite experienced and generally well educated. The questionnaire revealed that almost two-thirds (63.5%) had lobbied before 1984. One had lobbied since the 1956–1959 Legislature, and 28.1 percent either were or had been lobbyists in other states. All but one of the respondents had formal education beyond high school. An impressive 91.8 percent held at least a bachelor's degree, 24.6 had masters' degrees, 19.7 had law degrees, and one lobbyist had a doctorate.

The work load of an average lobbyist in Mississippi is specialized in coverage and concentrated in both time and target. While about 20 percent of lobbyists in the 1984, 1985, and 1986 legislative sessions represented more than ten interests each, some 60 percent represented only one. In the 1986 regular session 26.9 percent were somewhat concerned with fewer than ten bills, 54.3 percent with from ten to fifty, and 28.8 percent with over fifty. But 61.4 percent were vitally concerned with fewer than ten bills.

During the 1986 session 69.3 percent of lobbyists spent from three to six days a month lobbying legislators, whereas almost three-fourths (74.2%) reported only one to five days per month spent lobbying between regular sessions. There was also a considerable range in position of the targeted legislators. About seven lobbyists in ten (69.8%) spent at least 40 percent of their time with uncommitted legislators. Half (50.9%) spent a maximum of one-third of their time with legislators supporting their position, and about four out of five (79.6%) spent at most 20 percent of their time with legislators generally opposed to their position.

At the time of the survey the Mississippi Legislature had 174 members: The Senate had fifty-two, which included two blacks and no women; and the House of Representatives had 122, with eighteen blacks and four women.[36] These legislators were highly visible. For one thing, the number of people each one represented was smaller than in most states. Based on the Census Bureau's midcensus estimates, the representation ratio for the Senate was about one to 50,000 and for the House about one to 21,300, ranking the two chambers thirty-third and thirty-sixth, respectively, among the states. In so rural a state, then, almost all legislators are well known throughout their constituencies. Most act as lightning rods for any view on what the government should or should not do. They feel certain that they know their constituents' attitudes on virtually every subject and thus can ignore lobbyists' claims that some other view prevails.

Legislators' attitudes on the role of government in economic and social affairs are of considerable consequence for lobbyists. Of sixty-two legislators who classified themselves ideologically for the survey, none claimed to be "quite liberal," 6.5 percent were "somewhat liberal," 40.3 percent were "moderate," another 40.3 percent were "somewhat conservative," and 12.9 percent considered themselves "quite conservative." However vague and relative such categories may be, most legislators clearly distrust any interest that requires new and experimental economic or social policies, an attitude that seems to reflect the feelings of those who have elected them.

This dominant conservatism[37] is one more reason for the absence of any real two-party system in the Legislature, the basic cause of which goes back to the Reconstruction Era. It so effectively erases party lines that some Democratic presiding officers have appointed Republicans to chair standing committees. A significant result of this lack of competition, Morehouse theorizes, is the increased impact of pressure groups on the shaping of public policy.[38]

Nevertheless, this basic conservatism does not always cause the Legislature to oppose change or even fundamental experimentation. Mississippi was the first to adopt a statewide sales tax, the first with a policy of issuing bonds to attract industry, and the first to implement a program of reading-teaching assistants for the primary grades of all public schools. Ultimately, the Mississippi Legislature must be convinced, not simply told, that a change or new policy is necessary and proper, and the more fundamental the change, it seems, the nearer disaster the state must come to convince them.

The Techniques of Influence

Interest Groups and Election Efforts

Many interest groups seek to ensure that candidates favorable to their cause are elected, not only by supporting such candidates but by seeking out the well qualified and encouraging them to run. Yet not many interest groups have conducted electoral efforts in all races for statewide and legislative offices. Instead, a few major interests have concerned themselves with from one-third to one-half of Mississippi's races. Only the public-education group has mounted a fairly effective statewide effort to ensure the election of the "right" candidates.

In ranking the five interest groups they considered most effective at election time, 81.3 percent of legislators listed public education among those five, and 41 percent listed it as the most effective. Four other groups appeared on 30–40 percent of the replies, far behind the public-education group.[39] They were well ahead of the next cluster of six groups that appeared on 2–21 percent of replies. In all, thirty-six groups were listed by one or more legislator, including a first-place vote for Boy Scouts and Girl Scouts.

While fifty-four legislators (84.3% of those responding) were willing to rank groups they considered important at election time, only forty (62.5%) listed any that they considered helpful in their own election campaigns. A mere fourteen listed more than three, and twenty-six listed three or fewer. Nine respondents listed as interest groups only one or more from the categories family, friends, or voters in my district.

To a question on how interest groups had helped their campaigns, 79.9 percent of the legislators responding stated that they had been helped by financial contributions from such organizations. Only 56.3 percent of them reported being helped by interest groups' endorsements, 20.3 percent by campaign workers, and 18.8 percent by research or advice, or both, on strategy, provided by interest groups.

The Effects of the Legislative Setting on Lobbying Techniques

Interest groups seeking to influence legislation in Mississippi face limitations of both time and meeting place. The Legislature meets annually for ninety days, except for the 125-day session following the election of state officials every four years. Committee chairs are given office space, but it is often not much and some of the offices are two blocks away from the New Capitol. Other legislators can use vacant committee rooms for conferences with constituents and lobbyists. But for the most part, meetings between lobbyists and legislators actually occur in the corridors and stairwells of the Capitol or by accident or agreement elsewhere—a less than ideal setting for the exchange of ideas and information.

This inconvenience complicates an already existing problem: the lack of personnel for gathering independent information. Until the 1984 creation of a separate legislative budget office, there were only eight full-time legislative employees, except during sessions when some extra clerical and legal assistance was provided. The few librarians provided immeasurable help to committee chairs, but individual legislators had no research staff. Thus, unless a legislator has personal knowledge of a subject or friends to bring in needed information, he or she must rely on what can be gleaned, either directly or through committee members, from registered lobbyists. Perhaps an extreme view of this dependency was expressed by a lobbyist who added at the bottom of the questionnaire that "the state legislator would be lost without some professional assistance from the outside."

A few other elements of the legislative setting influence the legislator-lobbyist relationship and heighten the need for professional lobbying. One is the increased competition for the ears of legislators. The number of bills has reached a current annual high of twenty-eight hundred, compared to some eighteen hundred introduced biennially just before the 1972 start of annual sessions. Another is the schedule of deadlines now imposed on various stages of the legislative process. Lobbyists must stay ahead of these deadlines in both houses, even if they are able to get favorable committee action in the first place. Five of those lobbyists responding to the survey listed the deadline schedule as their greatest frustration in lobbying.

However, two features of the mechanics of the legislative setting now facilitate lobbyists' work. First, several years ago all information on the status of each bill introduced into the legislative process was computerized and made available to them. Second, the Mississippi Legislature has many standing committees, twenty-eight in each house. Since some 60 percent of lobbyists surveyed claimed to have represented only one interest group during the preceding three years, most lobbyists in Mississippi seem not only to have had a great chance to develop a rapport with members of the committee handling legislation affecting them but also have kept continually informed of propitious moments to approach those members.

Specific Tactics for Influencing the Legislature

Over the years the tactics of lobbyists seeking to influence Mississippi legislators have changed from the informal and social to an emphasis on providing the kind of information that will enable them to make reasoned decisions. As Representative Jim Simpson, veteran of six sessions and chair of the House Rules Committee at the time of the survey, said, "the old smoke-filled-room guy with a pocket full of cigars waiting to take everybody to lunch—he just doesn't cut it any more."[40] Interest groups still throw parties, but from all accounts these are social mixers designed to let lobbyists and legislators meet each other and relax together. The purported unwritten rule is that no one talks shop unless a legislator does so first.

In Table 12.2 today's views on effective lobbying techniques are reflected. Lobbying methods have had to change not only because of the changing legislative setting (more interest groups, more bills, and stricter time limits) but for other reasons. Many interest groups now employ "hired guns," as Representative Wes McIngvale refers to those defined as contract lobbyists (see Chapter 1). And raising legislators' salaries from $5,000 to $10,000, with a comparable increase in their expense allowances, has attracted more-discerning legislators, with the result that lobbying now consists mainly of supplying information to guide legislators in making thoughtful decisions, which lobbyists now regard as their chief function.

In ranking six possible services they could perform for legislators, 62.8 percent of the fifty-seven lobbyists who clearly indicated a single first-place vote on the questionnaire (as opposed to some who insisted on making two or more of the services their first choice) gave top priority to supplying technical information about their clients. Top priority was given by 5.9 percent to providing nontechnical client information. Thus, two-thirds of the lobbyists felt that their most important function was supplying information about clients and their fields. The services listed and the survey results are shown

Table 12.2 Lobbyists' Ranking of Most Effective Tactics

	Rank Order					Below
	1	2	3	4	5	5
Personal contacts with legislators in an office	43.4	34.0	11.3	5.7	3.8	1.9
Using my clients' membership to lobby personally	26.4	3.8	9.4	5.7	5.7	49.1
Mobilizing public opinion behind a bill	13.2	9.4	11.3	15.1	15.1	35.9
Joint lobbying with other interests or organizations	7.6	18.9	17.0	24.5	0.0	32.1
Appearing before legislative committees	5.7	13.2	24.5	22.6	13.2	20.8
Organizing a letter-writing campaign for my client	1.9	11.3	7.6	5.7	15.1	58.5
Personal contacts with public executives	1.9	5.7	3.8	3.8	17.0	67.9
Dealing with staffs of the Legislature or an executive	0.0	1.9	13.2	13.2	17.0	52.8
Personal contacts with senior civil servants	0.0	1.9	1.9	3.8	13.2	79.3
Totals (rounded)	100.0	100.0	100.0	100.0	100.0	100.0

Note: Percentages result from rank-ordering fifty-three valid responses to the survey.

on Table 12.3. Ninety-four percent of the responding lobbyists listed an information-related function as their greatest asset.

Legislators also listed the provision of information as lobbyists' most important function. Asked to rank seven services lobbyists provide, 34 percent of the fifty-four replying legislators gave top priority to a lobbyist's supplying information on his or her clients and their policy goals, while 31.9 percent chose research and getting technical information about clients' areas of interest. The services listed and the survey results are shown in Table 12.4.

Legislators overwhelmingly prefer that lobbyists use one of two means to impart their information. When asked to rank seven possible methods, 47.2 percent gave top priority to lobbyists' appearing at committee meetings, and 32.1 percent preferred to meet them in an office. More-complete results of this survey are given in Table 12.5. For comparison, the results of a similar survey of lobbyists are shown in Table 12.6.

As to the importance legislators give their own philosophical stand, more than half of those ranking factors that would lead them to support a measure gave first place to factors reflecting their own philosophies (see Table 12.7). When asked what would be necessary for them to support an issue they disagreed with philosophically, sixty-two legislators gave ninety-four responses. Of these, 73.4 percent would require that the proposal have strong support either among their own constituents or in the state at large. Thus, it would appear that lobbyists should stress ways in which their proposals will benefit the public in the legislator's district, in the state as a whole, or in both.

Legislators and lobbyists disagree on just how much lobbyists really influence decisions. Of the lobbyists asked to estimate their influence, only one rated it as less than "some," and almost four-fifths (79.6%) rated it either "determining" (33.3%) or "important" (46.3%). However, of the legislators estimating the percentage of their votes influenced by information provided by lobbyists, almost three-fifths (59.3%) reported 20 percent or less, with only five estimating over 50 percent. When asked to list the percentage of their votes determined by political pressure from interest groups, 71.8 percent of legislators estimated 10 percent or less and almost half (48.4%) estimated 5 percent or less.

Table 12.3 Services Provided by Lobbyists: Lobbyists' View

	Rank Order					
	1	2	3	4	5	6
Help legislators in research and getting technical information	62.8	21.6	5.9	9.5	2.4	0.0
Inform legislators on the attitude of their constituents	25.5	21.6	17.7	14.3	9.5	9.5
Provide legislators with nontechnical information about my clients	5.9	31.4	17.7	23.8	19.0	7.1
Help legislators build legislative support for their bills	5.9	17.7	23.5	26.2	16.7	7.1
Inform legislators about the attitudes of other legislators	0.0	5.9	21.6	16.7	31.0	23.8
Inform legislators about the attitudes of government agencies	0.0	2.0	13.7	9.5	21.4	52.4
Totals (rounded)	100.0	100.0	100.0	100.0	100.0	100.0

Note: Percentages under rank orders 1, 2, and 3 reflect the highest-ranked categories of the fifty-one valid responses rank-ordering at least three lobbyists' services. Those under rank orders 4, 5, and 6 reflect the lowest-ranked categories of the forty-two valid responses rank-ordering all lobbyists' services.

Table 12.4 Services Provided by Lobbyists: Legislators' Views

	Rank Order						
	1	2	3	5	6	7	
Provide me information on clients and their policy goals	34.0	17.0	12.8	13.5	5.4	10.8	
Help me in research and getting technical information	31.9	25.5	10.6	2.7	5.4	8.1	
Keep me informed on pending legislation	27.7	19.2	19.2	5.4	5.4	0.0	
Help me build legislative support for my bills	4.3	21.3	19.2	13.5	16.2	2.7	
Provide information on how my constituents are thinking	2.0	6.4	17.0	16.2	21.6	27.0	
Provide information about the attitudes of other legislators	0.0	4.3	17.0	18.9	29.7	18.9	
Keep me informed about attitude of government agencies	0.0	6.4	4.3	29.7	16.2	32.4	
Totals (rounded)	100.0	100.0	100.0	100.0	100.0	100.0	

Note: Percentages under rank orders 1, 2, and 3 reflect highest-ranked categories of the forty-seven valid responses rank-ordering at least three lobbyists' services. Those under rank orders 5, 6, and 7 reflect lowest-ranked categories of the forty-one valid responses rank-ordering all lobbyists' services.

Table 12.5 Methods of Gaining Access to Legislators: Legislators' Views

	Rank Order						
	1	2	3	5	6	7
Appearing at committee hearings	47.2	20.8	17.0	2.4	4.9	0.0
Meeting in an office	32.1	26.4	13.2	12.2	4.9	2.4
Formal submissions by lobbyists	5.7	15.1	24.5	7.3	12.2	22.0
Meeting with lobbyists socially	7.6	1.9	9.4	19.5	17.1	22.0
Telephone calls to legislators	3.7	22.6	20.8	14.6	7.3	4.9
Working through other groups or legislators	1.9	7.5	11.3	22.0	24.4	19.5
Chance meeting with a lobbyist	1.9	5.7	3.7	22.0	29.3	29.3
Totals (rounded)	100.0	100.0	100.0	100.0	100.0	100.0

Note: Percentages under rank orders 1, 2, and 3 reflect highest-ranked categories of methods of access of the fifty-three valid responses rank-ordering at least three methods. Those under rank orders 5, 6, and 7 reflect lowest-ranked categories of the forty-one valid responses rank-ordering all methods.

Table 12.6 Methods of Gaining Access to Legislators: Lobbyists' Views

	Rank Order					Below
	1	2	3	4	5	5
A scheduled meeting with a legislator	56.9	17.7	15.7	2.0	3.9	3.9
Giving testimony at committee hearings	17.7	13.7	21.6	15.7	11.8	19.6
Meeting with legislators at social occasions	11.9	9.8	7.8	9.8	13.7	47.1
Working through other groups or other legislators	3.9	11.8	11.8	11.8	21.6	39.2
Chance meeting with a legislator	3.9	7.8	5.9	9.8	17.7	54.9
Telephone calls to legislators	2.0	25.5	19.6	13.7	3.9	35.3
Formal submission of reports or position papers	2.0	9.8	7.8	15.7	11.8	52.9
Working through and/or with legislative aides	2.0	3.9	9.8	21.6	15.7	47.1
Totals (rounded)	100.0	100.0	100.0	100.0	100.0	

Note: Percentages under rank orders reflect rank-ordering of five methods of access felt to be most important, on fifty-one valid responses to the lobbyists' questionnaire.

Table 12.7 Determinants of Legislators' Support for Proposals

	Rank Order							
	1	2	3	4	5	6	7	8
It agrees with my philosophy	55.6	8.9	17.8	8.9	0.0	2.2	4.4	2.2
It has general public support	20.0	40.0	31.1	2.2	2.2	2.2	2.2	0.0
It has the support of a majority of my constituents (or seems to)	20.0	37.8	24.4	8.9	4.4	2.2	2.2	0.0
It is supported by the affected government agency	2.2	2.2	11.1	17.8	11.1	24.4	15.6	15.6
The concerned group is united on it	0.0	6.7	4.4	22.2	33.3	8.9	11.1	13.3
There are several groups that support it	0.0	2.2	8.9	26.7	26.7	20.0	13.3	2.2
A majority of the legislators seem to support it	0.0	2.2	2.2	8.9	8.9	17.8	33.3	26.7
It is supported by the governor	2.2	0.0	0.0	4.4	13.3	22.2	17.8	40.0
Totals (rounded)	100.0	100.0	100.0	100.0	100.0	100.0	100.0	100.0

Note: Percentages under rank orders reflect rank-ordering of the forty-five valid responses to the legislators' questionnaire.

Conclusion

Increases in both the number and variety of interest group organizations in Mississippi since World War II have been similar to those reported in the rest of the nation and have resulted in increased competition between lobbyists for the attention of the state's policymakers, especially legislators. Thus, lobbyists have had to become more professional, basing their efforts to obtain influence on facts and logic rather than on "the three Bs." Consequently, they have become almost indispensable sources of information for legislators without personal staffs upon whom to rely for data and assessment. As was found to be the case in another country, "clearly, one may claim that lobbyists are a legitimate and very necessary channel of communication between government and the community."[41]

Those increases have also brought more conflicting views to light. Since policymakers are more likely to procure facts and conclusions from differing perspectives, they can make better decisions. And in the Mississippi Legislature, virtually without party lines, the information provided by lobbyists is not filtered through the predispositions of party leaders to the legislators, as in the Morehouse model of a strong-party state. Thus, each legislator is freer to accept or reject interest groups' propositions according to his or her own political philosophy or concern for a constituency or the state.

Another consequence of the increase has been a closer approximation to reflecting all interests. How close that approximation is can be questioned in any state. But this question involves the things that are represented—not the types, techniques, or work loads of lobbyists, which parallel those of other states. And the things that are represented are rooted in the economic and social circumstances of each state.

Whatever differences exist among the states in the degree to which their interest group organizations reflect all of a state's interests, common among them is the prospect for greater interest group activity. The Mississippi survey returns showed that nearly 60 percent of both legislators and lobbyists in this state agreed that interest groups are destined to become considerably more important.

13

LOUISIANA

THE FINAL THROES
OF FREEWHEELING WAYS?

Charles J. Barrilleaux and Charles D. Hadley

Interest groups in Louisiana exert a strong influence on politics and public policies.[1] Given the nature of Louisiana's economy, oil and chemical companies and related interests have long been influential. Later, and in response to industrialization during this century, organized labor became a force in the state's politics.[2] New Orleans, the state's major city, has a twentieth-century history of bad relations with state government, although long represented by its port, tourist interests, and other lobbying efforts in Baton Rouge. The ability of these and other groups to influence public policy was abetted by the nonprofessional Legislature and by the tremendous power of the governor. Although recent changes are altering the interest group system, groups remain potent forces in state politics.

Louisiana politics is traditionalistic and personalistic, class-based and prone to manipulation by politicians with suspect motives and by monied interests since the ascension of Longism.[3] Lax laws regulating the behavior of organized groups and individual lobbyists reflect this cultural predisposition. Lobbyists must only register with the clerk of the House and the secretary of state; failure to do so may be punished as a misdemeanor offense. Louisiana is among only three states that do not require lobbyists to report expenditures, sources of income, or other information regarding their activities.

Although some of the most blatant activities of the corps of Louisiana lobbyists have been curtailed over the past twenty years, lobbyists continue to exert tremendous pressure on state politicians and to influence the state's public policies greatly. To provide background for recent Louisiana interest group politics, we briefly discuss contemporary Louisiana politics, focusing on the changes wrought by the adoption of a new state constitution in 1974, the emergence of blacks as a political force, the rise of the Republican party, and a growing legislative power relative to that of the governor.

Contemporary Louisiana Politics

Contemporary Louisiana politics has continuities with its colorful past, especially given the media attention focused on flamboyant oratory, raw political power, and political corruption. The state's political processes, both governmental and electoral, are under constant stress and continual change. Much of the contemporary political landscape was shaped during the gubernatorial terms of Democrat Edwin W. Edwards. With his narrow 1971/72 first and second primary and general election gubernatorial victories, Edwards produced many firsts. He was the first Catholic elected governor, first gubernatorial beneficiary of the emergent black vote produced by the federal Voting Rights Act of 1965, and the first governor elected outside traditional Long/anti-Long political bifactionalism.[4]

Edwards was reminiscent of the past because of his adherence to populist causes and his flamboyant style, and because he was a lightning rod for political change. As a reformer, he was responsible for the modernization of state government and politics with the writing and adoption of a new constitution, and with the writing, adoption, and implementation of the Open Elections System. As a lightning rod, he was partially responsible for the increasing number of Republicans in the Legislature and around the state, and for the growing independence of the Legislature as a counterbalance to the executive branch and to the governor himself.

Although a number of the changes in Louisiana politics spearheaded by Edwards have had positive impacts on the political system, not all were good. Many of the changes Edwards introduced to state government led to his direct political gain, despite their being packaged as reforms, and weakened the powers of the governor's office. Few who follow him in the near future will enjoy his degree of charisma, his political base, or the oil-related boom economy. Legislative independence grew dramatically under his more fiscally conservative reform successor, Democrat Charles E. "Buddy" Roemer, who assumed office in 1988. This legislative independence, coupled with Edwards's free spending in the waning days of his administration, despite falling oil revenues, contributed to the massive state budget deficits that defined immediate post-Edwards Louisiana politics.

The Emergence of Blacks and Black Groups

Although a large portion of the population, blacks have become a political force in Louisiana only in the past twenty years, during which early voter-registration efforts, part of the civil rights movement, bore fruit. Between 1948 and 1952 black voter registration increased from 28,000 to 108,000, from approximately 5.8 to 22.5 percent of the black voting-age population (BVAP). By 1960 the number stood at 160,000 or 31.1 percent. This early success was attributed to the racial tolerance of south Louisiana Catholics.[5] An additional five thousand blacks were registered between 1960 and 1964.

The 1965 passage and implementation of the federal Voting Rights Act ended the use of literacy tests, poll taxes, and complicated voter-registration application procedures. Further, because fewer than 50 percent of Louisiana's eligible black population was registered to vote in the 1964 presidential election, the U.S. attorney general sent federal registrars into the state to register all age-eligible blacks until that percentage cutoff was reached. The impact was dramatic. By 1966 black voter registration had reached 239,000, and by 1972, when Edwards won his hard-fought gubernatorial campaign, the number had nearly doubled to 377,000 (61.6% of BVAP). It stood at 561,000, or approximately 66.8 percent of the BVAP, in 1988. Although white voter registration increased as well, the registration gap between blacks and whites had narrowed from 45.8 percent in 1960 to less than 6 percent in 1988.[6]

Before the Voting Rights Act there was not one black elected official in Louisiana. The first ten appeared a year after the act, in 1966. Like the increase in black voter registration, the expansion of black elected officials came almost overnight, initially doubling every four years between 1968 and 1976; the respective numbers were fifty-three, 119, and 250. By 1988 it had reached 524.[7] From the late 1960s, when local black political organizations with the acronyms SOUL, COUP, BOLD, and TIPS competed alongside the voters' leagues and supported successful black as well as white candidates, their number rapidly expanded. Other predominantly black neighborhoods were organized. Over the years offshoots of the more successful groups splintered into even more organizations.

By 1983, 159 black political organizations reported sharing $1,572,055 in contributions to candidates, given in exchange for political support. Nearly 90 percent of the groups were located in New Orleans and Baton Rouge, cities with a disproportionate share of Louisiana's registered black voters. Nearly three-quarters of the funds came from candidates seeking statewide office; most came from gubernatorial candidate Edwin Edwards. Although it refused to file the required reports with the state, SOUL reportedly received $700,000 from Edwards to set up a sophisticated computerized system to contact registered black New Orleans voters with personalized appeals for election support.[8] BOLD, COUP, TIPS, and OPPVL were among the groups that received from $55,000 to $200,000 from candidates, as was LIFE, the organization of New Orleans' former mayor, Ernest N. Morial. Morial spawned factionalism among black political organizations. During his second term he used LIFE to elect his approved candidates to office at the expense of incumbents associated with SOUL, COUP, and TIPS.

Reform and Republicanism

With his thin 1971/72 electoral victory in mind, Governor Edwards advocated changing the elections system soon after he assumed office. Any proposed changes, however, waited until the 1975 legislative session, after the newly written constitution was approved by the voters and cleared for implementation by the U.S. Department of Justice. Over the opposition of good-government groups, major Louisiana newspapers, the fledgling Republican party, and prominent Democratic officials, Governor Edwards prevailed upon the Legislature to restructure the elections system and, after some difficulty, gained the U.S. Justice Department's approval for the new system in time for his own bid for reelection.

The Open Elections System restructured the ballot from columns headed by political parties' symbols, including the fabled state Democratic party's rooster (claimed by some to be worth 100,000 votes by itself), to blocks of political offices without party symbols. It forced all candidates, regardless of party affiliation, if any, to face each other in a primary election. If no candidate receives a majority of the votes cast, the top two vote-getters, regardless of party, face each other in a runoff election. As it favored Edwards, who sailed to an easy first primary victory with 62.3 percent of the vote, the system has proved to favor incumbent legislators[9] and other elected officials regardless of level of government. After its initial dampening effect on Republican aspirants for the Louisiana Legislature,[10] it became a law with which Republicans could live and prosper.

The Open Elections System and black political empowerment both strengthened Louisiana's Republican party. In the first case the party developed a strategy to encourage sitting conservative Democrats to convert to the Republican party. While its centerpiece was the protection for incumbents provided by the Open Elections System, the strategy included providing campaign support and promising not to oppose converts when they sought reelection. The process began slowly in 1977. By 1985 sixteen of the twenty-two Republican representatives and two of the party's three senators were converts. The conversion phenomenon reached all levels of government and became a prominent feature of the 1980s Republican presidential campaigns in Louisiana, alongside large-scale changes in voter registration. Between 1976 and 1988 the Republican share of registered voters increased from 3.7 to 16.4 percent. Far more dramatic, and parallel to those of blacks, were the increases, principally through conversion, in number of Republican elected officials. From fewer than fifty in 1975, they increased to 118 and 270 in 1981 and 1983, respectively, and to a high point of 345 in 1984.[11] In 1991 sitting Governor Roemer announced his switch to the GOP.

Changes in black political involvement led to increased black influence on state politics, at the same time aiding the state GOP cause. Although the GOP denies any allegations of using race as an issue, evidence suggests that Republicans are aware of the strategic importance of the black vote. During the 1986 U.S. Senate elections, in which incumbent Russell Long declined to run, the campaign of Republican U.S. Representative W. Henson Moore was stymied by publicity surrounding a national GOP-financed plan to target and purge ineligible voters from the rolls in predominantly black precincts.[12] In a 1989 special election the runoff for a state legislative seat in a New Orleans suburb was between two Republican aspirants. Although it was clouded because the loser was, to put it charitably, a lackluster candidate who made the mistake of championing a reduction of Louisiana's cherished Homestead Exemption (which renders the property tax all but meaningless as a revenue source), a former Ku Klux Klan grand wizard was elected on a platform of no taxes and white rights. Although the state and national Republican party organizations denied the ex-Klansman any financial or other support, his election may signal the degree to which race has divided Louisiana politics, especially in light of southern disaffection with the national Democratic party.[13]

Legislative Rebellion

The seeds for rebellion, in many respects, were sown in 1971 when court-appointed special master Edward J. Steimel drew up a single-member legislative districting plan approved by U.S. District Court Judge E. Gordon West. The common practice of multimember districts ended. Thrown into contests against each other in the 1972 elections, some legislators chose not to seek reelection; others did not survive. Fewer than 50 percent of the incumbents were returned. More important, the door was opened for the election of blacks and Republicans.[14] The new House was a reform-minded body that, among other procedural changes, restricted lobbyists to the back of the House chamber, as was the practice in the Senate. Both chambers required lobbyists, for the first time, to register.[15]

In many respects the 1979 gubernatorial election of Republican David C. Treen sparked insurrection in traditional Democratic ranks. When Public Service Commissioner Louis Lambert, backed by organized labor, edged out Lt. Gov. James E. Fitzmorris by 2,506 votes to join Treen in a runoff election, Fitzmorris alleged vote fraud. The lieutenant governor and fellow losing Democrats openly reacted by backing Treen against Lambert. All eventually received high-level positions in the Treen administration, which helped them to retire the financial and political debts incurred in the campaign preceding the gubernatorial primary election.[16] This Democratic defection was followed by a steady stream of conservative Democrats to the Republican party and by an increased willingness on the part of legislators to buck gubernatorial wishes.

Interest Groups, Lobbyists, and the Legislature

The 1972 state elections ushered in a new era for Louisiana's government. With respect to organized interest groups, outgoing Gov. John J. McKeithen, commenting on the possibility of a constitutional convention, labeled labor and teachers as the most powerful groups to be dealt with.[17] Victor Bussie, Louisiana AFL-CIO president, speaking of the continued attempt by reform-minded legislators to curb the power of organized labor by banning lobbyists from the House and Senate floors, noted: "We now have the most effective lobbying group in the nation, as far as state organizations. . . . But we'll lose all the other fights if we lose this one."[18] Organized labor went on to win a partial victory.

The reform-oriented legislators, dubbed Young Turks, were helped by the establishment of single-member state legislative districts in 1971 and by the resulting personnel changes from the 1972 state elections. They gained sufficient support to bring much-needed reform to rules governing the organization and operation of the House and, to a lesser extent, the Senate. In the House debate to adopt a rule banning lobbyists from the chamber, one opponent noted that lobbyists "are vitally needed in this state. They ought to be on hand when we need them."[19] While the rule failed (53 to 49), a compromise rule requiring lobbyists to remain three feet behind the rail at the back of the chamber passed (59 to 42). During the debate over a proposed Senate rule similar to the one defeated in the House, senators stressed the traditional role of lobbyists in the legislative process: They were "good men who only wanted to provide information." One member noted: "Nobody has to go over the rail to talk with a lobbyist if they don't want to. . . . I want to be informed. I don't want to cast an ignorant vote."[20] Status quo prevailed in a lopsided eleven-to-twenty-eight Senate vote, with lobbyists watching from the back of the chamber.

Organization and political support remain central to organized labor's political strength. During election campaigns, labor provides money and manpower to friendly legislators. Even back in the early 1970s, according to Bussie, "if a man in office has an acceptable voting record and runs for reelection, we support him regardless; it's an ironclad rule." During the legislative session, Bussie directs labor's lobbyists, beginning daily with a 6:00 A.M. strategy session. "We keep up with every bill introduced. We have an accurate voting record on labor, education, taxation, insurance rate legislation—anything that affects a workingman and woman. We're the group that does it." Bussie is the linchpin of labor's lobbying effort, personally on hand in the legislative chambers.[21]

The symbiotic 1960s–early 1970s organized labor–business community relationship, effected through the "good-government" Public Affairs Research Council (PAR), headed by Edward Steimel, and the Council for a Better Louisiana (CABL), had ended by 1976. In the 1970s what had become a traditional labor dominance of business and industry interests evolved into a fierce competition between them. Steimel had left PAR to head the newly formed Louisiana Association of Business and Industry (LABI). At Steimel's direction, LABI successfully galvanized enough forces to push the right-to-work law. Right-to-work legislation had been scuttled by Bussie and organized labor in 1956 with the help of the Longs, through the 1976 legislative session. The hesitant Gov. Edwin Edwards ceded to overwhelming public pressure and signed the law.[22]

Nine years later, in 1985, LABI successfully lobbied the Legislature to repeal Louisiana's prevailing-wage law (assumed to be union scale) only to have it vetoed by Governor Edwards. Given this scare, representatives of organized labor made a concerted effort between legislative sessions to have a long personal visit with every legislator who would see them. With these stronger ties developed with legislators, organized labor was better prepared for the industry-oriented 1986 Legislature.

Registered Interest Groups

At the end of the 1972 legislative session, the first in which lobbyists were required to register, there were sixty lobbyists. Nearly two-thirds (38) were associated with business and industry: fifteen with oil and gas companies; fourteen with industry groups; and nine with business associations. Powerful organized labor had seven lobbyists, teachers three, government associations five, and good-government groups four. Just over a decade later, by the end of 1985, over 328 lobbyists represented 380 organizations, from the Girl Scouts and League of Women Voters to the titans LABI and AFL-CIO.[23]

Although many were associated with national corporations and associations, eight out of ten interest groups were registered as having headquarters in Louisiana. Two-thirds of the lobbyists, moreover, were located in the state capital. Fewer than one in ten of the remaining lobbyists were located outside the state (see Table 13.1). Nearly three-quarters of the interest groups were represented by one lobbyist; a few were represented by more than three lobbyists; and only 5.1 percent had between four and twelve lobbyists. Despite all of the attention given to PACs, relatively few Louisiana interest groups (14.5%) had political action committees.

By classification, most Louisiana interest groups were the instruments of businesses or corporations (70.4%) followed distantly by professional or trade associations (15.3%).[24] Represented as well were educational, governmental, and political and religious groups, each with fewer than 4 percent. While business and industry-related interest groups appear to dominate Louisiana's interest group structure, some interests, including organized labor as described above, remain more important than others. From the available published sources in the late 1970s, Morehouse identified the oil companies and associations, gas pipeline interests, Louisiana Chemical Association, forest and rice industries, manufacturers association, Farm Bureau, and AFL-CIO as dominant in the Louisiana legislative pro-

Table 13.1 Characteristics of Louisiana Interest Groups, 1985

Location of headquarters	
(Percentage; N of groups = 380)	
In-state	78.9
Out-of-state	21.1
Location of lobbyists	
(Percentage; N of groups = 380)	
Baton Rouge	61.1
Baton Rouge and in-state	4.5
Baton Rouge and out-of-state	0.8
In-state	25.0
Out-of-state	7.6
In- and out-of-state	1.1
Size of staff	
(Percentage; N of groups = 380)	
1	72.4
2	11.3
3	11.3
4	1.8
5	1.3
6	1.1
9	0.3
10	0.3
12	0.3
Political Action Committee	
(Percentage; N of groups = 380)	
Yes	14.5
No	85.5
Classification	
(Percentage; N of groups = 378)	
Business or corporate	70.4
Professional or trade	15.3
Educational	3.7
Governmental	3.2
Political	2.4
Religious	1.3
Other [a]	3.7

[a] Includes such groups as the Girl Scouts and League of Women Voters.

Sources: List of lobbyists registered with the Louisiana House of Representatives, 1985; authors' survey.

cess.[25] Aggregated for all of the states, including Louisiana, with strong interest groups vis-à-vis legislatures, the dominant interests, as shown above, were business-related (75%). The remainder were equally divided among labor, farm, education, and government.[26]

Among the 266 interest groups associated with business and industry, the ten largest concentrations, in contrast to those listed by Morehouse, were the oil industry, insurance, medical community, retail trade, gas-related industry, general business, banking and finance, construction, chemical, and transportation interests. Together, they account for more than half of the registered interest groups; the petrochemical industry alone, including pharmaceuticals (2.6%), constitute 20.4 percent (see Table 13.2). Organizing interest groups by the size of their staffs (see Table 13.3) illustrates the more than two-to-one advantage business and industry lobbyists have over the others. Teachers, represented by the Louisiana Association of Educators (a National Education Association affiliate), had the largest lobbying staff (12), followed by LABI (10), and the AFL-CIO (9). When interest groups are arrayed by concentration, the forest and rice industries would drop from Morehouse's list. Teachers, government associations, and general contractors, when interest groups are arrayed by the size of lobbying staff, would be added. The data presented in Tables 13.1, 13.2, and 13.3 suggest the relative importance of interests in Louisiana's government and politics.

Influence

Presence is one thing, influence is another. According to Haynie, the mid-1970s witnessed the transition from legislative dominance by organized labor to that of organized business under the leadership of Steimel and LABI. More specifically, the passage of the right-to-work law in 1976, noted above, marks this shift in power. Under the banner of reform, LABI serves as the organizing force for business interests. It "provides much of the leadership for the business community's interests in Baton Rouge," says Haynie. "They have spearheaded the passage of such legislation as right-to-work, unemployment and workmen's compensation reform and the like by serving as an umbrella organization for the state's different business entities." Included within Haynie's business and interest category

Table 13.2 Louisiana Interest Groups, Ranked by Concentration, 1985

Rank	Groups	Concentration (Percentage)
1	Oil industry	8.5
2	Insurance interests	8.2
3	Medical interests	6.1
4	Retail trade	5.3
5	Gas-related industry	5.3
6	Miscellaneous business	5.3
7	Banking and finance	4.8
8	Construction	4.2
9	Chemical industry	4.0
10	Transportation	3.7

Sources: List of lobbyists registered with the Louisiana House of Representatives, 1985; authors' survey.

Note: Randy K. Haynie, a lobbyist with eighteen clients (one of the largest number of clients) varying from the oil, agrifuel, and pharmaceutical industries to a brewery, racetracks, and physical-fitness and interior-design associations, lists interest groups by relative order of importance as: business (broadly construed and including oil, gas, petrochemicals, timber, retail trade, and associations of these categories); labor; education (including labor and government-related associations); trial lawyers; local government; agriculture; seafood industry; Common Cause; environmentalists; public-interest groups; and legislative caucuses (see Randy K. Haynie and Richard E. Baudouin, eds., *Grass Roots Guide to Louisiana Politics,* vol. 2: *Lobbying the Louisiana Legislature, 1988–1992* [Baton Lafayette, La.: Louisiana Government Studies, 1988], xxxiii–xxxvi).

are the oil, gas, and chemical industries, contractors, timber industry (in north and central Louisiana), retail merchants (including finance and insurance), and chambers of commerce.

Organized-labor interests, because of their closeness to "key legislators" and committee control, particularly committees with jurisdiction over labor bills, "cannot be counted out of the process by a long shot. They are patient, steady and always looking to the future." Haynie also lists the educational establishment, Trial Lawyers Association (often linked with organized labor), local government, the Louisiana Farm Bureau, and the legislative caucuses (Acadiana, Rural, Black, Orleans, Jefferson, Shreveport, and now Republican) as categories of interest groups. Other interests he sees developing are the seafood industry, Common Cause, environmentalists, and public-interest groups.[27]

Political Action Committees

An important part of any political campaign is money and usually lots of it, especially in Louisiana political campaigns. A major

Table 13.3 Louisiana Interest Groups, by Lobby Staff Size, 1985

Number of Lobbyists	Interest Group	Affiliation
12	Louisiana Association of Educators	Organized labor
10	Louisiana Association of Business and Industry	Business
9	Louisiana AFL-CIO	Organized labor
6	Louisiana Municipal, School Board, and Police Jury (county commission) associations[a]	Government
	Texaco, Inc.	Business
5	Louisiana Chemical Association	Business
	Louisiana Farm Bureau	Agriculture
	Associated General Contractors of Louisiana	Business
	Gulf States Utilities	Business
	Louisiana Dental Association	Professional/Business

[a] The three government associations are tied.

Sources: List of lobbyists registered with the Louisiana House of Representatives, 1985; authors' survey.

source of those funds are PACs, which now must abide by a $5,000 limit on campaign contributions that took effect in 1990.[28] At a glance, Louisiana's PACs mirror its interest groups (see Table 13.4). Three-quarters of the registered PACs in the mid-1980s belonged to business and industry as opposed to organized labor (10.6%) and political entities (15%). Nearly half were associated with general business or the banking and finance communities. Other major PAC concentrations were in the medical, public utilities, petrochemical, insurance, and construction industries. The ten largest PACs, in fact, contributed nearly 60 percent of the $4,404,045 given in the 1983 state elections (see Table 13.5) to candidates for statewide and state legislative office, most of which went to the latter. Again, the dominance of business and industry is evident, especially general business PACs, which alone gave just over a quarter of the contributions. Other major PAC dollars came from the legal, banking, real estate, and oil interests, in addition to organized labor, which gave about 11 percent of the total contributions as well as its traditional supply of in-kind campaign resources including campaign workers.

Table 13.4 Louisiana PACs, Ranked by Concentration

	Category	Percentage
1	General business	22.1
2	Banking and finance	20.2
3	Unconnected[a]	15.3
4	Labor	10.6
5	Medical	7.7
6	Public utilities	7.7
7	Oil, gas, and chemical	4.8
8	Insurance	4.8
9	Construction	4.8
10	Real estate[b]	1.0

[a] Includes political party PACs, good-government, political, women's and personal committees.

[b] Legal interests tied with real estate for the tenth-ranked position.

Source: Records of the Division of Ethics Administration, Office of Finance Disclosure, State of Louisiana, Baton Rouge.

Table 13.5 Campaign Contributions of Louisiana PACs, 1983

Rank	Contribution (in Dollars)	PAC	Affiliation
1	805,051	Louisiana Political Action Council	LABI
2	439,367	Lawyers for Louisiana	Trial Lawyers Association
3	326,436	Louisiana Education and Economic Development PAC	Business
4	186,098	CERDES Fund	Organized labor
5	169,837	Thomas Jefferson Fund	Organized labor
6	163,693	Louisiana Realtors PAC	Business
7	110,000	Association for Competitive Banking (ABC/PAC)	Banking
8	107,955	OPERATE	Organized labor
9	104,350	Committee to Improve Local Government	First National Bank of Commerce
10	103,189	Louisiana Independent Producers and Royalty Owners (LAIPRO) PAC	Oil Interests

Source: Records of the Division of Ethics Administration, Office of Finance Disclosure, State of Louisiana, Baton Rouge.

In the 1987 state elections two PACs alone, Louisiana Political Action Council and Lawyers for Louisiana, respectively affiliated with LABI and the Trial Lawyers Association, contributed more than the fifteen largest PACs in 1983 ($3,006,226 versus $2,914,781). The largest nineteen PACs in 1987—those making contributions of about $50,000 or more—contributed $5,293,276, more than all PACs four years earlier. Comparing the largest PACs in the two most recent state elections (see Tables 13.5 and 13.6), organized labor was affiliated only with OPERATE, the PAC of its International Union of Operating Engineers in 1987, although Lawyers for Louisiana often supported labor candidates. The remaining seventeen had business affiliations. The tables also reflect shifting legislative or issue priorities. With the Legislature's legalization of statewide banking between the 1983 and 1987 elections, banking-industry PACs were no longer among the largest campaign contributors. The new large players were related to the medical field, bond industry, and public utilities.

Different PACs have different contribution strategies. LABI's political arm, Louisiana Political Action Council (LAPAC), contributed almost $1.6 million to nearly a hundred legislative candidates. According to LAPAC's Dick Schneider, "if a guy has a business record of voting with us 60 to 70 percent of the time or better, we support them." The PAC makes a conscientious effort to limit its contributions to 10 to 15 percent of a candidate's total budget, with the exception of "some rural legislators who couldn't raise any money and we put up big amounts."[29] This sentiment was mirrored by Lawyers for Louisiana, which contributed about $1.5 million, including $100,000 to six unopposed incumbents. It supported candidates who shared its values, based on "a discussion with candidates on their philosophy as it pertains to our issues [a prolabor position on workers' compensation reform, job safety, and product liability]."[30] Other PACs had narrower interests. For example, OPERATE was concerned with maintaining Louisiana's prevailing-wage law (union scale); Government and Business Alliance and Citipac focused on statewide officials and legislative leaders associated with the state Bond Commission; and Louisiana Pharmacy PAC focused its efforts during the legislative session itself on those legislators who supported regulation of mail-order drugs. The Louisiana Nurs-

Table 13.6 Louisiana PACs, Ranked by Campaign Contributions, 1987

Rank	Contribution (in Dollars)	PAC	Parent Organization
1	1,587,879	Louisiana Political Action Council (LAPAC)	LABI
2	1,418,347	Lawyers for Louisiana	Trial Lawyers Association
3	327,465	LAMPAC	Louisiana Medical Association
4	247,079	OPERATE	International Union of Operating Engineers
5	228,195	Chiropractors PAC of Louisiana	Chiropractors Association
6	191,771	Louisiana Pharmacy PAC	Pharmacists Association
7	187,218	Louisiana Home Builders PAC	Home Builders Association
8	154,504	Government and Business Alliance	Bond Attorneys Association
9	124,514	Louisiana Nursing Home PAC	Nursing Home Association
10	117,842	South Central Bell Louisiana PAC	South Central Bell Telephone Company
11	114,554	Gulf States Utilities PAC	Gulf State Utilities Company
12	110,308	Adams and Reese PAC	Law Firm (represents various tobacco interests)
13	95,185	LA Employees Committee on Political Action of LP&L	Louisiana Power and Light Company
14	89,558	BHK PAC	Law Firm (lobbyists)
15	76,121	Private Career Schools PAC	Private Career School Owners Association
16	64,561	Louisiana Association of Educators PAC	AFL-CIO affiliate
17	58,631	Council for Fiscal Reform PAC	LABI affiliate
18	51,316	Citipac	Tax-free bond industry
19	48,228	Louisiana Dental PAC	Dentists Association

Source: Bill McMahon, "Big Contributions make PACs a Power in State Government," Baton Rouge *Sunday Advocate*, May 15, 1988, 13A.

ing Home PAC concentrated contributions on six members of the nine-member Senate Finance Committee.[31] Gulf States Utilities PAC, on the other hand, hedged its bets by contributing to candidates who ran against each other.[32]

Lobbyists and Lobbying

Influence is more than PACs and campaign contributions, although those resources ensure access to decision makers.[33] More important is effectiveness, and experienced multi-client lobbyists have an advantage in that regard.[34] Nineteen of Louisiana's 328 lobbyists had six or more clients. With the exception of one firm that specialized in private colleges and universities (eight clients), and one lobbyist who specialized principally in insurance (nine clients), most represented diverse interests.

By 1988, moreover, Louisiana lobbyists had their own room in the State Capitol, where they could go to use telephones, do paperwork, or just have coffee and relax. They also had gained the privilege of using the House of Representatives' dining room.[35] A group of top lobbyists runs the Green House, an informal restaurant where legislators can get a free lunch, cigarettes compliments of the Tobacco Institute, and other favors, any Tuesday through Thursday during the legislative session. Parties and fund-raisers for legislators also are held at the Green House.[36] In fact, parties are an important adjunct to the legislative process. All major interest groups hold parties, some institutionalized, during the legislative session; a complete schedule for nearly every night of the eighty-five-day legislative session is published and available from the House of Representatives.[37]

Parties are important for both legislators and lobbyists because they provide the opportunity for new legislators to meet their peers, to have informal conversations with them as well as lobbyists, and to build relationships between legislators and lobbyists. According to one representative, parties provide "a good opportunity to get introduced to people and especially as a freshman an opportunity to meet my colleagues in an informal setting." At parties, "98 percent of the time there's no mention of any type of lobbying unless the lawmaker brings it up; . . . people think it could be burdensome on you after you have fought the [legislative] battles all day," indicated another representative. A senator and former lobbyist feels that "anytime you can get a legislator away from the back area of the chamber, . . . whether it's some place for lunch or at a reception, it's effective."[38] Louisiana Meat Association's President Fred Lafleur, commenting on that group's legislative barbecue, said: "We thought we needed to get to know one another better—get [lawmakers] in a casual atmosphere and let them know what our concerns are."[39] Most lobbyists would readily agree.

Lobbyists go out of their way to help legislators, themselves and with their constituents. For example, South Central Bell lobbyist George Sutton tries to help legislators solve telephone problems for constituents: "If I do a good job, I hope [legislators will] feel kindly toward me." Lobbyist M. L. "Bud" Mapes, one of the elite, takes every opportunity he can to help a legislator: "I learned a long time ago that when you put others first, they instantly and automatically put you first. And frankly, there's no known defense for that, if you're sincere with it."[40] In 1987 legislators loosened their code of ethics to permit each interest group to give them up to $300 per year in entertainment expenses, and in 1988 loosened it further to permit free trips in conjunction with speaking engagements. Lobbyists typically offer legislators "hunting and fishing trips, tickets to sporting events, golf course greens fees, complimentary products, loans and even business relationships that benefit legislators or their family members. Lobbying groups such as the building contractors, or industries that employ a lot of people, may respond to legislators' requests to hire supporters and other constituents."[41]

Lobbying, however, is far more than entertainment and favors with an eye to building personal relationships with legislators for the future. It involves the hard work of drafting, introducing, steering, and defending (or defeating) legislation. In Mapes's words, lobbying is divided into "blocking and tackling" and "razzle-dazzle." Blocking "involves putting bills together, explaining them to legislators and rounding up commitments." Tackling involves "knowing how to write a bill to put it in a certain [friendly] committee, moving it at the right time [either for committee or floor action] and calling in chits and votes."[42] An integral part of Mape's "razzle-dazzle" is putting together grass-roots organizations to mobilize when necessary, and careful selection of authors and coauthors for bills—legislative leaders who are "influential members of voting blocs."[43]

Said Mapes: "At the beginning of the session we are in our attack mode. We like to pick out the real bad [bills] and get rid of them first. Rather than dilly-dally, we get on it like a hen on a junebug." When two bills affecting assessors, a group he represents, got out of committee when a legislator left the committee to go to the restroom, Mapes quickly met "with his staff and several assessors to divvy up assignments" after checking his tally sheets for committed votes: "I want to just annihilate it. I want to absolutely kill it. I want to wipe it out so the next administration won't get any ideas about it." He did just that in the House later that day.[44]

Besides hard work, an important factor in lobbying success is honesty and information. New Orleans *Times-Picayune* Capitol Bureau reporter Bill Lynch attributed the success of the late Henri Wolbrette, who represented nine diverse clients including chemicals, waste disposal, national retail chains, and a major commercial bank, to "integrity." Information was the key, as Wolbrette "believed in selling his product, whoever the client might be, on the basis of facts without distortion." Lynch noted that "it was his passion for the details of the law that made him a successful lobbyist. When Wolbrette worked on a bill, either for or against, he knew every line of it, the meaning of every line and its impact on existing law." An essential ingredient of success was Wolbrette's willingness to step aside to let a legislator take credit for legislative action.[45]

Lobbying Through the Courts

While black people's access to the Louisiana political system was substantially enhanced with the voter registration brought about by the federal Voting Rights Act of 1965, federal court litigation under that act has increased their ability to get elected to public office through court-ordered redrawing of district boundaries. The first such action was twofold: an objection to the 1971 legislatively drawn multimember redistricting plan filed with the U.S. attorney general; and U.S. District Court suits consolidated and decided under *Bussie v. Governor of Louisiana* (333 F. Supp. 452 [E.D. La. 1971]). Both the U.S. attorney general and the court found that the legislative reapportionment plan discriminated against black voters, although the court acted earlier by engaging a special master to draw a single-member district plan for both houses of the Legislature. In doing so, the special master took into consideration the district's racial composition, after considering total population.[46]

More recently, the New Orleans U.S. District Court, in *Clark v. Edwards*, handed down a decision on August 15, 1988, that ruled Louisiana's judicial elections were racially polarized. This decision forced a political solution in which the state supreme court would keep its current seven white justices, allow one to seek reelection from the old New Orleans multimember district, and create a temporary New Orleans eighth district for a black justice. The justices would rotate so that only seven would hear and decide cases. Finally, when one of the two New Orleans–area white justices left the court, its number would revert to seven. It was also proposed that the state's five circuit courts of appeal would be redistricted, with some further divided into sections to create seven predominantly black districts. The seven current white appeals court judges in those districts would take "senior" status until eligible for retirement. Although the Legislature wrote this court reform into a constitutional amendment, passed it, and submitted it to the voters in an October 7, 1989, special election, it was not adopted.[47] The issue of judicial selection and districting continues under active consideration in *Clark v. Roemer* by the U.S. District Court in Baton Rouge at this writing.

The Darker Side

There also can be an invisible and questionable side to lobbying, an example of which recently surfaced. In 1982 Middle South Utilities, Incorporated (recently renamed Entergy Corporation) settled a lawsuit with Texaco, Incorporated, for $1.7 billion. The suit revolved around Texaco's alleged refusal to honor its long-term contract to supply natural gas to its subsidiary Louisiana Power and Light (LP&L). By the time the Public Service Commission (PSC) met and ordered LP&L to refund the settlement to its customers, the $587 million first installment had been used toward the construction of its Waterford 3 nuclear power plant and toward existing debt. Middle South Chairman of the Board Floyd Lewis discussed his company's immediate problem with former law school colleague and friend Edmund M. Reggie in a chance meeting at a Council for a Better Louisiana banquet in February 1983.

After several subsequent discussions and refusals to give aid, one of which occurred in Reggie's home, Reggie agreed to represent Middle South/LP&L before the PSC. There would be no fee if the PSC decision were not overturned. If it were, Reggie would receive $250,000 immediately and $100,000 per year for ten years. Lewis did not want to know how Reggie accomplished this goal nor did he want to be kept informed of Reggie's progress. Three weeks after their agreement the PSC decision was modified in LP&L's favor; only part of the Texaco settlement had to be repaid to LP&L customers. Reggie's fees, of course, were passed on to LP&L's and sister utility New Orleans Public Service's customers in the form of higher rates.

During Governor Edwards's trial for his alleged sale of hospital certificates of need (he was acquitted), Edwards revealed that Reggie split his LP&L fees with him "for legal services performed for LP&L before I was governor in 1983 and 1984." After this came to light, Middle South terminated the payments to Reggie two months later, after Reggie had collected more than $400,000, which he split with Edwards. Reggie, now under federal indictment for the mismanagement of his failed federal savings and loan, is suing for the balance of his fees.[48]

Conclusion

The 1970s appear to be a turning point for interest group politics in Louisiana for a number of reasons. But groups remain strong, as evidenced by a frustrated Governor Roemer's statement, made after he lost a legislative vote, a vote reversed several days later: "The lobbyists got to [House members]. Look, money talks, lunches talk, lobbying talks. . . . The special interests are now running the Legislature to the disadvantage of the people and the state."[49]

The professionalism of state legislators (enhanced by increased staff, the appointment of an independent budget officer, and the provision of offices), legislators' interest in reform, and the longevity they gain through the protection of incumbents offered by the Open Elections System helped change the face of interest group politics in Louisiana. Legislative caucuses and the Republican party came to play an important role in the legislative process. Organized labor declined, and organized business and industry came to play the dominant role. Specifically, AFL-CIO's Bussie and his lobbying operation became overshadowed by that of LABI and Steimel, who visibly marshaled his votes in the back of the legislative chambers. Steimel and LABI brought organization and effectiveness to business and industry interests, including the certainty of legislative access through PAC campaign contributions. Black political organizations are ascending in importance in Louisiana politics and are forcing changes in the political and governmental systems through the courts and through campaign activities. While lobbyists' information and integrity remain a key to the profession and its success, so does their organization of like-minded supporters in the Legislature. For the present, the melding of the growing number of Republican legislators with philosophically conservative, like-minded Democrats is in the ascendancy. This will, no doubt, have the effect of keeping traditional interests strong and stymying the increasing importance of social-issue groups.

PART III

CONCLUSION

14

CHANGE, TRANSITION, AND GROWTH IN SOUTHERN INTEREST GROUP POLITICS

Ronald J. Hrebenar

Two themes dominate our analysis of contemporary interest group activity in the southern states. The first is that great changes have occurred in the interest group scene in all southern states over the last twenty-five years or so. These parallel, to a large extent, the transformation that has taken place in southern politics in general during that period. In contrast, the second theme is one of lingering traditions within interest group politics. This, too, parallels another aspect of contemporary southern politics: The tremendous up-heavals of the recent past have affected some aspects of politics a lot more than others; and some remain relatively unaffected.

In this concluding chapter we endeavor to bring some systematic understanding to this apparent contradiction in recent developments in southern interest group life. In addition, we have two other, related goals. One is to synthesize the information in the chapters on the individual states to identify characteristics in such areas as the types of groups that are active, lobbyists, group power, and group tactics. Another is to seek an answer to a question we posed at the end of Chapter 1: How different is the South with regard to its interest group system? In pursuing answers to these questions we will from time to time be referring back to the analytical framework we developed in Chapter 1 and to several of the definitions and points we raised there.[1]

Public Disclosure of Lobbying Activity in the Southern States: Registered and Unregistered Groups

To appreciate fully the contemporary group scene in the southern states and to understand the changes that have taken place in recent years, we need to realize that the actual lobbying activity that takes place is much more extensive than an examination of public disclosure information about interest groups might lead us to believe. This is because several types of groups and interests are not required to register in the South. Consequently, as in all states, there are many unregistered or "hidden" groups and lobbies at work in southern state capitals.

In Table 1.1 we set out the four types of provisions that help provide some public monitoring of interest group activity: lobby laws; conflict-of-interest provisions; campaign-finance disclosure; and rules regulating the activities of PACs. While the first three types of laws existed in most southern states before the 1970s, they were usually weak and only laxly enforced. It took the Watergate affair of 1973/74 to generate a reformist movement across the nation against political corruption and in favor of more-extensive and stringently enforced public disclosure. This movement also included the regulation of PACs, which were burgeoning largely as a result of simultaneously declining parties, rising campaign costs, and the limits imposed on campaign contributions in many states. As we have seen in the chapters on individual states, the South was affected by this post-Watergate fervor, although less so than the Upper Midwest and the Northeast.

It is, however, state lobby laws that provide the most specific and comprehensive information about interest group activity. The thrust of these laws is to provide public information and throw light on group activities rather than to restrict or attempt to control these activities. Indeed, because of the provisions relating to the right to petition government in the First Amendment to the U.S. Constitution, and similar provisions in many state constitutions, attempts to restrict lobbying would run into some serious constitutional problems. Yet these laws vary considerably in their inclusiveness, their reporting requirements, and the stringency with which they are enforced.

In particular, the variations in who is and who is not required to register as a lobbyist under the various southern state laws produce a wide variation in the number of persons registering as lobbyists as well as those registering as lobbying organizations (that is, the employers or clients of lobbyists). Compare, for example, the registrations in Florida and in Georgia. In general the South has the least stringent lobby laws of any region of the nation. And even where such laws are apparently all-inclusive, as in the case of Florida, they are only laxly enforced.

The relative weakness of lobby laws in the South is explained by a combination of factors. The traditionalistic political culture, although now disappearing in most parts of the region, leaves a legacy of nonintervention by government. The individualistic political culture that is replacing the traditionalistic is also not particularly supportive of such restrictions. Then there is the fact that the power of some major interests has enabled them to forestall or weaken legislation regulating lobbies. After years of stalling and defeats for such provisions, only in 1988 and only through the initiative process did a comprehensive ethics law, which includes registration and reporting requirements for lobbies, pass in Arkansas.[2]

As we mentioned in considering our definition of an interest group in Chapter 1, the largest of the unregistered or hidden lobbies in the states is the state government itself, particularly its agencies, boards, and commissions, and local governments. Because of the South's increasing reliance on state and local governments, these are very significant lobbying forces even in those states with diversified economies (e.g., Florida and Virginia). Main, Epstein, and Elovich, writing of Georgia, emphasized the significance of governmental lobbies, none of which appears on any registration list. From our study of southern interest groups a rough estimate would be that as many as one-third of those "lobbyists" working the halls of state government in the South on any one day represent government. So, to obtain an accurate picture of interest group activity in the South we cannot ignore government even though studying its lobbying role presents problems because of the absence of information.

Interests Active in the Southern States Today

Of all the aspects of change in interest group life documented in the twelve southern states, the one that comes through most strongly is that, since the 1960s, there has been a considerable expansion in interest group activity. This expansion has had three dimensions: First, there has been a marked increase in the number of groups seeking to influence state government; second, the range of interests has also expanded as new interests, such as social-issue, public-interest, and single-issue groups, entered the political arena, and as traditional interests fragmented. Fragmentation has been particularly evident within the business and local-government lobbies. Individual corporations and businesses, and individual cities and special districts (especially school districts), have increasingly lobbied on their own. They have done so because, although they may remain part of an umbrella organization—chamber of commerce, trade association, municipal league—they see their specific interests as not being fully served by the umbrella group. The third dimension of this expansion is that groups are lobbying more intensively than was the case twenty or even ten years ago. They have more-regular contact with public officials and use more-sophisticated techniques. In states such as Mississippi and Virginia this is in part the result of the legislative body's moving from biennial to annual sessions.

Given the shortcomings of lobby-registration records, we use the definition set out in Chapter 1 to obtain as accurate a picture as possible of the variety of groups and interests operating in southern state capitals today. These diverse groups are set out in Table 14.1. Interests are listed on the basis of two criteria: (1) the extent of their presence in the twelve states (indicated as in all 12 states or in from 1 to 11 states); and (2) whether an interest is continually active in the states where it is present, or intermittently active in some or all states where it exists. Both in the continually and the intermittently active sections, interests are listed in order of the estimated intensity of their lobbying efforts across the region.

Well over half of the interests appear in the first column, indicating that they are present in all twelve states. Although not all are continually active, this means that a very broad array of interests, both public and private, operates in the South today. Nonetheless, it is probably true to say that as much as 75 percent of the lobbying effort in terms of time and money is attributable to the twenty interests listed first under "continually active."

The increasing prominence of several interests present in all twelve states is worthy of special mention. We have already noted individual cities and special local-government district and state agencies. The most prominent of state agencies in all southern states are the departments of education or public instruction, transportation (roads are a hot political issue, especially in the rural South), and state universities and colleges. Even though agriculture is declining in the South, departments of agriculture also figure prominently (except in Arkansas where the Farm Bureau unofficially fulfils that function). Even welfare departments (in Mississippi and Georgia among other states) are quite prominent—a significant sign of the changing times and political culture in the South.

Associated with this rise of government lobbying is the increased prominence of public-sector unions, particularly state and local employees' and teachers' unions. Ideological groups, which are also often single-issue groups such as antiabortionists, have also become quite active in recent years. Public-interest organizations, particularly good-government, senior citizen, and, most of all, environmentalist groups, are other forces that now have a presence in all southern state capitals. As might be expected, black American groups also have a presence in all twelve southern states.

Interests listed in the right-hand column tend to be newly formed groups, such as consumer and animal-rights groups; or those representing an interest concentrated in certain states, such as commercial fishing in the Gulf and Atlantic states.

By any definition or categorization this array of interests is no longer narrow, although it is important to note that the diversity of the group system varies from state to state. It is also important not to equate presence with power. Just because a group or interest is active in a southern state does not by itself assure its success in achieving its goals. As we shall see, some of the interests listed in Table 14.1 are very effective most of the time, while others have very little influence at all.

Table 14.1 Interests Active in the Southern States Today

Present in All Twelve States	Present in One to Eleven States
Continually Active	
Individual business corporations[a]	Health-care corporations
Local governmental units (cities, districts, etc.)	Agribusiness corporations
State departments, boards and commissions	Latino groups
Business trade associations[b]	Gaming/racetracks
Utility companies and associations (public and private)	Commercial fishing interests
Banks and financial institutions or associations	Sportsmen's groups (esp. hunting and fishing)
Insurance companies or associations	
Public employees' unions or associations (state and local)	
Universities and colleges (public and private)	
Schoolteachers' unions or associations	
Local governmental associations	
Farmers' organizations/commodity associations	
Traditional labor unions	
Labor associations (mainly AFL-CIO)	
Environmentalists	
Oil and gas companies or associations	
Hospital associations	
Tourism groups	
Mining companies	
Railroads	
Intermittently Active	
Doctors	Taxpayers groups
Trial Lawyers and State Bar associations	Native American groups

Retailers' associations
Contractors/real estate
Liquor interests
Communication interests (telecommunications, cable TV, etc.)
Truckers
Women's groups
Black American groups
Pro- and antiabortion groups
Religious groups
Senior citizens
Social-service groups and coalitions
Good-government groups (League of Women Voters, Common Cause)
American Civil Liberties Union
Federal agencies
Groups for the physically and mentally handicapped
Student groups
Nurses
Chiropractors
Parent Teachers associations
Veterans' groups
Moral Majority
Community groups
Pro- and anti–gun control groups

Animal rights groups
Welfare rights groups
Foreign businesses (esp. from Japan)
Children's rights groups
Media associations
Pro- and antismoking interests
Groups for the arts
Consumer groups

a   An unavoidably broad category that includes manufacturing and service corporations with the exception of those listed separately (e.g., private utilities and oil and gas companies; these and other business corporations were listed separately because of their frequency of presence across the southern states).

b   Another unavoidably broad category that includes chambers of commerce as well as specific trade associations (e.g., truckers, air carriers, manufacturers' associations).

Interest Groups' Influence
on Public Policy in the South

In Chapter 1 we pointed out that in the study of interest groups the concept of group power is used in two distinct but interrelated ways: It may refer to the power of specific or individual groups, interests, or lobbies; or to the power or impact of interest groups as a whole on the political system of a particular state.

Individual Groups and Interests

In Table 14.2 we set out a comparison between the most influential groups in each southern state as developed by Morehouse a decade ago, and the findings from our study.[3] Our listing (Hrebenar-Thomas) includes two entries for each state. Groups and interests in the first entry are assessed as being the most consistently influential during the 1980s. Those in the second entry are rising in power but not yet among the first rank; or declining in power; or ephemeral or only occasionally active. Comparing the Morehouse and the Hrebenar-Thomas lists, we can discern several trends regarding the influence of individual groups and interests in the southern states.

One major trend is that the days of states' being run by one or two dominant interests—the Big Mules in Alabama, the Bourbon planters, sewing-machine manufacturers and utilities in Arkansas, or the Big Four in Texas—are virtually gone. In other words, there are no longer any "company states." To be sure, many states still have a single prominent interest, such as the Farm Bureau in Tennessee, oil companies in Texas and Louisiana, and banks, utilities, and textiles in South Carolina. But these interests must share power with other groups. Thus, as the result of expanding political pluralism, the days when one interest could dictate policy on a wide range of issues appear to be gone forever. We should be careful, however, not to assume that the decline of the dominance of individual interests has also meant the decline of group systems as a whole. This has certainly not been the case.

As to the power status of the so-called traditional interests in the South—business, agriculture, education, local government, and, to a lesser extent, labor—three of these have maintained or enhanced their power while two appear to have lost ground. Education interests (especially schoolteachers), local governments, and business remain very influential.

Contrary to some predictions, increased political pluralism and fragmentation within the business community does not appear to have significantly affected its power. Certainly, in some instances such businesses as railroads and some natural-resource enterprises, such as mining in several states, have declined, but these have been replaced by service and other businesses among the ranks of the most powerful. What has maintained, and in most states enhanced, the power of business is the South's new obsession with economic development. As we have seen throughout this book, economic development is the priority in virtually every southern state; so a favorable business climate is a top priority for most politicians. This gives business interests a considerable advantage in the fight to gain access and influence. As a result, business interests are probably stronger in the South than in any other region of the nation. This continued power of entrenched business interests is one of the major threads of continuity in interest group life in the South.

On the other hand, agriculture and traditional labor appear to have suffered some loss of power, even though they still rank among the most influential interests in some southern states. Outside of Louisiana traditional labor has never been strong in the South. The region is the least unionized in the country, with South and North Carolina holding the forty-ninth and fiftieth positions in the nation, respectively, in regards to the percentage of unionized workers. But in the last ten years or so a new phase in the power of labor has emerged, exemplified by teachers' and state and local public employees' associations. The rise of state employees' associations is one of the most noteworthy phenomena in the changing configuration of group power in southern state capitals. It appears to be linked to the increased role of state and local governments since the 1960s. This rise has also enhanced the power of many state agencies, particularly departments of education and transportation and state university systems, although this is not a trend peculiar to the South (we mentioned it in Chapter 1 as one of the major trends in group activity in the other thirty-eight states).

Table 14.2 Most Effective Interest Groups in the Twelve Southern States

Morehouse Assessment	Hrebenar-Thomas Assessment
Alabama	
Farm Bureau Federation, utilities, highway interests, Associated Industries of Alabama	Alabama Education Association, Alabama Farmers Federation (ALFA), Alabama Cattlemen's Association, utilities (Alabama Power, South Central Bell, Alabama Gas Corporation), private transportation (road builders, concrete suppliers, car dealers, railroads, gasoline suppliers), Business Council of Alabama, Wholesale Beer and Wine Association, Alabama Retail Association
	Alabama League of Municipalities, Association of County Commissioners, Alabama State Employees Association, attorneys (State Bar, Trial Lawyers, District Attorneys), Alabama Central Labor Council, AFL-CIO, black American groups (esp. Alabama Democratic Conference, New South Coalition)
Arkansas	
Transport, agriculture, utilities, natural resources (oil, timber, bauxite), insurance, local government (County Judges Association, Arkansas Municipal League), labor, Chamber of Commerce, Arkansas Free Enterprise Association	Utilities (Arkansas Power and Light, Arkansas-Louisiana Gas, electric co-ops), Arkansas Education Association, Associated Industries of Arkansas, banks and financial institutions, State Highway Commission, governor's office, Department of Fish and Game, Arkansas Medical Association, Chamber of Commerce, Arkansas Poultry Federation

Railroads, Arkansas Farm Bureau, timber and pulp companies, local governments, insurance industry, AFL-CIO, state employees, lawyers (trial lawyers, State Bar Association), religious lobbies (esp. Baptists), Common Cause

Florida

Florida Association of Realtors, Associated Industries, Trial Lawyers, Florida Association of Insurance, governor's office, schoolteachers (Florida Teachers Profession/NEA, Florida Education Association), Homebuilders and Contractors Association, health groups (Florida Medical Association, Florida Dental Association, Florida Hospital League)

Farm Bureau, Florida Citrus Processors, Phosphate Council, banks and financial institutions (esp. Barnett Banks), liquor interests, Florida Power Corporation (utility), chain stores, racetracks, senior citizens, environmentalists, media groups, Committee of 100 (association of business and community leaders)

Georgia

Atlanta banks, business associations (esp. Business Council of Georgia), Medical Association of Georgia, Georgia Association of Educators, Department of Transportation, Coca-Cola, Delta Airlines

State Board of Regents, Georgia Municipal Association, Association of County Commissioners, Trial Lawyers

Associated Industries, utilities (Florida Power Corporation, Florida Power and Light), Farm Bureau, bankers, liquor interests, chain stores, racetracks, Phosphate Council

Atlanta business group, Citizens and Southern Bank, Coca-Cola, Fuqua Industries, Delta Airlines, Trust Company of Georgia, Woodruff Foundation, education lobby, Georgia Municipal Association

Kentucky

Coal companies, Jockey Club, liquor interests, tobacco interests, Kentucky Education Association, rural electric cooperatives

Kentucky Education Association, Farm Bureau, Chamber of Commerce, AFL-CIO and traditional unions, Kentucky Bankers Association, Kentucky Medical Association, Kentucky Utility Company, state universities

Kentucky Coal Association, Kentucky Retail Federation, Kentucky Hospital Association, Humana Hospitals, Associated Industries of Kentucky, Horsemen's Benevolent and Protective Association, Kentucky Thoroughbred Association, Prichard Group (a citizens' educational lobby), environmentalists (esp. Kentuckians for the Commonwealth)

Louisiana

Oil companies (Exxon, Chevron, Texaco, Gulf, Shell, Mobile, Mid-Continental Oil and Gas Association), gas pipeline interests, Louisiana Chemical Association, forest industry, rice industry, Louisiana Manufacturers Association, Farm Bureau, AFL-CIO

Louisiana Association of Business and Industry, Louisiana AFL-CIO, oil and gas industry, Louisiana Chemical Association, timber, wholesalers and retailers (esp. liquor and beverage companies), Louisiana Association of Educators (and the K–12 lobby in general), banking industry

Trial Lawyers, local government groups (esp. Louisiana Municipal Association, county commissioners), Louisiana Farm Bureau, seafood industry, environmentalists, public interest groups (esp. Common Cause), legislative caucuses

Mississippi

Mississippi Economic Council, Farm Bureau, manufacturers association, medical association, public school teachers, associations of local officials (county supervisors, mayors, sheriffs, etc.), segregationist groups (Citizens' Council, John Birch Society, Association for Preservation of the White Race, Women for Constitutional Government)

Mississippi Association of Educators, Mississippi Bankers Association, Mississippi Economic Council, utilities (esp. Mississippi Valley Gas, Mississippi Power and Light, South Central Bell), Mississippi State Medical Association, state agencies (esp. Agriculture, Highways, Education and Public Welfare departments), State Employees Association of Mississippi, Mississippi Manufacturers Association

Mississippi Farm Bureau, Mississippi Trial Lawyers Association, oil companies, insurance companies (esp. Alliance of American Insurers, Nationwide Insurance Company), National Association for the Advancement of Colored People, Mississippi Association of Supervisors, Mississippi Municipal Association, Mississippi AFL-CIO, Common Cause

North Carolina

Textile, tobacco, furniture, utilities, banks, teachers

Education (esp. schoolteachers—North Carolina Association of Educators), North Carolina Bankers Association and individual banks (esp. NCNB Corporation and Wachovia Bank), business organizations (esp. North Carolina Citizens for Business and Industry), State Employees Association of North Carolina, lawyers (North Carolina Bar Association, Academy of Trial Lawyers), North Carolina Medical Society, insurance, agriculture (esp. North Carolina

Local government lobby (esp. North Carolina Association of County Commissioners), utilities, North Carolina Beer Wholesalers Association, environmentalists (esp. Conservation Council of North Carolina), State Council for Social Legislation, Public School Forum of North Carolina, North Carolina Center for Public Policy Research (a private think tank)

South Carolina

Banks, utilities (esp. South Carolina Electric and Gas Company, Carolina Power and Light, Duke Power Company, Santee-Cooper, Electric co-ops), textiles (esp. South Carolina Textile Manufacturers Association), real estate, construction, waste management

Lawyers, Chamber of Commerce, health care (doctors, nurses, hospitals), schoolteachers, savings and loans, state universities and technical colleges, Governor's Office and state agencies, local governments (counties and municipalities), timber/paper, farm groups, environmentalists

Tennessee

Tennessee Farm Bureau, liquor lobby (Beverage Wholesalers, Malt Beverage Association), Tennessee Bankers Association, Tennessee Education Association, Tennessee Automotive Association, Tennessee Municipal League, lawyers (Bar Association, Trial Lawyers), Tennessee State Employees Association

Planters, textiles (DuPont, Stevens, Deering-Milliken, Fiberglass, Textron, Chemstrand, Lowenstein, Burlington, Bowaters), Electric and Gas Company, banks

Manufacturers association, County Services Association, Farm Bureau, Municipal League, Education Association, liquor lobby

Tennessee Manufacturers and Taxpayers Association, Tennessee Medical Association, Tennessee Business Roundtable, Tennessee Health Care Association, Insurers of Tennessee, Tennessee Press Association, Tennessee Road Builders Association

Texas

Chemical Council, Mid-Continent Oil and Gas Association, Independent Producers and Royalty Owners, State Teachers' Association, Manufacturer's Association, medical association, Motor Transport Association, insurance organizations

Texas Trial Lawyers Association, Texas Medical Society, Texas Realtors Association, Texas State Teachers Association, big oil (esp Texas Mid-Continent Oil and Gas Association)

Texas Motor Truck Association, Texas AFL-CIO, Independent Oil and Gas Producers Association, Texas Chemical Council, Texas Association of Business, Texas Savings and Loan Association

Virginia

Virginia Electric Power, Virginia Manufacturers Association, Chamber of Commerce, railroads

Utilities (esp. Virginia Power), manufacturers (esp. Virginia Manufacturers Association), railroads (esp. Norfolk Southern, CSX), Virginia Bankers Association, Virginia League of Savings Institutions, Virginia Retail Merchants Association, builders and developers, Virginia Trucking Association, University of Virginia, Virginia Polytechnic Institute, Virginia Education Association

Chamber of Commerce, George Mason University, James Madison University, environmentalists, American Civil Liberties Union

Sources: The Morehouse list is taken from Sarah McCally Morehouse, *State Politics, Parties and Policy* (New York: Holt, Rinehart and Winston, 1981), 108–11 by permission of the publisher. The Hrebenar-Thomas list was compiled from data supplied by the authors of the twelve chapters in this book.

Note: The designation "Education Association" or "Association of Educators" in the formal title of an organization indicates a schoolteachers' organization, usually the state affiliate of the National Education Association.

The various components of the health-care industry have also seen an increase in their power. Less significant but steady gains have been made by environmentalists and by senior citizens. Then there have been a series of successes by single-issue groups as diverse as anti-ERA groups and MADD. As it did in the rest of the states, the issue of tort reform, particularly the desire by many to place a cap on awards in damage suits, brought three of the best-financed and best-organized interests—doctors, lawyers, and insurance companies—into the ranks of the most effective interests in the South during the later 1980s.

The successes of other interests, including social-issue and minority groups, do not appear to have been significant enough across the southern states to emerge as a trend. In fact, noneconomic interests probably fare worse in the South than in any other region of the country. Once again we can trace this to the traditionalistic political culture, the continuing belief in laissez-faire economics, and the strong strain of conservatism that still dominates the region. Indeed, the changes in the configuration of group power across the South, as in the other states, has been far less dramatic over the last twenty-five years than the major expansion in group activity might lead us to assume. This is not surprising when we consider the lingering influences of the southern tradition. But perhaps even more important are the factors that constitute individual group power. The players in the game may have changed by the addition of new groups, but the rules of success, particularly command of resources and building up of long-term relationships with public officials, remain virtually unchanged.

In Table 14.3 we compare the most influential interests in the South, those in the fifty states as a whole, and those in the other three regions. From this we can see the dominance of certain economic interests in the South and the comparatively lower ranking of traditional labor. Once again, these differences reflect the economic goals and the conservative political culture of the region. But perhaps the most enlightening aspect of our comparison is the similarity in power of interests in the South, the other regions, and the fifty states overall.

Overall Group Power

While much important pioneering work has been conducted in attempting to assess overall group power, the methods vary and the results have been mixed and have left many unanswered questions.

The first such study, by Zeller, was based entirely on the assessments of political scientists. Nevertheless, Zeller established the principle that group strength was primarily a function of the strength of political parties and inversely proportionate to it.[4] Subsequent researchers built upon this and attempted to provide a more scientific basis. Morehouse, for example, used measures of party strength to define the relationship more accurately.[5] Zeigler and van Dalen, and Zeigler, added the variable of economic and social development.[6] As we noted in presenting our analytical framework in Chapter 1, these theories predicted the gradual transformation of strong group systems into moderate and eventually into weak systems as economic and social pluralism advanced.[7] The results from the Hrebenar-Thomas study enable us to suggest an alternative way of approaching an understanding of overall group power.

Most problematic is the categorization of states into strong, moderate, and weak group systems. First, this designation or terminology gives the mistaken impression that in some states groups are literally weak or virtually powerless, and therefore of little, if any, significance in state politics. However, even in states where groups are not all-powerful, certain organizations may exert considerable influence, such as the United Auto Workers (UAW) and auto makers in Michigan. A more accurate and informative way to designate the overall impact of groups is to use a terminology that avoids the mistaken impression that groups are not important but that conveys the degree of their significance in state public policy–making vis-à-vis other political institutions. One way to do this is to designate the impact of the group system as *dominant, complementary,* or *subordinate* in relation to other aspects of the system, or a combination of two of these.

What are the factors that determine the status of a group system in this regard? And is there a pattern of movement from one category to another? The inverse relationship between party strength and group impact does not always hold, and socioeconomic develop-

Table 14.3 The Forty Most Effective Interests, Nationally and by Region

National Ranking		South	Midwest	West	Northeast
			Overall Rank by Region		
1	Schoolteachers' organizations (predominantly NEA)	1	1	1	2
2	General business organizations (chambers of commerce, etc.)	3	4	3	1
3	Bankers' associations (includes savings and loan associations)	2	2	7	10
4	Manufacturers (companies and associations)	4	9[a]	8[a]	5[a]
5	Traditional labor associations (predominantly AFL-CIO)	10	3	8[a]	4
6	Utility companies and associations (electric, gas, telephone, water)	7	11	2	9
7	Individual banks and financial institutions	9	13	6	7
8	Lawyers (predominantly state bar associations and trial lawyers)	5	5	15	12
9	General local government organizations (municipal leagues, county organizations, etc.)	12	17[a]	4	5[a]
10	General farm organizations (mainly state farm bureaus)	8	6	11	26
11	Doctors	6	7	16	17[a]
12	State and local government employees (other than teachers)	11	20	5	8
13	Insurance (companies and associations)	22[a]	15	17	3
14	Realtors' associations	20[a]	14	22	11
15	Individual traditional labor unions (Teamsters, UAW, etc.)	27	8	23[a]	13
16	K–12 educational interests (other than teachers)	16	16	19	23[a]
17	Health-care groups (other than doctors)	28[a]	12	31	15
18	Agricultural commodity organizations (stockraisers, grain growers, etc.)	20[a]	23[a]	8[a]	NM[b]
19	Universities and colleges (institutions and personnel)	22[a]	17[a]	18	23[a]
20	Oil and gas (companies and associations)	19	23[a]	13[a]	30[a]
21	Retailers (companies and trade associations)	17[a]	9[a]	NM[b]	21
22	Contractors/builders/developers	13[a]	33[a]	20	16
23	Environmentalists	25[a]	26[a]	25[a]	14
24	Individual cities and towns	34[a]	23[a]	13[a]	20

25	Liquor, wine, and beer interests	17[a]	21	25[a]	30[a]
26	Mining companies and associations	28	22	12	NM[b]
27	Truckers and private transport interests (excluding railroads)	13[a]	28[a]	29[a]	27[a]
28	Public interest/good-government groups	25[a]	NM[b]	35	17[a]
29	State agencies	13[a]	28[a]	NM[b]	35[a]
30	Forest product companies	28[a]	NM[b]	23[a]	27[a]
31	Senior citizens	34[a]	31[a]	28	17[a]
32	Railroads	22[a]	31[a]	33[a]	NM[b]
33	Women and minorities	32[a]	NM[b]	21	35[a]
34	Religious interests	34[a]	NM[b]	27	23[a]
35	Sportsmen/hunting and fishing (includes anti–gun control groups)	34[a]	28[a]	NM[b]	22
36	Gaming interests (racetracks/casinos/lotteries)	32[a]	33[a]	32	30[a]
37	Antiabortionists and	NM[b]	19	NM[b]	NM[b]
	tourist industry groups[a]	NM[b]	33[a]	29[a]	27[a]
38	Newspapers/media interests and	31	33[a]	NM[b]	35[a]
	taxpayers' groups[a]	NM[b]	26[a]	33[a]	35[a]
39	Tobacco lobby	NM[b]	NM[b]	NM[b]	30[a]
40	Miscellaneous (all other groups mentioned)	34[a,c]	NOM[d]	NOM[d]	30[a,e]

[a] Tied ranking.

[b] Not mentioned as an effective interest in any state in the region.

[c] The only other groups mentioned in the entire region were legislative caucuses in Louisiana.

[d] No other groups were mentioned as effective in the region.

[e] The only two other groups mentioned in the region were Certified Accountants in Rhode Island and a group in Vermont for the mentally ill.

Source: Rankings are based on Appendix 1, "The Most Effective Interests in the Fifty States," and Table 4.2, "Ranking of the Forty Most Effective Interests in the Fifty States," in Clive S. Thomas and Ronald J. Hrebenar, "Interest Groups in the States," in Politics in the American States: A Comparative Analysis, 5th ed., ed. Virginia Gray, Herbert Jacob, and Robert B. Albritton (Glenview, Ill.: Scott, Foresman/Little, Brown, 1990), 144–45.

ment and increased professionalization in government does not always lessen the impact of groups on a state's political system. This is not to argue that these variables are not significant. Rather, it is to say that their effect on overall group power appears to be different than originally predicted.

For instance, it is generally the case that party strength has considerable influence on the overall impact of groups. However, while weak party systems are invariably accompanied by dominant group systems, strong parties do not always mean weak interest group systems, as Illinois and New York attest. Furthermore, increasing party strength may not result in a decrease in overall group influence, as recent developments in California demonstrate. There is no automatic progression from dominant to subordinate status resulting from socioeconomic development and increased professionalization of government. In fact, groups often increase their influence as such developments occur. All this leads us to conclude that party strength, and socioeconomic development and professionalization are not the only factors that influence overall group power, and in some circumstances may not be the most important variables. What is needed is a more extensive explanation. While we do not claim to have developed a definitive theory, a combination of quantitative and qualitative analysis of our data indicates that a more comprehensive understanding is provided by reference to the components of our analytical framework described in Chapter 1.

Each of the eight factors in this framework has some influence on overall group power. The problem is that the impact of each appears to vary from state to state and from time to time within a state; the combined influence of all eight factors will vary accordingly. For example, the moralistic political culture apparently moderates group influence in North Dakota in a situation that, with relatively weak parties and a fragmented policy-making system, would otherwise mean that groups would be dominant. In contrast, the same political culture does not have a similar restraining influence on group power in Oregon. Here the influences of multiple access through a highly fragmented policy-making system, and the needs of economic development, appear to be the most significant. And we have already noted how a particular policy preference such as economic development in the South, can work to offset influences resulting from increased group competition that might in other circumstances reduce the overall impact of groups.

Drawing on our research, we have classified the fifty states according to group impact on their respective state policy-making systems (see Table 14.4; for purposes of comparison, the table is organized by region, which enables us to place the South in perspective against the states as a whole).

States listed in the column labeled Dominant are those in which groups as a whole are the overwhelming and consistent influence on policy-making. The column labeled Complementary contains those states where groups tend to have to work in conjunction with or are constrained by other aspects of the political system. Most often this is the party system; but it could also be a strong executive branch, competition between groups, the political culture, or a combination of all these. The column labeled Subordinate represents a situation wherein the group system is consistently subordinated to other aspects of the policy-making process; there are no states that fall into this category, indicating that research reveals that groups are not consistently subordinate in any state. The column labeled Dominant/Complementary includes those states whose group systems alternate between the two situations or are in the process of moving from one to the other. And the same can be said for the column labeled Complementary/Subordinate.

With the exception of North Carolina, all the southern states appear in either the dominant or the dominant/complementary category, with six of the twelve under "dominant." As a region, the South's interest group systems are unsurpassed in their overall impact on public policy. Only the West comes close to the South in this regard, and not very close at that. So, despite many changes in southern life and politics in the last decade, with some minor exceptions these have not markedly affected the overall power of interest groups. In fact, in several southern states—South Carolina, Georgia, Florida, and Kentucky, for example—interest groups are perhaps more powerful than ever both individually and in their overall impact on state politics.

Table 14.4 Classification of Southern States by Overall Impact of Interest Groups, Compared to Other Regions

Dominant	Dominant/Complementary	Complementary	Complementary/Subordinate	Subordinate
		The South		
	Arkansas	North Carolina		
	Georgia			
	Kentucky			
	Texas			
	Virginia			
		The West		
Alaska	Arizona	Colorado		
New Mexico	California			
	Hawaii			
	Idaho			
	Montana			
	Nevada			
	Oregon			
	Utah			
	Washington			
	Wyoming			

Alabama
Florida
Louisiana
Mississippi
South Carolina
Tennessee

The Midwest

Illinois
Indiana
Iowa
Kansas
Michigan
Missouri
North Dakota
South Dakota
Wisconsin

Minnesota
Nebraska
Ohio
Oklahoma

The Northeast

Maine
Maryland
Massachusetts
New Hampshire
New Jersey
New York
Pennsylvania

Connecticut
Delaware
Rhode Island
Vermont

West Virginia

Interest Group Tactics and Lobbyists in the South

In the South, as elsewhere, the use and misuse of political power by railroad interests during the late nineteenth century contributed to a public legacy of distrust and suspicion of interest groups and particularly the lobbyists who represent them. Over the years this attitude was reinforced by the fact that, because of the crucial importance of government actions (or in the case of the South government inaction) to the goals and particularly the material benefits of many interest groups, interests have been willing to use almost any means at their disposal, sometimes illegal ones, to secure access to public officials and to influence governmental decisions. The populist opposition to the dominance of entrenched interests in the South also included a strong anti–special interest strain. Yet while these negative images live on, the passage of public-disclosure laws and a general increase in public awareness over the last twenty-five years have changed the way that groups and lobbyists do business.

The four direct avenues of access and influence that groups use are election campaigns, the legislature, the executive branch including the bureaucracy, and the courts. Public relations and media campaigns, and to a lesser extent demonstrations, sit-ins, and the like, form the major indirect tactics, the ultimate purpose of which is to enhance direct access and influence. By far the most common and still the most effective of group tactics is the use of one or more lobbyists. In fact, until very recently it was the only tactical device used by the vast majority of groups, and it remains the sole approach used by many groups today.

Overall the state capital lobbying community has become much more pluralistic and has advanced greatly in its level of professionalism during the last twenty years. In Table 14.5 the makeup of the contemporary lobbying community in the twelve southern states is set out. Contract lobbying appears to have made the greatest strides in professionalism; but in-house lobbyists, particularly those representing associations, have also made such advances. While the level of professionalism varies from state to state, its general increase among contract lobbyists is evidenced by several developments, including an increase in the number of those working at the job full-time; the emergence of lobbying firms, which often provide a variety of services and represent as many as twenty-five clients; and an increased specialization on the part of many contract lobbyists in response to the increasing complexity of government.

Does this mean that the "good ol' boy" wheeler-dealer wearing the traditional polyester suit has passed from the lobbying scene in southern state capitals? In the raw form that he used to exist, the answer is probably yes. However, the most successful lobbyists today are wheeler-dealers under a more sophisticated guise. Like the old wheeler-dealers, they realize the need for a multifaceted approach to establishing and maintaining good relations with public officials. This includes everything from participating in election campaigns to helping officials with their personal needs. But in addition this modern-day wheeler-dealer is very aware of the increased importance of technical information, the increased professionalism and changing needs of public officials, and the increased public visibility of lobbying. The result is a low-key, highly skilled, and effective professional who is a far cry from the old public stereotype of the lobbyist.

Here, too, lies an aspect of continuity in southern interest group politics. Despite both increased professionalism and an expanding lobbying community, personal contacts and long-standing relationships between lobbyists and policymakers remain a major ingredient of success. To be sure, this is also the case in all other states, but in the long tradition of personalized politics in the South, unfettered by strong parties and cohesive legislative or executive leadership, this key personal relationship is even more crucial.

Since the 1960s, increased competition between groups as their numbers expanded, the changing needs of public officials, and an increased public awareness of both the activities and potential of interest groups have spawned other tactical devices to supplement the work of the lobbyist. These include mobilizing grass-roots support through networking (sophisticated member-contact systems); public relations and media campaigns; building coalitions with other groups; and contributing workers and especially money to election campaigns, particularly by establishing a PAC. Yet it is important to note that such tactics are not viewed as a substitute for a lobbyist. Rather, they are employed as a means of enhancing the ability of the group's lobbyists to gain access to and influence public

Table 14.5 The Five Categories of Lobbyists: Their Recruitment,
Gender, and Approximate Percentage of the Capital
Lobbying Community in Southern States

1 Contract Lobbyists

Those hired on contract for a fee specifically to lobby; they often represent
more than one client. Approximately 10% represent five or more clients.

Recruitment: Many, especially the most successful, are former elected or
appointed state officials, usually legislators or political appointees, and
sometimes former legislative staffers. An increasing number are attorneys
from capital law firms, or public relations and media specialists. Some are
former in-house lobbyists. Few are former career bureaucrats.

Gender: Predominantly male (ranges from 85% to 95%, compared with
80–90% for the fifty states as a whole).

Percentage: From 15% to 25% of the state capital lobbying community
(This is about the same as the average for the fifty states).

2 In-house Lobbyists

Employees of an association, organization, or business who as part or all of
their job act as lobbyists. These represent only one client—their employer.

Recruitment: Most have experience in the profession, business, trade, etc.,
they represent, e.g., education, health care, oil and gas, retailing, labor union
activities. Much less likely than contract lobbyists to have been public
officials, although more likely to have been so in southern states.

Gender: Approximately 80% male and 20% female (compared with 75%
male, 25% female average for all fifty states).

Percentage: From 40% to 50% of the lobbying community—the largest
category in almost all state capitals (similar for the states as a whole).

3 Government Lobbyists and Legislative Liaisons

Employees of state, local, and federal agencies who as part or all of their job
represent their agency to the legislative and executive branches of state
government. These also represent only one interest. They include state
government agency heads and senior staff, both elected and appointed
officials of local governments, and some federal officials. Specifically to
monitor their relations with the legislature, most state agencies, and some
local governments and federal agencies, appoint a person designated as a
legislative liaison.

Recruitment: Often these are career bureaucrats with broad experience in
the agency or governmental unit that they represent. Some are political
appointees, and an increasing number are recruited from the ranks of
legislative staffers. No common recruitment pattern exists for government
lobbyists as a whole.

Gender: Approximately 25–35% are female; higher in more economically and socially diverse states. Tends to be lower in the South, but exact figures are difficult to acquire as many states do not require government personnel to register as lobbyists.

Percentages: Difficult to estimate because they are often exempted from registering. A rough estimate for all government lobbyists is between 25% and 40%. Tends to be higher in states where state and local government employment is highest, especially in the West. No exact figures are available for the South.

4 Citizen or Volunteer Lobbyists

Persons who, usually on an ad hoc and unpaid basis, represent citizens' and community organizations or informal groups. They rarely represent more than one interest at a time.

Recruitment: Too varied for meaningful categorization, but most are very committed to their cause.

Gender: Difficult to estimate, as many are not required to register as lobbyists. It appears that the majority, and in some states as high as 75%, are female.

Percentage: Estimated at 10 to 20% of the state capital lobbying community in the states as a whole. Probably less in the South because social-service/public-interest groups are less numerous.

5 Private Individual, "Hobbyist," or Self-styled Lobbyists

Those acting on their own behalf. Therefore, the only "organization" that they "officially" represent is themselves. They usually lobby for pet projects or direct personal benefits, or against some policy or proposal that they find particularly objectionable.

Recruitment: Other than self-recruitment, no common pattern.

Gender: Difficult to estimate, as usually, many are not required to, or do not, register as lobbyists. Probably most are male, especially in the South.

Percentage: Difficult to estimate, but probably less than 5%. May be higher in the South because of the personalized and formerly elitist nature of southern politics.

Source: Adapted for the South from Figure 2 in Clive S. Thomas and Ronald J. Hrebenar, "Interest Groups in the States," in *Politics in the American States: A Comparative Analysis,* 5th ed., ed. Virginia Gray, Herbert Jacob, and Robert B. Albritton (Glenview, Ill.: Scott, Foresman/Little, Brown, 1990), 150–51.

officials. Shrewd and experienced group leaders and lobbyists choose the most cost-efficient and politically effective method that they can to achieve their goals. In most cases this means establishing a legislator-lobbyist contact that involves a minimum of other group members. They employ the newer techniques only if absolutely necessary. This is partly because public relations campaigns, setting up networks, and contributing to election campaigns are all very costly. Equally important is that the more people involved in a campaign and the more complex the strategy, the harder it is to orchestrate. Nevertheless, for the reasons we related above, these new techniques are being widely and increasingly used.

Finally, it is important to note that group tactics and group activity at the state level do not usually take place in isolation. Either directly or indirectly, they are often connected with and affected by group activities at the federal and sometimes at the local level. Many state groups have national affiliates. NEA, for example, has an extensive and sophisticated national organization that provides all sorts of aid and advice to its state affiliates. State affiliates also sometimes participate in lobbying in Washington, D.C. At the same time, local chapters of state schoolteachers' associations often lobby local school boards. Large corporations, such as IBM and some oil companies, set general policies on political involvement that are followed by the state offices of these organizations. According to Zeigler, interstate cooperation and funding of groups has also increased.[8] We found that this is particularly the case with social issues such as abortion, gun control, and attempts to restrict smoking.

The Transition in Southern Politics and the Southern Interest Group System

The question that will perhaps be uppermost in the minds of experts on southern politics in regards to contemporary interest group life is to what extent the major transformation in southern politics in the period since the 1960s has had an impact on the interest group system in southern states. This question has received very little attention in the literature on southern politics. So far we have addressed it only incidentally in the chapters on individual states and in the Introduction and this concluding chapter. We now synthesize that analysis and consider the issue directly.

Of the numerous changes that have made themselves felt in southern life and politics over the last three decades, we single out six that have been particularly significant: (1) increased political participation by blacks and lower-income whites; (2) the rise of the Republican party, and the emergence, in most states, of two-party competition; (3) extensive reapportionment of state legislatures; (4) increased economic diversity and the decreasing importance of agriculture; (5) increasing urbanization accompanied by a growth of the middle class; and (6) increased demand for state and local governmental services and a consequently expanded role for these governments.

To deal with the last four of these first: as we have noted on several occasions in this book, each of them has had a considerable *direct* impact on interest group life in each of the twelve southern states. Together with the decline in the importance of agriculture, reapportionment has undermined the power of agricultural groups, of rural local governments, and of the "courthouse rings" and Bourbon interests that were so dominant in the first half of this century. And while the rural South is still a force politically, power has shifted to the expanding urban areas. This increased urbanization with its middle class has nurtured diversity in the groups operating in state capitals as well as contributed to an expanded number of active interests. The increasing demand for governmental services has had a similar result. In particular, it has spawned the rise of public-sector groups such as state and local employees, and helped enhance the power of teachers. All this increased governmental activity has also brought an array of, for the most part, unregistered groups onto the lobbying scene, most notably government agencies at both the state and local levels. The effect of economic diversity has also had its impact on southern interest group life. But this has worked less to change things than to reinforce the old pattern of the dominance of economic and especially business interests. This is also in part a consequence of the modern South's obsession with economic development.

In addition, the combined effects on interest group activity of these four developments in recent southern politics have worked to produce more competition between groups and the need for more-extensive and technically oriented information. This in turn has produced a higher degree of professionalism both in the organization and operation of lobbying campaigns and among those who engage in lobbying.

But what of the impact on southern interest group life of increased political participation by blacks and lower-income whites, and of increased party competition and the rise of the Republicans? Judging by the effects that these two developments have had on other areas of southern politics, such as campaign strategy, the operations of state legislatures, and the policy agenda, it might be assumed that they would also have had a major direct impact on interest group activity. The evidence does not support this, however. While there have probably been many *indirect* effects, and some minor direct consequences of these two developments on southern interest group life, their impact has been negligible.

If the rise of the Republicans had been substantial in state politics (as it has been in federal elections in the region) then one could assume that the strong party systems that would have resulted would have moderated the power of interest groups. But in no southern state have Republicans become strong enough to engender a strong party system that would then take over from interest groups the role of structuring state politics. Because the predominant southern ideological orientation is conservatism, Republicans offer a less clear choice in terms of policy orientation. Instead, in some respects, Republicans simply offer another form of old southern factionalism—just a variation on old Democratic politics. The continuing power vacuum in southern politics is filled by interest groups. So the rise of the Republican party in the South has done little to change the environment in which these groups operate.

More surprising is the fact that the major expansion in the political participation of blacks has not had a major impact on southern interest group life. Although at a closer look this is not so surprising, especially when one considers the nature of interest group activity and the ingredients for success, and the diversity of the black community in southern states. For blacks to have a major direct impact, in the form of powerful groups, they would require a cohesiveness and singleness of purpose, plus tremendous organizational skill. The black community is far from a monolith, however. Like other racial and ethnic minority groups, Chicanos and Native Americans, for example, blacks often subordinate their nebulous solidarity as an underprivileged group to the more specific goals of their occupational or personal interest. Thus black teachers often see themselves as teachers first and blacks second when it comes to securing political benefits. And a black industrial union worker may see himself or herself as being a member of the union before a member of the black community. Factionalism within the black community is also rife, as was well illustrated in the chapter on Alabama. For these, among other reasons, black American groups are not among the most prominent or powerful in southern states, although they certainly have a presence in all twelve. In this regard the success of black groups is on a par with other minority and civil rights groups in other parts of the country. Like these groups, blacks have increasingly used the courts to gain benefits that were not forthcoming from state legislatures or executive agencies.

How Different Are Interest Group Systems in the Southern States?

As with most aspects of its politics and government, the South's interest group systems and interest group politics exhibit both similarities and differences when compared to the other thirty-eight states. If we ask whether there are any features of interest group activity that are uniquely southern, the answer is probably no.

This is because, while there are certainly variations in group systems and activity between regions, these are essentially circumstantial rather than indigenous or uniquely regional. This is illustrated by the fact that Florida's interest group system is far more akin to the populous, and economically and socially diverse, states of the Northeast and Midwest than to those of, say, Arkansas or Alabama. As in any region of the country, it is a state's level of socioeconomic and political development that is the primary determining factor in shaping its interest group system, and less so the region in which it is located. For this reason, intraregional differences between states in the Peripheral South and the Deep South can be explained mainly by reference to differences in their economies and social makeup. Futhermore, developments in the past twenty-five years have tended to reduce differences in group systems and group politics across the states as these become more and more like their counterpart in Washington, D.C.

Nevertheless, despite some variations among the twelve states, today, as in the past, the South does manifest some common characteristics in its interest group systems, some of which set it apart from the rest of the nation. These circumstantial differences stem primarily from the nature of the southern historical experience and its current preoccupation with economic development, plus the feeling that it needs to catch up with the rest of the nation in such areas as education. Add to this its relatively weak political institutions, its populist tradition, and its strong conservatism and relatively low level of governmental professionalism. The result has been that southern group systems as a whole have been, and remain, very powerful. In this regard they are unsurpassed by those of any other region. In addition, southern systems have generally been among the least developed in terms of professionalism; and for a long time only a very narrow range of groups were represented in southern state capitals, thus making interest groups the preserve of a very few in terms of their role as vehicles of political participation. Both situations are changing, however, especially in the Peripheral South.

Yet, while there have been major developments over the last two decades in the diversity of groups operating in southern state capitals, resulting in increased political participation for causes and individuals not previously represented, the old, entrenched economic and institutional interests still exert the most consistent influence on public policy. These are primarily business and professional groups, as well as agencies of state and local governments. It is primarily their command of extensive resources that has enabled them to maintain, and in some cases enhance, their influence. So while the days of blatant corruption may be long gone, and more people are represented through interest groups, in the South as elsewhere groups are still far from being an ideal means of political participation.

Notes

Chapter 1. Understanding Interest
Group Activity in Southern State Politics

1. Paul Burka, "Power," *Texas Monthly* (December 1987):216.

2. Joel Garreau, *The Nine Nations of North America* (Boston: Houghton Mifflin, 1981), 130.

3. V. O. Key, Jr., *Southern Politics in State and Nation*, new ed. (Knoxville: University of Tennessee Press, 1984).

4. See, e.g., William C. Havard, ed., *The Changing Politics of the South* (Baton Rouge: Louisiana State University Press, 1972); Jack Bass and Walter DeVries, *The Transformation of Southern Politics: Social Change and Political Consequences Since 1945* (New York: Basic Books, 1976); Alexander P. Lamis, *The Two-Party South* (New York: Oxford University Press, 1984); and Earl Black and Merle Black, *Politics and Society in the South* (Cambridge, Mass.: Harvard University Press, 1987).

5. Black and Black, *Politics and Society in the South*, ch. 1, esp. 12–22.

6. John Gunther, *Inside USA* (New York: Harper and Brothers, 1951); Neal R. Peirce, *The Border South States of America* (New York: W. W. Norton, 1975), *The Deep South States of America* (New York: W. W. Norton, 1974), and *The Megastates of America* (New York: W. W. Norton, 1972); and Neal R. Peirce and Jerry Hagstrom, *The Book of America: Inside Fifty States Today* (New York: W. W. Norton, 1983).

7. Sarah McCally Morehouse, *State Politics, Parties and Policy* (New York: Holt, Rinehart and Winston, 1981), 112, Table 3.2.

8. For example, James Bolner, ed., *Louisiana Politics: Festival in a Laby-*

rinth (Baton Rouge: Louisiana State University Press, 1982) gives only incidental treatment to interest groups. In contrast, Diane D. Blair, *Arkansas Politics and Government: Do the People Rule?* (Lincoln: University of Nebraska Press, 1988), devotes ch. 6 to interest groups; as does Robert E. Botsch, author of ch. 5 in Luther F. Carter and David S. Mann, eds., *Government in the Palmetto State* (Columbia: Bureau of Government Research and Service, University of South Carolina, 1983).

9. See, e.g., chapters on Florida, Georgia, Kentucky, and Texas in Alan Rosenthal and Maureen Moakley, eds., *The Political Life of the American States* (New York: Praeger Publishers, 1984).

10. See, e.g., Tod A. Baker, Robert P. Steed, and Laurence W. Moreland, eds., *Religion and Politics in the South: Mass and Elite Perspectives* (New York: Praeger Publishers, 1983); Moreland, Baker, and Steed, eds., *Contemporary Southern Political Attitudes and Behavior* (New York: Praeger Publishers, 1982).

11. Harmon Zeigler, "The Florida Milk Commission Changes Minimum Prices," in *State and Local Government: A Case Book*, ed. Edward A. Beck (University: University of Alabama Press, 1963), 359–428; Joseph Stewart, Jr., and James F. Sheffield, Jr., "Does Interest Group Litigation Matter? The Case of Black Political Mobilization in Mississippi," *Journal of Politics* 49, no. 3 (August 1987):780–98.

12. Charles DeWitt Dunn and Donald E. Whistler, "Insiders and Outsiders: Lobbyists in the Arkansas General Assembly," paper presented to the Southern Political Science Association meeting, 1984.

13. L. Harmon Zeigler and Michael Baer, *Lobbying: Interaction and Influence in American State Legislatures* (Belmont, Calif.: Wadsworth, 1969); Charles G. Bell, Keith E. Hamm, and Charles W. Wiggins, "The Pluralistic Model Reconsidered: A Comparative Analysis of Interest Group Policy Involvement in Three States," paper presented to the American Political Science Association meeting, August–September 1985.

14. Belle Zeller, *American State Legislatures*, 2d ed. (New York: Thomas Y. Crowell, 1954), 190–91 and ch. 13, "Pressure Group Influence and Their Control"; L. Harmon Zeigler, "Interest Groups in the States," in *Politics in the American States: A Comparative Analysis*, ed. Virginia Gray, Herbert Jacob, and Kenneth N. Vines, 4th ed. (Boston: Little, Brown, 1983); L. Harmon Zeigler and Hendrik van Dalen, "Interest Groups in State Politics," in *Politics in the American States: A Comparative Analysis*, ed. Herbert Jacob and Kenneth N. Vines, 3d ed. (Boston: Little, Brown, 1976); and Morehouse, *State Politics, Parties and Policy*, ch. 3, "Pressure Groups Versus Political Parties."

15. William H. Hedrick and L. Harmon Zeigler, "Oregon: The Politics of

Power," in *Interest Group Politics in the American West*, ed. Ronald J. Hrebenar and Clive S. Thomas (Salt Lake City: University of Utah Press, 1987), 107; and Eleanor C. Main, Lee Epstein, and Debra L. Elovich, "Georgia: Business as Usual," Chapter 10.

16. David B. Truman, *The Governmental Process* (New York: Alfred A. Knopf, 1951), 33: "An interest group is any group that is based on one or more shared attitudes and makes certain claims on other groups or organizations in the society for the establishment, maintenance or enhancement of forms of behavior that are implied by the shared attitudes." Despite its insight, Truman's definition has been criticized for its emphasis on "shared attitudes" and the modes of political behavior that result from this. Subsequent work, especially that by Clark and Wilson and by Olson, persuasively challenges the notion that group members share common reasons for joining or maintaining membership in a group; or that all members are concerned or aware of the political goals of the group. See Peter B. Clark and James Q. Wilson, "Incentive Systems: A Theory of Organizations," *Administrative Science Quarterly* 6 (1961):219–66; Mancur Olson, *The Logic of Collective Action: Public Goods and the Theory of Groups* (Cambridge, Mass.: Harvard University Press, 1965); also see Terry M. Moe, *The Organization of Interests* (Chicago: University of Chicago Press, 1980).

17. For the provisions of the lobby laws in the fifty states see COGEL, *Campaign Finance, Ethics & Lobby Law Blue Book 1988–89: Special Report* (Lexington, Ky.: Council on Governmental Ethics Laws, Council of State Governments, 1988), 157–68.

18. C. Vann Woodward, *Origins of the New South, 1877–1913* (Baton Rouge: Louisiana State University Press, 1951), esp. ch. 1.

19. See, e.g., Havard, *The Changing Politics of the South*, 4; Bass and DeVries, *The Transformation of Southern Politics*, x; and Key, *Southern Politics in State and Nation*.

20. Ira Sharkansky, *Regionalism in American Politics* (Indianapolis, Ind.: Bobbs-Merrill, 1970), 4; and Key, *Southern Politics in State and Nation*, 6.

21. Key, *Southern Politics in State and Nation*, 5.

22. Morehouse's listing of the most significant groups in state politics, in *State Politics, Parties and Policy*, 108–12, was based largely on secondary sources, particularly the series of books on the regions of the United States by Neal R. Peirce (see her list of sources, 112). An updated version of Morehouse's table was produced by Michael Engel, *State and Local Politics: Fundamentals and Perspectives* (New York: St. Martin's Press, 1985), 241–42. Most of the updating appears to be based on Peirce and Hagstrom, *The Book of America*.

23. See Clive S. Thomas and Ronald J. Hrebenar, "Interest Groups in the

States," in *Politics in the American States: A Comparative Analysis*, ed. Virginia Gray, Herbert Jacob, and Robert B. Albritton, 5th ed. (Glenview, Ill.: Scott, Foresman/Little, Brown, 1990), 123–58.

Chapter 2. Kentucky:
Adapting to the Independent Legislature

1. Sarah McCalley Morehouse, *State Politics, Parties and Policy* (New York: Holt, Rinehart and Winston, 1981), 108.

2. John H. Fenton, *Politics in the Border States* (New Orleans: Houser Press, 1957), 41–67.

3. Malcolm E. Jewell and Phillip W. Roeder, "Partisanship in Kentucky: 1979–1986," in *The South's New Politics: Realignment and Dealignment*, ed. Robert H. Swansbrough and David M. Brodsky (Columbia: University of South Carolina Press, 1988).

4. Michael Baer, Phillip W. Roeder, and Lee Sigelman, "Public Opinion in Kentucky," in *Kentucky Government and Politics*, ed. Joel Goldstein (Bloomington, Ind.: College Town Press, 1984), 188–204.

5. Official lists of registered agents from the *Legislative Record*, 1974, 1990.

6. *Lexington Herald-Leader*, August 12, 1986, sec. 3, p. 8.

7. Ibid.

8. Dennis O'Keefe, "Interest Group Contributions in Kentucky's 1983 Gubernatorial and Senatorial Elections," paper presented at the annual meeting of the Kentucky Political Science Association, 1986.

9. This section is based in large part on interviews conducted in 1986 with lobbyists and legislators.

10. Morehouse, *State Politics, Parties and Policy*, 108.

11. Jack E. Bizzel, "Interest Groups, Lobbying Tactics, and Issues: 1984 Kentucky General Assembly," manuscript (1984), 2.

Chapter 3. Tennessee: New Challenges
for the Farm, Liquor, and Big Business Lobbies

1. For an excellent analysis of the increasing competitiveness of elections in Tennessee see Earl Black and Merle Black, *Politics and Society in the South* (Cambridge, Mass.: Harvard University Press, 1987); and Robert H. Swansbrough and David M. Brodsky, eds., *The South's New Politics: Re-*

alignment and Dealignment (Columbia: University of South Carolina Press, 1988).

2. The mail survey of state legislators was conducted December 1986–January 1987. Sixty-one of the 132 legislators responded (43 representatives and 18 senators) for a response rate of 46.2 percent.

3. L. Harmon Zeigler, "Interest Groups in the States," in *Politics in the American States: A Comparative Analysis*, ed. Virginia Gray, Herbert Jacob, and Kenneth N. Vines, 4th ed. (Boston: Little, Brown, 1983), 97–131.

4. Sarah McCally Morehouse, *State Politics, Parties and Policy* (New York: Holt, Rinehart and Winston, 1981), 109.

5. Jim O'Hara, "Big Dinner Tabs Scarce on Lobbyists' 'Gift' Lists," *Nashville Tennessean*, June 27, 1984, D3.

6. Ibid.

7. Ibid.

8. See the list of registered lobbyists, Office of the Secretary of State, Division of Elections.

9. Lee Greene, David Grubbs, and Victor Hobday, *Government In Tennessee*, 4th ed. (Knoxville: University of Tennessee Press, 1982), 16.

10. This finding corresponds with the conclusion of L. Harmon Zeigler and Michael Baer, *Lobbying: Interaction and Influence in American State Legislatures* (Belmont, Calif.: Wadsworth, 1969), 82.

11. Morehouse, *State Politics, Parties and Policy*, 109.

12. Rebecca Ferrar, "Consumer Groups Grow More Powerful," *Knoxville News-Sentinel*, April 13, 1987, A-1, 8.

13. Nicholas Henry, *Governing at the Grassroots*, 3d ed. (Englewood Cliffs, N.J.: Prentice-Hall, 1987), 76.

14. This finding is based on our survey of legislative staff opinions on the importance of factors in determining interest group influence. The mail questionnaire was administered December 1986–January 1987.

15. Ferrar, "Consumer Groups Grow More Powerful," A-8.

16. Based on responses to a mail questionnaire directed to the sixty-one lobbyists who represent the major state associations. Twenty-nine lobbyists, or 47.5 percent, responded to the questionnaire. Pearson correlation coefficients for lobbyist's length of tenure and rating of legislators' receptivity indicated a positive relationship; however, these were not statistically significant at the .05 level.

17. Morehouse, *State Politics, Parties and Policy*, 109.

18. Ann O'M. Bowman and Richard Kearney, *The Resurgence of the States* (Englewood Cliffs, N.J.: Prentice-Hall, 1986), 22–27.

19. Zeigler, "Interest Groups in the States," 115.

20. L. Harmon Zeigler and Hendrik van Dalen, "Interest Groups and

State Politics," in *Politics in the American States: A Comparative Analysis,* ed. Herbert Jacob and Kenneth N. Vines, 3d ed. (Boston: Little, Brown, 1976), 105–9.

Chapter 4. Virginia:
A New Look for the "Political Museum Piece"

The author wishes to thank his colleagues Arthur Gunlicks and Thomas Morris for their helpful comments.

1. V. O. Key, Jr., *Southern Politics in State and Nation* (New York: Vintage Books, 1949), 19.

2. Ralph Eisenberg, "Virginia: The Emergence of Two-Party Politics," in *The Changing Politics of the South,* ed. William C. Havard, (Baton Rouge: Louisiana State University Press, 1972), 41.

3. Key, *Southern Politics in State and Nation,* 19.

4. See, for example, John L. McGlennon, "Virginia's Changing Party Politics, 1976–1986," in *The South's New Politics: Realignment and Dealignment,* ed. Robert H. Swansbrough and David M. Brodsky (Columbia: University of South Carolina Press, 1988), 56–76.

5. Larry Sabato, "Virginia Politics: A Republican Dream Come True," in *A Virginia Profile, 1960–2000,* ed. John V. Moeser, (Palisades Park, N.J.: Commonwealth Books, 1981), 41.

6. Unless otherwise indicated, all references to lobbyist and group figures and activities are based on the records of the secretary of the commonwealth for the year or years indicated, and on interviews with lobbyists, reporters, legislators, legislative staff, agency officials, and academic authorities, conducted between 1984 and 1987.

7. Virginia Department of Economic Development, *How the Virginia Economy Compares* (Richmond: VDED, December 1985), 15a.

8. Quoted in J. Harvie Wilkinson, III, *Harry Byrd and the Changing Face of Virginia Politics, 1945–1966* (Charlottesville: University Press of Virginia, 1968), 157.

9. See, for example, Larry Sabato, *Virginia Votes: 1979–82* (Charlottesville: Institute of Government, University of Virginia, 1983), 84.

10. Russell L. Hanson, "The Intergovernmental Setting of State Politics," in *Politics in the American States,* ed. Virginia Gray, Herbert Jacob, and Kenneth N. Vines, 4th ed. (Boston: Little, Brown, 1983), 39.

11. Lawrence J. O'Toole, Jr., and Robert S. Montjoy, *Regulatory Decision Making: The Virginia State Corporation Commission* (Charlottesville: University Press of Virginia, 1984), 275–80.

12. L. Harmon Zeigler and Hendrik van Dalen, "Interest Groups in the States," in *Politics in the American States*, ed. Herbert Jacob and Kenneth Vines, 3d ed. (Boston: Little, Brown, 1976), 114.

13. See records of the secretary of the commonwealth, the Virginia State Bar, and *Martindale-Hubbard Law Directory*, vol. 6 (Summit, N.J.: Martindale-Hubbard, 1984 and 1985).

14. Charles David Hounshell, "The Legislative Function of the Virginia General Assembly," Ph.D. diss., University of Virginia, Charlottesville, 1950, 326.

15. Stephen C. St. John, "Power, Elitism, and Lawyers," Honors Thesis, University of Richmond, 1974, 124–32.

16. Zeigler and van Dalen, "Interest Groups in the States," 114.

17. *Richmond Times-Dispatch*, January 4, 1981, A-2.

18. *Washington Post*, February 21, 1985, C-1.

19. *Richmond-Times Dispatch*, July 29, 1985, B-1.

20. *Washington Post*, March 13, 1982, A-9.

21. Virginia Joint Legislative Audit and Review Commission, *Vehicle Cost Responsibility in Virginia*, Senate Document 13, 1982, 45–85; on the education issue, see, e.g., *Richmond Times-Dispatch*, January 22, 1986, A-6.

22. Jeffrey M. Berry, *The Interest Group Society*, 2d ed. (Boston: Scott, Foresman, 1989), 39.

23. See Chapter 1, note 22.

24. Belle Zeller, *American State Legislatures* (New York: Greenwood Press, 1954), 190–91; and L. Harmon Zeigler, "Interest Groups in the States," in *Politics in the American States*, ed. Herbert Jacob and Kenneth Vines, 1st ed. (Boston: Little, Brown, 1965), 114.

25. Key, *Southern Politics in State and Nation*, 26–27.

26. Wilkinson, *Byrd and the Changing Face of Virginia Politics*, 39.

27. O'Toole and Montjoy, *Regulatory Decision Making*, ch. 3.

28. Ibid., 87.

29. Benjamin Muse, *Virginia's Massive Resistance* (Bloomington: Indiana University Press, 1961), 106–10.

30. Sarah McCally Morehouse, *State Politics, Parties and Policy* (New York: Holt, Rinehart and Winston, 1981), 111; Zeigler and van Dalen, "Interest Groups in the States," 102.

31. O'Toole and Montjoy, *Regulatory Decision Making*, 338.

32. Ibid., 342; for background on the SCC changes, see esp. chs. 8–11.

33. *Richmond Times-Dispatch*, September 18, 1984, A-1. For example, proposed rules covering open burning, dust emissions, and the reactivation of emission units were dropped, while regulations addressing toxic chemical substances for which the Environmental Protection Agency had not set

federal standards were relaxed. A fuller treatment of this case can be found in John Whelan, "Interest Groups in Virginia," paper delivered at the annual meeting of the Southern Political Science Association, Atlanta, November 6–8, 1986.

34. *Richmond Times-Dispatch*, January 4, 1981, A-2.

35. For background, see Frederick P. Kozak, "Public Employee Collective Bargaining in Virginia: Perspectives and Direction," *University of Richmond Law Review* 11 (1977):431–45.

36. *Commonwealth of Virginia v. County Board of Arlington, et al.*, 217 Va. 558 (1977).

37. The VEA takes credit for achieving legislatively such things as duty-free lunch periods; class-size limitations; improved grievance procedures; salary increases; and protection and improvement of retirement benefits. See, e.g., "Legislative Successes," *Virginia Journal of Education* 77 (May 1984):6.

Chapter 5. North Carolina:
Interest Groups in a State in Transition

The author is grateful for the assistance of Terri Johnson and Elide Vargas in the research for and preparation of this chapter.

1. Jon Healey, "Bill Holman: Environmental Lobbyist Feels the Tide Turning," *Winston-Salem Journal*, May 10, 1987, A-13; "Of Legislators and Lobbyists: The Biennial Rankings of Effectiveness and Influence," *North Carolina Insight* (September 1986):52–56.

2. For a useful theoretical framework in which to understand the context of interest group activity, see Chapter 1 of this volume and Clive S. Thomas and Ronald J. Hrebenar, "Interest Groups in the States," in *Politics in the American States: A Comparative Analysis*, ed. Virginia Gray, Herbert Jacob, and Robert Albritton, 5th ed. (Glenview, Ill.: Scott, Foresman/Little, Brown, 1990), 123–58.

3. See Jack D. Fleer, Roger C. Lowery, and Charles L. Prysby, "Political Change in North Carolina," in *The South's New Politics: Realignment and Dealignment*, ed. Robert H. Swansbrough and David M. Brodsky (Columbia: University of South Carolina Press, 1988), 99–111; Jack D. Fleer, "North Carolina," in *The 1984 Presidential Election in the South: Patterns of Southern Party Politics*, ed. Robert P. Steed, Laurence W. Moreland, and Tod A. Baker (New York: Praeger Publishers, 1986); and Jack D. Fleer, *North Carolina Politics: An Introduction* (Chapel Hill: University of North Carolina Press, 1968), esp. 125–63.

4. Milton S. Heath, Jr., "Fifty Years of the General Assembly," *Popular Government* 46 (Winter 1981):20–26; Jack Betts, "The Coming of Age of the N.C. General Assembly," *North Carolina Insight* 4, no. 4 (1981):12–16; and Ann Morris, "The 800 Pound Gorilla: Meet Liston Ramsey—Mountain Populist and Unlikely King of Our Capitol Hill," *North Carolina Independent* 3 (February 1–14, 1985):1, 12.

5. Thad L. Beyle, "The Power of the Governor of North Carolina: Where the Weak Grow Strong—Except for the Governor," *North Carolina Insight*, 12, no. 2 (1990):27–45; and Thad L. Beyle, "Governors," in Gray, Jacob, and Vines, *Politics in the American States*, 217–30.

6. This discussion draws heavily from Bill Finger, "Making the Transition to a Mixed Economy," *North Carolina Insight* 8, nos. 3–4 (April 1986):3–21; and *The Future of North Carolina: Goals and Recommendations for the Year 2000*, report of the Commission on the Future of North Carolina (Raleigh, 1984), ch. 2, "Economy." An additional perspective is provided in Paul Luebke, *Tar Heel Politics: Myths and Realities* (Chapel Hill: University of North Carolina Press, 1990), esp. ch. 4.

7. For regional trends see Earl Black and Merle Black, *Politics and Society in the South* (Cambridge, Mass.: Harvard University Press, 1987), esp. chs. 2, 3.

8. Advisory Commission on Intergovernmental Relations (ACIR), *The Question of State Government Capability* (Washington, D.C.: GPO, 1985), 200–10.

9. Office of Budget and Management, *Post-Legislative Budget Summary, Biennium, 1989–91* (Raleigh, November 1989), 1–4.

10. North Carolina State Government, *Statistical Abstract*, 5th ed. (Raleigh, 1984), 343; ACIR, *State Government Capability*, 309.

11. *North Carolina Insight* (April 1986):6, 12.

12. Response of the secretary of state to the Legislative Research Commission, Committee on Legislative Ethics and Lobbying, January 24, 1986, 3.

13. See also *North Carolina Law Review* 25, 458.

14. Milton C. Jordan, "Black Legislators: From Political Novelty to Political Force," *North Carolina Insight* 12, no. 1 (1989):40–54, 58.

15. Questionnaires were sent to all members of the North Carolina General Assembly and 150 legislative agents registered with the Office of the Secretary of State. Responses from fifty-one legislators and fifty-two agents provide the basis for the survey analysis. The author is grateful to those who responded.

16. See Larry J. Sabato, *PAC Power: Inside the World of Political Action Committees* (New York: W. W. Norton, 1984), esp. ch. 1; and Ruth S. Jones,

"Financing State Elections," in *Money and Politics in the United States: Financing Elections in the 1980s*, ed. Michael Malbin (Chatham, N.J.: Chatham House Publishers, 1984), 172–214.

17. General Statutes of North Carolina, Article 22A, Chapter 163; and *Manual of Regulations and Reporting Instructions* (Raleigh: Campaign Reporting Office, State Board of Elections, January 1988).

18. Ken Eudy, "PAC Contributions Win Attention From Candidates," *Charlotte Observer*, June 16–20, 1985, 1, 4.

19. Ibid.; and Jim Morrill, "Lobbyists Escalate 'Arms Race'," *Charlotte Observer*, April 9, 1989, A-1, 8.

20. Ken Eudy, "Political Balance Sheet," *Charlotte Observer*, June 16–20, 1985, 1, 5. See also Morrill, "Lobbyists Escalate 'Arms Race'."

21. Morrill, "Lobbyists Escalate 'Arms Race'."

22. North Carolina Center for Public Policy Research, "1983–84 Governor's Race Contribution Analysis," manuscript, n.d. The author is grateful to Jim Bryan and Ran Coble of the center for making this data available.

23. Ibid.

24. "The Money Behind Martin: Does it Signal a New Era for the State's GOP?," *North Carolina Independent* 3 (March 1–14, 1985):5–6.

25. "Legislators Get Scores of Goodies," *Winston-Salem Journal*, February 24, 1987, A-5.

26. See note 15, above.

27. North Carolina Center for Public Policy Research, "Ex-Legislators, Lawyers Still Are Most Influential Lobbyists," manuscript, July 21, 1986; and *News and Observer* (Raleigh), August 7, 1990, B-1. 1986.

28. "Rating the Lobbyists," *Winston-Salem Journal*, July 22, 1986, 14; see also *News and Observer* (Raleigh), August 7, 1990, B-1.

29. North Carolina Center for Public Policy Research, "Ex-Legislators, Lawyers Still Are Most Influential Lobbyists."

30. *News and Observer* (Raleigh), July 22, 1986, 20C. See also "Lobbying is Serious Business to Zeb Alley," *Winston-Salem Journal*, June 26, 1990, 24.

31. Ann Morris, "Mr. Big: Sam Johnson is Raleigh's Consummate Lobbyist," *North Carolina Independent* 3 (June 8–21, 1985):10–11.

32. Barry Yeoman, "Who Runs N.C.?" *North Carolina Independent* 4 (July 4–17, 1986):6–8.

33. Belle Zeller, *American State Legislatures* (New York: Thomas Y. Crowell, 1954), 190–91; and Sarah McCally Morehouse, *State Politics, Parties and Policy* (New York: Holt, Rinehart and Winston, 1981), 109.

34. John Wahlke et al., *The Legislative System* (New York: John Wiley and Sons, 1962), 322; and L. Harmon Zeigler and Michael Baer, *Lobbying: Interaction and Influence in American State Legislatures* (Belmont, Calif.: Wadsworth Publishing, 1969), 37.

35. Wahlke et al., *The Legislative System*, 322; and Daniel J. Elazar, *American Federalism: A View from the States* (New York: Thomas Y. Crowell, 1966), 92–97.

36. L. Harmon Zeigler, "Interest Groups in the States," in *Politics in the American States: A Comparative Analysis*, ed. Virginia Gray, Herbert Jacob, and Kenneth N. Vines, 4th ed. (Boston: Little, Brown, 1983), 112.

37. Morehouse, *State Politics, Parties and Policy*, 112.

38. William Crotty, *The Party Game* (New York: W. H. Freeman, 1985), 102–3.

39. Malcolm Jewell, *Representation in State Legislatures* (Lexington: University Press of Kentucky, 1982), 26; and Council of State Governments, *The Book of the States*, various editions.

40. Zeigler, "Interest Groups in the States," 122.

Chapter 6. Florida: The Changing Patterns of Power

1. "Special Report on Florida's Establishment," *Florida Trend* 28, no. 12 (November 1969):17–18.

2. This discussion is taken from William E. Hulbary, Anne E. Kelley, and Lewis Bowman, "A Political Mid-Elite in a Transitional Party Setting: Florida in the 1980s," paper presented at the fourteenth World Congress of the International Political Science Association, Washington, D.C., August 28–September 1, 1989, 32.

3. LeRoy Collins, "Remembering Florida's Pork Choppers," *St. Petersburg Times*, September 2, 1985, 19A.

4. Bill Cox, "The Game is Politics and the Prize is Power," *Florida Trend* 18, no. 1 (March 1986):35.

5. Robert Barnes, "Things Are Changing in the Capitol," *St. Petersburg Times*, June 2, 1985, 10B.

6. Scholarly literature on Florida's special-interest groups is very sparse. See L. Harmon Zeigler, "The Florida Milk Commission Changes Minimum Prices," reprinted in *State and Local Government: A Case Book*, ed. Edward W. Beck (Tuscaloosa: University of Alabama Press, 1963), 359–428; William C. Havard, ed., *The Changing Politics of the South* (Baton Rouge: Louisiana State University Press, 1972), 160–62; and Manning Dauer, ed., *Florida's Politics and Government*, 2d ed. (Gainesville: University Presses of Florida, 1984), 64–72. Some general treatments of Florida politics, including special-interest groups are V. O. Key, Jr., *Southern Politics in State and Nation* (New York: Vintage Books, 1949), ch. 5; Jack Bass and Walter DeVries, *The Transformation of Southern Politics* (New York: Basic Books, 1976), ch. 6; Havard, *The Changing Politics of the South*, ch. 3; Alexander

Lamis, *The Two-Party South* (New York: Oxford University Press, 1984), ch. 13; and Robert H. Swansbrough and David M. Brodsky, eds., *The South's New Politics* (Columbia: University of South Carolina Press, 1988), ch. 3.

7. Allen Morris, *Reconsiderations* (Tallahassee: Florida House of Representatives, 1982), 138–39.

8. George Thurston, "Is Business Too Powerful?" *Florida Trend* 23, no. 2 (June 1980):13.

9. Bud Wylie, "CC/FLA Proposes Tougher Law for Gift Givers and Takers," *Common Cause Florida Frontline* (April 1981):1.

10. Anne E. Kelley, *Modern Florida Government* (Lanham, Md.: University Press of America, 1983), 117.

11. Genie Stowers, "Interest Groups and Public Policy in the American States," paper presented at the American Political Science Association meeting, New Orleans, August 1985.

12. Joint Center for Political Studies, *Black Elected Officials: A National Roster* (Washington, D.C.: Joint Center for Political Studies Press, 1988), 9–19, 105–15.

13. Bass and DeVries, *The Transformation of Southern Politics*, 135.

14. Ibid., 132.

15. Dauer, *Florida's Politics and Government*, 359.

16. Morris, *Reconsiderations*, 15.

17. James MacGregor Burns, J. W. Peltason, and Thomas E. Cronin, *Government by the People*, 11th ed. (Englewood Cliffs, N.J.: Prentice-Hall, 1981), 193–94.

18. Our results are based on mail surveys sent to all legislators (160) and a selected group of influential lobbyists (62). The overall response rate was 56 percent (52% for the legislators and 61% for the lobbyists).

19. Ann Driscol, "Sources of Legislators' Campaign Contributions," *St. Petersburg Times*, March 31, 1985, 5D–6D; and Ann Driscol and David Dahl, "Campaign Gifts to Legislators Hit $10 Million," *St. Petersburg Times*, March 29, 1987, 1D–5D.

20. Ibid.

21. Florida, Department of State, Division of Elections, *1974 Compilation of Aggregate Amounts Contributed in Excess of One Hundred Dollars* (Tallahassee: Department of State, May 9, 1975), 10; and *1976 Compilation of Total Reported Contributions and Expenditures for Candidates and Committees* (Tallahassee: Department of State, 1977), 19.

22. The 1970–81 data comes from "Lobby Registrations," August 14, 1986; *Lobbying in Florida: 1984–86*; and John B. Phelps, *Lobbying in Florida* (Tallahassee: Florida Legislature, Office of the Clerk, 1988–90), 1–51.

23. Clive S. Thomas, "Interest Groups in Alaska: Oil Revenues, Region-

alism and Personalized Politics," in *Interest Groups in the American West*, ed. Ronald J. Hrebenar and Clive S. Thomas (Salt Lake City: University of Utah Press, 1987), 18.

24. Morris, *Reconsiderations*, 132.

25. One way to approach interest group activity in the legislative process is by asking legislators what groups they perceive as powerful; see Thomas Dye, *Politics in States and Communities*, 2d ed. (Englewood Cliffs, N.J.: Prentice-Hall, 1973), 155–57; and John C. Wahlke et al., *The Legislative System* (New York: John Wiley and Sons, 1962), 311–42.

26. In our study we used the reputational approach; see Floyd Hunter, *Community Power Structure* (Chapel Hill: University of North Carolina Press, 1953); Robert Dahl, *Who Governs?* (New Haven, Conn.: Yale University Press, 1961); David B. Truman, *The Governmental Process* (New York: Knopf, 1951); and Nelson W. Polsby, *Community Power and Political Theory* (New Haven, Conn.: Yale University Press, 1980).

27. Morris, *Reconsiderations*, 140.

28. L. Harmon Zeigler, "The Effects of Lobbying: A Comparative Assessment," *Western Political Quarterly* 22 (March 1969):122.

29. Ibid., 122.

30. Samuel C. Patterson, "Legislators and Legislatures in the American States," in *Politics in the American States: A Comparative Analysis*, ed. Virginia Gray, Herbert Jacob, and Kenneth N. Vines, 4th ed. (Boston: Little, Brown, 1983), 171.

31. Eric Uslander and Ronald Weber, *Patterns of Decision Making in State Legislatures*, (New York: Praeger Publishers, 1977).

32. John Taylor, "Inside Tallahassee: A New Team Is Playing For Power," *Florida Trend* 28, no. 1 (March 1986):49.

33. Ibid., 51.

34. Ibid.

35. John Naisbitt, *Megatrends: Ten New Directions Transforming Our Lives* (New York: Warner Books, 1982), 7–8.

36. Sarah McCally Morehouse, *State Politics, Parties and Policy* (New York: Holt, Rinehart and Winston, 1981), 108.

37. Hulbary, Kelley and Bowman, "A Political Mid-Elite in a Transitional Party Setting," 36.

Chapter 7. Texas: The Transformation from Personal to Informational Lobbying

1. Arnold Vedlitz, James A. Dyer, and David B. Hill, "The Changing Texas Voter," in *The South's New Politics: Realignment and Dealignment*, ed.

Robert H. Swansbrough and David M. Brodsky (Columbia: University of South Carolina Press, 1988), 43–49.

2. Daniel J. Elazar, *American Federalism: A View From The States*, 2d ed. (New York: Thomas Y. Crowell, 1972), 84–126. Our discussion of the Texas political culture draws significantly from Beryl E. Pettus and Randall W. Bland, *Texas Government Today*, rev. ed. (Homewood, Ill.: Dorsey Press, 1979), 6–16.

3. James E. Anderson, Richard W. Murray, and Edward L. Farley, *Texas Politics: An Introduction*, 4th ed. (New York: Harper and Row, 1984), 103.

4. Ibid.

5. Ibid.; Richard Kraemer and Charldean Newell, *Texas Politics*, 3d ed. (St. Paul, Minn.: West Publishing, 1987), 103.

6. Information contained in this paragraph was taken from Kraemer and Newell, *Texas Politics*, 97–98.

7. Ibid., 95.

8. Ibid.

9. Information contained in the remainder of this section, unless otherwise noted, was taken from Texas Secretary of State, *1986 Political Funds Reporting and Disclosure Directive* (January 1986).

10. Candace Romig, "Placing Limits on PACs," *State Legislatures* (January 1984):20.

11. Edward C. Olson, "Political Reform in Texas: Big Money Still Talks," in Eugene W. Jones, Joe E. Ericson, Lyle C. Brown and Robert S. Trotter, Jr., *Practicing Texas Politics*, ed. Eugene W. Jones et al., 6th ed. (Boston: Houghton Mifflin, 1986), 181–82.

12. Wendell M. Bedichek and Neal Tannahill, *Public Policy in Texas* (Glenview, Ill.: Scott, Foresman, 1982), 140.

13. Brent Manley, "Some of the State's Top Arm-Twisters," in Jones et al., *Practicing Texas Politics*, 226–27.

14. Raul Reyes and Patti Kilday, "High-Tech Powers State's Top Lobbyists," *Times Herald* (Dallas), March 1, 1987, A-17.

15. Ibid.

16. Cited in "Legislators Draw Fire for Gifts From Special Interests," *Austin American-Statesman*, July 24, 1986.

17. R. G. Ratcliffe, "PACs Put up $4.7 Million to Push Issues," *Houston Chronicle*, January 4, 1987, 1-1.

18. Ibid.

19. John R. Wright, "PACs, Contributions, and Roll Calls: An Organizational Perspective," *American Political Science Review* 79 (1985):400–14.

20. See Larry J. Sabato, *PAC Power: Inside The World of Political Action Committees* (New York: W. W. Norton, 1985). See also Gary C. Jacobson,

Money in Congressional Elections (New Haven, Conn.: Yale University Press, 1980); J. Davis Gopoian, "What Makes PACs Tick?" *American Journal of Political Science* 28 (1984): 259–77; and Wright, "PACs, Contributions, and Roll Calls."

21. Ruth Jones and Thomas J. Norris, "Strategic Contributing in Legislative Campaigns: The Case of Minnesota," *Legislative Studies Quarterly* 10 (1985):89–105.

22. The Trial Lawyers were especially active in the 1990 primary campaigns, supporting challengers to incumbents who had supported business and other interests on successful workers' compensation reform legislation in 1989. The group was very unsuccessful in these efforts, leading one Austin-based political newsletter to predict a sharp reduction in the group's influence in legislative affairs in future sessions. See "Trial Lawyers at the Precipice," *Quorum Report: The Journal of Political Texas* (April 6, 1990): 2–7.

23. This section draws heavily from a series of newspaper articles written about Texas lobbyists in 1981 by Jackie Calmes of the Austin bureau of the Harte-Hanks newspaper chain. See the following articles in the *Bryan–College Station Eagle*: "The Lobby: Any Comparison to Team Sports is Entirely Appropriate," May 17, 1981, 1A, 3A; "The Lobby: Its Members Wage War When Others Won't," May 18, 1981, 1A; "The Lobby: Women Compete in Persuasion Game," May 19, 1981, 1A; and "Would You Buy a Car from a Lobbyist?" May 19, 1981, 5A.

24. "Would You Buy a Car from a Lobbyist?"

25. "The Lobby: Any Comparison to Team Sports is Entirely Appropriate," 3A.

26. Reyes and Kilday, "High-Tech Powers State's Top Lobbyists."

27. Ibid.

28. Richard C. Elling, "The Relationship Among Bureau Chiefs, Legislative Committees and Interest Groups: A Multistate Study," paper presented at the American Political Science Association Meeting, 1983, 8.

29. Ibid., 18, 20, 22.

30. Ibid., 18, 20.

31. David Prindle, *Petroleum Politics and the Texas Railroad Commission* (Austin: University of Texas Press, 1981), 158.

32. Ibid., 170–71.

33. James W. Lamare, *Texas Politics: Economics, Power and Policy*, 2d ed. (St. Paul, Minn.: West Publishing, 1985), 147.

34. Jones et al., *Practicing Texas Politics*, 213; Kraemer and Newell, *Texas Politics*, 101.

35. Prindle, *Petroleum Politics and the Texas Railroad Commission*, 203.

36. Quoted in Kraemer and Newell, *Texas Politics*, 100; original source of the ad was *The Texas Almanac and State Industrial Guide, 1970–1971* (Dallas: A. H. Belo, 1970), 425.

37. Glenn Abney and Thomas P. Lauth, "Interest Groups in the States: A View of Subsystem Politics," paper presented at the American Political Science Association meeting, 1986, table 3.

38. Elling, "The Relationship Among Bureau Chiefs, Legislative Committees, and Interest Groups," 12.

39. Ibid.

40. The phrase *triumph of many interests* is borrowed from a typology found in L. Harmon Zeigler and Hendrik van Dalen, "Interest Groups in State Politics," in *Politics in the American States: A Comparative Analysis*, ed. Herbert Jacob and Kenneth N. Vines, 3d ed. (Boston: Little, Brown, 1976), 95–110.

41. See Clifton McCleskey et al., *The Government and Politics of Texas* (Boston: Little, Brown, 1982), 159. See also Pettus and Bland, *Texas Government Today*, 12; Anderson, Murray, and Farley, *Texas Politics*, 142; Kraemer and Newell, *Texas Politics*, 117; and Richard L. Cole and Delbert A. Taebel, *Texas Politics and Public Policy* (San Diego, Calif.: Harcourt Brace Jovanovich, 1987), 82.

42. Anderson, Murray, and Farley, *Texas Politics*, 142.

43. William G. Smith, "Early Start on the Eleventh Hour," *Texas Business* (December 1986):39–41.

Chapter 8. Arkansas: The Politics of Inequality

1. For the most comprehensive analysis of Arkansas politics and government, see Diane D. Blair, *Arkansas Government and Politics: Do the People Rule?* (Lincoln: University of Nebraska Press, 1988).

2. U.S. Bureau of the Census, *Statistical Abstract of the United States: 1986* (Washington, D.C.: GPO 1985), 393, 418. Arkansas per capita data are taken from publications of the University of Arkansas Center for Research and Public Policy, Demographic Research.

3. Jim Lester, *A Man for Arkansas: Sid McMath and the Southern Reform Tradition* (Little Rock: Rose Publishing, 1976), 70–75.

4. For an excellent analysis of this election, see Gary H. Brooks, "Hattie and Huey: A Re-examination of the Arkansas Senatorial Primary of 1932," *Arkansas Political Science Journal* 3 (1982):1–19.

5. The distinction between populist and progressive is confounded in Arkansas by the dominance of the populist style and the frequency with

which these two ideologies form coalitions in opposition to corporate power and intransigent government officials. The negative nature of the coalition gives it a distinctly populist flavor, even though components of the coalition, such as the League of Women Voters or even the NAACP, may have their base in Arkansas' small urban middle class and other elements usually associated with the progressive tradition.

6. Jim Ranchino, *Faubus to Bumpers: Arkansas Votes, 1960–1970* (Arkadelphia, Ark.: Action Research, 1972).

7. Jack Bass and Walter DeVries, *The Transformation of Southern Politics: Social Change and Political Consequences Since 1945* (New York: New American Library, 1977), 87–106; Arthur English and John J. Carroll, "Local Party Organization and the Transformation of Southern State Policies: The Case of Arkansas' Pulaski County," *Journal of Campaigns and Elections* 3 (Summer 1982):36–43; Richard E. Yates, "Arkansas: Independent and Unpredictable," in *The Changing Politics of the South*, ed. William C. Havard (Baton Rouge: Louisiana State University Press, 1972), 233–93; Alexander P. Lamis, *The Two Party South* (New York: Oxford University Press, 1984), 121–30; and Diane D. Blair and Robert L. Savage, "The Appearance of Realignment and Dealignment in Arkansas," in *The South's New Politics: Realignment and Dealignment*, ed. Robert H. Swansbrough and David M. Brodsky (Columbia: University of South Carolina Press, 1988), 127–39.

8. These data are based on responses to a 1986 mail questionnaire sent to the 370 registered lobbyists and 134 members of the General Assembly. Ninety-two, or 25 percent, of the lobbyists and fifty-five, or 41 percent, of the legislators responded.

9. Similar data for the 1983 Assembly were collected by Charles DeWitt Dunn and Donald E. Whistler, "Insiders and Outsiders: Lobbyists in the Arkansas General Assembly," paper presented at the meeting of the Arkansas Political Science Association, February 1984.

10. These categories are adapted from L. Harmon Zeigler and Michael Baer, *Lobbying: Interactions and Influence in American State Legislatures* (Belmont, Calif.: Wadsworth Publishing, 1969).

11. Arthur English and John J. Carroll, "Outsiders and the Amateur Legislature: A Case Study of Legislative Politics," *Arkansas Political Science Journal* 6 (Winter 1985):22–34.

12. Standards of acceptable conduct in Arkansas have changed considerably over the years. Ralph Craft reported that before the mid-1960s some legislators received "direct subsidies" from interest groups, while others used their legislative powers for the purposes of blackmail; *Strengthening the Arkansas Legislature* (New Brunswick, N.J.: Rutgers University Press, 1972), 174–75.

13. V. O. Key, Jr., *Southern Politics in State and Nation* (New York: Random House, 1949), 148. Key concluded that race was the key variable in explaining southern politics. For an interesting and informative view of how southern politics have been reshaped since midcentury, see Earl Black and Merle Black, *Politics and Society in the South* (Cambridge, Mass.: Harvard University Press, 1987).

14. This relationship is argued generally for the states by Sarah McCally Morehouse in *State Politics, Parties and Policy* (New York: Holt, Rinehart and Winston, 1981), 116–18.

15. Arthur English and John J. Carroll, "Why Parties are Weak in Arkansas," *Party Line* 21 (Fall 1986):7–10.

16. Data were collected by mail questionnaire.

17. Arthur English and John J. Carroll, *Citizens Manual to the Arkansas General Assembly* (Little Rock: Institute of Politics and Government, 1983), 45.

18. Arthur English and John J. Carroll, "Constitutional Reform in Arkansas: The 1979–1980 Convention," *National Civic Review* 71 (May 1982): 247–48.

19. See the discussion of "professional" and "amateur" lobbyists in Dunn and Whistler, "Insiders and Outsiders."

20. U.S. Bureau of the Census, *Statistical Abstract of the United States: 1986*, 51.

21. Donald T. Wells, "The Arkansas Legislature," in *Power in American State Legislatures: Case Studies of the Arkansas, Louisiana, Mississippi, and Oklahoma Legislatures*, ed. Alex B. Lacy, Jr. (New Orleans: Tulane University, 1967), 7–9; English and Carroll, *Citizens Manual*, 45.

22. These trends are discussed by David Vogel in "The Power of Business in America: A Re-appraisal," *British Journal of Political Science* 13 (January 1983):19–43.

23. Interviews were completed with thirty-two members of the seventy-seventh General Assembly in the closing days of the session in 1989. They were asked to rate the groups that were influential from session to session in the Assembly. The groups that received the most mentions in rank order were the AEA; business groups, particularly the Chamber of Commerce; the utilities; particularly AP&L; the Poultry Federation; the Farm Bureau; and the Highway Commission. The Arkansas Bar Association along with the Trial Lawyers and the Arkansas Medical Association were also mentioned frequently. No mentions were made of any good-government group, and the governor received only one mention.

24. For a comparative analysis of interest groups in the fifty states, see Clive S. Thomas and Ronald J. Hrebenar, "Interest Groups in the States,"

in *Politics in the American States: A Comparative Analysis*, ed. Virginia Gray, Herbert Jacob, and Robert Albritton, 5th ed. (Glenview, Ill.: Scott, Foresman/Little, Brown, 1990), 123–58.

Chapter 9. South Carolina: The Rise of the New South

1. V. O. Key, Jr., *Southern Politics in State and Nation* (New York: Alfred A. Knopf, 1949), 150.

2. Ibid., 139.

3. William Blough, "Local Government in South Carolina," in *Government in the Palmetto State*, ed. Luther F. Carter and David S. Mann (Columbia: Bureau of Government Research and Service, University of South Carolina, 1983), 168. Also see Key, *Southern Politics in State and Nation*, 150 52.

4. Key, *Southern Politics in State and Nation*, 152.

5. David S. Mann, "Mr. Solomon Blatt: Fifty Years in the South Carolina State Legislature (An Oral History)," paper delivered at the South Carolina Political Science Association Meeting, Aiken, S.C.: March 1–2, 1985.

6. Key, *Southern Politics in State and Nation*, 154–55.

7. Neal R. Peirce, *The Deep South States of America* (New York: W. W. Norton, 1972), 380–434; Jack Bass and Walter DeVries, *The Transformation of Southern Politics: Social Change and Political Consequences Since 1945* (New York: Basic Books, 1976), 248–83; and Neal R. Peirce and Jerry Hagstrom, *The Book of America: Inside 50 States Today* (New York: W. W. Norton, 1983), 423–37.

8. Peirce, *The Deep South States*, 419. Back in the 1970s these traditional interests so dominated the scene that they were able to discourage the location of a Phillip Morris plant in South Carolina because it was a unionized company that "might drag the union here and raise wage rates"; Fred Monk, "Columbia in Motion Scores a Touchdown," *The State* (January 26, 1986): G-1.

9. See Cole Blease Graham, Jr., "Partisan Change in South Carolina," in *The South's New Politics: Realignment and Dealignment*, ed. Robert H. Swansbrough and David M. Bradsky (Columbia: University of South Carolina Press, 1988), 159.

10. Peirce, *The Deep South States*, 413–14.

11. Ibid., 412–13, 415; Bass and DeVries, *The Transformation of Southern Politics*, 250; and Peirce and Hagstrom, *The Book of America*, 432–33. Chester Bain notes the importance of economic diversification; see "South Carolina: Partisan Prelude," in *The Changing Politics of the South*, ed.

William C. Havard (Baton Rouge: Louisiana State University Press, 1972), 592.

12. Bass and DeVries, *The Transformation of Southern Politics*, 251; and Peirce, *The Deep South States*, 391–402.

13. Bass and DeVries, *The Transformation of Southern Politics*, 265.

14. Peirce, *The Deep South States*, 410–11; and Peirce and Hagstrom, *The Book of America*, 432.

15. Bass and DeVries, *The Transformation of Southern Politics*, 279.

16. Perice, *The Deep South States*, 424–25.

17. Sarah McCally Morehouse, *State Politics, Parties and Policy* (New York: Holt, Rinehart, and Winston, 1981), 109, 112.

18. Peirce and Hagstrom, *The Book of America*, 432–33.

19. Alexander Lamis, *The Two-Party South* (New York: Oxford University Press, 1984), 70.

20. Randolph C. Martin, "Background Paper: Economic Opportunities for the People of South Carolina" (The Commission on the Future of South Carolina, August 1988), 13–14.

21. *Operation Baseline: An Audit of South Carolina's Economy* (Columbia, S.C.: State Chamber of Commerce, November 1985), 5–8 of the "Executive Summary."

22. *South Carolina Business* (South Carolina Chamber of Commerce, 1986).

23. Martin, "Economic Opportunities," 10.

24. Telephone interview with the South Carolina State Development Board.

25. *Operation Baseline*, 24–25.

26. Martin, "Economic Opportunities," 13.

27. *Operation Baseline*, 26.

28. Ibid., 20–21.

29. Frank Heflin, "Trail of Poverty: The 'New Plantation System' Creates a Permanent Underclass," *The State* (August 19, 1990):1-A, 13-A.

30. David F. Kern, "Barbers, Cosmetologists Oppose Joint Regulation," *The State* (December 13, 1985):2-C.

31. Peirce, *The Deep South States*, 422.

32. Bill Hughes, "Study Shows Decline in Farmland Value," *The State* (January 26, 1986):1-G, and "S.C. Losing 1,000 Farms Every Year, Survey Finds," *The State* (August 1, 1990):1-A.

33. David F. Kern, "Taxes On Timberlands Raising Questions," *The State* (May 18, 1986):4-B.

34. Robert E. Botsch, "You Can't Have It Both Ways: The Difficulties of

Unionization in the South," in *Perspectives on the American South*, ed. Merle Black and John Shelton Reed, vol. 1 (New York: Gordon and Breach, 1981), 173–86.

35. Richard C. Kearney, "Local Government Unionization and Collective Bargaining in South Carolina," in *Local Government in South Carolina: Problems and Perspectives*, ed. Cole Blease Graham and Charlie B. Tyer (Columbia, S.C.: Bureau of Government Research and Service, 1984), 60–61, 67.

36. Jan Collins Stucker, "Taking Department of Energy To Task," *The State Magazine* (July 28, 1986): 8–11.

37. Robert E. Botsch, "Organizing the Breathless: The Politics of Brown Lung," paper delivered at the Southern Political Science Association Convention, Memphis, Tennessee, 1981.

38. Robert E. Botsch, "Interest Group Money in South Carolina House Elections," *Common Cause South Carolina* (November 1983), 2.

39. Robert E. Botsch, "Campaign Financing in South Carolina: The 1981–82 House Elections," *Public Affairs Bulletin* (Columbia, S.C.: Bureau of Government Research and Service, University of South Carolina, January 1984), 13. Less-comprehensive unpublished studies of the 1988 legislative elections by John Crangle of South Carolina Common Cause reconfirmed this pattern of giving.

40. Jerry Adams, "Who Is 'Hootie,' And Why Does His Support Matter?" *The State* (February 9, 1986):1-D.

41. Mabashir Salahuddin, "Medical Group Targets Legislators," *The State* (April 28, 1986):1, 4-B.

42. Cindi Ross Scoppe, "Give and Take at the State House," *The State* (August 12, 1990):1, 6-A.

43. Ibid.

44. Ibid.

45. Cindi Ross Scoppe, "The Legislature's Dirty Little Secret," *The State* (August 19, 1990):1-A, 11-A.

46. Scoppe, "Give and Take at the State House."

47. Results of this survey were previously reported in Robert E. Botsch, "Interest Group Politics in South Carolina," in Carter and Mann, *Government in the Palmetto State*, 72–73.

48. David F. Kern, "Landlord-Tenant Act May Reduce Lawsuits," *The State* (July 8, 1986):1-A.

49. These innovations made 42,000 additional citizens eligible for Medicaid, guaranteed access for the poor to all state hospitals, both public and private, and set up a prenatal care program for high-risk women who are not

on welfare but could not otherwise afford such care on their own. See John Herbers, "South Carolina Extends Health Care for Its Poor," *New York Times*, March 31, 1986.

50. Bruce Smith, "Group to Lobby for Setbacks," *The State* (July 12, 1986):2-B.

51. Botsch, "Organizing the Breathless."

52. Frank Monk, "Political Realities Hit State Chamber," *The State* (July 20, 1986):1-G.

53. *Operation Baseline*, 1.

54. Richard Riley, "State Can Be Proud of Its Economic Climate," *The State* (December 8, 1985):3-B.

55. Lois Duke, "Beyond Money: Lobbying on a Shoe-String," paper delivered at the Southern Political Science Association meeting, Atlanta, Ga.; November 6–8, 1986.

56. Robert E. Botsch, Jerry Seigler, and Amy Boyette, *Education, Training, and Consulting Needs of South Carolina Industry: The Two South Carolinas* (Aiken, S.C.: University of South Carolina and Aiken Survey Research Services, June 1990).

57. Earl Black and Merle Black, *Politics and Society in the South* (Cambridge, Mass.: Harvard University Press, 1987), 29.

58. Fred Monk and David F. Kern, "Mack 'Flat Likes' S.C.," *The State* (January 23, 1986):1, 6-A.

59. Francis M. Thomas, "Community and Economic Development", in Graham and Tyer, *Local Government in South Carolina*, 135–52.

Chapter 10. Georgia: Business as Usual

1. Jack Bass and Walter DeVries, *The Transformation of Southern Politics: Social Change and Political Consequences Since 1945* (New York: American Library, 1976), 137–57. See also Lawrence R. Hepburn, "Georgia," in *The Political Life of the American State*, ed. Alan Rosenthal and Maureen Moakley (New York: Praeger, 1984), 171–95, for a discussion of how consensus politics operates in most state and local decision making.

2. V. O. Key, Jr., *Southern Politics in State and Nation* (New York: Vintage Books, 1949), 106–9.

3. Bass and DeVries, *The Transformation of Southern Politics*, 150.

4. Hepburn, "Georgia," 174.

5. Numan V. Bartley, "Georgia Governors in an Age of Change," in *Georgia Governors in an Age of Change: From Ellis Arnall to George Busbee*, ed.

Harold P. Henderson and Gary L. Roberts (Athens: University of Georgia Press, 1988), 293.

6. Hepburn, "Georgia," 178.

7. Floyd Hunter, *Community Power Structure* (New York: Doubleday, 1963).

8. Elites who are still in office or working in the public arena often do not wish to be identified. All of our interviews were conducted with people currently involved in the Georgia political process. We assured them the confidentiality they requested. We found that all of the persons interviewed were extremely candid with us and gave us willingly of their time; the interviews ranged from forty-five minutes to two hours. Some of the lobbyists we interviewed were from the following groups: Medical Association of Georgia; Georgia Association of Educators; Petroleum Council; Georgia Business Council; Georgia Power; Georgia Legal Services; Georgia Council for Children; and American Association of Retired Persons.

9. Sarah McCally Morehouse, *State Politics, Parties and Policy* (New York: Holt, Rinehart and Winston, 1982), 108.

10. The county-unit system provided that a candidate in a primary election who won a plurality of votes carried that county's unit votes. Each county was allotted two unit votes for each member that it elected to the Georgia House of Representatives. The eight most populous counties each had six unit votes, while the 121 least populous counties cast two units each. See Numan V. Bartley, *From Thurmond to Wallace: Political Tendencies in Georgia, 1948–1968* (Baltimore, Md.: Johns Hopkins University Press, 1970), 11–15. A federal district court held the county-unit system unconstitutional in 1962, finding "invidious discrimination" in the unequal weighing of votes (*Gray v. Sanders*, 372 U.S. 368).

11. A. L. May, "Campaign Could Wake Up Voters, Shape Decade: Young Candidacy, GOP Hopes, TV Ads May Make '90 Governor's Race Unique," *The Atlanta Journal and The Atlanta Constitution*, January 1, 1990, A-1 (hereafter cited as *Journal/Constitution*).

12. Margaret L. Usdansky, "The Burgeoning Burbs: Growth is Leaving City Behind," *Journal/Constitution*, August 29, 1990, E-1.

13. Bill Shipp, "Governor Harris Loses by a Split Decision," *Journal/Constitution*, July 16, 1986, C-1.

14. Thomas G. Walker and Eleanor C. Main, "Georgia," in *The 1984 Presidential Election in the South: Patterns of Southern Party Politics*, ed. Robert P. Steed, Laurence W. Moreland, and Tod A. Baker (New York: Praeger, 1985), 96–122.

15. May, "Campaign Could Wake Up Voters, Shape Decade," A-7.

16. Alexander P. Lamis, *The Two-Party South* (New York: Oxford University Press, 1984).

17. George D. Busbee, "Inauguration Speech," *Journal of the Senate of the State of Georgia*, Regular Session, 1 (January 1, 1975):53.

18. David K. Secrest, "Young Draws 2,000 in S. Georgia," *Journal/Constitution*, June 11, 1990, D-1.

19. Michael B. Binford, "Georgia: Political Realignment or Partisan Revolution," in *The South's New Politics: Realignment and Dealignment*, ed. Robert H. Swansbrough and David M. Brodsky (Columbia: University of South Carolina Press, 1988), 175.

20. Ibid., 186.

21. May, "Campaign Could Wake Up Voters, Shape Decade," A-7.

22. A *Journal/Constitution* survey of June 24, 1990 (see p. D-9) revealed that 45 percent of all voters identified themselves as Democrats, 27 percent as Republicans, and 24 percent as Independents. Three-fourths of black voters thought of themselves as Democrats. Republicans have made the greatest inroads among whites. One-third of white voters identified with the Republican party, the same number who considered themselves Democrats.

23. Hepburn, "Georgia," 190.

24. Earl Black and Merle Black, *Politics and Society in the South* (Cambridge, Mass.: Harvard University Press, 1987), 306.

25. See also Dinker I. Patel and Joyce Bullock, *Campaign Finance and Lobby Law Blue Book 1988–1989* (Lexington, Ky.: Council of State Governments), 157.

26. The registration is $5 and is valid for only one regular or extraordinary session of the General Assembly. A picture identification badge must be worn by all lobbyists. Lobbyists are prohibited from contingency-basis lobbying; offering or proposing anything that may be reasonably construed to influence improperly a legislator's official acts, decisions, or votes; and from being on the floor of either the House or Senate chamber while they are in session.

27. The short, forty-day session mandated by the state constitution means that lobbyists have very little time to respond to legislative action; the best lobbyists line up their support ahead of time.

28. See Henderson and Roberts, *Georgia Governors in an Age of Change*. This book is an in-depth study of each of the administrations of these governors. Although Georgia changed greatly during the period covered, all of these governors had economic development and education as their primary policy goals.

29. Leslie W. Dunbar, "The Changing Mind of the South: The Exposed Nerve," *Journal of Politics* 26 (February 1964):20.

30. Joe Frank Harris, "Visions for a Better Georgia," in Henderson and Roberts, *Georgia Governors in an Age of Change*, 299–300.

31. Legislators receive a salary of $12,000 per year plus the annual cost-of-living raise granted to state employees, as well as $59 per diem when they are on committee business or when the General Assembly is in session.

32. *Members of the General Assembly of Georgia* (Atlanta: Senate Public Information Office and House Public Information Office, 1989).

33. Hepburn, "Georgia," 179.

34. The 1986 election was the last year in which campaign contributions were unlimited under Georgia law.

35. Peter Mantius and David Secrest, "What Do the 'Sugar Daddies' Get for Their Money?" *Journal/Constitution*, May 27, 1990, D-1.

36. Young raised approximately $3.1 million, compared to Zell Miller's $4.1 million.

37. Numan V. Bartley, *The Creation of Modern Georgia* (Athens: University of Georgia Press, 1983), 200.

Chapter 11. Alabama: Personalities and Factionalism

1. Belle Zeller, *American State Legislatures*, 2d ed. (New York: Thomas Y. Crowell, 1954), 190–91.

2. Patrick Cotter distributed these Capstone poll data at the 1983 Alabama Political Science Association annual meeting; no numbers were given.

3. V. O. Key, Jr., *Southern Politics in State and Nation* (Knoxville: University of Tennessee Press, 1984), 57.

4. Joint Center for Political Studies, *Black Elected Officials* (New York: Unipub, 1984), 14–15.

5. Key, *Southern Politics in State and Nation*, 37.

6. See also Amy Herring, "Hunt May Use Proceeds for Personal Debts," *Montgomery Advertiser*, January 22, 1987, 1; and editorial, "Top of the Agenda," ibid., January 23, 1987, 14A.

7. Alabama, Secretary of State, *An Elections Guide for Candidates and Political Committees* (n.d.), 6.

8. See Curt Anderson, "Ethics Commission Support Weakened," *Opelika-Auburn News*, January 4, 1987, A-5.

9. See *The Book of the States 1986–87*, vol. 26 (Lexington, Ky.: Council of State Governments, 1986), 114, where the entry for the tally of gubernatorial vetoes in Alabama reads "N.A." (not available). Similarly, the primitive level of political research in Alabama is illustrated by the enrolling clerk in the secretary of state's office who kept private track of the fate of bills. When she retired the bill tabulation retired with her.

10. These examples are from the Code of Alabama, 1975 (1986 Supp.), Title 40, ch. 9, "Exemptions from Taxation and Licenses."

11. Rep. Jimmy Clark, quoted by Sam Duvall and Michele MacDonald, "Election Casts a Shadow on Special Session," *Birmingham News*, September 7, 1986, 1, 6A.

12. Sarah McCally Morehouse, *State Politics, Parties and Policy* (New York: Holt, Rinehart and Winston, 1981), 108.

13. See BCA and AABI registration cards, filed with the clerk of the Alabama House and the secretary of the Senate for the 1986 session.

14. *Metropolitan Life Insurance Co. v. Ward*, 470 U.S. 869 (1985). One sentence from this opinion reads: "Alabama's purpose constitutes the very sort of parochial discrimination that the Equal Protection Clause was intended to prevent" (878).

15. ALFA's insurance companies have fourteen hundred employees and 675,000 policies in effect. See "Ed Lowder" (obituary), *Montgomery Advertiser*, February 18, 1987, 14A; and Coke Ellington, "Ed Lowder Remains Modest," *Alabama Journal and Advertiser*, July 9, 1986, 6B.

16. See AEA's registration form with the Alabama Ethics Commission, October 1986.

17. See Mitchell's registration form with the Alabama Ethics Commission, October 1986.

18. Bessie Ford, "Ex-legislators Swarm House Floors as Lobbyists," *Alabama Journal and Advertiser*, April 1, 1984, B-1.

19. Morehouse, *State Politics, Parties and Policy*, 139.

20. *Mayberry v. State of Alabama*, 419 So. 2nd 262 (1982).

21. A celebrated observation by the late Jesse Unruh, former speaker of the House and state treasurer of California.

22. Personal interview with Mel Cooper, executive director, Alabama Ethics Commission, April 15, 1983. Christine S. Sermons, "Political Action Committees and the Alabama State Senate," paper presented at the Alabama Political Science Association meeting, 1982, found that total Alabama Senate campaign contributions reported rose from $1.2 million in 1978 to $1.8 million in 1982, and the proportion of PAC money in Senate races from 14 to 31 percent. For the 1986 elections, see note 25, below.

23. Information on AVOTE is taken from its July 14, 1986, statement, filed by Paul Hubbert at the Alabama secretary of state's office. See also Julie Lindy, "Teachers' Lobby Funded by Automatic Deductions," *Alabama Journal and Advertiser*, November 25, 1984, 6A; Betty Cork, "AEA Power: State Teachers' Lobby Wields Great Influence in Legislature," ibid., April 7, 1985, 1C, 6C; and Robert Dunnavant, "Hubbert Plans to Run for Governor," *Birmingham News*, May 23, 1989, 1B.

24. *Rules of the House of Representatives of Alabama, 1983*, Legislative Document no. 1, 23.

25. See David L. Martin, "PAC Money in State Legislative Elections: An Alabama Report," *Comparative State Politics Newsletter* 8, no. 4 (August 1987):18–21.

26. Bessie Ford, "Outsiders Are Now Insiders on Legislative Committees Most Likely to Screen Business' Bills," *Business Alabama Monthly* (March 1987):8–9.

27. Amy Herring, "Primary Costs Top $8 Million," *Montgomery Advertiser*, June 3, 1990, 1; and Steve Prince, "Less Than a Third of Those Registered Vote," *Alabama Journal*, June 27, 1990, 1

28. Key, *Southern Politics in State and Nation*, 47.

29. "New South Claims Clout Over Older Rival ADC," *Montgomery Advertiser*, June 27, 1986, 5A; and Nancy Dennis, "For Nearly 20 Years, Joe Reed Has Made a Difference as State Dean of Black Politics," *Alabama Journal and Advertiser*, February 19, 1984, 1–2F.

30. See Frank Bass, "Blacks Proclaim Unity," *Alabama Journal and Advertiser*, February 8, 1987, 1; Raad Cawthon, "Blacks 'on back of bus' in Alabama Politics, Protestors Say," *Atlanta Constitution*, February 5, 1987, 33; and Robin Tower, "Black Democrats Map March on Alabama Capitol," *New York Times*, February 13, 1987, 10.

31. See Grant Thornton Accountants and Management Consultants, *General Manufacturing Climates* (June 1986), which purports to rank states according to their presumed business attractiveness in respect to laws, taxes, and regulation.

32. Compare Bruce Ritchie, "Republicans Top List of Pro-Business Lawmakers," *Alabama Journal and Advertiser*, April 20, 1986, 7B, and Amy Herring, "Labor Endorses Candidates," ibid., April 20, 1986, C1, listing candidates endorsed by COPE (Committee on Political Education) of the Alabama Labor Council, AFL-CIO.

33. Key, *Southern Politics in State and Nation*, 36–37.

34. Quoted in Ritchie, "Republicans Top List of Pro-Business Lawmakers."

35. Quoted in Amy Herring, "PACs Special Interest Groups Key to Baxley, Graddick Election Bids," *Alabama Journal and Advertiser*, June 15, 1986, 1.

36. Quoted in San Duvall and Michele MacDonald, "Graddick Victory Could Mean New, Pro-Business Era," *Birmingham News*, June 29, 1986, C-1.

37. The 1986 Alabama gubernatorial race spawned some eighteen separate court proceedings. For a summary, see David L. Martin, "The 1986 Ala-

bama Democratic Primaries: A Contest Without a Winner," *Comparative State Politics Newsletter* 7, no. 4 (August 1986):2–4; Martin, "Republicans Resurgent in Alabama," ibid. 7, no. 6 (December 1986):2; and Patrick. R. Cotter and James Glen Stovall, "The 1986 Election in Alabama: The Beginning of the Post-Wallace Era," *Political Science* 20, no. 3 (Summer 1987):655–64.

38. "Klan Backs Graddick for Governor," *Opelika-Auburn News*, June 3, 1986, 2. Indicative of changing racial attitudes in Alabama, virtually all ten statewide candidates endorsed by the Ku Klux Klan repudiated the endorsement.

39. Duvall and MacDonald, "Graddick Victory Could Mean New, Pro-Business Era."

40. Personal interview with John Dorrill, Jr., executive director, Alabama Farm Bureau, December 11, 1986, and Graddick campaign contribution report for the June 24, 1986, runoff election, Alabama secretary of state's office. Since he withdrew a week before the November 4, 1986, general election, under Alabama law Graddick did not have to file a disclosure statement for his write-in campaign.

41. John Dorrill, Jr., executive director of the Alabama Farm Bureau, interviewed on "For the Record," Alabama Public Television, January 26, 1987.

42. Office of the Alabama Secretary of State, "Political Action Committees Filing Under Alabama Statutes," lists Local Fair Share Committee as c/o O. H. Sharpless III (executive director of the Association of County Commissions of Alabama) and Vote Yes Alabama Committee's, chair as, Elvin L. Stanton; treasurer, Ferrell Patrick. Upon passage of Amendment 450, subsequent political compromise promised a percentage to the counties and cities.

43. Phillip Rawls, "Folsom, Chairmen Share Common Financial Backers," *Opelika-Auburn News*, February 11, 1987, A-5.

44. See Amy Herring, "Special Interests Still Control House, Legislator Says," *Montgomery Advertiser*, January 19, 1987, 2A; Phillip Rawls, "Business Lobbies Supported Most Clark Appointees," ibid., January 28, 1987, 2A; and Brooks Boliek, "PAC Money Buys Access, Not Votes, Lawmakers Say," *Montgomery Advertiser and Alabama Journal*, October 30, 1988, B-1.

45. James D. Thomas and William H. Stewart, *Alabama Government and Politics* (Lincoln: University of Nebraska Press, 1988), 129.

46. Key, *Southern Politics in State and Nation*, 305.

47. Patrick R. Cotter and James Glen Stovall, "Political Change in Alabama," in *The South's New Politics: Realignment and Dealignment*, ed. Robert H. Swansbrough and David M. Brodsky (Columbia: University of South Carolina Press, 1988), 155.

Chapter 12. Mississippi: An Expanding Array of Interests

1. A picture similar in both content and in the reaction it evoked to the South is referred to in John Shelton Reed, "For Dixieland: The Sectionalism of *I'll Take My Stand,*" in *A Band of Prophets, The Vanderbilt Agrarians After Fifty Years,* ed. William C. Havard and Walter Sullivan (Baton Rouge: Louisiana State University Press, 1982), 45.

2. For an analysis of this pattern see Clive S. Thomas and Ronald J. Hrebenar, "Changes in the Number and Types of Interest Groups and Lobbies Active in the States," *Comparative State Politics Newsletter* 10 (April 1989):28–36; and by the same authors, "Interest Groups in the States," in *Politics in the American States: A Comparative Analysis,* ed. Virginia Gray, Herbert Jacob, and Robert Albritton, 5th ed. (Glenview, Ill.: Scott, Foresman/Little, Brown, 1990), 129–31.

3. David B. Ogle, *Strengthening the Mississippi Legislature, An Eagleton Study and Report* (New Brunswick, N.J.: Rutgers University Press, 1971), 170.

4. L. Harmond Zeigler and Hendrik van Dalen, "Interest Groups in State Politics," in *Politics in the American States: A Comparative Analysis,* ed. Herbert Jacob and Kenneth N. Vines, 3d ed. (Boston: Little, Brown, 1976), 94–112.

5. V. O. Key, Jr., *Southern Politics in State and Nation* (New York: Random House, 1949), 231.

6. Neal R. Peirce, *The Deep South States of America* (New York: Basic Books, 1976), 207.

7. James C. Cobb, *The Selling of the South: The Southern Crusade for Industrial Development, 1936–1980* (Baton Rouge: Louisiana State University Press, 1981), 8.

8. "Business Indicators," *Mississippi Business Journal* 12 (August 13, 1990):37.

9. Jack Bass and Walter DeVries, *The Transformation of Southern Politics* (New York: Basic Books, 1976), 188.

10. This idea came from a lecture given by Professor Harold J. Laski at the London School of Economics and Political Science in the fall of 1945. See also note 37.

11. John Ray Skates, *Mississippi, A Bicentennial History* (New York: W. W. Norton, 1979), 166.

12. Jack W. Gunn, "Religion in the Twentieth Century," in *A History of Mississippi,* ed. Richard Aubrey McLemore (Jackson: University and College Press of Mississippi, 1973), 2, 477.

13. *Clarion-Ledger* (Jackson, Miss.), December 3, 1982, April 26, 1983, and January 12, 1985.

14. Stephen D. Shaffer, "Changing Party Politics in Mississippi," in *The South's New Politics: Realignment and Dealignment*, ed. Robert H. Swansbrough and David M. Brodsky (Columbia: University of South Carolina Press, 1988), 189–203.

15. Much of the information on black interest groups was obtained from personal interviews with Leroy Brooks (first black elected in this century to the County Board of Supervisors in Lowndes County), Mississippi State, Miss., August 28, 1986, and with Representative Tyrone Ellis (1986 chair of the Black Caucus), Starkville, Miss., September 4, 1986.

16. On August 22, 1990, this last-named organization obtained the nation's first judgment against a state employment service for a county office's actions in race and sex discrimination. The $6.16 million judgment included a $3.425 million portion for interest in the twenty-year-old case, which could rise to $5.8 million by the May 7, 1991, deadline the judge gave the Legislature for payment of the judgment. See the Jackson *Clarion-Ledger*, August 23, 1990.

17. In a report released August 22, 1990, by the U.S. Department of Commerce, Mississippi was ranked last again in per capita income—the fifty-fifth consecutive year for such a ranking.

18. Jackson *Clarion-Ledger*, April 15, and June 7, 10, 15, 25, and 26, 1986.

19. Personal interview with Bryan Baker, head of the Department of Animal Science, Mississippi State University, August 27, 1986.

20. Peirce, *The Deep South States of America*, 204.

21. Telephone interview with Thomas Knight, state AFL-CIO president, Mississippi State University, Jackson, Miss., September 5, 1986.

22. The information on the state supreme court used here came from interviews with two of the court's nine justices: Justice Lenore L. Prather (first female justice), Mississippi State University, September 15, 1986; and Justice James L. Robertson, Jackson, Miss., June 18, 1987, and July 20, 1989.

23. Kay L. Schlozman and John T. Tierney, *Organized Interests and American Democracy* (New York: Harper and Row, 1986), ch. 14.

24. Glenn Abney and Thomas P. Lauth, *The Politics of State and City Administration* (Albany: State University of New York Press, 1986), 103.

25. Depending on what is defined as a state agency, the number ranged from 120 to 210 when tabulated in January 1977; see Thomas E. Kynerd, *Administrative Reorganization of Mississippi Government, A Study in Politics* (Jackson: University Press of Mississippi, 1978), 154–57.

26. Abney and Lauth, *The Politics of State and City Administration*, 101–2.

27. Charles A. Marx, chair and director of the State Tax Commission, illustrated this point in a personal interview in Jackson, Miss., June 18,

1987. He and the two other commissioners, he said, receive scores of representations from companies, friends, and politicians on behalf of truck drivers who have received penalties assessed by a weighing station, against overweight trucks. The commissioners, he declared, have no choice but to stand behind the penalties assessed by an established scale of penalties. But, he pointed out, those interests whose representatives (lobbyists) present adequate data and reasoning at a commission hearing for establishing the rule on weights can play a part in shaping the rule the commissioners must enforce.

28. Schlozman and Tierney, *Organized Interests and American Democracy*, 264.

29. Karl Wiesenburg, *Let's Look at Our Legislature* (Pascagoula, Miss.: Advertiser Printing, 1958), 2.

30. Ibid., 1.

31. A five-page questionnaire consisting of twenty-seven items, a modified form of the lobbyists' questionnaire developed by Clive S. Thomas for use in Alaska, was mailed in June 1986 to 141 individual lobbyists registered with the secretary of state's office. There were sixty-four valid returns (46.1%), which were utilized in this study.

32. A nine-page questionnaire consisting of forty-eight items, a modified form of the legislators' questionnaire developed by Clive S. Thomas for use in Alaska, was mailed to the 174 legislators in June 1986. Valid replies were received from sixty-four legislators (36.8%), which serve as the basis for much of the information used in this chapter.

33. Ogle, *Strengthening the Mississippi Legislature*, 170.

34. Mississippi, Secretary of State, *Lobbying in Mississippi: Regulations and Registration* (August 1, 1985).

35. Jackson *Clarion-Ledger*, June 1, 1985.

36. The 1990 legislature has the same total memberships, but in the Senate there were two blacks and three women, and in the House there were twenty-one blacks and five women.

37. An excellent discussion of the nature and political implications of this pervasive conservative attitude throughout the South can be found in Earl Black and Merle Black, *Politics and Society in the South* (Cambridge, Mass.: Harvard University Press, 1987), ch. 10.

38. Sarah McCally Morehouse, *State Politics, Parties and Policy* (New York: Holt, Rinehart and Winston, 1981), 116–18.

39. These were BIPEC (39.6%), organized labor (35.4%), health—including doctors and health-care facilities (33.3%), and state employees (31.3%). The six interests in the 10 to 21 percent cluster were Mississippi Bankers Association (20.8%), Mississippi Manufacturers Association (20.8%),

NAACP (16.7%), churches (16.7%), local officials (10.4%), and lawyers (10.4%).

40. *Clarion-Ledger*, March 23, 1986.

41. Canada, Ministry of Consumer and Corporate Affairs, *Lobbying and the Registration of Paid Lobbyists, A Discussion Paper*, 1985, 3.

Chapter 13. Louisiana:
The Final Throes of Freewheeling Ways?

We received support for this research from the College of Liberal Arts and the Computer Research Center, University of New Orleans.

1. Sarah McCally Morehouse, *State Politics, Parties and Policy* (New York: Holt, Rinehart and Winston, 1981), 108; Clive S. Thomas and Ronald J. Hrebenar, "Interest Groups in the States," in *Politics in the American States*, ed. Virginia Gray, Herbert Jacob, and Robert Albritton, 5th ed. (Glenview, Ill.: Scott, Foresman/Little, Brown, 1990).

2. Allan P. Sindler, *Huey Long's Louisiana: State Politics, 1920–1952* (Baltimore, Md.: Johns Hopkins University Press, 1956), 248–86; Jack Bass and Walter DeVries, *The Transformation of Southern Politics: Social Change and Political Consequence Since 1945* (New York: Basic Books, 1976), 181–85.

3. On Longism, see Edward T. Jennings, "Some Policy Consequences of the Long Revolution and Bifactional Rivalry in Louisiana," *American Journal of Political Science* 21 (May 1977):225–46; Perry H. Howard, "Louisiana: Resistance and Change," in *The Changing Politics of the South*, ed. William C. Havard (Baton Rouge: Louisiana State University Press, 1972), 544–49; Earl Black and Merle Black, *Politics and Society in the South* (Cambridge, Mass.: Harvard University Press, 1987), 27; and Bass and DeVries, *The Transformation of Southern Politics*, 164–72.

4. John Wildgen, "Voting Behavior in Gubernatorial Elections," in *Louisiana Politics: Festival in a Labyrinth*, ed. James Bolner (Baton Rouge: Louisiana State University Press, 1982), 320–44; Alexander P. Lamis, *The Two-Party South* (New York: Oxford University Press, 1984), 107–19; and Bass and DeVries, *The Transformation of Southern Politics*, 172–76. Cf. V. O. Key, Jr., *Southern Politics in State and Nation* (New York: Alfred A. Knopf, 1949), 168–79.

5. John H. Fenton and Kenneth N. Vines, "Negro Registration in Louisiana," *American Political Science Review* 60 (September 1957): 704–13.

6. Charles D. Hadley, "Louisiana," in *The 1984 Presidential Election in the South*, ed. Robert P. Steed, Laurence W. Moreland, and Tod A. Baker (New York: Praeger, 1986), 22–24; and Hadley, "Louisiana: Race, Re-

publicans and Religion," in *The 1988 Presidential Election in the South*, ed. Laurence W. Moreland, Robert P. Steed, and Tod A. Baker (New York: Praeger, 1990), Table 6.1. For black voter-registration data alone, see Hadley, "The Transformation of the Role of Black Ministers and Black Political Organizations in Louisiana Politics," in *Blacks in Southern Politics*, ed. Laurence W. Moreland, Robert P. Steed, and Tod A. Baker (New York: Praeger, 1987), 136.

7. *Black Elected Officials: A National Roster* (Washington, D.C.: Joint Center for Political Studies Press, 1989), 9.

8. Dudley Clendinen, "Computer-Aided Black Network Won Louisiana For Jackson," *New York Times*, May 7, 1984, B-9.

9. Patrick F. O'Connor, "The Legislature," in Bolner, *Louisiana Politics*, 53.

10. Thomas A. Kazee, "The Impact of Electoral Reform: 'Open Elections' and the Louisiana Party System," *Publius* 13 (Winter 1983):134–36.

11. For a thorough examination of the Open Elections System, see Charles D. Hadley, "The Impact of the Louisiana Open Elections System Reform," *State Government* 58 (Winter 1986):152–57.

12. Hadley, "Louisiana: Race, Republicans and Religion."

13. See James O'Byrne, "Duke: Anatomy of an Upset," *Times-Picayune* (New Orleans), March 8, 1989, 1, A-14–A-15. On the decline of Republicanism, cf. Wayne Parent, "The Rise and Stall of Republican Ascendency in Louisiana Politics," in *The South's New Politics: Realignment and Dealignment*, ed. Robert H. Swansbrough and David M. Brodsky (Columbia: University of South Carolina Press, 1988), 204–17.

14. O'Connor, "The Legislature," 46–53.

15. Louisiana Revised Statutes 24:51–55, Amended by Acts 1978, No. 759.

16. Hadley, "The Impact of the Louisiana Open Elections System Reform," 154.

17. "Governor: Edwards Must Bow to Teachers, Labor," *Times-Picayune*, April 10, 1972, sec. 1, 16.

18. John Roberts, "Lobbyist Ban Idea Attacked," *Times-Picayune*, April 17, 1972, sec. 1, 8.

19. Quoted in Gene Bourg, "Reformers Win Only Half Loaf," *States-Item* (New Orleans), May 9, 1972, 1. See also James H. Gillis, "Henry Is Named House Speaker," *Times-Picayune*, May 9, 1972, sec. 1, 1–2.

20. Quoted from and in "Anti-Lobbyist Bill Again Fails As They Stand in Background," *States-Item*, May 11, 1972, 48. See also C. M. Hargroder, "Senate Refuses to Curb Lobbyists and the Public," *Times-Picayune*, May 11, 1972, sec. 1, 11; L. Harmon Zeigler and Michael A. Baer, *Lobbying: Interaction and Influence in American State Legislatures* (Belmont, Calif.:

Wadsworth, 1969), 126–28, 164–67; Harold W. Stanley, *Senate vs. Governor, Alabama 1971* (University: University of Alabama Press, 1975), 68–72.

21. Neal R. Peirce, *The Deep South States of America* (New York: W. W. Norton, 1972, 1974), 74–75.

22. Peirce, *The Deep South States*, 71–77; Neal R. Peirce and Jerry Hagstrom, *The Book of America* (New York: W. W. Norton, 1983), 499.

23. "Records Show 60 Lobbyists," *Times-Picayune*, August 22, 1972, sec. 1, 8.

24. Compiled from the 1985 Louisiana House of Representatives report, which lists all registered interest groups and their lobbyists. By 1989 the number of registered lobbyists had grown to 387. See Zack Nauth, "Lobbyists Sitting in Catbird Seat in Baton Rouge," *Times-Picayune*, June 12, 1989, 1, A-8.

25. Morehouse, *State Politics, Parties and Policy*, 108. See also L. Harmon Zeigler, "Interest Groups in the States," in *Politics in the American States*, ed. Virginia Gray, Herbert Jacob, and Kenneth N. Vines, 4th ed. (Boston: Little, Brown, 1983), 103.

26. Louisiana's interest groups in the mid-1980s, with the exception of the petrochemical industry, are not too different from those in Florida during the early 1960s. See William C. Havard and Loren P. Beth, *The Politics of Mis-Representation* (Baton Rouge: Louisiana State University Press, 1962), 220–27.

27. Randy K. Haynie and Richard E. Baudouin, Jr., eds., *Grass Roots Guide to Louisiana Politics:* vol. 1, *Lobbying the Louisiana Legislature* (Lafayette: Louisiana Governmental Studies, 1984), xxxiii–xxxvi (the quotations are from xxxiii, xxxiv), and vol. 2, *Lobbying the Louisiana Legislature, 1988–1992* (Lafayette: Louisiana Governmental Studies, 1988), ix–x, 13–31. The remainder of the volumes profile each legislator. On the relative relationship of organized labor and business interest groups, see Zeigler, "Interest Groups in the States," 99.

28. For an analysis of PACs in the 1983 state elections, see Charles D. Hadley and Rainer Nick, "The Two Step Flow of State Campaign Funds: PACs As Donors *and* Receivers In Louisiana," *The Western Political Quarterly* 40 (March 1987):65–77. At the time of writing, there was little experience with this $5,000 PAC contribution limit.

29. Bill McMahon, "LABI Has Financial Clout . . . and Uses It," *Sunday Advocate* (Baton Rouge), May 15, 1988, 12A.

30. Bill McMahon, "Lawyers' PAC Spent over $1.4 Million in '87," *Morning Advocate* (Baton Rouge), May 16, 1988, 1, 4A.

31. Bill McMahon, "PACs Formed with Legislative Agendas," *Morning Advocate*, May 20, 1988, 13A; and McMahon, "Health Care Industry Woos State Lawmakers," *Morning Advocate*, May 18, 1988, 5A.

32. Bill McMahon, "GSU PAC Plays Both Sides of the Fence," *Morning Advocate*, May 19, 1988, 11A.

33. See Charles D. Hadley and Charles J. Barrilleaux, "The Organization of Interests in an American State: Questioning Interest Groups & PACs as Interchangeable Indicators," *Polity* 21 (Spring 1989):598–605.

34. L. Harmon Zeigler and Hendrik van Dalen, "Interest Groups in State Politics," in *Politics in the American States*, ed. Herbert Jacob and Kenneth N. Vines, 3d ed. (Boston: Little, Brown, 1976), 107.

35. Haynie and Baudouin, *Grass Roots Guide*, vol. 2, 14.

36. Zack Nauth, "Lobbyists Bank on a Good Back Scratch from Legislators," *Times-Picayune*, June 13, 1989, A-8.

37. Ibid.

38. Quoted in Marsha Shuler and Carl Redman, "EBR's Legislators Attend Parties but Less Than Most Others," *Sunday Advocate*, June 5, 1988, 18A.

39. Quoted in Marsha Shuler and Carl Redman, "Parties Part of Lawmaking for Louisiana Legislators," *Sunday Advocate*, June 5, 1988, 1, 18A–19A.

40. Lobbyists quoted in Nauth, "Lobbyists Bank on a Good Back Scratch from Legislators," A-8; and Zack Nauth, "Razzle-dazzle Keeps Show Rolling in B.R.," *Times-Picayune*, June 14, 1989, A-2.

41. Nauth, "Lobbyists Bank on a Good Back Scratch from Legislators," A-8.

42. Nauth, "Razzle-dazzle Keeps Show Rolling in B.R.," A-2.

43. Haynie and Baudouin, *Grass Roots Guide*, vol. 2, 27–28.

44. Quoted in Nauth, "Razzle-dazzle Keeps Show Rolling in B.R.," See also Haynie and Baudouin, *Grass Roots Guide*, vol. 2, 27–31.

45. Bill Lynch, "Eulogy for an Honest Lobbyist," *Times-Picayune*, July 22, 1986, A-9.

46. Stanley A. Halpin, Jr., and Richard L. Engstrom, "Racial Gerrymandering and Southern State Legislative Redistricting," *Journal of Public Law* 22 (1973):52–57.

47. Jack Wardlaw, "The Rocky Road Toward an Eight-man Supreme Court," *Times-Picayune*, June 4, 1989, B-7; Allan Pursnell, "House OKs 8th District Justice Bills; Senate OKs Courts Overhaul," *Morning Advocate*, June 2, 1989, 10A; and Richard L. Engstrom, "When Blacks Run for Judge: Racial Divisions in the Candidate Preferences of Louisiana Voters," *Judicature* (August–September 1989).

48. Mark Schleifstein, "Refund: How Lobbyist Got $1 Million Deal," *Times-Picayune*, July 23, 1989, 1, A-2 (Edwards is quoted on A-2).

49. Quoted in Zack Nauth, "Lobbyists Show Muscle in Tax Fight," *Times-Picayune*, March 4, 1989, 1, A-8.

Chapter 14. Change, Transition, and Growth in Southern Interest Group Politics

1. The data used in this chapter to compare the South with the other three regions of the country are taken from the twelve state chapters in this book and from the Hrebenar-Thomas study. The most complete results for the fifty states published from this study to date can be found in Clive S. Thomas and Ronald J. Hrebenar, "Interest Groups in the States," in *Politics in the American States: A Comparative Analysis*, ed. Virginia Gray, Herbert Jacob, and Robert B. Albritton, 5th ed. (Glenview, Ill.: Scott, Foresman/Little, Brown, 1990).

2. Diane D. Blair, *Arkansas Politics and Government: Do the People Rule?* (Lincoln: University of Nebraska Press, 1988), 109–12.

3. Morehouse's assessment was based on thirteen books and one journal article on state politics. She relied heavily on the series of books on the subregions of the country by Neal R. Peirce. An updated version of the Morehouse table was produced by Michael Engel, *State and Local Politics: Fundamentals and Perspectives* (New York: St. Martin's Press, 1985), 241–42. Most of the updating, however, appears to be based on Neal R. Peirce and Jerry Hagstrom, *The Book of America* (New York: W. W. Norton, 1983). The Hrebenar-Thomas listing is the first based on original research in all fifty states.

4. Belle Zeller, *American State Legislatures*, 2d ed. (New York: Thomas Y. Crowell, 1954), 190–93.

5. Sarah McCally Morehouse, *State Politics, Parties and Policy* (New York: Holt, Rinehart and Winston, 1981), 107–17.

6. L. Harmon Zeigler and Hendrik van Dalen, "Interest Groups in State Politics," in *Politics in the American States: A Comparative Analysis*, ed. Herbert Jacob and Kenneth N. Vines, 3d ed. (Boston: Little, Brown, 1976), 94–110; and L. Harmon Zeigler, "Interest Groups in the States," in *Politics in the American States: A Comparative Analysis*, ed. Virginia Gray, Herbert Jacob, and Kenneth N. Vines, 4th ed. (Boston: Little, Brown, 1983), 111–15.

7. Two other studies have attempted to assess aspects of overall group power in the fifty states: Wayne L. Francis, *Legislative Issues in the Fifty States: A Comparative Analysis* (Chicago: Rand McNally, 1967); and Glen Abney and Thomas P. Lauth, "Interest Group Influence in the States: A View of Subsystem Politics," paper delivered at the 1986 Annual Meeting of the American Political Science Association. However, both based their assessments on studies of only one aspect of the process: Francis concentrated on the legislature, while Abney and Lauth based their listing on a survey of administrators.

8. Zeigler, "Interest Groups in the States," 117–18.

SELECTED BIBLIOGRAPHY

Both general background works and specific sources for exploring southern interest groups are listed in this selected bibliography. The sources are divided into four sections: General Treatments of Southern Politics and Society; General Works on Interest Groups; Sources on State Interest Groups; and The Politics and Interest Group Systems of Individual Southern States.

General Treatments of Southern Politics and Society

The sources in this section are divided into three categories: works on southern history, economics, and society; comparative analyses of southern politics; and state-by-state treatments of southern politics. The first category comprises books that provide a background for understanding the context of southern politics and interest groups. In addition, some works in this first category include the South as part of a national focus where politics is just one of several topics covered. Titles in the second and third categories do not usually include Kentucky as a southern state.

Works on Southern History, Economics, and Society

Black, Merle, and John Shelton Reed, eds. *Perspectives on the American South*. 2 vols. New York: Gordon and Breach, 1981 and 1983.

Cash, W. J. *The Mind of the South*. New York: Vintage Books, 1941.

Cobb, James C. *The Selling of the South: The Southern Crusade for Industrial Development, 1936–1980*. Baton Rouge: Louisiana State University Press, 1981.

Dunn, Joe P., and Howard L. Preston, eds. *The Future South: A Historical Perspective for the Twenty-first Century.* Urbana and Chicago: University of Illinois Press, 1991.

Garreau, Joel. "Dixie." In *The Nine Nations of North America.* Boston: Houghton Mifflin, 1981.

Grantham, Dewey W. *The Life and Death of the Solid South: A Political History.* Lexington: University of Kentucky Press, 1988.

Gunther, John. *Inside USA.* New York: Harper and Brothers, 1951.

Lawson, Stephen F. *Black Ballots: Voting Rights in the South, 1944–1969.* New York: Columbia University Press, 1976.

Peirce, Neal R. *The Border South States of America.* New York: W. W. Norton, 1975.

———. *The Deep South States of America.* New York: W. W. Norton, 1974.

———. *The Megastates of America.* New York: W. W. Norton, 1972.

———, and Jerry Hagstrom. *The Book of America: Inside Fifty States Today.* New York: W. W. Norton, 1983.

Reed, John Shelton. *The Enduring South: Subcultural Persistence in Mass Society.* Chapel Hill: University of North Carolina Press, 1986.

———. *One South: An Ethnic Approach to Regional Culture.* Baton Rouge: Louisiana State University Press, 1982.

———. *Southerners: The Social Psychology of Sectionalism.* Chapel Hill: University of North Carolina Press, 1983.

Sale, Kirkpatrick. *Power Shift: The Rise of the Southern Rim and Its Challenge to the Eastern Establishment.* New York: Random House, 1975.

Stanley, Harold W. *Voter Mobilization and the Politics of Race.* New York: Praeger, 1987.

Woodward, C. Vann. *Origins of the New South, 1877–1913.* Baton Rouge: Louisiana State University Press, 1951.

Comparative Analyses of Southern Politics

Baker, Tod A., Robert P. Steed, and Laurence W. Moreland, eds. *Religion and Politics in the South: Mass and Elite Perspectives.* New York: Praeger Publishers, 1983.

Bartley, Numan V., and Hugh D. Graham. *Southern Politics and the Second Reconstruction.* Baltimore, Md.: Johns Hopkins University Press, 1975.

Billington, Monroe Lee. *The Political South in the Twentieth Century.* New York: Scribner's, 1975.

Black, Earl, and Merle Black. *Politics and Society in the South.* Cambridge, Mass.: Harvard University Press, 1987.

Kousser, J. Morgan. *The Shaping of Southern Politics: Suffrage Restrictions and the Establishment of the One-Party South 1880–1910.* New Haven, Conn.: Yale University Press, 1974.

Moreland, Laurence W., Tod A. Baker, and Robert P. Steed, eds. *Contemporary Southern Political Attitudes and Behavior.* New York: Praeger Publishers, 1982.

Moreland, Laurence W., Robert P. Steed, and Tod A. Baker, eds. *The 1988 Presidential Election in the South: Patterns of Southern Party Politics.* New York: Praeger Publishers, 1990.

Paulson, Darryl, ed. *Contemporary Southern Politics.* Washington, D.C.: College and University Press, 1975.

Steed, Robert P., Laurence W. Moreland, and Tod A. Baker, eds. *The Disappearing South?* Tuscaloosa: University of Alabama Press, 1989.

———. *The 1984 Presidential Election in the South: Patterns of Southern Party Politics.* New York: Praeger Publishers, 1986.

———. *Party Politics in the South.* New York: Praeger Publishers, 1980.

State-by-State Treatments of Southern Politics

Barone, Michael, and Grant Ujifusa. *The Almanac of American Politics, 1984, 1986, 1988, 1990.* Washington, D.C.: National Journal, 1983, 1985, 1987, 1989.

Bass, Jack, and Walter DeVries. *The Transformation of Southern Politics: Social Change and Political Consequences Since 1945.* New York: Basic Books, 1976.

Fenton, John H. *Politics in the Border States.* New Orleans: Houser Press, 1957.

Havard, William C., ed. *The Changing Politics of the South.* Baton Rouge: Louisiana State University Press, 1972.

Key, V. O., Jr. *Southern Politics in State and Nation.* New ed. Knoxville: University of Tennessee Press, 1984 (1st ed. New York: Alfred A. Knopf, 1949).

Lamis, Alexander P. *The Two-Party South.* New York: Oxford University Press, 1984 (expanded ed., 1988).

Swansbrough, Robert H., and David M. Brodsky, eds. *The South's New Politics: Realignment and Dealignment.* Columbia: University of South Carolina Press, 1988.

General Works on Interest Groups

Most of the books in this section focus on interest groups at the national level. However, all explore the basic theory of interest groups and some contain chapters, sections, or examples of interest group politics in the states.

Berry, Jeffrey M. *The Interest Group Society*. 2d ed. Glenview, Ill.: Scott, Foresman, 1989.

Cigler, Allan J., and Burdett A. Loomis, eds. *Interest Group Politics*. 3d ed. Washington, D.C.: CQ Press, 1991.

Garson, G. David. *Group Theories of Politics*. Beverly Hills, Calif.: Sage Publications, 1978.

Hrebenar, Ronald J., and Ruth K. Scott. *Interest Group Politics in America*. 2d ed. Englewood Cliffs, N.J.: Prentice-Hall, 1990.

Ippolito, Dennis S., and Thomas G. Walker. *Political Parties, Interest Groups and Public Policy: Group Influence in American Politics*. Englewood Cliffs, N.J.: Prentice-Hall, 1980.

Key, V. O., Jr. *Politics, Parties and Pressure Groups*. 5th ed. New York: Thomas Y. Crowell, 1964.

Lowi, Theodore J. *The End of Liberalism: The Second Republic of the United States*. 2d ed. New York: W. W. Norton, 1979.

Mahood, H. R. *Interest Group Politics in America: A New Intensity*. Englewood Cliffs, N.J.: Prentice-Hall, 1990.

Moe, Terry M. *The Organization of Interests: Incentives and the Internal Dynamics of Political Interest Groups*. Chicago: University of Chicago Press, 1980.

Petracca, Mark P., ed. *The Politics of Interests: Interest Groups Transformed*. Boulder, Colo.: Westview Press, 1992.

Schattschneider, E. E. *The Semisovereign People: A Realist's View of Democracy in America*. New York: Holt, Rinehart and Winston, 1960.

Schlozman, Kay Lehman, and John T. Tierney. *Organized Interests and American Democracy*. New York: Harper and Row, 1986.

Truman, David B. *The Governmental Process*. 2d ed. New York: Alfred A. Knopf, 1971.

Wootton, Graham. *Interest Groups: Policy and Politics in America*. Englewood Cliffs, N.J.: Prentice-Hall, 1985.

Zeigler, L. Harmon, and Wayne G. Peak. *Interest Groups in American Society*. 2d ed. Englewood Cliffs, N.J.: Prentice-Hall, 1972.

Sources on State Interest Groups

Abney, Glen, and Thomas P. Lauth. "Interest Group Influence in the States: A View of Subsystem Politics." Paper delivered at the Annual Meeting of the American Political Science Association, Washington, D.C., 1986.

Bell, Charles G., Keith E. Hamm, and Charles W. Wiggins. "The Pluralistic Model Reconsidered: A Comparative Analysis of Interest Group Policy Involvement in Three States." Paper delivered at the Annual Meeting of the American Political Science Association, New Orleans, 1985.

COGEL (Council on Governmental Ethics Laws). *Campaign Finance, Ethics & Lobby Law Blue Book 1990.* Lexington, Ky.: COGEL, Council of State Governments, 1990.

Gray, Virginia, and David Lowery. "Interest Group Politics and Economic Growth in the American States." *American Political Science Review* 82, no. 1 (March 1988): 109–31.

Hrebenar, Ronald J., and Clive S. Thomas, eds. *Interest Group Politics in the American West.* Salt Lake City: University of Utah Press, 1987.

———. *Interest Group Politics in the Midwestern States.* Ames: Iowa State University Press, forthcoming.

———. *Interest Group Politics in the Northeastern States.* University Park: Pennsylvania State University Press, forthcoming.

Hunter, Kennith G., Laura Ann Wilson, and Gregory G. Brunk. "Societal Complexity and Interest Group Lobbying in the American States." *Journal of Politics* 53, no. 2 (May 1991): 486–503.

Hyde, Mark S. and Richard W. Alsfeld. "Role Orientations of Lobbyists in a State Setting: A Comparative Analysis." Paper delivered at the Annual Meeting of the American Political Science Association, New Orleans, 1985.

Lowery, David, and Virginia Gray. "The Deep Structure of State Interest Group Systems I: Interest Group System Density." Paper delivered at the Annual Meeting of the American Political Science Association, San Francisco, 1990.

———. "The Deep Structure of State Interest Group Systems II: The Diversity of Interests." Paper delivered at the Annual Meeting of the Midwest Political Science Association, Chicago, 1991.

Morehouse, Sarah McCally. "Pressure Groups Versus Political Parties." In *State Politics, Parties and Policy.* New York: Holt, Rinehart and Winston, 1981.

Nice, David C. "Interest Groups and Policymaking in the American States." *Political Behavior* 6, no. 2 (1984): 183–96.

Thomas, Clive S. "Interest Groups and Lobbying." In *Politics and Public*

Policy in the Contemporary American West, ed. Clive S. Thomas. Albuquerque: University of New Mexico Press, 1991.

———, and Ronald J. Hrebenar. "Changing Patterns of Interest Group Activity: A Regional Perspective." In *The Politics of Interests: Interest Groups Transformed,* ed. Mark P. Petracca. Boulder, Colo.: Westview Press, 1992.

———. "Interest Groups in the States." In *Politics in the American States: A Comparative Analysis,* ed. Virginia Gray, Herbert Jacob, and Robert B. Albritton. 5th ed. Glenview, Ill.: Scott, Foresman/Little, Brown, 1990.

———. "The Nationalization of Interest Groups in the American States." In *Interest Group Politics,* ed. Allan J. Cigler and Burdett A. Loomis. 3d ed. Washington, D.C.: CQ Press, 1991.

———. "A New Look at Lobbyists and the Lobbying Community in the American States." Paper presented at the annual meeting of the American Political Science Association, San Francisco, 1990.

———. "The Regulation of Interest Groups and Lobbying in the Fifty States: Some Preliminary Findings." Paper presented at the annual meeting of the Midwest Political Science Association, Chicago, 1991.

Wiggins, Charles W., and William P. Browne. "Interest Groups and Public Policy Within a State Legislative Setting." *Polity* 14, no. 3 (Spring 1982): 549–58.

Wilson-Gentry, Laura Ann, and Kennith Hunter. "Institutional Influences on Interest Group Form." Paper presented at the annual meeting of the Midwest Political Science Association, Chicago, 1991.

Zeigler, L. Harmon. "Interest Groups in the States." In *Politics in the American States: A Comparative Analysis,* ed. Virginia Gray, Herbert Jacob, and Kenneth N. Vines. 4th ed. Boston: Little, Brown, 1983.

———, and Michael Baer. *Lobbying: Interaction and Influence in American State Legislatures.* Belmont, Calif.: Wadsworth, 1969.

Zeigler, L. Harmon, and Hendrik van Dalen. "Interest Groups in the States." In *Politics in the American States: A Comparative Analysis,* ed. Herbert Jacob and Kenneth N. Vines. 3d ed. Boston: Little, Brown, 1976.

Zeller, Belle. "Pressure Group Influence and Their Control." In *American State Legislatures.* 2d ed. New York: Thomas Y. Crowell, 1954 (see also 190–91).

The Politics and Interest Group Systems of Individual Southern States

Alabama

Carlson, Jody. *George C. Wallace and the Politics of Powerlessness.* New Brunswick, N.J.: Transaction Books, 1981.

Cotter, Patrick R., and James Glen Stovall. "The 1986 Election in Alabama: The Beginning of the Post-Wallace Era." *Political Science* 20, no. 3 (Summer 1987): 655–64.

Farmer, Hallie. *The Legislative Process in Alabama.* University: University of Alabama Bureau of Public Administration, 1949.

Hackney, Sheldon. *Populism to Progressivism in Alabama.* Princeton, N.J.: Princeton University Press, 1969.

Martin, David L. *Alabama's State and Local Governments.* 2d ed. London and Tuscaloosa: University of Alabama Press, 1985.

———. "PAC Money in State Legislative Elections: An Alabama Report." *Comparative State Politics Newsletter* 8, no. 4 (August 1987): 18–21.

Stewart, William H., Jr. *The Alabama Constitutional Convention: A Pragmatic Approach to Constitutional Revision.* University: University of Alabama Press, 1975.

Thomas, James D., and William H. Stewart. *Alabama Government and Politics.* Lincoln: University of Nebraska Press, 1988.

Arkansas

Anderson, Peg. *Government in Arkansas.* Little Rock: League of Women Voters of Arkansas, 1989.

Blair, Diane D. *Arkansas Politics and Government: Do the People Rule?* Lincoln: University of Nebraska Press, 1988.

Donovan, Timothy P., and Willard B. Gatewood, eds. *The Governors of Arkansas.* Fayetteville: University of Arkansas Press, 1981.

Dunn, Charles DeWitt, and Donald E. Whistler. "Professional and Amateur Lobbyists in the Arkansas General Assembly." *Arkansas Political Science Journal* 8 (1987): 27–40.

English, Arthur, and John J. Carroll. *A Citizen's Manual to the Arkansas General Assembly.* Little Rock: Institute of Politics and Government, 1983.

Hinshaw, Jerry E. *Call the Roll: The First One Hundred Years of the Arkansas Legislature.* Little Rock: Rose Publishing, 1986.

Johnston, Phyllis F. *Bill Clinton's Public Policy for Arkansas: 1979–1980*. Little Rock: August House, 1983.

Ledbetter, Calvin R., Jr., et al. *Politics in Arkansas: The Constitutional Experience*. Little Rock: Academic Press of Arkansas, 1972.

Lester, Jim. *A Man for Arkansas: Sid McMath and the Southern Reform Tradition*. Little Rock: Rose Publishing, 1976.

Nunn, Walter, ed. *Readings in Arkansas Government*. Little Rock: Rose Publishing, 1973.

Ranchino, Jim. *Faubus to Bumpers: Arkansas Votes, 1960–70*. Arkadelphia: Action Research, 1972.

Savage, Robert L., and Diane D. Blair. "Regionalism and Political Opinion in Arkansas: An Exploratory Survey." *Arkansas Political Science Journal* 5 (1984): 59–85.

Ward, John L. *The Arkansas Rockefeller*. Baton Rouge: Louisiana State University Press, 1978.

Florida

Colburn, David R., and Richard K. Sher. *Florida's Gubernatorial Politics in the Twentieth Century*. Tallahassee: University Press of Florida, 1980.

Dauer, Manning, ed. *Florida's Politics and Government*. 2d ed. Gainesville: University Presses of Florida, 1984.

Decker, James D. "A Factor Analysis Examination of Interest Group Activity at the State Level: The Case of Florida." Paper presented at the annual meeting of the Midwest Political Science Association, Chicago, 1991.

Huckshorn, Robert J., ed. *Government and Politics in Florida*. Gainesville: University Presses of Florida, 1991.

Kelley, Anne E. *Modern Florida Government*. Washington, D.C.: University Press of America, 1983.

St. Angelo, Douglas. "Florida." In *The Political Life of the American States*, ed. Alan Rosenthal and Maureen Moakley. New York: Praeger, 1984.

Zeigler, L. Harmon. "The Florida Milk Commission Changes Minimum Prices." In *State and Local Government: A Case Book*, ed. Edward W. Beck. University: University of Alabama Press, 1963.

Georgia

Bartley, Numan V. *The Creation of Modern Georgia*. Athens: University of Georgia Press, 1983.

———. *From Thurmond to Wallace: Political Trends in Georgia.* Baltimore, Md.: Johns Hopkins University Press, 1970.

Henderson, Harold P., and Gary L. Roberts. *Georgia Governors in an Age of Change: From Ellis Arnall to George Busbee.* Athens: University of Georgia Press, 1988.

Hepburn, Lawrence. "Georgia." In *The Political Life of the American States,* ed. Alan Rosenthal and Maureen Moakley. New York: Praeger, 1984.

Kentucky

Bizzel, Jack E. "Interest Groups, Lobbying Tactics and Issues: The 1984 Kentucky General Assembly." Unpublished manuscript, 1984.

Goldstein, Joel, ed. *Kentucky Government and Politics.* Bloomington, Ind.: Tichenor Publishing, 1984.

Jewell, Malcolm E., and Everett W. Cunningham. *Kentucky Politics.* Lexington: University of Kentucky Press, 1968.

Jewell, Malcolm E., and Penny M. Miller. *The Kentucky Legislature: Two Decades of Change.* Lexington: University Press of Kentucky, 1988.

Jewell, Malcolm E., and Phillip W. Roeder. "Partisanship in Kentucky: 1979–1986." In *The South's New Politics: Realignment and Dealignment,* ed. Robert H. Swansbrough and David M. Brodsky. Columbia: University of South Carolina Press, 1988.

Landy, Marc. "Kentucky." In *The Political Life of the American States,* ed. Alan Rosenthal and Maureen Moakley. New York: Praeger, 1984.

———. *The Politics of Environmental Reform: Controlling Kentucky Strip Mining.* Baltimore, Md.: Johns Hopkins University Press, 1976.

Miller, Penny M., and Malcolm E. Jewell. *Political Parties and Primaries in Kentucky.* Lexington: University Press of Kentucky, 1990.

O'Keefe, Dennis. "Interest Group Contributions in Kentucky's 1983 Gubernatorial and Senatorial Elections." Paper presented at the Annual Meeting of the Kentucky Political Science Association, Lexington, 1984.

Louisiana

Bolner, James, ed. *Louisiana Politics: Festival in a Labyrinth.* Baton Rouge: Louisiana State University Press, 1982.

Carleton, Mark T., Perry H. Howard, and Joseph B. Parker, eds. *Readings in Louisiana Politics.* 2d ed. Baton Rouge: Claitor's Publishing, 1988.

Hass, Edward F. *DeLesseps S. Morrison and the Image of Reform: New Or-*

leans Politics, 1946–1961. Baton Rouge: Louisiana State University Press, 1974.

Haynie, Randy K., and Richard E. Baudouin, eds. *Grass Roots Guide to Louisiana Politics.* Vol. 2: *Lobbying the Louisiana Legislature, 1988–1992.* Baton Rouge: Louisiana Government Studies, 1988.

Howard, Perry H. *Political Tendencies in Louisiana.* Rev. and expanded ed. Baton Rouge: Louisiana State University Press, 1971.

Kane, Harnett T. *Louisiana Hayride.* New York: William Morrow, 1941.

Kurtz, Michael L., and Morgan D. Peoples. *Earl K. Long: The Saga of Uncle Earl and Louisiana Politics.* Baton Rouge: Louisiana State University Press, 1990.

Liebling, A. J. *The Earl of Louisiana.* New York: Simon and Schuster, 1961.

Louisiana Legislative Council. *Louisiana: Its History, People, Government and Economy.* Research Study, no. 7. Baton Rouge: State of Louisiana, 1955.

Maginnis, John. *The Last Hayride.* Baton Rouge: Gris Gris Press, 1984.

Sindler, Allan P. *Huey Long's Louisiana: State Politics, 1920–1952.* Baltimore, Md.: Johns Hopkins University Press, 1956.

Williams, T. Harry. *Huey Long.* New York: Alfred A. Knopf, 1970.

Mississippi

Blake, Edward L. *Farm Bureau in Mississippi, A History of the Farm Bureau Federation.* Jackson: Farm Bureau Federation, 1971.

Campbell, Leslie C. "Legislative Tactics of a Mississippi Professional Organization." *Public Administration Survey* 13 (1966): 1–6.

Colby, David C. "Black Power, White Resistance and Public Policy: Political Power and Poverty Program Grants in Mississippi." *Journal of Politics* 47 (1985): 579–95.

Dittmer, John. "The Politics of Mississippi Movement, 1954–1964." In *The Civil Rights Movement in America,* ed. Charles W. Eagles. Jackson: University Press of Mississippi, 1986.

Jones, Melvin E. "Mississippi Pressure Groups and Their Influence on the State Legislature." M.A. thesis, University of Southern Mississippi, Hattiesburg, 1967.

Kirwan, Albert D. *Revolt of the Rednecks, Mississippi Politics: 1876–1925.* Lexington: University of Kentucky Press, 1951.

McElvaine, Robert S. "Claude Ramsey, Organized Labor, and the Civil Rights Movement in Mississippi, 1959–1966." In *Southern Workers and Their Unions, 1880–1975: Selected Papers, The Second Southern Labor*

History Conference, 1978, ed. Merl E. Reed, Leslie S. Hough, and Gary M. Fink. Westport, Conn.: Greenwood Press, 1981.

McLemore, Leslie B. "The Mississippi Freedom Democratic Party: A Case Study of Grass Roots Politics." Ph.D. diss., University of Massachusetts, Amherst, 1971.

Schuelar, Donald G. *Preserving the Pascagoula.* Jackson: University Press of Mississippi, 1980.

Skates, John Ray. *Mississippi, A Bicentennial History.* New York: W. W. Norton, 1979.

Stewart, Joseph, Jr., and James F. Sheffield, Jr. "Does Interest Group Litigation Matter? The Case of Black Political Mobilization in Mississippi." *Journal of Politics* 49 (1987): 780–98.

Wirt, Frederick M. *Politics of Southern Equality: Law and Social Change in a Mississippi County.* Chicago: Aldine, 1970.

North Carolina

Beyle, Thad L., and Merle Black, eds. *Politics and Policy in North Carolina.* New York: MSS Information Corporation, 1975.

Durden, Robert E. "North Carolina in the New South." In *The North Carolina Experience: An Interpretive and Documentary History,* ed. Lindley S. Butler and Alan D. Watson. Chapel Hill: University of North Carolina Press, 1984.

Escott, Paul D. *Many Excellent People: Power and Privilege in North Carolina. 1850–1900.* Chapel Hill: University of North Carolina Press, 1985.

Fleer, Jack D. *North Carolina Politics: An Introduction.* Chapel Hill: University of North Carolina Press, 1968.

Kersey, Marianne M., and Ran Coble, eds. *North Carolina Focus: An Anthology on State Government, Politics, and Policy.* Raleigh: North Carolina Center for Public Policy Research, 1990.

Luebke, Paul. *Tar Heel Politics: Myths and Realities.* Chapel Hill: University of North Carolina Press, 1990.

Snider, William D. *Helms and Hunt: The North Carolina Senate Race, 1984.* Chapel Hill: University of North Carolina Press, 1984.

South Carolina

Botsch, Robert E. "Campaign Financing in South Carolina: The 1981–82 House Elections." In *Public Affairs Bulletin.* Columbia: Bureau of Government Research and Service, University of South Carolina, January 1984.

———. "Government's Role in the Future of South Carolina: A Background Paper." Written for the Commission on the Future of South Carolina, chaired by Lt. Gov. Nick Theodore, 1988.

———. "Interest Group Politics in South Carolina." In *Government in the Palmetto State*, ed. Luther F. Carter and David S. Mann. Columbia: Bureau of Government Research and Service, University of South Carolina, 1983.

———. "Organizing the Breathless: The Politics of Brown Lung." Paper presented at the Southern Political Science Association meeting, Atlanta, 1981.

Carter, Luther F., and David S. Mann, eds. *Government in the Palmetto State*. Columbia: Bureau of Government Research and Service, University of South Carolina, 1983.

Duke, Lois. "Beyond Money: Lobbying on a Shoe-String." Paper presented at the Southern Political Science Association meeting, Atlanta, 1986.

Tyer, Charlie B., and S. Jane Massey. *Government in the Palmetto State: Perspectives and Issues*. Columbia: Bureau of Government Research and Service, University of South Carolina, 1988.

Tennessee

Freeman, J. Leiper. *Political Change in Tennessee, 1948–1978: Party Politics Trickles Down*. Knoxville: University of Tennessee Bureau of Public Administration, 1980.

Greene, Lee S. *Lead Me On: Frank Goad Clement and Tennessee Politics*. Knoxville: University of Tennessee Press, 1982.

———, David Grubbs, and Victor Hobday. *Government in Tennessee*. 4th ed. Knoxville: University of Tennessee Press, 1982.

Swansbrough, Robert H. *Political Change in Tennessee*. Knoxville: University of Tennessee Bureau of Public Administration, 1985.

Texas

Anderson, James E., Richard Murray, and Edward Farley. *Texas Politics: An Introduction*. 4th ed. New York: Harper and Row, 1984.

Bedichek, Wendell M., and Neal Tannahill. *Public Policy in Texas*. Glenview, Ill.: Scott, Foresman, 1982.

Jones, Eugene W. et al. *Practicing Texas Politics.* 6th ed. Boston: Houghton Mifflin, 1986.

Kraemer, Richard H., and Charldean Newell. *Texas Politics.* 3d ed. St. Paul, Minn.: West Publishing, 1987.

Pettus, Beryl E., and Randall W. Bland. *Texas Government Today: Structures, Functions, Political Processes.* Rev. ed. Homewood, Ill.: Dorsey Press, 1979.

Prindle, David. *Petroleum Politics and the Texas Railroad Commission.* Austin: University of Texas Press, 1981.

Virginia

Eiseman, Dale. "Behind the Scenes: Legislators and Lobbyists." *Richmond Times-Dispatch,* January 4–6, 1981, A-1.

Morris, Thomas R. "From 'Old Virginny' to the 'New Dominion': Two Decades of Public Policymaking in Virginia." In *A Virginian Profile, 1960–2000,* ed. John V. Moeser. Palisades Park, N.J.: Commonwealth Books, 1981.

———, and Larry Sabato, eds. *Virginia Government and Politics: Readings and Comments.* 3d ed. Richmond and Charlottesville: Virginia Chamber of Commerce and University of Virginia Institute of Government, 1990.

O'Toole, Lawrence, and Robert S. Montjoy. *Regulatory Decision Making: The Virginia State Corporation Commission.* Charlottesville: University Press of Virginia, 1984.

Sabato, Larry. *Virginia Votes: 1983–1986.* Charlottesville: University of Virginia Institute of Government, 1987.

Wilkinson, J. Harvie, III. *Harry Byrd and the Changing Face of Virginia Politics, 1945–1966.* Charlottesville: University Press of Virginia, 1968.

CONTRIBUTORS

CHARLES J. BARRILLEAUX is associate professor of policy sciences and public administration at Florida State University. He has contributed, authored, and coauthored articles on state politics and policy to the *American Journal of Political Science, The American Political Science Review, Polity*, and other journals.

ROBERT E. BOTSCH is professor of politics at the University of South Carolina at Aiken, where he also directs USCA Survey Research Services. He was awarded his doctorate from the University of North Carolina in 1977. His teaching areas include southern politics, South Carolina politics, and parties and interest groups. He wrote *We Shall Not Overcome: Populism and Southern Blue Collar Workers* (1982).

JOHN J. CARROLL is professor of political science at the University of Massachusetts at Dartmouth. After receiving his Ph.D. from Brown University, he taught at the University of Detroit, where he served as chair of the department. His research on interest groups, business and politics, and constitutional reform has been published in *Polity, Western Political Quarterly, Legislative Studies Quarterly*, and other journals.

DEBRA L. ELOVICH is senior policy analyst in the Office of Senate Research of the State Senate of Georgia. She specializes in health, aging, and human-resources policy.

ARTHUR ENGLISH is associate professor of political science at the University of Arkansas at Little Rock. His Ph.D. is from Brown University. His research on Arkansas politics, constitutional reform, and legislative politics has been published in the *Midsouth Political Science Journal, The Arkansas Lawyer, Arkansas Business, The Journal of Politics,* and other journals. He is coauthor with John J. Carroll of *A Citizen's Manual to the Arkansas General Assembly.*

LEE EPSTEIN is an associate professor of political science at Washington University, St. Louis. She is the author of *Conservatives in Court* (1985) and coauthor of *Public Interest Law Groups* (1989). She has published articles in political science and law journals on interest groups, the U.S. Supreme Court, and judicial decision making.

JACK D. FLEER is professor and chair of the Department of Politics at Wake Forest University. He received his Ph.D. from The University of North Carolina at Chapel Hill. His publications include *North Carolina Politics: An Introduction* (1968) and chapters on North Carolina in *The 1984 Presidential Election in the South* (1986) and (as co-author) in *The South's New Politics: Realignment and Dealignment* (1988). He has also published articles on campaign finance in professional journals.

DAVID H. FOLZ is a member of the Political Science Department at the University of Tennessee, Knoxville, from where he also received his Ph.D. He teaches state and local politics, public management, and research methodology. His research on state and local government management and policy issues has appeared in several journals of public administration and public policy.

PATRICIA K. FREEMAN is a member of the Political Science Department at the University of Tennessee, Knoxville. Her Ph.D. is from the University of Wisconsin-Milwaukee. She teaches courses in public policy, organization theory, and American government. Her research on several state government issues has appeared in numerous journals of political science and public policy.

CHARLES D. HADLEY is research professor of political science at the University of New Orleans. He is currently completing a coauthored Louisiana government and politics book for the Center for the Study of Federalism's fifty-state series published by the University of Nebraska Press.

KEITH E. HAMM teaches political science at Rice University. He has published numerous professional articles and book chapters on state politics. His major research has dealt with such topics as committee decision making in state legislatures, interest groups and lobbying, formation of subgovernments, and gubernatorial transitions. Currently he is working on a study of state legislative committee assignments and their impact on public policy. He is past vice-president of the Southwestern Political Science Association.

THOMAS H. HANDY (Ph.D., University of Texas) is a native Mississippian who retired after teaching for thirty-three years at Mississippi State University. He wrote chapters in *Mississippi Government and Politics* and *Mississippi Government and Politics in Transition* (forthcoming). He has been Mississippi public administration intern director, 1986–1988; Mississippi Political Science Association president, 1987–1988; and a correspondent for *The Municipal Yearbook* since 1976.

RONALD J. HREBENAR is professor of political science at the University of Utah. His research and teaching focuses on interest groups, political parties, public policy, and Japanese politics. He has published several books and articles, including *Interest Group Politics in America* (2d ed., 1990). He was a Fulbright-Hays scholar in Japan during 1982–1983.

MALCOLM E. JEWELL is professor of political science at the University of Kentucky. His Ph.D. is from Pennsylvania State University. His teaching and research interests include the legislative process and political parties and elections, both at the national and state levels. Two of his recent coauthored books are *The Legislative Process in the U.S.* (4th ed.) and *The Kentucky Legislature.*

ANNE E. KELLEY, Ph.D., is associate professor of political science at the University of South Florida, and director of interns in practical politics. She is a former chair of the Florida Elections Commission. Among her publications are *Modern Florida Government* and the following coauthored works: "Party Sorting at the Grassroots:

Stable Partisans and Party Changers Among Florida's Precinct Officials," in Robert Steed et al., eds., *The Disappearing South?* (1989); "Gender, Party and Political Ideology: The Case of Mid-Elite Party Activists in Florida," *Journal of Political Science* (1989); "No Contest, But Continuing Change: Florida in 1988," in Laurence W. Moreland, Robert P. Steed, and Tod A. Baker, eds., *The 1988 Presidential Election in the South* (1989).

ELEANOR C. MAIN is associate vice-president for graduate studies at Emory University, where she is also a member of the Political Science Department. She has published articles on urban and state politics and policy.

DAVID L. MARTIN (Ph.D., Claremont Graduate School) is professor of political science at Auburn University, Auburn, Alabama. His recent books include *Running City Hall: Municipal Administration in America* (2d ed., 1990) and *Alabama's State and Local Governments* (2d ed., 1985). He edited the seventh edition of *Capitol, Courthouse and City Hall* (1988).

PENNY M. MILLER is a member of the Political Science Department at the University of Kentucky, where she received her Ph.D. She teaches courses on the legislative process, state and local government, and American political parties and elections. Her coauthored books include *The Kentucky Legislature: Two Decades of Change* (1988) and *Political Parties and Primaries in Kentucky* (1990).

ELLA L. TAYLOR is a Ph.D. candidate at Rutgers University. Presently she is an instructor at the University of South Florida, Tampa.

CLIVE S. THOMAS is professor of political science at the University of Alaska, Juneau, and director of the University of Alaska Legislative Internship Program. His publications include works on interest groups, legislative process, and state politics, the latest of which is *Politics and Public Policy in the Contemporary American West* (1991). He has been a volunteer lobbyist and teaches seminars on lobby organization and tactics.

JOHN T. WHELAN, a University of Pittsburgh Ph.D., is a member of the Political Science Department at the University of Richmond, where he teaches courses on American government, legislative process, and the presidency. He has written about Virginia government, directed a state legislative internship program, and served as an analyst on Virginia elections for ABC TV network news.

CHARLES W. WIGGINS is a member of the political science faculty at Texas A&M University, where he has served as the director of the master of public administration program. He has published several books, chapters, and articles on state politics, including ones dealing with the legislative process, interest groups and lobbying, and gubernatorial transitions. He is active in several professional organizations and has served as president of the Southwestern Political Science Association.

INDEX